Women in Chinese Martial Arts Films of the New Millennium

Women in Chinese Martial Arts Films of the New Millennium

Narrative Analyses and Gender Politics

Ya-chen Chen

LEXINGTON BOOKS
Lanham • Boulder • New York • Toronto • Plymouth, UK

Published by Lexington Books
A wholly owned subsidiary of The Rowman & Littlefield Publishing Group, Inc.
4501 Forbes Boulevard, Suite 200, Lanham, Maryland 20706
http://www.rowman.com

Estover Road, Plymouth PL6 7PY, United Kingdom

Copyright © 2012 by Lexington Books

Excerpts from Lin, Shuen-Fu, and Stephen Owen, *The Vitality Of The Lyric Voice*
© 1986 Princeton University Press reprinted by permission of Princeton University Press.

All rights reserved. No part of this book may be reproduced in any form or by any electronic or mechanical means, including information storage and retrieval systems, without written permission from the publisher, except by a reviewer who may quote passages in a review.

British Library Cataloguing in Publication Information Available

Library of Congress Cataloging-in-Publication Data
Chen, Ya-chen.
  Women in Chinese martial arts films of the new millennium : narrative analyses and gender politics / Ya-chen Chen.
    p. cm.
  Includes bibliographical references and index.
  ISBN 978-0-7391-3908-0 (cloth : alk. paper)—ISBN 978-0-7391-3910-3 (electronic)
  1. Martial arts films—China—History and criticism. 2. Feminism and motion pictures. 3. Motion picture producers and directors—China—Interviews. 4. Screenwriters—China—Interviews. 5. Women in motion pictures. I. Title.
  PN1995.9.H3C54 2012
  791.43'6522—dc23   2011050518

♾™ The paper used in this publication meets the minimum requirements of American National Standard for Information Sciences—Permanence of Paper for Printed Library Materials, ANSI/NISO Z39.48-1992.

Printed in the United States of America

Contents

Preface	vii
Acknowledgments	xvii
Introduction	
Toward Social-Cultural and Historical Readings: "Chinese Cinematic Martial Arts Feminism" and Its Limitation in the Narrative of Martial Arts Films	1

Part 1: Narrative Analyses of Chinese Women and Gender Concerns

1	The Fox, Dragon, and Lotus in *Crouching Tiger Hidden Dragon*	31
2	To (En)gender the Gendered History in *Hero*	47
3	There Is a Beauty in the Door(way) of Flying Daggers	69
4	Women Who Do Not Practice Martial Arts in *Seven Swords*	83
5	Cinderella, Sleeping Beauty, and Snow White in *The Promise*	97
6	The Chinese Hamlet's Two Women and Shakespeare's Chinese Sisters: Qing Nü and Wan'er in *The Banquet*	115
7	Traffic of Madwomen in the Chinese Royal Attic: Gender Concerns in *Curse of the Golden Flower*	133

Part 2: Integrated Analyses about the Limitation of Feminist Emancipation

8	Let's Make a Wish: Women's Wishes under the Cinematic Pen(is) from *A Touch of Zen* to *Crouching Tiger Hidden Dragon*, *Hero*, *House of Flying Daggers*, and *The Promise*	153
9	Phallocentric Teacher-Student Complex: From *Legend of the Mountain*, *Crouching Tiger Hidden Dragon*, and *Hero* to *Seven Swords*	175

10 A Chinese Cinematic Martial Arts Room of Pygmalion's Own   195

Part 3: Interviews

11 Interview with Chung Ling, King Hu's Spouse and Screenwriter   217

12 Interview with Pan Hua, a Female Classmate and Peer-Director of Zhang Yimou, Chen Kaige, Tian Zhuangzhuang, Wu Ziniu, Li Shaohong, Hu Mei, and Peng Xiaolian   221

13 Interview with Tsai Kuo-jung, a Coplanner and Screenwriter of Ang Lee's *Crouching Tiger Hidden Dragon*   229

14 Interview with Wang Wei, a Judge in the Golden Horse Film Festival   235

Appendices   243
Selected Bibliography   277
Index   291
About the Author   295

Preface

The ratio of award-winning male and female filmmakers and screenwriters has been truly unbalanced in Chinese-language and global film industry from the early twentieth century to the present. The gender issues in this book do vibrate my heart, especially because of my decades-long experience as a director in Chinese film studios.

The Fourth-Generation Filmmaker in China
Wu Tianming

從二十世紀初到目前為止，華語電影市場以及全球電影工業男女導演、編劇等得獎比例確實仍然十分懸殊。而本書中所論述的性別議題，對照數十載華語片廠與導演經驗，特別引發本人心有同感。

中國第四代導演吳天明

从二十世纪初到目前为止，华语电影市场以及全球电影工业男女导演、编剧等得奖比例确实仍然十分悬殊。而本书中所论述的性别议题，对照数十载华语片厂与导演经验，特别引发本人心有同感。

中国第四代导演吴天明

This book focuses on narrative analyses of gender politics and investigates how feminist the Chinese martial arts films of the new millennium are. Among all the books on martial arts films, this monograph exclusively focuses on feminist/gender aspects of Chinese martial arts film texts in the new millennium. Although there are numerous books on martial arts films in the Sino-Western publication market, seldom do they share the same kind of purely feminist research insistence and standpoints with this monograph. For example, none of the following publications on martial arts films share the same feminist emphasis as this book: David West's *Chasing Dragons: An Introduction to the Martial Arts Film* (London and New York: I. B. Tauris, 2006), John Overall's *Other Reviews: Kung Fu, Cult, Horror Cinema & Anime 1991-2006* (Liskeard: Exposure, 2006), Jia Leilei's *Zhongguo wuxia dianying shi* (*History of Chinese Martial Arts Films*) (Beijing: Wenhua yishu, 2005), Chen Mo's *Zhongguo wuxia dianying shi* (*History of Chinese Martial Arts Films*) (Beijing: Chinese Film Press, 2005), P. T. J. Rance's *Martial Arts* (London: Virgin, 2005), Leon Hung's *Kung Fu Cult Masters* (London: Wallflower, 2003), Jia Leilei's *Wu zhi wu: zhongguo wuxia dianying de xingtai yu shenhun* (*The Dance of Martial Arts: Forms and Souls of Chinese Martial Arts Films*) (Zhengzhou: Henan renmin, 1998), Bey Logan's *Hong Kong Action Cinema* (Woodstock, NY: Overlook Press, 1996), Bill Palmer's *The Encyclopedia of Martial Arts Movies* (Metuchen, NJ: Scarecrow Press, 1995), François Armanet's *Ciné Kung Fu* (Paris: Ramsay, 1988), and Marilyn D. Mintz's *The Martial Arts Films* (Rutland VT: C.E. Tuttle, 1983). Even when some authors, such as Zhang Zhen in the sixth chapter in *Amorous History of the Silver Screen: Shanghai Cinema 1896-1937* (Chicago: University of Chicago Press, 2005) or Rikke Schubart in *Super Bitches and Action Babes: The Female Hero in Popular Cinema 1970-2006* (Jefferson, NC: McFarland Press, 2007) show interest in women whom Chinese martial arts films include, they do not share the same research methods with this monograph.

Overview and Introduction

The cinematic world of martial arts offers ancient Chinese women the freedom to enjoy literacy, education, critical thinking, talent, ambition, job market, career, and the right to choose their spouses and decide their fates. I create a term for this: Chinese cinematic martial arts feminism. The practice of Chinese cinematic martial arts feminism is incomplete, however. This book aims to unmask not merely the feminism that female protagonists take pleasure in but also the limitation that filmmakers inadvertently set up for their female protagonists' feminist liberation. It highlights the patriarchal maximum limitation or restriction of women's rights and feminism. The camera lenses are like the glass ceiling of Chinese cinematic martial arts feminism.

Chapter Outline
Part One
Every chapter in Part One analyzes the story plot in a Chinese martial arts film. The main goal of Part One is to show the feminism that female protagonists enjoy and the gender problems that female protagonists face in every film.
Chapter One
The Fox, Dragon, and Lotus in *Crouching Tiger Hidden Dragon*
This chapter is a narrative analysis of the love stories of the three female protagonists in *Crouching Tiger Hidden Dragon*: Jade Fox, Yü Jiaolong (literal translation: jade, as well as a delicate and attractive dragon), and Yü Xiulian (literal translation: a graceful lotus, which symbolizes spiritual purity, lack of pollution, and dignity in traditional Chinese culture). I contend that the names of the three female martial arts characters in this film imply two different aspects of romantic love: carnal love and spiritual love. Jade Fox and Yü Jiaolong, whose names include animals, happen to experience erotic love and have physical contacts with men, while Yü Xiulian, whose name indicates a lotus, insists on Platonic, or purely spiritual love, for Li Mubai. Both Jade Fox and her disciple, Yü Jiaolong, intend to have business deals of martial arts and sex with men. Jade Fox has a sexual relationship with Jiang Nanhe, Li Mubai's teacher, and tries to exchange sex for more advanced martial arts skills, such as the secret manual of kung fu. Yü Jiaolong shows interest in Li Mubai, tries to seduce him, and learns his art of fencing. Yü Xiulian stops Yü Jiaolong from touching or accessing Li Mubai's sword as if she were preventing Li from any aggressor's beastly behavior or protecting his sword from any dirt. In fact, with her name symbolizing how an elegant and clean lotus rises from mudflats, Yü Xiulian is thwarting the third party's animalistic or beastly "pollution" of her pure, lofty, and lotus-like Platonic love for Li Mubai. At the end of the film, Yü Jiaolong's transformation from Jade Fox's apprentice to Li Mubai's trainee indicates her farewell to Jade Fox's and her past animal nature, and wins her repaired friendship and spiritual sisterhood with Yü Xiulian.
Chapter Two
To (En)gender the Gendered History in *Hero*
In this chapter, I argue that *Hero*, which is directed by the *qinguo ren* (a citizen/descendent of the Qin State) named Zhang Yimou, is a *qinguo ren*'s rethinking and (en)gendering of the Qin State's historical story of the assassination of Ying Zheng, the king of the Qin State—in other words, a *qinguo ren*'s filmic "*Book of Qin* in *The Stratagems of the Warring States.*" In addition, Zhang Yimou emphasizes heroines in his filmic versions of the historical story so that what he (en)genders is "gendered history." Flying Snow and Moon are as heroic and significant as men in this gendered history. In the film, Flying Snow mirrors Gao Jianli, who heroically tried to kill Ying Zheng

and avenge Jing Ke. In addition, Flying Snow's alias, accompanied by Broken Sword's designation, represents the *jiangshan* (literally, rivers and mountains; metaphorically, the territory), which signifies the *tianxia* (the plebs under heaven). Moon's name symbolizes time because the moon is infinite. It also refers to the future generations that look on Ying Zheng to see whether he keeps his promise or simply eats his words after the death of Flying Snow, Broken Sword, Long Sky, and Nameless.

Chapter Three
There Is a Beauty in the Door(way) of Flying Daggers

I begin the third chapter with the interrelation between Zhang Yimou's *House of Flying Daggers* and the poem by Li Yannian that Xiaomei sings in the film. Xiaomei, like the *jiaren* (beauty) who conquers the city and country in Li Yannian's poem, is unequaled and irreplaceable though there are many xiaomei (literally, little sisters or young girls) in the House of Flying Daggers. Li Yannian is probably unaware that the *jiaren* in his poem is not given any chance to make her own decision after the emperor of the Han Dynasty shows his romantic love for her; however, Zhang Yimou compensates Xiaomei by making her a martial arts lady in the Tang Dynasty, one of the most feminist dynasties in ancient China, giving her the opportunity to have two admirers, and allowing her the power and freedom to decide her destiny. Playing the game of *xianren zhilu* (fairies point out the way), which indicates that she needs fairies to show her a way out of the romantic triangle, Xiaomei is given plenty of time to balance between and respond to her two admirers. She serves as the entrance and exit of the love triangle. Her hymen is like the door of it, and her vagina is like the doorway to it. Although *feidaomen* (literally, the door of flying daggers) is the Chinese name of the House of Flying Daggers, it also indicates how Xiaomei functions as a door, brings her two admirers into the romantic triangle, and then guides them out of it by killing herself with a flying dagger. This chapter was published as a journal article in *Asian Cinema: A Publication of the Asian Cinema Studies Society* 16:2 (fall/winter 2005): 277-291.

Chapter Four
Women Who Do Not Practice Martial Arts in *Seven Swords*

This chapter affirms that women without martial arts backgrounds should not be neglected in martial arts films though the most impressive characters in martial arts films are usually people who do weapon practice. It aims to focus on the two women in *Seven Swords* who do not practice martial arts, Liu Yüfang and Lüzhu, and to propose that they contribute as much as all the knights in the film. Compared with all the people who practice martial arts in the film, Liu Yüfang and Lüzhu seem weak, fragile, and unable to make significant achievements; however, Liu Yüfang risks her life to help Wu Yuanying and Han Zhibang rescue Fu Qingzhu and enables Fu Qingzhu to ask for the swordsmen's help in Tianshan. Liu Yüfang is also the only adult to fight against the enemy agent, Qiu Dongluo, and save all the children in the village. Lüzhu tells Chu

Zhaonan the secret about the military budget in order to help the seven swordsmen win their battle against Fenghuo Liancheng.

In addition to the survival of the village, the film includes love stories of Liu Yüfang and Lüzhu. For instance, Lüzhu has two male admirers, Fenghuo Liancheng and Chu Zhaonan; the woman fighter among Fenghuo Liancheng's twelve troopers also shows her obsession with Lüzhu. Liu Yüfang loves both Han Zhibang and Chu Zhaonan and decides to stick to Han Zhibang after she realizes that Chu Zhaonan and Lüzhu love each other. The love triangles and lesbianism enrich the film and support my argument that even people who do not practice martial arts are important for martial arts films. Women who do not do weapon practice in martial arts films are not simply decorative and trivial roles. They can be significant roles.

Chapter Five
Cinderella, Sleeping Beauty, and Snow White in *The Promise*

In this chapter, I aim to point out that Chen Kaige combines, problematizes and rewrites the love stories of Cinderella, Snow White, and Sleeping Beauty in *The Promise*. The goddess, Manshen, turns Qingcheng (literally, to conquer the city; metaphorically, a pretty woman who conquers the city with her appearance) into a beauty, whose name matches the reality. This is the Cinderella motif. When Qingcheng is doomed to gain no true love, Kunlun serves as a Prince Charming who runs faster than the light to rescue her from the curse. This includes the motifs of Snow White and Sleeping Beauty. In addition, Chen Kaige problematizes the archetypal patterns of Cinderella, Snow White, and Sleeping Beauty by adding the complex love triangle that Qingcheng, Kunlun, and Guangming form. This chapter was published as a journal article in *Mediascape: Journal of Cinema and Media Studies* 1:3 (Summer 2007).

Chapter Six
The Chinese Hamlet's Two Women and Shakespeare's Chinese Sisters:
Qing Nü and Wan'er in *The Banquet*

This chapter investigates the first martial arts film and cinematic adaptation of William Shakespeare's *Hamlet* by Feng Xiaogang: *The Banquet*. In this film, Prince Wuluan is modeled after Hamlet; Qing Nü, Ophelia; Emperor Li, Hamlet's uncle; Empress Wan'er, the queen in the Shakespearian drama. I focus on two female protagonists in this story: Qing Nü and Empress Wan'er. Qing Nü's romantic love for Prince Wuluan draws on the first translated poem with different historical backgrounds of both heterosexual and same-sex love in the Chinese literary tradition: *Yüeren ge* (*A Song from Yüe*). Empress Wan'er in *The Banquet* parallels Empress Wu Zetian, the only female ruler in imperial Chinese history. Both Wan'er's life story in *The Banquet* and Wu Zetian's life story include their beloved's Freudian complexes: both Prince Wuluan and Li Zhi display an Oedipus complex, which reminds the audience of the famous research on Shakespeare's *Hamlet* and Oedipus. Both Qing Nü and Wan'er are Shakespeare's talented Chinese sisters. Unfortunately, just like Judith

Shakespeare's fate foreseen by feminists, both Qing Nü and Wan'er die without any happy ending with Prince Wuluan and final success of their career in stage-performance and political kingship.

Chapter Seven
Traffic of Madwomen in the Chinese Royal Attic:
Gender Concerns in *Curse of the Golden Flower*

The final film text in this book is Zhang Yimou's *Curse of the Golden Flower*. In this story, there are three female protagonists: the queen, the king's first wife, and Jiang Chan. I contend that all of these women are victims of what Gayle Rubin calls "traffic in women." The queen is the daughter of the king of Liang—namely, the Princess of Liang. The king marries her only because of royal pedigree and because her father, the king of Liang, can help him obtain the political leadership of the state. She seems to be nothing but a tool of which the king takes advantage to advance politically or exchange for his political status. According to the queen, the king loves only his first wife; however, even the king's first wife does not think the king really loves her, because he betrays her by exchanging her life for the political power that follows his marital relation with the queen. The queen is viewed as the object that the king "buys" from the king of Liang Jiang at the cost of his first wife's "death." Jiang Chan is no exception to the traffic of women. Doctor Jiang knows of her love affair with the crown prince and indirectly encourages her to deepen this romantic relationship to benefit the Jiang family in the royal palace. Doctor Jiang's ideal is therefore to "sell" Jiang Chan to the crown prince in exchange for a higher political status and more royal honor for his whole family in the future.

Part Two

This part offers integrated analyses of Chinese martial arts films. It aims to highlight the assertion that the feminism that female protagonists enjoy in films is not unlimited. The limitation is like a glass ceiling that hinders the ongoing increase of women's freedom and selfhood.

Chapter Eight
Let's Make a Wish: Women's Wishes under the Cinematic Pen(is) from *A Touch of Zen* to *Couching Tiger Hidden Dragon*, *Hero*, *House of Flying Daggers*, and *The Promise*

I begin this chapter with narrative analytical questions about women's sacrifice of themselves or the loss of their lives in film texts. This chapter aims to provide a possible answer to the question of women's sacrifice: women's wishes under the cinematic pen(is). In ancient China, most women could hardly make wishes of their own, and it was even more of a luxury for their wishes to come true, because they were under patriarchal control. In the martial arts films, filmmakers compensate the women by letting them make wishes; however, there is a strong self-destructive, self-sacrificing, or suicidal tendency in their wishes: Yang Huizhen's voluntary offer of herself in *A Touch of Zen* as a birth machine without any extensive romance with Gu Xingzhai, Yü Jiaolong's struggles to leave the restrictions of home but her ironical leap into the abyss to make Xiao Hu's dream about returning home come true in *Crouching Tiger Hidden Dragon*, Jade Fox's and Yü Jiaolong's seduction of Jiang Nanhe and Li Mubai to fulfill their strong desire to learn the secret kung fu of Wudang in *Crouching Tiger Hidden Dragon*, Flying Snow's sacrifice of her life to help Nameless assassinate the king in *Hero*, Moon's insistence on her suicidal fight against Flying Snow to avenge her dead master at the cost of her life in *Hero*, Xiaomei's choice of no man and suicide to stop Jin and Liu from killing each other in *House of Flying Daggers*, and so on. Even Qingcheng's wish is to access true love in *The Promise*; she is eventually doomed to depend on her male savior, Kunlun, to change her fate. I argue that these wishes are not wishes of these ancient Chinese women's own but wishes under filmmakers' cinematic pen, and that the pen is a male one. Moreover, the cinematic pen can even be symbolically compared to the pen(is) that signifies filmmakers' unconscious desires to cinematically sculpt or dominate female protagonists' selfless sacrifices for men. These wishes under the cinematic pen(is) lead to various sorts of phallocentrism or male pride that indirectly or directly highlights women's sacrifice for, need of, or dependence on men.

Chapter Nine
Phallocentric Teacher-Student Complex: From *Legend of the Mountain*, *Crouching Tiger Hidden Dragon*, and *Hero* to *Seven Swords*

This chapter aims to unmask and problematize the phallocentrism hidden in the teacher-student relationships in *Legend of the Mountain*, *Crouching Tiger Hidden Dragon*, and *Hero*. These films have men with academic sculpting power at a higher social status and women to be cultivated at a lower social status. This indirectly reflects the unconsciously patriarchal wish to enjoy the higher status and controlling power over the female sex, just like the filmmakers' cinematic sculpting power over the ancient Chinese women included in the kung fu movies.

The portrait of female teachers and their students in *Crouching Tiger Hidden Dragon* and *Seven Swords* is the foil to the highly honored or successful male teachers in *Legend of the Mountain*, *Crouching Tiger Hidden Dragon*, and *Hero*. It includes the lack of cinematic focus on students' sacrifice for female teachers in the same way female students reward male teachers as well as female students' successful careers free from the "glass ceiling" of workplaces. This phallocentric teacher-student complex reflects gender inequality. It is not a coincidence for all the successful teachers in the films to be male and the less successful teachers to be female, because the patriarchal gender ideology favors men to occupy the teaching positions at higher social statuses and women to be placed at the students' relatively lower statuses. Neither is it an accident for highly respected teachers to have female students who seduce them, have sex with them, or take care of their everyday lives in the films because the male-centered social trends tend to take male privilege for granted by turning women into scapegoats for men's sexuality and assistant-like or secretary-like caretakers, again, at a lower status to help men deal with trivial issues.

Chapter Ten
A Chinese Cinematic Martial Arts Room of Pygmalion's Own

This chapter offers Sino-Western comparative support for my argument about the incompleteness of Chinese cinematic martial arts films. The Sino-Western comparative readings of the gender issues touch upon and begin with my adoption of Plato's "cave" theory in *The Republic*. In Plato's theory, viewers face the screen on the front wall in the cave to see the images projected onto the wall. The director handles puppets behind the fire or source of light in the back of the cave so that the images of his puppets can be projected onto the wall. The screen on the front wall in the cave is like the theatrical screen to show Chinese martial arts films, and the cave is like a movie theater. The director mirrors the filmmakers who produce the Chinese kung fu films of the new millennium. The puppets are compared to actresses who play the roles of ancient Chinese women included in the cinematic martial arts world. When viewers see the ancient Chinese women and the feminist freedom and compensation that they enjoy in *Crouching Tiger Hidden Dragon* on the theatrical screen, they may agree that some women's rights truly are given to the ancient Chinese women according to the images shown on the screen. Once the viewers turn their heads around to see what happens behind them; however, they will discover the truth that the extent of ancient Chinese women's freedom and the degree of feminism in these kung fu films depend on the control of the filmmakers behind the scene. What the ancient Chinese women in the martial arts world or the puppet-like actresses can do outside of the scope of the directors' consent is little. In addition to Plato's "cave" theory, I draw on the Greco-Roman myth of Pygmalion, George Bernard Shaw's *Pygmalion* (*My Fair Lady*), and Virginia Woolf's advocacy of "a room of one's own" in my theorization. The relationship between the director and the puppet parallels that between the sculptor named Pygmalion and the ivory fair lady under his control as well as that between the linguist and the fair lady into whom he turns a countryside flower girl. The Chinese kung fu films shown in the cave-like theater equal a room of the director's or Pygmalion's own, not ancient Chinese fair ladies' own.

Part Three
Interviews

This part includes information and opinions of four interviewees regarding the academic arguments that this book includes. All the interviews were completed in June and July 2009.

Chapter Eleven is an interview with Chung Ling in Hong Kong. She offers her viewpoints mainly as King Hu's spouse and screenwriter. Chapter Twelve is an interview with Pan Hua in Beijing. She is a female classmate and peer-director of the most well-known fifth-generation filmmakers, including Zhang Yimou, Chen Kaige, Tian Zhuangzhuang, Wu Ziniu, Li Shaohong, Hu Mei, and Peng Xiaolian. Chapter Thirteen is an interview with Tsai Kuo-jung in Taipei. He is a co-planner and screenwriter of Ang Lee's *Crouching Tiger Hidden Dragon*. Chapter Fourteen is an interview with Wang Wei in Taipei. He speaks as a judge in the Taipei Golden Horse Film Festival. All the interviewees are also professors teaching undergraduate and graduate courses related to literature, drama, and cinema in diverse universities.

Ya-chen Chen
陳雅湞
陈雅浈

Acknowledgments

Professor Wendy Larson gave an invited speech about three female protagonists in Ang Lee's *Crouching Tiger Hidden Dragon* in early May 2005. This speech inspired me to rethink gender issues in Chinese martial arts films. Professor Chung Ling, who assisted Director King Hu to produce *Legend of the Mountain*, was my advisor when I pursued my first master's degree. Stanford University provided abundant academic resources to me when I initiated early drafts of chapters in this book. Professor John C. Y. Wang's classical Chinese literary courses, which I audited, also helped me a lot.

I thank the following colleagues: Professors Janet Neipris, Virginia Sanchez-Korrol, Nicholas Boston, Jerry W. Carlson, Natasha Gordon-Chipemberc, Vanessa Y. Perez Rosario, Sarah E. Ryan, Drew Hopkins, Hope Hartman, Joyce Gelb, and Dorothy Kehl. In addition, I owe my gratitude to Mr. Wang Wei, Mr. Tsai Kuo-jung, Professor Pan Hua, Mr. Simon Xiaomin Chen, Ms. Maxine Lu, Professor Emily Yue-yu Yeh, Professor Sheldon H. Lu, my students, my interviewees, and all the other people who gave me a hand before this book came out. Dr. Kan-lin Hsiung offered not only technical support but also spiritual support to me. Ms. Joyce Berry is like my American grandmother, and the entire Berry family provided more warmth to me than my Asian family members. I am grateful for Professor John A. Lent (editor of *Journal of Asian Cinema*), Mr. Brian Hu (editor of *Mediascape: Journal of Cinema and Media Studies*), and Professor Alexander C. Y. Huang (guest editor of a special issue of *Borrowers and Lenders: Journal of Shakespeare and Appropriation*) because they permit my inclusion of revised articles in this book.

Ya-chen Chen
陳雅湞
陈雅浈

Introduction
Toward Social-Cultural and Historical Readings:
"Chinese Cinematic Martial Arts Feminism" and Its Limitation in the Narrative of Martial Arts Films

This book is an excavation of underexposed gender issues in Chinese martial arts films since the dawn of the new millennium, focusing mainly on the contradictory and troubled feminism[1] in the film narratives. In this book, the film narratives under examination include the following kung-fu films: *Crouching Tiger Hidden Dragon* (2000), directed by Ang Lee (b. 1954), *Hero* (2002), directed by Zhang Yimou (b. 1951), *House of Flying Daggers* (2003), directed by Zhang Yimou, *Seven Swords* (2005), directed by Tsui Hark (b. 1952), *The Promise* (2005), directed by Chen Kaige (b. 1952), *The Banquet* (2006), directed by Feng Xiaogang (b. 1958), and *Curse of the Golden Flower* (2007), directed by Zhang Yimou (See appendices). It also touches upon the plots of two of the earliest award-winning Chinese martial arts films, *A Touch of Zen* (1971)[2] and *Legend of the Mountain* (1979),[3] both directed by King Hu (1932-1997).

"Chinese Cinematic Martial Arts Feminism" and Its Limitation

In the cinematic world of martial arts films, one regularly finds representations of women of Ancient China released from the constraints of the patriarchal social order to revel in a dreamlike space of their own. They are free to develop themselves, protect themselves, and even defeat or conquer men. This world not only frees women from the convention of foot-binding,[4] but it also "unbinds" them in terms of literacy, education, critical thinking, talent, ambition, career, financial difficulties, domestic toil, opportunities to socialize and interact with different men, and the freedom or right to choose their spouse and decide their fate. I refer to this as "Chinese cinematic martial arts feminism." In the conventions of Chinese literary discourse, the dreamlike space of martial arts is the *jiang hu* (literally, rivers and lakes; figuratively, the rarified realm of the scholar-official or, in the world of kung fu, of martial arts masters). Just as rivers and lakes never limit flows of water, the *jiang hu* should also never restrict women's rights and feminist emancipation. The *jiang hu* should be a world without constraints where male and female martial arts masters practice in a world of infinite justice and chivalry. In the *jiang hu*, as in kung fu films, infinite justice includes perfect gender equality, freeing Chinese women from the restrictions and injustices of the patriarchal social order. The liberation enjoyed by female martial arts masters and the ideal of the *jiang hu* permeate the entire Chinese culture. In Chinese literature, mythology, legend, fairy tales, poetry, fiction and drama of every dynasty,[5] as in television serials, and martial arts films women in the *jiang hu* enjoy many aspects of the above-mentioned feminism.

However, I suggest that the liberation afforded women in "Chinese cinematic martial arts feminism" is never sustaining or complete. The freedom which male Chinese filmmakers offer their female protagonists is not without constraints. After relishing their apparent liberation from patriarchal restrictions, most female protagonists in these films ultimately return to conventional roles in the male-dominated social order. The lives of many of these liberated female protagonists end in death, often in suicide or slaughter, their lives sacrificed for the restoration or preservation of the patriarchal order. It may be no coincidence that, of the seven award-winning Chinese martial arts films of the new millennium, female protagonists die in more than half—*Hero*, *House of Flying Daggers*, *The Banquet*, and *Curse of the Golden Flower*. It is as if death were the inevitable consequence of defying the patriarchal order—the price exacted by patriarchal society for feminist deliverance. Even though some of the other films have open endings and thus do not necessarily include female protagonists' death or suicide, they often feature female protagonists' self-sacrifice, such as Yü Jiaolong's leap into the abyss only to make Luo Xiaohu's wish come true in *Crouching Tiger Hidden Dragon*, Liu Yüfang's decision to stay in the village and take care of children for villagers in *The Seven Swords*, and Yang Huizhen's pregnancy and childbirth only to fulfill Gu Shenzhai's mother's wish in *A Touch of Zen*.

This book aims to reveal the feminism in which female protagonists take pleasure as well as the constraints placed upon their full feminist liberation which award-winning, male filmmakers inadvertently or deliberately impose upon their female protagonists. It highlights the presence of a glass ceiling marking the maximal exercise of feminism and women's rights which the patriarchal order is willing to accept. As such, these films are to be seen, not as celebrations of feminist liberation, but as enunciations of the patriarchal authority that suffuses "Chinese cinematic martial arts feminism."

Multi-Disciplinary Approaches

In order to prepare readers for the subsequent exploration of the limits on feminist liberation imposed by China's leading male filmmakers, this chapter presents a multidisciplinary overview of the cultural context in which the films under examination were produced, touching upon relevant historical, socio-cultural, literary, ethnic, geographical, and philosophical materials. The interdisciplinary academic perspective adopted here locates this book at the intersection of Asian/Chinese Studies, Women and Gender Studies, Socio-Cultural Anthropology, Classical and Modern Chinese Literary Studies, Sino-Western Comparative Literary Studies, Ancient and Modern History, Film and Media Studies, Philosophy, and Pedagogy, among others. The broad range of literary, socio-cultural, historical, philosophical, and pedagogical materials upon which it draws affords this book an analytic purchase upon film construction and plot narrative that bridges Film Studies, Feminist/Gender Studies, Martial Arts Studies, and so on.

Chinese Dynasties and Martial Arts Films: Socio-Historical "Establishing Shots"

This book begins the preparation with some social and historical "establishing shots."[6] First, it offers a brief overview of the cycle of dynasties that frame China's history, in order that we may meaningfully situate the films under consideration in the dynastic period in which each film's narrative is set. According to longstanding tradition enshrined in legend, fairy tales and oral and Classical literature, the Xia is the first true Chinese dynasty, conventionally dated as beginning in the twenty-second century B.C.E. and continuing until the sixteenth century B.C.E.[7] The Xia was succeeded by the Shang Dynasty (sixteenth-eleventh century B.C.E.): the earliest dynasty that archaeologists, anthropologists and historians have been able to verify.[8] The Shang was succeeded by the Zhou Dynasty, conventionally divided between the Western Zhou (1056-771 B.C.E.) and the Eastern Zhou (771-256 B.C.E.), the latter, in turn, further divided between the Spring and Autumn Era and the Warring States Era. Zhang Yimou locates *Hero* exactly at the end of the Eastern Zhou,[9] depicting events surrounding the consolidation of power by the first Emperor of Qin, who came to power in 221 B.C.E., establishing a dynasty that ended in 206 B.C.E. Although among the briefest of China's dynasties, it was of world-historic significance as the first unified and centralized multi-ethnic state in Chinese history. Both Zhang Yimou's *Hero* and Tony Siu-Tung Ching's *The Terracotta Warriors* (1989) address the political ambitions of the first Qin emperor. From the collapsing Qin arose the Han Dynasty—divided between the Former or Western Han (201-25 C.E.) and the Latter or Eastern Han (25-220 C.E.)—and the Era of the Three Kingdoms—referring to the splintering of China under the rules of the Wei (220-265 C.E.) the Shu (221-263), and the Wu (222-280).[10] Notably, the Han dynasty provided the ethnonym by which China's dominant ethnic group identifies itself, with ethnic Chinese referring to themselves as the people of Han.

After the decline of the Three Kingdoms came the Wei (386-534), the Western Jin (265-317), the Eastern Jin (317-420); the Northern Dynasties (386-581) and Southern Dynasties (420-589), and the Sui (581-618). Replicating the earlier sequence of the Qin and Han Dynasties, the short-lived Sui was followed by the much longer and significant Tang dynasty, which ruled the realm which the Sui had reconsolidated from 618-907. Like the Han, the Tang Dynasty long has been a touchstone of Chinese cultural identity with Chinese people historically using the term "Tang" to identify themselves, and to signify traditional Chinese-style clothing and the Chinese communities they established overseas (the conventional Chinese terms for San Fransisco's Chinatown, the earliest consolidated Chinese immigrant community in North America, is "*tang ren jie*," or "Streets of the People of the Tang"). The Tang is the only dynasty in which a woman ruled as empress, Wu Zetian (624-705), and thus perhaps constitutes one of the most pro-feminist dynasties in imperial China. As such, it is significant that Zhang Yimou chose the late Tang dynasty to locate *House of Flying Daggers*, which centers upon the story of a woman's love triangle, the quality of which he conveys with a poetic phrase from the Han Dynasty: *qingguo qingcheng* (a woman beautiful enough to bring down the city and the nation).

The Tang was followed by divided rule under the Five Dynasties (907-960) in the north and the Ten Kingdoms (902-979) in the south, in which one can discern traces of residual feminism from the Tang. Feng Xiaogang's *The Banquet* is not only a Chinese parody of Shakespeare's *Hamlet* but also a cinematic parody of the political ambitions of Wu Zetian, conveyed through the story of the female protagonist's career in the Five Dynasties and Ten Kingdoms period. Zhang Yimou's *Curse of the Golden Flower* also falls in the Five Dynasties and Ten Kingdoms period. Similar to Feng Xiaogang's caricature of the female protagonist's schemes to acquire political power for herself and her lover in *The Banquet*, Zhang Yimou's *Curse of the Golden Flower* tells the story of a powerful woman who plots to rescue herself and establish a new dynasty to be headed by her favorite son.

The Five Dynasties and Ten Kingdoms period was followed by yet another powerful dynasty, the Song (960-1279), which restored centralized rule over a reconsolidated China and ushered in a period of unprecedented economic and commercial expansion. Notably, it was during the Song that the practice of foot-binding was popularized. At the same time, however, the Song was plagued by military incursions launched by the various non-Han peoples on its northern and western peripheries. Rulers with non-Han or foreign heritage established several states in regions conquered from the Song, such as the Liao (907-1125), the Jin (1115-1234), and the Western Xia (1038-1127). In 1127, Genghis Khan seized all of northern China. In 1279, Kubilai Kahn completed the conquest, vanquishing the Song and establishing the Mongol Yuan dynasty (1206-1368). Less than a century later, in 1368, with China's economy and transport infrastructure collapsing under the inadequate rule of the Mongolians, a Han-led millenarian movement overthrew the Mongolian court, restoring Chinese political rule with the founding of the Ming Dynasty (1368-1644). This is perhaps the dynasty which King Hu likes most. Many of his successful films are placed in the Ming Dynasty, including *Come Drink with Me* (1966), *A Touch of Zen* (1971), and *Legend of the Mountain* (1979) which, in turn, inspired Chang Che's *Golden Swallow* (1968).

Like the Song, the Ming was conquered by non-Han peoples from the north, with the Manchurians from the northeast vanquishing the Ming court and establishing their own dynasty, the Qing (1616-1911), which is also the final Chinese dynasty. Tsui Hark's *Seven Swords* and Ang Lee's *Crouching Tiger Hidden Dragon* both take place in this dynasty. The genre of Chinese martial arts films conventionally includes films that are set before the end of the Qing Dynasty, with films that include fighting and kung fu but are set after the end of the Qing dynasty conventionally referred to, not as Chinese martial arts films, but instead as action films. As such, Chen Kaige's *The Promise* is identified as a martial arts film, even though there is no indication as to the specific dynasty in which the story is situated, because the hairstyles and costumes suggest that the story took place before the Qing Dynasty.

Chinese Martial Arts Studies, Education, Demonstration, Performance and Films

Martial arts developed from hunters' struggles with beasts in pre-historic times.[11] In the Paleolithic and Neolithic age, stones were fashioned into weapons. Later on, military, political, athletic and recreational demands converged to foster the development of martial arts and initiated the use of bronze, iron, wooden, and steel weapons: arrows, spears, swords, daggers, sticks, etc. *Yuenü jian* (the sword of the lady in the Yue State) that Feng Xiaogang's *The Banquet* includes, for instance, was well-known in the Eastern Zhou Dynasty.[12] Archery started before the Qin and Han Dynasties, as conveyed in legends of a great archer who shot nine of the ten suns from the sky This legend concerns a shift in calendric conventions, from the earliest ten-day week, which survived in the *xun* (□), to the enumeration of days in each monthly cycle by the sexegenary cycle of *tiangan* (□□) and *dizhi* (□□), while his wife stole his elixir and became a beauty on the Moon. Early in the Qin and Han Dynasties, there were already various forms of martial arts, including kick-boxing, fencing, and pugilism (boxing with the fists), among others. Later dynasties developed more varieties, i.e. *qigong* (a series of actions and deep breathing aimed at accumulating, circulating, and maximizing the vital energy in the body) and *tai chi chuan* (an internal martial art that features slow flowing movements).

The terms most frequently used to refer to Chinese martial arts are *wuxia* (武俠) and *kung fu* (功夫). The character, *wu* (武), contains two word-roots: stop (止) and sword (戈). The word, *xia* (俠), refers to the noble code of chivalry and the strong spirit of justice with which it is associated. The term, *kung fu*, is not limited to martial arts, but is used to refer to training, diligence or earnest effort applied to a wide range of activities. The true meaning of martial arts is not to fight but to work diligently to stop violence and pursue justice or peace. From the standpoint of "Chinese martial arts feminism," the ultimate justice includes the gender equality that women deserve. The violence which the noble spirit of chivalry aims to stop includes patriarchal violence and discrimination against women in their access to education, physical or athletic instruction, martial arts training, and profession.

In Chinese martial arts tales, one inevitably comes upon at least one of three legendary mountains—Song Mountain, Wudang Mountain or E Mei Mountain. Situated in Henan province, Song Mountain is the site where, in 495-496, Buddhist monks of the Northern Wei Dynasty established the renowned Shaolin temple for the purpose of kung fu training. Although King Hu does not always specify which Buddhist temples are featured in his martial arts films, he invariably associates martial arts with Zen Buddhism, the form of Buddhism practiced at Shaolin temple. The temple attained its greatest renown as a preeminent center of kung fu training in 620, when monks who trained at Shaolin aided Li Shimin (599-649) to defeat his enemy and strengthen the foundation of the Tang Dynasty (618-907). In the Song Dynasty, the reputation of Shaolin martial arts was already unequaled.[13] The masters of Shaolin Temple gradually institutionalized Chinese martial arts training, eventually establishing training centers or demonstration sites in Hong Kong and Shanghai. At the main temple and the branch training facilities, monks offered a variety of martial arts training programs for students at every level, including summer camps for adolescents, after-school sessions for children, short-term and semester-long sessions, college-level athletic classes, eventually even adding bilingual (Chinese-English) kung fu classes for foreign students, tourists, or overseas Chinese.

In martial arts tales which do not feature Song Mountain and its world renown Shaolin temple, one is likely to encounter either. Wudang Mountain in Hubei or E Mei Mountain in Sichuan. Wudang Mountain is where Ang Lee concludes his first martial arts film, *Crouching Tiger Hidden Dragon*. According to martial arts legend, Daoist monks at Wudang Mountain developed alternate forms of martial arts, most notably *tai chi chuan*, said to have been developed by Zhang Sanfeng. Although there is no reliable historical evidence to substantiate the story, the martial arts novels of Jin Yong (b. 1924), such as *The Return of the Condor Heroes* (1959) and *Heaven Sword and Dragon Sabre* (1961), purport that Zhang Sanfeng was born in 1247, during the final years of the Southern

Song Dynasty, and that Zhu Yuanzhang (1328-1398), the founding, Taizu Emperor of the Ming Dynasty (1368-1644), heard tales about Zhang and searched for him, without success.

In Chinese martial arts history, the form of martial arts taught on E Mei Mountain began with a type of boxing developed by Situ Xuankong during the Warring States Era (476-221 B.C.E.) of the Eastern Zhou.[14] For "Chinese martial arts feminism," E Mei Mountain is of particular significance, as it was home of a school of martial arts training for women, instructed by Daoist nuns. As such, the training center on E Mei Mountain exemplifies the insistence upon women's rights attributed to Chinese martial arts, lending historical credibility to tales in which the training of women martial arts masters features prominently and professional women martial arts instructors serve as major characters. Although training at Song Mountain and Wudang Mountain is led by Buddhists and Daoist monks, respectively, both martial arts schools now are co-ed, offering admittance both to men and women.

Although Song Mountain, Wudang Mountain and E Mei Mountain are the most renowned centers of martial arts training, demonstration and performance of kung fu was hardly limited to these three mountains. In ancient China, displays of martial arts were not merely combats against animals or enemies for the purpose of self-defense or service to the monarch but also were a form of physical exercise and a performing art, featured along with dancing and singing, entertainment, street-corner skits or on-stage vaudeville acts. Martial arts masters participated in these spectacles to make a living, or even to compete for a spouse. They also were hired to attract customers or promote commercial products, particularly medical elixirs. They could be seen in plazas, marketplaces, temples, public parks, theaters or amphitheaters. One might witness a performance in a city or in the countryside, at a temple festival, a private party, the palace of a wealthy family, or alongside the road. The history of martial arts demonstration and performance can be traced back to the gladiatorial battles with animals or enemies in pre-historic times and subsequently the cultural festivals held in every Chinese dynasty. In all these venues, the performers might be either male or female, a fact which lends further credence to the gender egalitarianism in "Chinese martial arts feminism."

Of course, it was not until the introduction of film-making technology in the final years of the Qing that it became possible to document the tradition of martial arts performance on film. Although the first Chinese film appeared in 1907, at the end of the Qing Dynasty[15] and Lai Man-wai had his wife serve as the first actress in Chinese film in 1913, the first Chinese martial arts film was not shown until the late 1920s.[16] In the history of Taiwanese film industry, the first martial arts film in Taiwan was *Luo Xaiohu and Yü Jiaolong* in 1959.[17] The theme of this kung fu movie happened to be the same as one of the most significant parts of Ang Lee's *Crouching Tiger Hidden Dragon* in 2000.

Across Film Studies, Feminist/Gender Studies and Literary Studies

Historically speaking, there have been at least five waves of Chinese martial arts film. The first wave includes hundreds of kung fu movies that followed the first Chinese martial arts film, *The Burning of Red Lotus Temple*, directed by Zhang Shichuan (1890-1954) in 1928. The second wave is comprised of two strands of works produced in Hong Kong, namely a film series about Huang Feihong (1847-1925) and another group of films based on the post-1949 martial arts novels by Jin Yong and Liang Yüsheng (1924-2009).[18] The third wave, in the 1960s and 1970s, includes King Hu's award-winning martial arts films and the works of other filmmakers, such as Zhang Che (1922-2002). The fourth wave is mainly comprised of films featuring true martial arts masters, such as Bruce Lee (1940-1973), Jackie Chan (b. 1954), and Jet Li (b. 1963). The fifth wave was inaugurated with the release of Ang Lee's award-winning *Crouching Tiger Hidden Dragon*, which ushered in the current era of martial arts film production under China's most prominent directors.

Works from each of these successive waves of Chinese martial arts film provide rich "playgrounds" for feminist theorists to explore gender issues. On the one hand, female martial arts masters in the films are indeed released from many of the constraints of China's patriarchal society, such as foot-binding and illiteracy. Yet on the other hand, chauvinist clichés continue to haunt the cinematic representation of the *jiang hu*. For example, in many instances female martial arts masters are forced to cross-dress as men, thus enunciating the impossibility for women to function openly as women, and thus as equals. Women's necks, shoulders, chests, arms, legs or feet are inevitably exposed because of wounds and medication. Men suck and remove the blood from women's gashes after fights. In the aftermath of fights set in the dead of winter, men and women masters embrace one another for warmth. Typically, women's martial arts skills are diminished after men have discovered their true gender. In addition to the heterosexual tensions that invariably arise in martial arts films, television serials and novels, characters often must negotiate other forms of sexual tension—such as the gender confusion that arises when women masquerade as men or the farcical homosexuality of a swordsman whose love interest turns out to be a man disguised as a woman. In this, even Disney's martial arts cartoon, *Mulan*, is no exception. Mulan's career, achievements and adventure are not focused on once her colleagues discover that she is female, and her romantic love becomes central.

In English-language academic literature, Western feminist scholars seldom explore the diverse gender issues in Chinese kung fu works. Nor do prominent Western film critics display a strong theoretical background in Chinese gender studies,[19] overlooking entirely the many gender issues in cinematic representations of the Chinese martial arts world. This book seeks to remedy this oversight on the part of eminent film critics and renowned Western feminist scholars, by examining the narratives of martial arts films purely from the theoretical purchase of critical feminism. Our critical analysis of gender relations in Chinese martial arts tales of the new millennium calls into question the purported feminism of these works. Most famous Western film critics do not digest the narrative of martial arts films purely from feminist theoretical standpoints, and most renowned Western feminist scholars do not do research on gender issues in Chinese martial arts films. This book offsets this situation by examining and analyzing the gender problem of how feminist Chinese martial arts film can be at the beginning of the new millennium.

Film studies and literary studies often converge, especially in narrative analyses and critical readings of storylines, though feminist concerns may not be most film critics' main focus and martial arts stories may not be what most literary scholars concentrate on. Shakespearean theatricality, for instance, is a *locus classicus* of the convergence of literary studies, theater studies, performance studies, film studies, and (multi)media studies. One of the chapters in this book centers on Feng Xiaogang's Chinese cinematic adaptation and reinterpretation of William Shakespeare's *Hamlet*. Other chapters likewise are situated at the academic junction of the above-mentioned disciplines. Indeed, on the whole, this book is located theoretically and analytically at this juncture, particularly at the crossroads of feminist literary studies and Chinese film studies.

It is interesting that professional terms acceptable in literary studies are sometimes taboo in film studies and historical studies. For example, literary analyses, literary criticism, literary interpretations, textual analyses, and hermeneutics are all acceptable terms in literary studies; however, most scholars in film studies hesitate to use "literary analyses" as a professional phrase, replacing it instead with the alternate term, "narrative analyses."[20] Evidently, performing deep textual analyses of film plots as in literary studies runs the risk of appearing as if one is unaware that the works under examination are merely motion pictures, not literary works. Some historians might discount literary works and films for their distorted or exaggerated rendering of history. This book attempts to negotiate the points of contention among these academic fields, underscoring the concerns they share, despite their conflicting terms and research methods.

Creation of the New Term, "Chinese Martial Arts Feminism": Beyond Different Waves of Modern Feminism in Chinese-Speaking Areas

In current academic publications about feminism in Chinese-speaking areas, researchers mention at least three waves of Mainland Chinese feminism, three waves of Hong Kong feminism, and three waves of Taiwanese feminism.[21] It is undoubted for Chinese feminists to welcome the fourth wave and more future waves, but how about feminist developments and gender studies in ancient China? Before the first wave of modern Chinese feminism, was there any belief or practice to alleviate the gender inequality in ancient Chinese dynasties? Yes, the Tang Dynasty is probably a good example. This book highlights a special kind of ancient Chinese belief since the Tang Dynasty: women's empowerment in the imaginary world of martial arts through the Tang Dynasty's legends (*chuanqi*: a story-telling literary genre shorter than but similar to modern Chinese writers' martial arts fictions). Because it is not uncommon for researchers to create special names for some of their research subjects, just like the terms to name numerous waves of feminism, I create a brand new term for this ancient Chinese belief of women's power and potentiality in the imaginary world of kung fu: "Chinese martial arts feminism."[22] In order to prepare readers for the exploration of "Chinese martial arts feminism," the following paragraphs include some background information about gender problems in ancient China, exceptional feminist practice and alternative women's empowerment in some Chinese dynasties, the Tang Dynasty's legends about martial arts ladies, and gender problems of kung fu stories since the Tang Dynasty's legends.

Women and Gender Inequality in Ancient and Imperial China

In the mainstream of ancient Chinese society, the male-dominated socio-cultural norms equated women with inferior, beast-like, demon-like, and yet ultimately tame-able creatures. The following offers a brief chronology of the status of women in Chinese society.

The patriarchal tradition in China is traced to the pre-historic legendary reigns of Fuxi, Shennong, and the Yellow Emperor, who (sometimes together with Suiren, who is attributed with the mastery of fire) are considered the founders of Chinese civilization. Shennong initiated the Chinese herbal medical system. Fuxi invented fishing nets and devised the *bagua* (eight diagrams) by which he unlocked the secrets of the universe. In some mythological stories, Fuxi's body looks like a dragon, an important early totemic creature for the Chinese. An alternate creation myth concerns Pangu, a giant who formed the world by separating the sky from the ground. This division was then sealed by Pangu's consort, Nüwa, who arrayed the heavens with colorful stones, thereby creating the rainbow. Nüwa is conventionally depicted with a snake-like tail, indirectly associating her with animal-like creatures. Elsewhere, she is depicted having sex with Fuxi.

The Yellow Emperor is regarded as the collective ancestor of the Chinese people. It was he who brought his people the secrets of fire,[23] taught them to cook foods, invented musical instruments, devised the earliest version of China's lunar calendar, and introduced mathematics. Chinese polygamy—invariably a man with many women rather than a woman with many men—also appears first in legends of the Yellow Emperor, who is said to have had four wives and ten concubines. His most famous wife was Leizu, who is attributed with the innovations in the spinning and weaving of silk. Thus, the conventional gender hierarchy and the normative gender division of labor of classical and imperial China are traced to the very founders of Chinese civilization, consigning women thenceforth to toil in cloistered isolation in the domestic sphere.

The system of Chinese pictographic writing devised during the Shang Dynasty reinforced this gender inequality, as can be discerned in the Chinese character, *nü* (女), "woman," which has been traced to cave drawings from Neolithic times: These early images evoke a person kneeling down, whose hands are held forward, either to show subservience or to serve food to a (male) master. Numerous characters that have negative meanings, such as *jian* (奸), signifying treachery, contain the "radical" or word-root of *nü*.

According to historical records, the Shang Dynasty is perhaps the first dynasty in which women were used as scapegoats when male emperors or the state faced crises. A similar tale is told of the final monarch of the Xia, whose defeat to the Shang is likewise attributed to the distracting wiles of his favorite concubine. The final Shang monarch, Zhou (1105-1046 B.C.E.), was notorious for his ineffectual reign, which male historians long have attributed to his favorite spouse, Daji, whose beauty distracted Zhou from governing. The chauvinism of this account was deepened in popular legend and novels, where Daji is depicted as a she-devil or the transformation of a fox.

The Zhou Dynasty in no way alleviated the unbalanced gender ideology it inherited from the Shang. The kings, policy-makers and thinkers of the period all were male, including every king and governor from the 1056 to 771 B.C.E., and every thinker from Confucius (551-479 B.C.E.), to Laozi (600-470 B.C.E.), Sunzi (535-? B.C.), and Zhuangzi (369-286 B.C.E.). Confucius[24] himself, one of the most influential educators and philosophers in world history, did not have any female students; he apparently saw no reason to address the overall lack of female teachers and students during his lifetime. In fact, the relatively high doorsills of Confucian temples were designed specifically to prevent women and animals from entering.

In Confucian culture, the guiding precepts for the disciplining of women was captured in the "three obediences and four virtues." These general behavioral codes, which now serve as clear evidence of the entrenched gender inequality of ancient China, served for millennia as the "golden rule" for ancient "women's studies," the principal device by which women were disciplined and controlled in imperial China. The three obediences first appeared in the Zhou Dynasty. Mencius (either 372-289 B.C.E. or 385-303/302 B.C.E.), Confucius' best student and perhaps the most important Confucian scholar after Confucius, fashioned the "three obediences" to regulate women. The three obediences dictate that a woman must obey her father before marriage, her husband after marriage, and her sons after her husband's death. These rules originated in conventions concerning the appropriate length of a woman's mourning period following the death of her father and husband, gradually becoming a normative code insuring women's lifelong subordination to men.

The "four virtues" refer to women's propriety in speech, countenance, merit, and virtue. They were derived from written records of the behavioral rules of royal spouses in the Zhou Dynasty. Soon, aristocratic families, eager to emulate the ruler, also instructed their daughters in the four virtues, which they considered the most significant elements of family education to prepare their daughters for marriage. The behavioral code enshrined in the four virtues gradually spread to the whole of Chinese society, with almost every dynasty in imperial China endorsing the teaching. For current feminist scholars, the "four virtues" deepened and broadened women's institutionalized subordination to the patriarchy and further limited women's rights to decide their fates, with parents or matchmakers deciding their future marital lives, expectations of unconditional tolerance of husbands' polygamy and adultery, and everlasting filial piety for biological parents and parents-in-law, including unquestionable forbearance for the mistreatment or abuse of parents and parents-in-law, moral insistence on women's chastity including expectations that a woman commit suicide to avoid rape and endure everlasting widowhood after her husband's death, and so on. In current feminist viewpoints, the deprivation of women's education and the barriers to cultivating her talent and pursuing a career all were enshrined in the so-called women's virtues, as emblems of the male-centered view that talent-less women are virtuous—or rather, that a woman with no other life recourse is more readily controllable. The so-called virtues ensured women's status at the bottom of the social ladder and institutionalized their imprisonment within the patriarchal order. It is in light of these normative features of China's imperial culture that I view female protagonists in Zhang Yimou's *Hero* as enjoying a certain degree of "Chinese cinematic martial arts feminism," as evidenced in their literacy, education, cultivation of talent, freedom to pursue a career, and to realize ambitions, while making life decisions in regards to both romantic relations and life course.

The Han Dynasty witnessed one of many climaxes in Chinese patriarchy. Li Yannian's (?-87 B.C.) poetic lines about *qingcheng qingguo* (a woman beautiful enough to bring down the city and the nation) is an example. Zhang Yimou's *House of Flying Daggers*, Chen Kaige's *The Promise*, and Feng Xiaogang's *The Banquet* all evoke this poetic phrase. A court musician, Li Yannian, presented a musical poem about his sister's beauty to the Wu Emperor (156-87 B.C.E.) of the Western Han Dynasty.

Beifang you jiaren (In the North there is a beauty)
Jueshi er duli (Unique and Unequal)
Yigu qing ren cheng (With a glance, she collapses the castle because of her beauty)
Zaigu qing ren guo (At the second glance, she conquers the nation)
Ning buzhi qingcheng yu qingguo (I'd rather have no idea about the collapse of

the castle and the nation)
Jiaren nan zai de (The beauty cannot be regained)

This musical poem resulted in the romantic relationship between the Wu Emperor and Lady Li. Enticed by Li Yannian's evocative verse, the Wu Emperor had Li Yannian's sister brought to the royal palace, where he married her, bestowing upon her the title of Lady Li. For his gift, Li Yannian was rewarded with a promotion. Thenceforth, the poetic phrase, *qingcheng qingguo*, became a standard expression used to describe women of exceptional beauty. However, from a feminist standpoint, this poetic phrase only served to legitimate the sexist use of women's beauty to vindicate male leaders for their failure to safeguard their realm. This may account for the female protagonist's retort in Feng Xiaogang's *The Banquet*. Wan'er, the female protagonist in *The Banquet*, talks back to and corrects Emperor Li, who recites this poem, by emphasizing that everything should be his own responsibility, not hers.

If some current feminist anthropologists, such as Gayle Rubin, compare marriage to traffic in women,[25] Lady Li was not the only woman in Chinese history to have been "trafficked." Many emperors, in the Han Dynasty and later periods, married their royal daughters to the kings of neighboring states and adopted their daughters, such tactical exchanges serving as conventional elements of diplomacy. Wang Zhaojun (*ca.* 50-? B.C.E.) and Princess Wencheng (623-680) are but two of many other examples of the tactical trafficking in women in Chinese culture. Wang was married to the ruler of Xiongnu, an allied state to the west of the Han domain, in 33 B.C.E. Princess Wencheng was married to the ruler of the South Asian state of Tufan (around Nepal), in 640.

Ban Zhao (45-117 C.E.), a female historian, wrote *Lessons for Women* and emphasized women's four virtues.[26] This work initially was composed as a collection of motherly instructions for her own daughter. Yet it gradually became one of the most widely used sexist treatises in China, a "gender studies textbook" for women used throughout the history of imperial China. The other canonical text in the patriarchal curriculum for Chinese women was *Biographies of Chaste Women*, written by Liu Xiang (77-6 B.C.E.). This "gender studies text" promotes women's self-sacrifice, and implicitly denigrates any woman who acts out of her own self-interest or ambition. These works devised for the purpose of disciplining and controlling women unequivocally identified the Han Dynasty as a period in which sexism flourished. Although current social norms no longer endorse the gender inequality enshrined in the works of Ban Zhao and Liu Xiang, women's disinclination to demand equal rights and their propensity to assent to expectations that they sacrifice themselves for the patriarchal order and submit to sexist norms, unfortunately, still appear to resonate in the works of China's leading male filmmakers, as can be discerned in the tragic ends to which they condemn their powerful, liberated feminist protagonists, as in Ang Lee's *Crouching Tiger Hidden Dragon*, Tsui Hark's *Seven Swords*, Feng Xiaogang's *The Banquet*, and Zhang Yimou's *House of Flying Daggers*, *Curse of the Golden Flower*, and *Hero*.

The Han Dynasty also witnessed the introduction of the practice of castrating male servants and hence staffing the inner quarters at the court with eunuchs—a practice devised to foreclose upon any romantic relations that might arise between male servants and royal spouses or concubines. The castration was perpetuated for the subsequent two millennia, until the end of the Qing Dynasty in 1911. The practice underscores the fact that polygamy in imperial China was practiced mainly to legitimate men's sexuality with more than one woman and not to fulfill the desires of women to pursue relations with more than one man.

The Tang Dynasty, as noted, appears to have been a period of greater feminism than perhaps any other time in imperial China. Still, by late in the Tang Dynasty, the conventional patriarchal order was restored, in the wake of socio-political crises and incursions by forces from neighboring states. Once again, women became the scapegoats when emperors failed to manage the realm effectively. Yang Yühuan (719-756) is one such example. She won the love of both the Xuanzong Emperor (685-721) and his son, Li Mao. In the end, however, the Xuanzong Emperor was compelled to demand Yang to commit suicide, in response to the condemnation of Yang by court officials, who blamed her for distracting the emperor with her beauty, thereby causing him to fail to act swiftly and effectively to quell civil unrest.

The practice of foot-binding first appears in written records of the Han Dynasty, returning a millennium later in the Song. In the Han, the practice appears in the *Record of the Grand Historian*, one of the most significant of China's historical works. The Grand Historian himself, Sima Qian (145/135-86 B.C.), reports the practice of foot-binding in Linzi, capital of the state of Qi, in present-day Shandong province. It was in the Song, however, that foot-binding gained widespread popularity. Su Dongpo (1037-1101), an eminent Song poet, mentioned the "steps of a lotus" in his poem, "Pusa man." From the Song onward, women's feet, tightly bound since early childhood, that measured no more than three Chinese inches (9.4 cm, or 3.7 inches) in length were defined as "golden lotuses," while larger bound feet were named "silver lotus" and "iron lotus."[27] Though popularized in the Song, legends traced foot-binding back to the Shang Dynasty. Mythological tales relate that Daji, the vixen attributed with bringing down the Shang, never completed her transformation from fox to woman. To conceal her true nature, she covered her fox feet with white fabric, which she explained by purporting that binding feet with white fabric increased a woman's charm and beauty. This, it is said, resulted in the popularization of women's foot-binding from the royal palace to ordinary folks.

Regardless of when ancient Chinese people began to bind their daughters' feet, foot-binding is widely considered as a striking emblem of the condition of subjectivity suffered by women in imperial China. It effectively immobilized Chinese women, adversely affected their physical health and barred them from any pursuit that would take them outside the severely constrained limits of walking distance.

On the whole, the Song Dynasty (960-1279), and particularly the Southern Song (1127-1279), was more Confucian and less feminist than the Tang (although legendary accounts of the female warriors of the Yang family during the Northern Song appear as singular exceptions). It was in the Song that there first appeared a popular romantic mythological tale about the love between a scholar and a white snake. According to the legend, this white snake transformed itself into a beautiful woman with an academic background and advanced skills in medicine and pharmacology, in which she was aided by a female servant, who was actually a green snake who had been similarly transformed. This tale has been recounted ever since, sometimes even appearing in present-day television serials and feature films. The tale serves literally to demonize professional career women with advanced academic training or mastery of specialized fields such as medicine, pharmacology, midwifery, or martial arts. They are portrayed as serpents, for whose deceit—and conceit—they deserve the tragic fates they suffer. This trope resonates, for instance, in the female protagonists in Zhang Yimou's *Curse of the Golden Flower*, who are possessed of a mastery of medicine and pharmacology and whose lives, as if in consequence, end in tragic deaths. Similarly, Jade Fox, the female kung fu instructor in Ang Lee's *Crouching Tiger Hidden Dragon* dies a miserable death, reduced in her final scene to a writhing creature crawling, beast-like on the ground. The animal included in her name, fox, doubles the denigration and demonization of her. The tragic ends these strong female characters suffer may reflect the degree to which the patriarchal tradition continues to inform the creative vision of China's award-winning filmmakers, preventing them from allowing their strong professional women characters to survive and supporting my argument that the feminism these male filmmakers offer is never more than partial and limited, as yet far from complete.

The Ming Dynasty continued the Confucian tradition and the resolute patriarchal order of the Song Dynasty. As in the Song, the Ming cleaved to the patriarchal orthodoxy with particular steadfastness at times when they faced military threats from powerful neighboring states. The Song and the Ming also shared the same high demands for women's chastity, and concern for the cultivation of womenly virtues, fearing that the pure Han blood might be tarnished as a result of their women's sexual relations with foreign men.

Strange Tales from a Chinese Studio by Pu Songling (1640-1715)[28] is one of the most well-known literary works of the Ming Dynasty. It relates beautiful women with ghosts, foxes and negative supernatural power. It also furthered the longstanding patriarchal tradition of using women and their beauty as scapegoats for the failures of men—whether in their immoral sexuality, premarital sex, extramarital affairs, sexual irresponsibility, or setbacks in their careers.

The Qing Dynasty was established by the non-Chinese Manchurians, and yet they proved far more Confucian than the Mongolians, founders of the Yuan Dynasty. Although the Qing Taizong Emperor (1592-1642) tried to stop foot-binding in 1638, his goal was not feminism but to assert physical control over the Han people. The same can be said for the anti-foot-binding campaign of the Japanese colonizers in Taiwan. The object of the Japanese colonizers was not to benefit Taiwanese women or advance the cause of feminism, but to dominate

Taiwanese women. Generally speaking, most women in the Qing still did not enjoy as much feminist freedom as women in the mid-Tang until nearly the end of the Dynasty. Parental control of arranged marriages, men's polygamous sexual liberties, cultural exigencies of widowhood after a husband's death, and women's lack of power to decide their own destiny continued to shape the lot of ordinary women throughout the Qing Dynasty. Empress Dowager Cixi (1835-1908), politically speaking, was the most powerful woman in the Qing Dynasty. Yet, during her reign, the Qing lost many wars, was forced to consent to unequal treaties, and accelerated the precipitous decline that began with the Opium War of 1839-1842. Like the tragic endings which the powerful women of legend invariably suffer, Cixi became a target of public criticism.

Exceptional Feminist Activism and Alternative Gender Practices in Imperial China

Although it is undeniable that China's mainstream culture in the imperial era did not treat women and men equally, there were some exceptional feminist ventures or alternative gender practices in imperial China. What this book mainly focuses on is the feminism that appears in award-winning Chinese martial arts film. I call it "Chinese cinematic martial arts feminism," which I contend is also an exceptional feminist activism or alternative gender practice in the imaginary and cinematic world of martial arts. However, before moving on to the feminism in the award-winning martial arts films in the twentieth and twenty-first centuries, I must first provide readers with a brief chronological outline of other exceptional feminist activism or alternative gender practices in imperial China.

Perhaps the most irrefutable examples are provided by the matrilineal tribes of pre-historic China, some of which have survived to the present day. The Mosuo people of Yunnan and Sichuan provinces, for instance, still practice their distinctive matrilineal system in the present-day. The Zhabei people of Tibet also continue to observe a similar matrilineal system. Among these peoples, women serve as household heads, and children belong to mothers and bear their mothers' surnames. Fathers are entirely insignificant in the families where their descendents are raised; they are even expected to return to their original homes and live with their birth mothers after the birth of their children. Upon attaining adulthood, sons inherit nothing, with virtually all household assets passing to the daughters.

Another group distinctive for their gender practices is the Lahu people of Yunnan. They do not practice matrilineal descent, but their traditions strongly insist upon an equal sharing of responsibilities by men and women. The gender parity extends even to the spirit world, with their deities always represented in a pairing of god and goddess, never with a god or a goddess alone. Temples likewise always are headed by couples, in contrast to leadership exclusively by men or women, as among the Han. The metaphor by which the Lahu convey their conventions of gender parity is the pairing of chopsticks, because "chopsticks only work in pairs."[29]

The original *yin* and *yang* suggests a similar understanding of the interdependence of the sexes. As initially conceived, the concept aimed to achieve universal harmony through the healthful synergy of *yin* and *yang*. The earliest written enunciation of the cosmological principles grounding the understanding of *yin* and *yang* date to the Zhou Dynasty, though the rough outline of this concept can be traced to much earlier. *Yang* stands for the solar, bright, heavenly, clear, masculine, hard, hot, energetic or positive power of the universe, while *yin* represents the lunar, dark, earthly, muddy, feminine, soft, cold, inactive or sometimes negative supernatural power. The harmony of the universe requires the equilibrium of *yin* and *yang*. The same principle of harmony is at the foundation of traditional Chinese medicine.

The Tang Dynasty is one of the most feminist dynasties in the whole Chinese history. Generally speaking, women in the mid Tang Dynasty enjoyed more freedom than women in other dynasties. Still, the period was not without cases of abused women or institutionalized gender inequality. It is a matter of historical record that some princesses and royal spouses in the Tang married twice, thrice, or even four times and had their own male consorts without enduring the constraints of forced chastity or virginity. Donning men's sportswear, riding horses, participating in physical exercise and athletics, learning kung fu, organizing army troops, socializing with various men, having extramarital affairs, and, in fashion, exposing their neck, shoulders and the upper part of their chest. For aristocratic women of the Tang, such practices were not in the least uncommon.

Wu Zetian (624-705) was the only woman ever to reign as emperor in the whole of China's imperial history. Entering the palace at the age of thirteen, she won the love of both the Taizong (599-649) and Gaozong Emperors (628-683). Building on the favor she enjoyed, she gradually acquired political power, ultimately consolidating her authority to reign from 690 to 705. During her reign, women were permitted to compete in the national examinations and serve as court officers. Shangguang Wan'er (664-710), for instance, was her favorite female officer at the court. Although the dynasty that she created, Da Zhou, was short-lived, her life story provides an intriguing instance of exceptional feminist activist practice which current feminists or scholars never fail to cite.[30]

Another domain where women were able to flourish was that of the women hired to instruct the daughters of aristocratic and wealthy elite during the Ming dynasty and other periods.[31] Until the introduction of Western-style schools to educate girls and train women teachers late in the nineteenth century, teachers of the inner chambers were among the only positions open to literate women. Most historians and Chinese feminists still firmly believe that the proportion of educated women and career women in imperial China, including the late Qing Dynasty, was minuscule.

As noted, state objections to foot-binding were first promulgated early in the Qing Dynasty. Still, the effective eradication of the practice was not achieved until the Republican era (1911-present) in Mainland China, and under Japanese colonial rule in Taiwan (1895-1945). Throughout the imperial period, however, most Hakka women, non-Han women, and women in Chinese martial arts stories did not practice foot-binding. As such, they constitute examples of exceptional feminist practice in imperial China.

Early in the Republican era, the ratio of educated women began rapidly to increase, although the vast majority of women remained illiterate. A limited number of female students were able to travel abroad for further studies. Following their return to China, many of these women joined in the various reform movements of the time, such as Qiu Jin (1875-1907), who called herself "the female knight of Jianhu"; Sophie H. Chen (1890-1976), who was the first female overseas student that the Qing government sent to the U.S. and also the first female professor at Beijing University (1910), where she taught the history of Chinese higher education; Cai Axin (Tsai, Ah-hsin 1899-1990), who was the first Taiwanese woman to earn a Ph.D. degree in medical studies; Soong Qingling (1893-1981), who married the national father of the Republic of China; and Soong Mei-ling (1897-2003), who was the first Chinese woman to give a speech on behalf of the Chinese government in the U.S. Congress.

Tang Dynasty's Legends and Chinese Cinematic Martial Arts Feminism

Although *The Records of Grand Historian*, by Sima Qian, touched upon some notable women in his biographies of chivalric peoples of the Han Dynasty, it was in the Tang Dynasty that the earliest legends about female martial arts masters were composed.[32] The Tang legends also provided the archetypes for subsequent developments of novelettes, short stories, novels, and romantic epics in the Ming and Qing Dynasties.

In Tang Dynasty legends, two women martial arts masters—Nie Yinniang and Hong Fu Nü—stand out. Beyond these two exceptional women masters, other women kung fu adepts such as Hong Xian Nü and Hong Xiao Nü are also featured prominently in Tang legends. Nie Yinniang trained in martial arts under a nun beginning at the age of ten to become the master swordswoman featured in *The Biography of Nie Yinniang*. She selected a man who made mirrors to be her husband, requesting her father directly to marry her to this chosen man. She defeated various kinds of mysterious experts with unequaled martial arts skills and requested a low-rank governmental official position for her husband as the reward.

Tang legends identify Hong Fu Nü as a concubine of a militarist named Li Jing (571-649). As related in *The Biography of Qiu Ran Ke*, by Du Guangting (850-933), Hong Fu Nü cooperated with Qiu Ran Ke (literally, someone with curly hair; probably someone of foreign or Western heritage) and Li Jing, and assisted the Taizong Emperor of the Tang in strengthening the Tang realm.

Nie Yinniang and Hong Fu Nü both violated almost all the behavioral codes for women in the patriarchal order of imperial China. First, they undertook extensive athletic and kung fu training from an early age—opportunities that were inconceivable for most women in imperial China. The story-teller unconsciously affirmed his awareness of this exceptional condition by choosing an unusual nun, rather than an ordinary male teacher, as Nie Yinniang's kung fu instructor, at a time when most educators in ancient China were male. At the same time, the choice of a nun to serve as Nie Yinniang's kung fu instructor resonated with legendary accounts of the Daoist nun masters of E Mei Mountain. Hong Fu Nü's martial arts skills distinguished her from almost all the women in imperial China. Both Nie Yinniang and Hong Fu Nü fought against other martial arts masters, most of whom were male, winning combat after combat against them. This also contradicted the most popular presumption that women were weaker than men in terms of physical strength and athletic skill. In terms of literacy, most women masters in martial arts legends are literate. Nie Yinniang and Hong Fu Nü were not portrayed as illiterate women.

Second, the freedom to choose one's own spouses was inconceivable for most Chinese women, with parents always asserting the prerogative to arrange the marriages of their children. Yet, as we have seen, Nie Yinniang selected her own spouse, whom she surpassed in skill and renown. The most incredible thing to most women in imperial China was that her father consented to her request, thus relinquishing his parental right to arrange a marriage for her that served his interests. In terms of Confucian codes of filial piety, it was the duty of sons and daughters to obey their parents—never for parents to comply with the wishes of their children. This aspect of Nie Yinniang's story stands in complete opposition to Confucian norms. In ancient China, it was common for women never to have seen, much less to know, their husbands prior to the wedding day. Most women could little imagine having the freedom to select their favorite mate from among different candidates.

Although Hong Fu Nü was a concubine under the polygamous marital system, she freely socialized, interacted and worked alongside men. Most women in any period other than the Tang Dynasty, were not free to do so. Because Qiu Ran Ke is described as a man with curly hair, it is possible that the author intended to suggest that he was of foreign or Western heritage. In other words, Hong Fu Nü interacted and collaborated not only with ordinary Chinese men but also perhaps a foreigner or Westerner. To have ordinary Chinese and foreign or Western male colleagues was certainly far beyond what most women in imperial China expected their life stories to include.

Third, Nie Yinniang obviously surpassed her husband in skill and accomplishment. This implies that her husband was weak or deficient in fulfilling the conventional role of master of the family in patriarchal point of view, with Nie Yinniang coming across as the true household head, even succeeding in securing a government post for her husband, a final emasculating feat. For most women in imperial China, this degree of status in marital and family life could never be more than a luxurious daydream.

Fourth, the legends of both Nie Yinniang and Hong Fu Nü mention nothing concerning their children. This, of course, was highly unusual for most women in imperial China, especially considering that women who produced no sons were certain to suffer the rebukes and abuse of husband and in-laws and were likely to be abandoned.

Fifth, Nie Yinniang and Hong Fu Nü never suffered familial discord with parents-in-law, sisters-in-law, or other relatives. They also never were burdened with domestic chores. Such conditions were far indeed from the reality of life for the vast majority of Chinese women, a dream most women dared not indulge.

With reference to the "three obediences," Nie Yinniang contravened almost every part of them. Her father assented to *her* spousal choice. Nor, clearly, did she obey her husband. Instead, her husband clearly deferred to her in the management of their household and depended on her to find a government position. Finally, the omission of any mention of a son suggests that Nie Yinniang also violated the last of the three obediences. The legend of Hong Fu Nü takes the reader even further from the norm, with no information concerning her parents or her offspring, hence providing no touchstones by which to assess her life in terms of the "three obediances," other than the relation with her husband, itself overshadowed by his evident alterity.

Comparable violations of the patriarchal code for Chinese women are featured in most martial arts stories, including those written by Jin Yong and Liang Yüsheng. In this, award-winning Chinese martial arts films featuring female protagonists have proven no exception. Except for the character of Jade Fox in Ang Lee's *Crouching Tiger Hidden Dragon*, each female protagonist in the films under consideration is portrayed as literate. Even Jade Fox is depicted as having attained advanced mastery of martial arts. The character of Jiang Chan in Zhang Yimou's *Curse of the Golden Flower* is even a medical doctor. Flying Snow in Zhang Yimou's *Hero* is a female master of calligraphy, and Liu Yüfang is a teacher. In Feng Xiaogang's *The Banquet*, Qing Nü is the chief manager of theatrical performance in the royal palace and Wan'er is a politician. All of these characters defy the Chinese patriarchal preference for talent-less and hence more controllable women.

The exceptional education of these female protagonists is matched by their active social lives. Each of these powerful women has a broad range of acquaintances, socializing, interacting, and working with a number of men. The virtues of virginity, chastity and the prohibition of premarital sexuality that are central features of the patriarchal code for the women of imperial China appear in no way to hinder the social activities or sexual relations of these female protagonists, as witnessed in the sexual union of Yü Jiaolong and Luo Xiaohu's in Ang Lee's *Crouching Tiger Hidden Dragon*; of Qingcheng and the General in Chen Kaige's *The Promise*; of Broken Sword and Flying Snow and Moon in Zhang Yimou's *Hero*; of Xiaomei and Jin in *House of Flying Daggers*; and the union of

Jiang Chan and the crown prince in *Curse of the Golden Flower*. In addition, almost all the female protagonists in award-winning Chinese martial arts films share Nie Yinniang's and Hong Fu Nü's freedom from troubles of parental domination, arranged marriages, spousal abuse, or abusive parents-in-law, sisters-in-law or other relatives, and, like their Tang predecessors, are unencumbered by housework.

To have many male acquaintances and colleagues and to engage in physical battles with men—much less to prevail in those struggles—though unimaginable for the vast majority of Chinese women, were not impossible for female protagonists in award-winning Chinese martial arts films. On the contrary, most female protagonists appear familiar with all of these feats, taking them for granted. Even if it is not extremely surprising for martial arts women to defeat men, it is feminist enough for male filmmakers to allow even female characters without martial arts skills also to vanquish male rivals, such as when Liu Yüfang kills the male betrayer in Tsui Hark's *Seven Swords* or when Qingcheng conquers all the soldiers on the roof of the castle in Chen Kaige's *The Promise*.

The Limitation of "Chinese Cinematic Martial Arts Feminism"

Although almost all the comparisons and contrasts between the Tang Dynasty's legends and award-winning Chinese martial arts films bear witness to the feminist freedoms the female protagonists enjoy, the "Chinese cinematic martial arts feminism" that I have described is not complete, but remains only partial.

With the inevitable tragic endings or suicidal self-sacrifice of female protagonists in award-winning Chinese martial arts films in the twentieth and twenty-first centuries, these films actually fall short of the feminism of the Tang Dynasty legends, where the ending remains open. Nie Yinniang and Hong Fu Nü, at least, do not perish in selfless sacrifice, suicide or miserable death. One wonders why it is that award-winning Chinese male filmmakers in the twentieth and twenty-first centuries are not willing to be generous enough to allow at least the same open endings, or even to hazard a happy ending for their female protagonists. Does this indicate that award-winning male filmmakers' camera lens and screen frames are in fact a type of hidden glass ceiling that constrains their female protagonists' feminism within the parameters of their own vision of the social order? Does this imply that award-winning male filmmakers' "cinematic eyes" are less feminist and hence more sexist than the "literary pen" of the male writers and story-tellers of the Tang Dynasty? Is the *jiang hu* (the imaginary world of martial arts) wider and more feminist in the legends of the Tang Dynasty than in the award-winning Chinese martial arts films? If these female protagonists on the silver screen can hear this book's "voiceover" about their incomplete or partial "Chinese cinematic martial arts feminism," will they be willing to accept without question the limitations that their filmmakers impose upon their feminist freedom? Perhaps Qingcheng still has an opportunity to talk back to these award-winning male filmmakers, because the ending of her story is an open one. As for female protagonists whom award-winning filmmakers "sentence to self-sacrificing or tragic deaths," Wan'er in Feng Xiaogang's *The Banquet* would undoubtedly like to represent them and have her retort to these award-winning male filmmakers, considering the retort she already delivered to Li Yannian's scapegoating poem. This book cannot bring them back to life, but at least it can shed light upon the limits of their feminist freedom and their female predicament.

Conclusion

In summation, most female protagonists in the award-winning Chinese martial arts films under examination in this book indeed enjoy a certain degree of "Chinese cinematic martial arts feminism." Still, the extent of the feminist freedom they are permitted is determined by the filmmaker. Whether by deliberate choice or by the unconscious tug of the residual patriarchal order that continues to constrain the lives of Chinese women, these award-winning filmmakers have encumbered and constrained full attainment of the promise of "Chinese cinematic martial arts feminism."

References

Braester, Yomi. "Chinese Cinema in the Age of Advertisement: The Filmmaker as a Cultural Broker." *China Quarterly* 183 (September 2005): 549-564.

Chen, Chen. *Gong Fu (Kung Fu)*. Beijing: Wenhua yishu, 2006.

Chan, Felicia. "Crouching Tiger Hidden Dragon: Cultural Migrancy and Translatability." *Chinese films in Focus: 25 New Takes*. Chris Berry edt. London: BFI, 2003, pp. 56-64. This article also appears in Chris Berry's *Chinese Films in Focus II*. Basingstoke: BFI / Palgrave MacMillan, 2008, pp. 73-81.

Chan, Kenneth. "The Global Return of the *Wu Xia Pian* (Chinese Sword-Fighting Movie): Ang Lee's *Crouching Tiger Hidden Dragon*." *Cinema Journal* 43.4 (2004): 3-17.

Chen, Shan. *A History of Chinese Martial Arts Heroes*. Shanghai: San Lian Shu Dian, 1992.

Clements, Jonathan. *Wu: The Chinese Empress Who Schemed, Seduced and Murdered Her Way to Become a Living God*. Stroud: Sutton, 2007.

Du, Shanshan. *Chopsticks Only Work in Pairs*. New York: Columbia University Press, 2002.

Guo, Zhiyu. *Zhongguo wushu shi jian bian (Concise History of Chinese Martial Arts)*. Beijing: Renmin tiyu, 2007.

Han, Yunbo. *The Culture of the Martial Arts Hero*. Chongqing: Chongqing Publishing Company, 2004.

Huang, Qi. *The Martial Arts Hero in Ancient China*. Taipei: The Commercial Publishing Company, 1998.

Jay, Jennifer W. "*Crouching Tiger Hidden Dragon:* (Re)packaging China and Selling the Hybridized Culture in an Age of Transnationalism." *Reading Chinese Transnationalisms: Society, Literature, and Films*. Maria Ng and Philip Holden edt. Hong Kong: Hong Kong University Press, 2006.

Ko, Dorothy. *Teachers of the Inner Chamber: Women and Culture in Seventeenth-Century China*. Stanford: Stanford University Press, 1994.

---. *Cinderella's Sisters: A Revisionist History of Footbinding*. Berkeley: California University Press, 2005.

---. *Every Step a Lotus: Shoes for Bound Feet*. Berkeley: University of California Press, 2001.

Li, Ning and Bailong Jiang. *Zhongguo wushu shi lue* (*A Brief Historical Survey of Chinese Martial Arts*). Beijing: Renmin tiyu, 2003.

Li, Zongwei. *Tangren chuanqi* (*Legends of People in the Tang Dynasty*). Beijing: Zhonghua, 2004.

Luo, Lichun. *A History of Chinese Martial Arts Fiction*. Liaoning: People's Publishing Society, 1990.

Mann, Susan and Yu-yin Cheng. *Under Confucian Eyes: Writings on Gender in Chinese History*. Berkeley: University of California Press, 2001.

Mao, Yinkun. *Sichuang wushu da chuan* (*Complete Collections of Martial Arts in Sichuan*). Chengdu: Sichuan keji, 1989.

Pu, Songling. *Strange Tales from a Chinese Studio*. John Minford trans. London: Penguin, 2006.

Rothschild, N. Harry. *Wu Zhao: China's Only Woman Emperor*. New York: Pearson Longman, 2008.

Rubin, Gayle. "The Traffic in Women: Notes on the 'Political Economy' of Sex." *Toward an Anthropology of Women*. Rayna Reiter edt. New York: Monthly Review Press, 1975, pp. 157-210.

Wang, Georgette and Emily Yueh-yu Yeh. "Globalization and Hybridization in Cultural Products: The Cases of *Mulan* and *Crouching Tiger, Hidden Dragon*." *International Journal of Cultural Studies* 8.2 (2005): 175-193.

Yau, Kinnia Shuk-ting. *Japanese and Hong Kong Film Industries: Understanding the Origins of East Asian Film Networks*. London: Routldge, 2010.

Yu, Zhijun. *Zhongguo tuantong wushu shi* (*History of Traditional Chinese Martial Arts*). Beijing: Renmin University Press, 2006.

Yu, Shuiqing. *Zhongguo wushu shi gaiyao* (*Historical Outline of Chinese Martial Arts*). Wuhan: Hubei kexue jishu, 2006.

Yun, Youke. *Jianghu cong tan* (*Legends of Jiang Hu*). Tianjin: Baihua wenyi, 1996.

Zhang, Jihe. *The Martial Arts Hero in Chinese Literary History*. Beijing: Chinese Social Science Press, 1994.

Zhang, Yingjin. "Chinese Cinema and Transnational Cultural Politics: Reflections on Film Festivals, Film Productions, and Film Studies." *Journal of Modern Literature in Chinese* 2.1 (July 1998): 105-32.

Zhang, Youhe. *Tang Song chuanqi xuan* (*Selected Legends of the Tang and Song Dynasties*). Beijing: Renmin wenxue, 1998, p. 221.

Zheng, Qunyuan. *History of Martial Arts Heroes*. Shanghai: Shanghai Literary Publishing Society, 1999.

Zhou, Weiliang. *Zhongguo wushu shi* (*History of Chinese Martial Arts*). Beijing: Gaodeng jiaoyu, 2003.

Notes

1. "Feminism" is a frequently seen word in modern languages or a well-known concept in modern societies. It means women's rights equal to men in terms of political, economic, intellectual, sexual and all the other aspects. I choose this word in this book in order to refer to the emancipation that women enjoy in the film text.

2. The film was awarded the Technical Grand Prize and nominated for the Palme d'Or at the 1975 Cannes Film Festival. This was the first Chinese martial arts film to win the international award after King Hu obtained strong support and solid training through film networks in both Hong Kong and Taiwan. Kinnia Shuk-ting Yau's *Japanese and Hong Kong Film Industries: Understanding the Origins of East Asian Film Networks* can supply useful background information about how Hong Kong film studios nurtured King Hu and his Chinese martial arts films.

After this film, Ang Lee's *Crouching Tiger Hidden Dragon* became the second Chinese martial arts film to be the globally well-known and award-winning introducer of Chinese martial arts culture to the non-Chinese world. For details, consult Jennifer W. Jay's "*Crouching Tiger Hidden Dragon:* (Re)packaging China and Selling the Hybridized Culture in an Age of Transnationalism"; Georgette Wang and Emily Yueh-yu Yeh's "Globalization and Hybridization in Cultural Products: The Cases of *Mulan* and *Crouching Tiger Hidden Dragon*"; and Kenneth Chan's "The Global Return of the *Wu Xia Pian* (Chinese Sword-Fighting Movie): Ang Lee's *Crouching Tiger Hidden Dragon*." Other scholarly discourses can be found in numerous publications, such as the following: Yomi Braester's "Chinese Cinema in the Age of Advertisement: The Filmmaker as a Cultural Broker"; Zhang Yingjin's "Chinese Cinema and Transnational Cultural Politics: Reflections on Film Festivals, Film Productions, and Film Studies"; and Felicia Chan's "*Crouching Tiger Hidden Dragon*: Cultural Migrancy and Translatability," etc.

3. In 1979 Golden Horse Film Festival, this film won the following awards: best feature film, best director, best photographer, best sound-recording, and best music.

4. See my explanation of foot-binding in the later part of this chapter.

5. Consult the following publications:
Chen Shan's *A History of Chinese Martial Arts Heroes*, Han Yunbo's *The Culture of the Martial Arts Hero*, Huang Qi's *The Martial Arts Hero in Ancient China*, Luo Lichun's *A History of Chinese Martial Arts Fiction*, Zhang Jihe's *The Martial Arts Hero in Chinese Literary History*, and Zheng Qunyuan's *History of Martial Arts Heroes*.

6. An "establishing shot" in films or television shows is usually the first shot of a new scene to inform viewers of where the story begins or where actions are taken.

7. Chiang Nan, Li Han-hsiang, and Ku Sen-lin's film, *Lady from the Moon* (1954), portrays a fairy tale about a beauty on the Moon in this dynasty.

8. The story about the Emperor Zhou and his concubine, Daji, is probably the most frequently seen topic for multi-media representation about this dynasty.

9. The first Chinese film to include an actress, *Zhuangzi Tests His Wife* (1913) directed by Lai Man-wai, coincidentally situates the story plot in the Eastern Zhou Dynasty.

10. Li Han-hsiang's *Beyond the Great Wall* (1964) portrays the cross-national marital relationship between the Han Dynasty and Xiongnu through Wang Zhaojun (52-19 B.C.). His *Diao Chan* (1958) is a film about Diao Chan (around 164 B.C.-?), one of the most famous female spies during the Era of Three Kingdoms and one of the four most

beautiful women in imperial China according to legends. Formal historical records mention an attractive servant who had similar experience but did not specify whether this woman was named Diao Chan. In 2008 and 2009 *Red Cliff* I and II, films directed by John Woo (b. 1946), tells the stories between Wu and Shu during the Era of Three Kingdoms.

11. See Zhou Weiliang's *Zhongguo wushu shi* (*History of Chinese Martial Arts*). (Beijing: Gaodeng jiaoyu, 2003), 10.

12. Consult Zhijun Yu's *Zhongguo tuantong wushu shi* (*History of Traditional Chinese Martial Arts*). (Beijing: Renmin University Press, 2006), 75-77.

13. See Li Ning and Jiang Bailong's *Zhongguo wushu shi lue* (*A Brief Historical Survey of Chinese Martial Arts*). (Beijing: Renmin tiyu, 1996), 46.

14. See the following publications about Chinese martial arts: Zhou Weiliang's *Zhongguo wushu shi* (*History of Chinese Martial Arts*); Mao Yinkun's *Sichuang wushu da chuan* (*Complete Collections of Martial Arts in Sichuan*); Chen Chen's *Gong Fu* (*Kung Fu*); Yu Zhijun's *Zhongguo tuantong wushu shi* (*History of Traditional Chinese Martial Arts*); Yu Shuiqing's *Zhongguo wushu shi gaiyao* (*Historical Outline of Chinese Martial Arts*); Guo Zhiyu's *Zhongguo wushu shi jian bian* (*Concise History of Chinese Martial Arts*); Li Ning and Jiang Bailong's *Zhongguo wushu shi lue* (*A Brief Historical Survey of Chinese Martial Arts*); and Yun Youke's *Jianghu cong tan* (*Legends of Jiang Hu*).

15. Hu An's *Shadow Magic* (2000) tells a story about the birth of the first Chinese film.

16. Although Western audiences without Asia-related background knowledge may oversimplify Chinese martial arts films and mistake them as something Chinese, martial arts films are not as authentically Chinese as live shows of kung fu since the pre-historical era to Chinese people, especially when most Chinese filmmakers, photographers, technicians and staff in film studios, and even professional screenwriters must have a great deal of knowledge about all the equipments, terms, technology, processing, and skills from the West. Many Chinese filmmakers have deep connections with the West. For example, Ang Lee earned his graduate degree from New York University and finished many films entirely outside of Chinese-speaking areas. His wife used to be also an overseas Taiwanese student in the US and completed her degree in the University of Illinois in Urbana Champaign. Influential French and Italian films enthralled Tsai Ming-liang (b. 1957). Wang Quan'an (b. 1965) hired a multi-lingual actress—Yu Nan (b. 1978), who speaks Mandarin Chinese, English and French—as the female protagonist in his award-winning film, *Tuya's Marriage* (2007).

17. In 1968, Taiwan produced 128 martial arts films, and 548 kung fu movies from 1971 to 1977.

18. On January 27, 2009, the *Beijing News* gives the following brief summary of Liang's life:

> Liang Yüsheng was born Chen Wentong on March 22, 1924, to an educated family in Mengshan, Guangxi. After the anti-Japanese war was won, Liang went to Guangzhou's Lingnan University to study international economics. After graduating he became editor of the supplement to Hong Kong's *Ta Kung Pao* (newspaper). In 1954, a dispute in the martial arts world between the White Crane style and [Wu

style] Tai-chi escalated from a war of words in the newspaper to an actual fight between the heads of the two schools. Lo Fu, who was general editor of the New Evening Post at the time, serialized Liang's *The Dragon Fights the Tiger* to capitalize on martial arts fever. This novel is seen as the beginning of "new martial arts." Over the three decades beginning in 1954, when he started writing "new martial arts novels," through 1984, when he declared that he was "putting away his sword," Liang wrote 35 novels in 160 volumes, totally 10 million Chinese characters.

In an interview with Lo Fu published a few years ago in *Southern Metropolis Daily*, journalist Li Huaiyu provides some details about newspaper politics at the time Liang started writing:

> *The New Evening Post*'s big news headline on that day was "Two fighters face off at 4 o'clok before 5,000 Hong Kong spectators." Having a flash of inspiration, Lo Fu persuaded Liang Yüsheng to write a martial arts novel. The day after the fight, New Evening Post ran a notice that it would serialize martial arts fiction to satisfy readers' desire for fighting. The following day, *The Dragon Fights the Tiger*, the product of "one day of planning" on Liang's part, began publication. Later, Lo invited Louis Cha to "join the fight," and thus the book and the sword shook the world.
>
> Lo: There was the new *Commercial Daily*, you see, and they saw the readers the *New Evening Post* was getting by running Liang's martial arts fiction, so they asked if he could write for them. We had to agree to that, because we had to support the *Commercial Daily*, you know. We had launched it as a leftist newspaper to take over from *Ta Kung Pao* and *Wen Wei Po*, which had been involved in a lawsuit with the Hong Kong government that accused *Ta Kung Pao*, *Wen Wei Po*, and *New Evening Post* of instigating social unrest. The three papers could potentially have been shut down, so we immediately began plans for another paper, the *Commercial Daily*. But when we had it about ready, the lawsuit ended with the other papers not getting shut down. So the *Commercial Daily* carried on, but we decided to turn it into a more neutral paper to attract more readers. The content would be more plebian and not so leftist. Since martial arts attracted readers, we naturally let Liang write for them. But we had to have it too, so we immediately found Louis Cha, who was quite happy to do it.

19. Dai Jinhua (b. 1959), a well-known scholarly film critic who earned her doctoral degree in comparative literature and comes to film studies with a solid feminist academic background, may be a singular exception. However, thus far, she has yet to be anthologized or well received in Western or English-speaking academy as other academic celebrities, such as Gayatri C. Spivak (b. 1942).

20. I thank Jerry W. Carlson and Nicholas Boston for their reading responses and suggestions in professional viewpoints of film studies.

21. Generally speaking, most scholars think that the May Fourth Movement initiated Mainland Chinese feminism in 1919. The second wave of feminism in Mainland China started because of the establishment of the People's Republic of China in 1949, and the United Nations' Fourth World Women's Congress was the landmark of the third wave Mainland Chinese feminism in 1995. The early wave of Hong Kong feminism began in the post-war era to the mid 1970s. The second wave of Hong Kong feminism was influ-

enced by the second wave of Western feminism, starting around 1975 and lasting for around a decade. The third wave of Hong Kong feminism featured post-colonial and de-colonial characteristics after the mid 1980s. As for most feminists' rough historical outline of Taiwanese feminist activism, the first wave of Taiwanese feminism occurred in the Japanese colonial era. The lifting of Martial Law began the second wave of it in 1987. Some feminists believe that the third wave of Taiwanese feminism went together with the Democratic Progressive Party's social movements. For details, consult Ya-chen Chen's *The Many Dimensions of Chinese Feminism*. New York: Palgrave MacMillan, forthcoming.

22. I am grateful for all the scholarly participants in the FFPP (Faculty Fellowship Publication Program) grant workshop hosted by Virginia Sanchez-Korros at the City University of New York in spring 2009. They read my book chapters and encouraged me to create my own term: "Chinese martial arts feminism."

Zhong Xueping's academic monograph, *Mainstream Culture Refocused: Television Drama, Society, and the Production of Meaning in Reform-Era China*, is a supportive illustration about scholars' creation of their own new terms for their research subjects. In this book, Zhong Xueping created the following new names for different kinds of Mainland Chinese television drama: "emperor drama," "anticorruption drama," "youth drama," and "family-marriage drama," etc. For details, consult Zhong Xueping's *Mainstream Culture Refocused: Television Drama, Society, and the Production of Meaning in Reform-Era China*. Honolulu: University of Hawaii Press, 2010.

23. In some mythological stories, Suiren is the first Chinese person to start fires and cook foods.

24. Susan Mann and Yu-yin Cheng, *Under Confucian Eyes: Writings on Gender in Chinese History*. (Berkeley: University of California Press, 2001).

25. Gayle Rubin, "The Traffic in Women: Notes on the 'Political Economy' of Sex." *Toward an Anthropology of Women*. ed. Rayna Reiter. (New York: Monthly Review Press, 1975), 157-210.

26. Ironically, Ban Zhao was herself extremely accomplished as a scholar, so much so that, following the death of her elder brother, Ban Gu (32-92 C.E.), she completed his monumental unfinished History of the Han Dynasty.

27. Dorothy Ko, *Cinderella's Sisters: A Revisionist History of Footbinding*. (Berkeley: California University Press, 2005).

28. Songling Pu, *Strange Tales from a Chinese Studio*. trans. John Minford. (London: Penguin, 2006).

29. Shanshan Du, *Chopsticks Only Work in Pairs*. (New York: Columbia University Press, 2002).

30. For instance, N. Harry Rothschild, currently an associate professor of history at the University of North Florida, wrote *Wu Zhao: China's Only Woman Emperor* in 2008. Even Jonathan Clements, a British scriptwriter, published a book about Wu Zetian in 2007.

31. Dorothy Ko, *Teachers of the Inner Chamber: Women and Culture in Seventeenth-Century China*. (Stanford: Stanford University Press, 1994). Also consult Ko's *Every Step A Lotus: Shoes for Bound Feet*. (Berkeley: University of California Press, 2001).

32. See Li Zongwei's *Tangren chuanqi* (*Legends of People in the Tang Dynasty*). (Beijing: Zhonghua, 2004). Also consult Zhang Youhe's *Tang Song chuanqi xuan* (*Selected Legends of the Tang and Song Dynasties*). (Beijing: Renmin wenxue, 1998), 221.

PART 1

NARRATIVE ANALYSES OF CHINESE WOMEN AND GENDER CONCERNS

Chapter One
The Fox, Dragon, and Lotus in *Crouching Tiger Hidden Dragon*

In *Crouching Tiger Hidden Dragon*,[1] there are three female protagonists: Jade Fox, Yü Jiaolong ("jade appealing dragon"), and Yü Xiulian ("graceful lotus," symbolizing dignity, spiritual purity and lack of pollution).[2] I contend that their names imply two different aspects of romantic love: carnal love and spiritual love. Jade Fox and Yü Jiaolong—whose names, it should be noted, both include animals—experience erotic love and have physical contact with men, while Yü Xiulian, whose name indicates a lotus, insists on Platonic or purely spiritual love for Li Mubai. Both Jade Fox and her disciple, Yü Jiaolong, attempt to negotiate exchanges of martial arts and sex. Jade Fox has a sexual relationship with Jiang Nanhe, Li Mubai's teacher, with whom she attempts to exchange sex for more advanced martial arts skills, such as those contained in the secret manual of kung fu. Yü Jiaolong shows interest in Li Mubai and tries to seduce him, so as to learn his art of fencing, while the virtuous Yü Xiulian stops Yü Jiaolong from touching or gaining access to Li Mubai's sword, as if she were rescuing Li from a savage predator and protecting his sword from defilement. In fact, from her name, evoking the elegant and pristine lotus that rises from mudflats, the viewers understand that Yü Xiulian is thwarting the "pollution" of her pure and lofty, lotus-like Platonic love for Li Mubai. At the end of the film, Yü Jiaolong's transformation from apprentice and co-conspirator of Jade Fox to dutiful student of Li Mubai and attentive recipient of Yü Jiaolong's sisterly counsel indicates her break with Jade Fox and with her erstwhile animal nature, by which she restores her friendship and spiritual sisterhood with Yü Xiulian.

Jade Fox and Jiang Nanhe

Jade Fox eschanges sexual relationships and physical intimacy for Jiang Nanhe's martial arts skills. Virginity, sexuality, and carnal desire are the currency with which Jade Fox negotiates access to Jiang Nanhe's advanced kung fu training. This narrative link between female seduction and fox spirits probably derives from Chinese mythology and legends. In traditional Chinese culture, it is widely believed that fox spirits, after meditation for hundreds or thousands of years in mountainous caves, acquire uncanny shape-shifting powers, enabling them to attain human form and to appear as mysteriously beguiling ladies.

In Chinese tradition, fox spirits are not unlike faeries in Euro-American legend or Pandora in Greco-Roman mythology, irresistibly appealing women who bring harm to men.[3] They are enchanting demons, alluring she-devils, extraordinarily sexy women with easy virtues. Classical Chinese literary works, such as *Liaozhai zhiyi* (*Strange Stories from a Chinese Studio*)[4] and *Fengshen yanyi* (*The Investiture of the Gods*),[5] include different versions of stories that evolve from similar archetypal patterns of fox spirits. Sometimes fox spirits are depicted as mythical women with remarkable powers, such as kung fu or sorcery. Examples include "Hu jia nü" (Fox marries off his daughter),[6] "Chou hu" (Ugly Fox),[7] and "Fengxian" (Fengxian)[8], from Liaozhai zhiyi, and "A Banquet for Specters in the Palace," the twenty-fifth chapter of *Fengshen yanyi*.

On the night of the thirteenth day . . . [Daji] assumed her original form, [namely, a fox] and traveled on a gust of wind beyond the south gate . . . to the grave mound . . . She was welcomed by the nine-headed pheasant . . . [Daji] thought of a plan . . . to transform into immortals and fairies and attend the banquet on the Happy Terrace. . . . Just then, they heard a great wind howling around them and realized that the immortals had already arrived. The foxes . . . had absorbed the essences of heaven, earth, the sun and moon for hundreds of years, and were now capable of assuming the likeness of immortals.[9]

Fox spirits are invariably female. According to folklore, good fox spirits would like to partake of the romantic love and carnal ecstasy that human beings enjoy while evil fox spirits want to exchange sex for the vital, "yang" essence which men discharge in sexual climax to counter-balance their own "yin" energy and thereby gain immortality. The men who consent to have sex with fox spirits are usually married, thereby betraying their orthodox sexual bonds. Neither are they sexually responsible for fox spirits.

Jade Fox's exchange of sex for Jiang Nanhe's martial arts skills is strikingly similar to the notorious business-like sexual transactions of evil fox spirits. The question remains, however, as to whether there is any true romantic love in the exchanges between Jade Fox and Huang Nanhe or, for that matter, between fox spirits and the men who have sex with them. But whether, in *Crouching Tiger Hidden Dragon*, Jade Fox can be seen as a sort of evil fox spirit demands further examination. Whether the fox spirits indeed truly are wicked also calls for further scrutiny. Why? Viewers must also wonder at Jiang Nanhe's willingness to use Jade Fox as nothing but a sex object, while taking no sexual responsibility and entirely discarding her feelings, ultimately failing to honor his agreement to teach her advanced kung fu skills. Although it may well be dishonorable for Jade Fox, and fox spirits, to exchange their sexuality for what they truly want, it is no less disgraceful for Jiang Nanhe (and the consorts of fox spirits) to partake of the sexual indulgences offered to them while withholding the vital masculine skills or essence from Jade Fox and the pretty women whom fox spirits turn into.

In the business deals of sex, if Jade Fox and fox spirits are labeled as evil, then Jiang Nanhe and the men who have sex with fox spirits can hardly be absolved of their sexual irresponsibility, lack of morality, and adultery.

From a feminist point of view, Chinese men historically tended to blame their immoral love affairs, extramarital sexual behaviors, lack of faith for legal wives, and betrayal of wedlock on fox spirits. Most legends of fox spirits have been told, written, revised, or recorded by men, which may well account for the conventional characterization of the fox spirits as active initiators of sexual relationships, thus making them scapegoats for the immoral, adulterous behavior of dishonorable men. Surely, men cannot reasonably be absolved of blame for their sexual trysts with fox spirits, nor can the illicit encounters be convincingly blamed solely upon the fox spirits, or the female forms into which they transform. It is rather the men who must be held accountable. Not only do they partake of the forbidden sexual pleasure, but they then proceed to demonize or denigrate their female sexual partners, shift all the blame onto fox spirits, denying any responsibility for their actions, as if they were no more than innocent victims. Even if fox spirits be reduced to the status of sex object valued for nothing more than the fleeting sexual gratification that they provide for men, to cast them aside once their lust has been satisfied and denigrate them as evil or monstrous is the most glaring of double standards—and this, without even addressing the profound sexism of the gross objectification of women upon which this defense is predicated.

Because of the age-old Confucian code concerning the pricelessness of women's virginity, which must be defended even unto suicide from falling prey to the carnal appetites of men, Chinese women were exhorted to value their chastity as highly as their lives. A woman's fertility was to be consecrated to the service of only one man, remaining true to him even should he die before their marriage was consummated. Once a Chinese woman gave her sexuality to a man, severe social and cultural sanctions intervened to disallow her to offer herself to another. Virginity was especially significant for Chinese women's reputations. Its importance was equated with the value of a woman's life, as neither can be recuperated once it is spent. In light of these views, Jade Fox can be seen to have paid an extremely high price for Jiang Nanhe's secret manual of advanced kung fu, sacrificing her very virginity, the most valuable attribute a woman can possess in offering herself to Jiang Nanhe. Giving the cost to her virtue, she naturally presumes that Jiang Nanhe will honor their bargain and provide her the secret manual. Yet, even after accepting the sacrifice which Jade Fox offered him, Jiang Nanhe neither offers the secret manual of kung fu nor teach her any advanced martial arts techniques. At minimum, gender parity should mean that, when men are given what they want from women, women should also be provided that which they desire. Yet, Jiang Nanhe brazenly defies this rule of gender parity. Is it any wonder, then, that Jade Fox is enraged in response and seeks to visit vengeance upon Jiang Nanhe. Even if one views Jade Fox as equivalent to a sex worker, exchanging her body for a value she deem equivalent to her virtue, this cannot excuse Jiang Nanhe, as her customer, to refuse payment once he has sated his lust.

Yü Jiaolong and Li Mubai

Yü Jiaolong's attitude toward Li Mubai is similar to that of Jade Fox toward Jiang Nanhe. She loosens the buttons on her garment along the neck and chest, revealing the upper frontier of her undergarments, and whispers seductively to Li Mubai, all in an effort to be persuade him to train her in swordsmanship in exchange for sex. Her approach to Li Mubai is actually not very different from Jade Fox's seduction of Jiang Nanhe, offering sex in exchange for Jiang's martial arts skills.

Parallel Narratives of Sexual Exchange for Kung Fu

Wherein lies the symmetry in these two parallel narratives? Yü Jiaolong is Jade Fox's disciple.[10] She may well have been schooled in the tactic of exchanging sex for martial arts skills by Jade Fox. Still, there is a disparity in their power relations. Jade Fox teaches Yü Jiaolong martial arts, yet she is illiterate and hence depends on Yü Jiaolong's literacy to gain access to the teachings contained in kung fu manuals. This dependence upon Yü Jiaolong exposes Jade Fox to the risk that she might inadvertently divulge the value of Jiang Nanhe's kung fu secrets to Yü Jiaolong. As Jiang Nanhe's disciple, Li Mubai inherits his master's secret of swordplay after Jiang dies. With this shift in power relations, Yü Jiaolong devises a plan to learn the secret from Li Mubai by means of sexual seduction.

The film's narrative, therefore, is constructed upon parallel master-apprentice relationships, neatly aligned along the axis of gender. On the one hand is the relationship between Jade Fox and Yü Jiaolong and, on the other, that between Jiang Nanhe and Li Mubai. Structurally, then, there is an equivalence posited between Jade Fox and Jiang Nanhe, in that both are teachers, and between Yü Jiaolong and Li Mubai, as apprentices. And yet this equivalence is immediately disrupted, since Jade Fox seeks to become the apprentice of Jiang Nanhe, while Yü Jiaolong hopes to become Li Mubai's apprentice. Hence, both women disavow their rightful status by seeking to subordinate themselves to men who should be considered their equal and counterpart, and doing so by yielding that which is most precious to the sexuality of woman to the basest sexuality of men. Thus, Jade Fox seduces Jiang Nanhe in an attempt to exchange her body for Jiang Nanhe's kung fu, and Yü Jiaolong seduces Li Mubai in an effort to induce Li Mubai to teach her secrets of his swordplay.

Structurally speaking, then, the film narrative is mounted upon parallels and disjunctures among the four principal roles of Jade Fox, Jiang Nanhe, Yü Jiaolong, and Li Mubai. First, the master-apprentice relationship between Jade Fox and Yü Jiaolong parallels that between Jiang Nanhe and Li Mubai. Second, Jade Fox's seductive strategies to exchange her body for Jiang Nanhe's martial arts parallel Yü Jiaolong's seduction of Li Mubai in exchange for his instruction in advanced kung fu.

Carnal Passion and the Bestiality of Names

Yet another parallel is hidden in the names of Jade Fox and Yü Jiaolong. The names of both women contain the names of mythical animals. Jade Fox is designated by the cunning and solitary fox while Yü Jiaolong[11] is designated by the auspicious yet inscrutable dragon. She identifies herself as a flying dragon, possessed of a mastery swordsmanship by which she will defeat Eagle Sung and Flying Couger Li, as if the dragon by which she is named endows her with the same degree of supremacy the dragon enjoys over all other creatures. As she proclaims:

> I am the invincible sword goddess,
> Armed with the incredible Green Destiny.
> Be you Li or South Crane,
> Lower your head and ask for my mercy.
> I am the desert dragon.
> I leave no trace.
> Today I fly over the Er-mei.
> I topple Wudang.

The mythologized animals evoked in the names of these characters are no mere narrative flourish, but reveal deeper levels of homology and resonance among the characters; for, as we discover, the man to whom Yü Jiaolong already has given herself is named by the most ferocious of creatures. His name is Luo Xiaohu, whose given name, Xiaohu, refers to a small tiger. This union brings together two of the most powerful mythological creatures in Chinese culture, evoking images of uncanny supernatural power. Lest the viewers overlook these name plays, Ang Lee has Li Mubai characterize martial arts as the "world of tigers and dragons." The three characters who are named by mythologized creatures are also those who violate orthodox morality to have illicit sexual relations. The designation of these three characters by mythologized creatures that embody untamable cosmic forces—creatures which, in their wildness and violence, are beyond all measures of constraint—evokes the unbridled sexuality of the characters they thus name. Like the beasts whose names they bear, these characters act outside of all social constraints and cultural injunctions. Never will they submit to the discipline of society's moral codes, nor yield to the confining strictures of cultural convention. These creatures, I contend, are invoked to denote the unbridled sexuality of these characters thus named, positioning them in violent defiance of cultural norms.

Spiritual Love: Yü Xiulian and the Name of the Lotus

It is in the lotus invoked in the name of Yü Xiulian that the untamable creatures that haunt the names of Jade Fox, Yü Jiaolong, and Luo Xiaohu find their foil. The word, *lian*, refers to a lotus blossom. Combined with *xiu*, the character's given name signifies a graceful or elegant lotus, which connotes dignity, loftiness, and spiritual purity, undefiled by pollution and untarnished by social stigma. In classical Chinese literature, the lotus signifies a self-disciplined and righteous person with a good character, a sound education, and a strong and steady personality. Its blossom is anthropomorphized as *hua zhi jünzi*, "a gentleman—or, here, a gentle person—of noble character and integrity."

The resonance of such a gentle person with the lotus is discernible in the following ode to the lotus penned by the Northern Song Neo-Confucian philosopher and cosmologist Zhou Dunyi (1017-1073): It repels pollution even after emerging from the sludge or mud (signifying its refusal to wallow in the mire of wickedness). It purifies itself in clear ripples, but refrains from appearing overly seductive in its beauty. Its stems are hollow while its outer sheath forms a stalk that is sturdy and upright. (That is to say, the person who personifies the lotus remains upright and virtuous regardless of the context.) The lotus is simple and without ambition: it does not seek to climb nor does it spread itself with a profusion of lateral branches. (In other words, the person who personifies the lotus does not seek to curry favor with people of high power, wealth or status. Nor does this person become entangled in side issues or raise any unexpected difficulties.) Its fragrance spreads out far and wide, and its aroma remains always pleasant and never overwhelms. It stands upright and still, an aura of grace surrounding it. It deflects all irreverence or wantonness. Those who see it can only gaze at it from the shores of the pond or swamp, admiring its still, pure beauty, which remains always out of reach.[12]

The lotus by which the character of Yü Xiulian is named evokes her capacity for spiritual love. Her great virtue, for instance, is revealed by her enduring devotion to her deceased betrothed. In full accordance with Confucian codes on female virtue, she keeps his spirit tablet in her closet and reserves a space in her heart for him. A similar kind of love is also available to Li Mubai, for the romantic love Yü Xiulian feels for Li Mubai is sublimated into a spiritual, Platonic, divine love. In her physical interactions with Li Mubai, she displays the self-discipline and restraint demanded of an honorable Confucian woman. This internalized, spiritual exalting love is the absolute inverse of the carnal desire that draws Luo Xiaohu to Yü Jiaolong and the purely sexual encounter between Jade Fox and Jiang Nanhe.

From the vantage of Yü Xiulian's spiritual mysophobia, Yü Jiaolong's seduction of Li Mubai seems to "pollute" his loftiness and spiritual purity. For example, when Yü Xiulian prohibits Yü Jiaolong from touching Li Mubai's sword, she does so to safeguard the sword from defilement, giving expression to the spiritual ideals which she and Li Mubai have in common. By protecting the sword, she, in essence, defends their spiritual love against the "pollution" by the carnal bestiality of Yü Jiaolong. Her battles with Yü Jiaolong, are waged in defense of the spiritual purity and chaste virtue of Yü Xiulian's sublimated love for Li Mubai.

Li Mubai: Yearning for Purity

The spirituality and purity of sublimated love is also invoked in the name of Li Mubai. The character, *mu*, refers to the pleasant feeling of wonder, aspiration and yearning for some esteemed or idealized state or objective. That objective is given in the second character, *bai*, "white" or "whiteness," which, in this context, suggests purity, righteousness, and spirituality. It evokes the pristine petals of the lotus repelling the mud of the swamp. The name, Mubai, clearly suggests that Li Mubai longs for the purity and chastity embodied by Yü Xiulian. It conveys to the audience that Li Mubai's love for Yü Xiulian is a divine, spiritual love. When Yü Xiulian remarks that "to repress one's feelings only makes them stronger," Li Mubai agrees and confesses his spiritual love for her: "You're right, but I don't know what to do. I want to be with you." This is probably also why Yü Jiaolong's seductive strategies and plans to exchange her carnal love for martial arts skills fail.

On the other hand, the excessive self-discipline required to attain the lotus-like spiritual purity upon which Yü Xiulian and Li Mubai insist may also be seen as a form of classism or cultural conceit, which may repress freedom, deaden critical thinking, and devour originality, creativity, individualism, adventurousness, and any true feelings that flow from the depths of the human heart. Lu Xun's "Diary of a Madman" (1918), a seminal work of China's early literary modernist movement, vividly depicts this by depicting traditional Chinese culture, with its strict rules and rigid codes, of being cannibalistic. Yü Xiulian and Li Mubai both clearly know which part of them is "devoured" by the constraints of culture. For instance, Yü Jiaolong imagines that Yü Xiulian and Li Mubai enjoy complete freedom in the world of martial arts and openly envies them; however, Yü Xiulian reveals her frustration at the cultural constraints that prevent her and Li Mubai from consummating their love for one another, even after her fiancé's death. This is perhaps why both Yü Xiulian and

Li Mubai arrange the reunion of Yü Jiaolong and Luo Xiaohu in Wudang, so as to allow them enough freedom to enjoy their romantic relationship, although it violates the strict and rigid societal and familial regulations Yü Jiaolong faces in her home. They are actually helping Yü Jiaolong and Luo Xiaohu negotiate the rigid familial and socio-cultural structures and strike a balance between the "cannibalistic" cultural norms and the wild, uncontrollable animal nature their names signify.

Film critics have written that Ang Lee "illustrates the inevitable conflicts and negotiations between individuals bound by familial and societal obligations . . . [He] demonstrates the struggles of individuals."[13] It is indeed true that the "common thread in [almost] all [Ang Lee's] films is the family facing change,"[14] and that *Crouching Tiger Hidden Dragon* conforms with Ang Lee's previous work: "Well-crafted . . . films [about the dynamics of parent-child conflicts] could succeed in both winning awards and generating profits."[15] If the wild savagery of the animals by which Yü Jiaolong and Luo Xiaohu are named and the "cannibalistic" culture of Yü Xiulian and Li Mubai are like two poles, Ang Lee juxtaposes them with "spice, [and] seasoning that . . . liven up"[16] the screen. In Ang Lee's films, generations and cultures do not compromise, coalesce, fuzzily melt, but rather achieve a tense, polite, and somehow bracing remove.[17]

Domesticating the Wild and Savage Beasts

Among the three animals, the dragon and tiger[18] are usually the animals to be tamed by kung fu masters. Such is the case, for instance, in the story of Wu Song's defeat of the tiger in "Wu Song Kills a Tiger on Jingyang Ridge," one of the most renowned episodes in Shi Nai'an and Luo Guanzhong's *Shuihuzhuan* (*Outlaws of the Marsh*).[19]

> There was a fierce tiger with a white forehead and bulging eyes on Jingyang Ridge. It came out at night, and had already killed nearly thirty strong men. . . . Both hungry and thirsty, the big animal clawed the ground with its front paws, sprang up and hurtled forward. . . . [Wu Song] kicked the beast in the face and eyes, again and again. The tiger roared, pushing back two piles of yellow earth and digging a pit before it with its claws. Wu Song pushed the animal's muzzle into the pit . . . After sixty or seventy blows, the tiger lay motionless, panting weakly, blood streaming from eyes, mouth, nose and ears . . . [Wu Song] then beat the animal till it breathed no more.[20]

The kung fu technique named *xianglong shiba zhang* (eighteen palms to defeat the dragon) in Jin Yong's martial arts novel, *Tianlong babu* (*Demi-Gods and Semi-Devils*),[21] is also representative of the taming of wild creatures, as is the novel *Yitian tulong ji* (*The Heaven Sword and Dragon Saber*),[22] in which the *tulong dao* (dragon saber) is the saber used to slaughter the dragon.

In *Crouching Tiger Hidden Dragon*, Yü Jiaolong is the "dragon" that Li Mubai tames.[23] She is the "dragon" that is disciplined to the way of righteousness and spiritual purity to which the "lotus," Yü Xiulian, and Li Mubai cleave. Yü Jiaolong, as the tamed "dragon," is transformed from a cunning "dragon" trained by Jade Fox to an apprentice of spiritual rectitude.

In literary terms, Yü Jiaolong is a "round character," a character who undergoes transformation as the story develops. The central narrative of Yü Jiaolong's transformation thus makes the film into a cinematic "bildungsroman,"[24] a story about a protagonist's growth or spiritual metamorphosis from mental immaturity or emotional weakness to psychological maturity or adulthood.

Li Mubai's success in taming Yü Jiaolong contrasts with Jiang Nanhe's refusal to accept Jade Fox as a student as well as his failure in teaching her. In subduing Yü Jiaolong, Jade Fox's disciple, and turning her into a good and righteous person, Li Mubai puts an end to the teacher-student relationship between Jade Fox and Yü Jiaolong. He thereby also puts an end to the expansion of Jade Fox's foxiness. By making the extension of Jade Fox's foxiness impossible, this also indirectly "kills" Jade Fox. Since Li Mubai's ambition after Jiang Nanhe's death is to avenge Jiang by killing Jade Fox, his conquest of Yü Jiaolong is actually one of the ways to take revenge on Jade Fox for the death of Jiang Nanhe, a vengeance completed when he kills Jade Fox. Although Li Mubai, later on, is "killed by [Jade Fox] by accident and dies with regret on his last breath" and thus seems to fail "as a traditional . . . hero,"[25] he still successfully avenges Jiang Nanhe by vanquishing Yü Jiaolong, "taking her back from the evil Jade Fox to what he calls the 'right path,'"[26] and stopping Jade Fox from perpetuating her foxiness across generations.

After being tamed by Li Mubai, Yü Jiaolong's transformation also influences her relationship with Luo Xiaohu as well as Luo Xiaohu himself. Yü Jiaolong's decision to leave Luo Xiaohu and commit suicide leads their relationship to a deeper spiritual level. Although Luo Xiaohu misses, waits for, and seeks to elope with Yü Jiaolong, thereby suggesting that he continues to feel carnal desire for Yü Jiaolong, this is coupled with a growing spiritual love. Yü Jiaolong's transformation under the guidance of Li Mubai and the suicide, which brings the story of her love for Luo Xiaohu to its tragic end, underscore the spiritual nature of their love and minimize the carnal passion with which their love began. In addition, Luo Xiaohu's nickname includes the character, *yün*, which signifies clouds, as well as the phrase, *bantian*, which means "half the sky." The clouds themselves may be seen to forecast the loftiness which his love for Yü Jiaolong ultimately will attain, while the reference to "half the sky" may suggest that the other half of Luo Xiaohu's lofty, spiritual love for Yü Jiaolong remains earthbound, firmly rooted in carnal desire.

That is to say, Li Mubai's taming of the "dragon" sublimates the love between Yü Jiaolong and Luo Xiaohu from carnal and earthy love to spiritual, divine love, bringing it more closely into alignment with the spiritual love between Yü Xiulian and Li Mubai. It transforms Yü Jiaolong from a practitioner of the foxy techniques learned from Jade Fox to a follower of the lofty spirituality and lotus-like purity of Yü Xiulian.

Because of Li Mubai's taming, Yü Jiaolong is drawn further and further from the clutches of Jade Fox's foxiness and ever closer to the lotus-like purity, integrity and virtue of Yü Xiulian. She is drawn further and further from the crafty fox and closer and closer to the pristine clarity of the lotus. This is discernible in the spiritual sisterhood that forms between Yü Jiaolong and Yü Xiulian, indicated, for example, when Yü Xiulian gives her hairpin to Yü Jiaolong in order to enable Yü Jiaolong to win trust and assistance from people in her own home. The sorority of these two female characters, strengthened by their common hope to rescue Li Mubai, also evokes a parallel with Yü Xiulian's love for Li Mubai.[27] After Li Mubai's death, the sisterly bond between the two women is given ritual expression when Yü Xiulian puts Li Mubai's sword on Yü Jiaolong's head and offers her sisterly guidance to Yü Jiaolong. Afterwards, Yü Jiaolong accepts Yü Xiulian's advice: "Be true to yourself." Therefore, she decides to embrace the path of faithfulness and virtue as in the legend that Luo Xiaohu told her.

> We have a legend. Anyone who dares to jump from the mountain, God will grant his wish. Long ago a young man whose parents were ill, so he jumped. He did not die. He was not even hurt. He floated away, far away, never to return. He knew that his wish had come true. If you believe, it will come true. An elder once said, "Faith makes wishes come true."

Yü Jiaolong requires Luo Xiaohu to make a romantic wish that she can share with him, and then jumps into the abyss in order to make their romantic dream come true: the romantic dream that they return to the desert together again. She jumps into the abyss, believing that her jump can enable their romantic dream to be realized in the future.

The romantic dream that Yü Jiaolong and Luo Xiaohu share parallels the spiritual love that Li Mubai and Yü Xiulian share, as when Li Mubai says to Yü Xiulian at the end of the film: "My spirit will be with you." Yü Jiaolong's decision to jump into the Wudang abyss in the final scene of the film stands in sharp contrast to the final part of the lyric that shows her original identity as a flying dragon from the desert: "I toppled Wudang." Instead of toppling Wudang, Yü Jiaolong jumps into the abyss in the Wudang mountainous area. Yü Jiaolong's leap signifies her yearning to free herself of the familial obligations and cultural codes that prevent her from fulfilling her desires. Ang Lee uses the scene of "flying"[28] to denote this freedom, which she realizes in her leap. By "the end of the movie, [she is so] . . . immersed in the mysterious atmosphere of Zen metaphysics as to renounce her love as well as her life... because of the profound influence of Li [Mubai]."[29] This can be seen as the final Wudang teaching that Li Mubai imparts through his own death, further guided by Yü Xiulian's sisterly advice, and shaped by Luo Xiaohu's romantic dream: a young couple's magical return to the desert with the help of the gods, instead of a dragon's solitary return to the desert.

Conclusion

Jade Fox, Yü Jiaolong, and Yü Xiulian are three significant female protagonists in *Crouching Tiger Hidden Dragon*. Jade Fox embodies the animal indicated in her name in so far as her strategy of seduction in exchange for Jiang Nanhe's secret of swordplay evokes the seduction of the sultry vixens into which fox spirits are depicted to transform themselves in order to partake of the "yang" essence they obtain from men during sex. These sinister attributes are cast in sharp clarity by their contrast to Yü Xiulian, whose lofty purity and virtue are indicated by the "lotus" included in her name. Li Mubai, the male protagonist caught between these women, foreshadows his ultimate choice in his own name, which tells of one who exalts and yearns for the purity and perfection of whiteness, as of the white petals of the lotus. Yü Jiaolong is likewise caught between the two poles of carnal bestiality and lofty virtue. Although Yü Jiaolong's name also indicates the wild, creature nature of the dragon, she is a "round character," gradually transforming from Jade Fox's foxy disciple to a tamed "dragon" under the sturdy tutelage of Li Mubai and Yü Xiulian. Chinese martial arts movies sometimes include tales of dragons that must be slain or tamed by martial arts masters.[30] The narrative of the young "dragon," Yü Jiaolong, who is transformed through civilizing discipline makes the film something of a *bildungsroman*.[31]

In addition to the dragon, the tiger is usually the animal that gives way to heroic warriors in classical Chinese literature or Chinese martial arts novels. The tiger in Luo Xiaohu seems to be no exception. He follows Li Mubai's advice and waits for Yü Jiaolong in Wudang. As a consequence, by the end of the film, his carnal desire for Yü Jiaolong is tamed and humanized, enriched and exalted by spiritual love. Thus, the animals and the lotus in the character's names foreshadow the story of *Crouching Tiger Hidden Dragon*.

References

Abrams, M. H. *Glossary of Literary Terms* (Eighth Edition). Boston: Thomson Wadsworth, 2005.
bell hooks. *Black Looks: Race and Representation*. Boston: South End Press, 1992, p. 21.
Berry, Michael. "Ang Lee: Freedom in Films." *Speaking in Images: Interviews with Contemporary Chinese Filmmakers*. New York: Columbia University Press, 2005, p. 327; 347.
Chan, Felicia. "*Crouching Tiger, Hidden Dragon:* Cultural Migrancy and Translatability." *Chinese Films in Focus: 25 New Takes*. Chris Berry edt. London: British Film Institute, 2003. p. 62.
Chen, Jingliang and Zou Jianwen. *Bainian zhongguo dianying jingxuan* (*The Best of Cenennial Chinese Cinema*). Beijing: Chinese Academy of Social Science, 2005, p. 227.
Dariotis, Wei Ming and Eileen Fung. "Breaking the Soy Sauce Jar: Diaspora and Displacement in the Films of Ang Lee." *Transnational Chinese Cinemas: Identity, Nationhood, Gender*. Sheldon Hsiao-peng Lu edt. Honolulu: University of Hawaii Press, 1997, p. 187.
Feng, Xiaosheng Lin. "Chow Yun-fat: Hong Kong's Modern TV." *Chinese Film Starts*. Mary Farquhar and Yinjing Zhang edt. London: Routledge, 2010.
Jin, Yong. *Tianlong babu* (*Demi-Gods and Semi-Devils*). Beijing: Wenhua yishu, 1998.
---. *Yitian tulong ji* (*The Heaven Sword and Dragon Sabre*). Hong Kong: Minghe she, 1985.
---. *Xueshan feihu* (*Fox Volant in the Snowy Mountain*). Hong Kong: Chinese University Press, 1996.
Kim, L. S. "*Crouching Tiger Hidden Dragon:* Making Women Warriors—A Transnational Reading of Asian Female Action Heroes." *Jump Cut: A Review of Contemporary Media*. 48 (Winter 2006): http://goo.gl/y05QA.
Lyons, Donald. "Passionate Precision: Sense and Sensibility." *Film Comment* 32.1 (1996): 36-42, p. 40.
Lo, Kwai-cheung. *Chinese Face/Off: The Transnational Popular Culture of Hong Kong*. Urbana: University of Illinois Press, 2005, pp. 186-187.
Morris, Gary. "Beautiful Beast: Crouching Tiger Hidden Dragon." *Bright Lights Film Journal* 31 (2001): http://brightlightsfilm.com/31/crouchingtiger.html.
Mulvey, Laura. "The Myth of Pandora: A Psychoanalytical Approach." *Feminisms in the Cinema*. Laura Pietropaolo and Ada Testaferri edt. Bloomington: Indiana University Press, 1995, p. 3.
Pu, Songling. *Liaozhai zhiyi* (*Strange Stories from a Chinese Studio*). Beijing: Beijing shi yue wen yi, 1997.
---. *Liaozhai zhiyi* (*Strange Stories from a Chinese Studio*). Herbert A. Giles's English trans. New York: Boni and Liveright, 1925.
Sang, Tze-lan Deborah. "Wang Dulu de jingwei nüxing chengzhang xiaoshuo" (The Bildungsroman of Beijing Women by Wang Dulu). *Beijing: Dushi xiangxiang yü wenhua jiyi* (*Beijing: Urban Imagination and Cultural Memory*). Chen Pingyuan and David Der-wei Wang edt. Beijing: Beijing University Press, 2005, pp. 210-212.

---. "Women's Work and Boundary Transgression in Wang Dulu's Popular Novels." *Gender in Motion: Divisions of Labor and Cultural Change in Late Imperial and Modern China*. Bryna Goodman and Wendy Larson edt. Lanham, MD: Rowman & Littlefield, 2005, pp. 289-291.

Shi, Nai'an and Luo Guanzhong. *Shuihuzhuan (Outlaws of the Marsh)*. Sidney Shapiro trans. Volume I. Bloomington: Indiana University Press, 1981, pp. 353-356.

Stone, Judy. "Ang Lee." *Eyes on the World: Conversations with International Filmmakers*. Los Angeles: Silman-James, 1997, p. 597.

Xü, Zhonglin. *Fengshan yanyi (The Creation of the Gods)*. Beijing: Xinshijie (New World Press), 2000.

Yang, Jeff. *Once Upon A Time in China*. New York: Atria, p. 103.

Zhang, Yingjin. *Chinese National Cinema*. New York: Routledge, 2004, p. 278.

Notes

1. I base this article on the film, *Crouching Tiger Hidden Dragon*, directed by Lee Ang, not Wang Dulu's martial arts novel entitled *Crouching Tiger Hidden Dragon*. Nevertheless, since the characters whose names contain the terms for "dragon," "fox," and "lotus" appear in the original novel and the film adaptation, the arguments presented here are applicable to both. Wang Hui-Ling, James Schamus, and Ah Cheng wrote adaptations of Wang Dulu's original story for Ang Lee. For details, see Ang Lee's statements in Michael Berry's "Ang Lee: Freedom in Film" in *Speaking with Images: Interviews with Contemporary Chinese Filmmakers*. (New York: Columbia University Press, 2005), 347.

2. L. S. Kim's discussion of these three female protagonists in her article, "*Crouching Tiger Hidden Dragon:* Making Women Warriors—A Transnational Reading of Asian Female Action Heroes" in *Jump Cut: A Review of Contemporary Media*. 48 (Winter 2006): http://www.ejumpcut.org/archive/jc48.2006/womenWarriors/index.html (online data accessed in July 2009). I do not disagree with Kim's argument concerning the presence of Orientalism in Li Ang's work. My aim in this article, however, is to present an exegesis of the names of the three female protagonists.

3. Consult Laura Mulvey's "The Myth of Pandora: A Psychoanalytical Approach" in *Feminisms in the Cinema*.

4. Consult Pu Songling's *Liaozhai zhiyi (Strange Stories from a Chinese Studio)*. Beijing: Beijing shi yue wen yi, 1997; see also Herbert A. Giles's English translation published by Boni and Liveright in New York in 1925.

5. Consult Xü Zhonglin's *Fengshen yanyi (The Investiture of the Gods)*. (Beijing: Xinshijie / New World Press, 2000).

6. See Pu Songling's *Liaozhai zhiyi (Strange Stories from a Chinese Studio)*, 42-43.

7. See Pu Songling's *Liaozhai zhiyi (Strange Stories from a Chinese Studio)*, 825-826.

8. Fengxian is the name of a beautiful lady, who is a transformed fox spirit.

9. See Xü Zhonglin's *Fengshen yanyi (The Investiture of the Gods)*, 492-499.

10. Felicia Chan notes: "As the 'queen' of the [martial arts] films in the 1960s, Cheng [Pei-pei (Zheng Peipei)] symbolically makes way for a new generation of actor the way Jade Fox must make way for her disciple," Yü Jiaolong. See Felicia Chan's "*Crouching*

Tiger, Hidden Dragon: Cultural Migrancy and Translatability" in *Chinese Films in Focus: 25 New Takes*. ed. Chris Berry. (London: British Film Institute, 2003), 62.

11. Ang Lee's choice of Zhang Ziyi for the role of "dragon" made her into a new Chinese female superstar, the natural successor of Zheng Peipei, Gong Li, and Michelle Yeoh. See Jeff Yang's *Once upon A Time in China*. (New York: Atria), 103. Zhang Ziyi has at least once expressed her gratitude to Ang Lee in public.

In an address concerning women in Chinese martial arts films delivered in May 2005, Wendy Larson presented Zheng Peipei, Michelle Yeoh, and Zhang Ziyi, the three female leads in *Crouching Tiger Hidden Dragon*, as representatives of three successive generations: Zheng Peipei represents the first generation; Michelle Yeoh the second, and Zhang Ziyi the third.

In his review of the film, Gary Morris cites Ang Lee's remarks concerning women in his film:

> People tend to look down on the genre. Some may have thought it strange that I could just drop what I normally do and make something like a B-movie. And as I was doing it, there was no escape. I had to bring in drama, I had to bring in women, I had to bring in beauty and whatever I feel added quality to it. It became an Ang Lee movie.

See Gary Morris's "Beautiful Beast: Crouching Tiger Hidden Dragon." in *Bright Lights Film Journal* 31 (2001): http://brightlightsfilm.com/31/crouchingtiger.html (online data accessed in May 2007). Also consult L. S. Kim's "*Crouching Tiger Hidden Dragon* Making Women Warriors—A Transnational Reading of Asian Female Action Heroes" in *Jump Cut: A Review of Contemporary Media* 48 (Winter 2006): http://goo.gl/y05QA (online data retrieved in April 2011).

Concerning the film, Michael Berry remarked: "Produced with international funding and starring Hong Kong superstars Chow Yun-fat and Michelle Yeoh alongside veterans like Zheng Peipei and new comers like Chang Chen and Zhang Ziyi, *Crouching Tiger [Hidden Dragon]* both resurrected the *wuxia* [martial arts] genre and created a new model for pan-Asian film production." For details, consult Michael Berry's *Speaking in Images: Interviews with Contemporary Chinese Filmmakers*. (New York: Columbia University Press, 2005), 327. As for scholarly research related to Chow Yun-fat, consult "Chow Yun-fat: Hong Kong's Modern TV."

12. This is my English translation and annotation according to my understanding of Zhou Dunyi's "Ai Lian Shuo" (On My Preference for the Lotus) in the Song Dynasty.

13. Consult Wei Ming Dariotis and Eileen Fung's "Breaking the Soy Sauce Jar: Diaspora and Displacement in the Films of Ang Lee" in *Transnational Chinese Cinemas: Identity, Nationhood, Gender*, 187.

14. See Judy Stone's "Ang Lee" in *Eyes on the World: Conversations with International Filmmakers*. (Los Angeles: Silman-James, 1997), 597.

15. Consult *Chinese National Cinema*. (New York: Routledge, 2004), 278.

16. bell hooks, *Black Looks: Race and Representation*. (Boston: South End Press, 1992), 21.

17. Donald Lyons, "Passionate Precision: Sense and Sensibility" in *Film Comment* 32.1 (1996): 40.

18. Jin Yong's *Xueshan feihu* (*Fox Volant in the Snowy Mountain*) also includes a person, named "Fox Volant," "Flying Fox," who tries to take revenge. However, Fox Volant has nothing to do with taming beast. See Jin Yong's *Xueshan feihu* (*Fox Volant in the Snowy Mountain*). (Hong Kong: Chinese University Press, 1996).

19. See Pu Songling's *Liaozhai zhiyi* (*Strange Stories from a Chinese Studio*). Beijing: Beijing shi yue wen yi, 1997, 825-826. Also consult Chapter Twenty-Three in Sidney Shapiro's translation of Shi Nai'an and Luo Guanzhong. *Shuihuzhuan* (*Outl aws of the Marsh*), 353-356.

20. See Pu Songling's *Liaozhai zhiyi* (*Strange Stories from a Chinese Studio*). (Beijing: Beijing shi yue wen yi, 1997), 825-826.

21. Consult Jin Yong's *Tianlong babu*. (Beijing: Wenhua yishu, 1998).

22. Yong Jin, *Yitian tulong ji* (*The Heaven Sword and Dragon Sabre*). (Hong Kong: Minghe she, 1985).

23. In "Women's Work and Boundary Transgression in Wang Dulu's Popular Novels," Sang Tze-lan argues that Yü Jiaolong "defies father, mother, teacher, brother, and husband to search for personal freedom and to test her own prowess. Not even her illicit male lover, Luo Xiaohu, can subdue her and make her surrender to domesticity." For details, consult this article in *Gender in Motion: Divisions of Labor and Cultural Change in Late Imperial and Modern China*. eds. Bryna Goodman and Wendy Larson. (Lanham, MD: Rowman & Littlefield, 2005), 289-291.

In this, Sang Tze-lan appears to base her argument on the original novel version of *Crouching Tiger Hidden Dragon*, by Wang Dulu, rather than the film version of the same story by Lee Ang. I base my argument on the film version of *Crouching Tiger Hidden Dragon*, and therefore contend that Li Mubai tames Yü Jiaolong and that Yü Jiaolong becomes Yü Xiulian's sisterly advisee at the end of the film. Lo Kwai-cheung's interpretation of Yü Jiaolong's change in the film, for instance, is similar to mine. In *Chinese Face/Off*, Lo likewise contends that Li Mubai recruits Yü Jiaolong "as his own disciple...Li's death seems to be a blow to" her and changes her. Lo also thinks that "by the end of the movie, [Yü Jiaolong is so]... immersed in the mysterious atmosphere of Zen metaphysics as to renounce her love as well as her life... because of the profound influence of Li [Mubai]." See *Chinese Face/Off*. (Urbana: University of Illinois Press, 2005), 186-187.

24. Consult Deborah Tze-lan Sang's "Wang Dulu de jingwei nüxing chengzhang xiaoshuo" (The Bildungsroman of Beijing Women by Wang Dulu) in *Beijing: Dushi xiangxiang yü wenhua jiyi* (*Beijing: Urban Imagination and Cultural Memory*), 210-212.

25. Consult Felicia Chan's "*Crouching Tiger, Hidden Dragon*: Cultural Migrancy and Translatability" in *Chinese Films in Focus: 25 New Takes*, 62.

26. Consult *Chinese Face/Off: The Transnational Popular Culture of Hong Kong*. (Urbana: University of Illinois Press, 2005), 186.

27. See *Bainian zhongguo dianying jingxuan* (*The Best of Cenennial Chinese Cinema*). (Beijing: Chinese Academy of Social Science, 2005), 227.

28. Michael Berry, "Ang Lee: Freedom in Film" in *Speaking in Images: Interviews with Contemporary Chinese Filmmakers*. (New York: Columbia University Press, 2005), 343.

29. Kwai-cheung Lo, *Chinese Face/Off: The Transnational Popular Culture of Hong Kong*. (Urbana: University of Illinois Press, 2005), 187.

30. In East Asian mythologies, dragons are not necessarily malevolent and represent the controlling power or authority. Some of them are related to water, rain or ocean. In imperial China, the dragon usually represented the emperor while the phoenix symbolized the empress.

31. *Bildungsroman* is a novelistic genre. It usually refers to life stories of all-round self-development from childhood to adulthood or even death. For details, consult M. H. Abram's *Glossary of Literary Terms*.

Chapter Two
To (En)gender the Gendered History in *Hero*

At the Beijing press conference for the first release of Zhang Yimou's film *Hero* on December 14, 2002, Zhang Yimou and higher authorities of the Chinese government had 200 male undergraduate students with impressive physique recreate scenes depicting the Qin state's[1] high level of respect for the movie's heroic swordsman, Nameless (Li Lianjie/Jet Lee).[2] The students wore military uniforms of the Qin state, held spears, and repeatedly shouted "Feng."[3] According to Chinese news reports, this portrayal greatly impressed the journalists who attended the press conference. However, one of the most frequent critiques of Zhang Yimou's *Hero* in China is that *ciqin* (assassinating Ying Zheng, the King of the Qin state) is a clichéd story. What kinds of fresh and surprising elements can Hero add to this hackneyed story to amaze viewers? In this article, I contend that Zhang Yimou brings at least two new and fabulous things to the table. First, Zhang Yimou rethinks and problematizes the complication of making choices and deciding history about *ciqin*. Second, Zhang Yimou highlights that heroines are as heroic and significant as heroes though ancient Chinese historical records about *ciqin* seldom include the importance of women.

I argue that Zhang Yimou, as a descendent of the Qin state,[4] repeatedly reconsiders and (en)genders various complicated versions of the story about *ciqin*, one of the most famous parts of the Qin history. If *Zhanguo ce* (*The Stratagems of the Warring States*) is a collection of each state's records of her own history and *The Book of Yan* is the Yan state's version of her own history, *Hero*, which is directed by the *qinguo ren* (a citizen of the Qin state)[5] named Zhang Yimou, is a *qinguo ren*'s rethinking and (en)gendering of the Qin state's historical story about *ciqin*—in other words, a *qinguo ren*'s filmic "*Book of Qin* in *The Stratagems of the Warring States*."

In addition, Zhang Yimou emphasizes heroines[6] in his filmic versions of the historical story so that what he engenders is "gendered history." If history is only stories written or engendered by historians from different perspectives and standpoints, there may not be authentic and genuine versions of stories in historical records. Under this circumstance, which history is the true history and, which history is not the true history, is no longer a question. There may not be true history. Male-centered or chauvinist historians in ancient China could, of course, engender stories about *ciqin* that exclude or underestimate women; however, Zhang Yimou, as a director who is good at filming women and telling stories about women, can absolutely engender stories about *ciqin* that include or serve as the foil to heroic women—namely, Zhang Yimou's "gendered history within his *qinguo ren*'s filmic *Book of Qin* in *The Stratagems of the Warring States*."

Problematization of Making Choices and Deciding History

Historians early in the Yan state of the Warring States era, the Qin Dynasty,[7] and all the following dynasties posited the story of *ciqin* in their written records. Likewise, other filmmakers have already portrayed the story in their films.[8] What can possibly be new in Zhang Yimou's *Hero*? How problematical *ciqin* can be is exactly the new side of the story that Zhang Yimou brings. Zhang Yimou successfully rethinks the failure to assassinate Ying Zheng and emphasizes how thorny it is to make choices and decide the history of warring states. That is to say, although *ciqin* is truly a hackneyed story in China, Zhang Yimou's *Hero* brings something new to the table, namely, the problematization of making choices and deciding history.

If, as I have posited, Zhang Yimou problematizes the process of making choices and deciding the history, how does he go about it? Likewise, if Zhang Yimou truly reconsiders in the film the already well-known history of the failure to assassinate Ying Zheng, how does he do it? He does this first by presenting the protagonists' differing versions of the same story and, second, by allowing the same story to be told over and over again. These are Zhang Yimou's principle strategies of problematizing the well-worn story of *ciqin*: "*Hero* is a film about storytelling, or, to put it more abstractly, a film that puts narrativity itself into question. . . . Instead of a struggle *within* narrative, *Hero* stages a struggle *among* narratives."[9]

At the Beijing press conference for the film, Zhang Ziyi (the actress who plays Moon) summarized the film and said that there are two fake versions and a true version of the story. According to her, the first version of Nameless and the version of Ying Zheng (played by Chen Daoming) are the two fake versions: the true version is the final version that Nameless and Ying Zheng together figure out, and also the depiction that includes the romantic relation between Broken Sword (Liang Chaowei/Tony Chiu-wai Leung) and Flying Snow (Zhang

Manyu/Maggie Man-yuk Cheung) and their initial conspiracy to assassinate Ying Zheng. These two fake versions and the true story in the film create Zhang Yimou's cinematic reconsideration of *ciqin*.

In addition, Zhang Yimou uses five colors, one for each version of the story and for each protagonist's telling of his or her version of the story. Zhang Yimou, formerly a cinematographer, is undoubtedly sensitive to colors in films.[10] He "always knows what he wants and retains the necessary focus to make sure he gets it."[11] *Hero* is "the culmination of Zhang's obsession with colors."[12] At the Beijing press conference, Zhang confessed that Akira Kurosawa indirectly influenced his plans for color in the film. He also revealed that he attributed the success of the marvelous colors to his Japanese costume designer: She produced more than one hundred shades of red when he called for red in the film.

A number of viewers and film critics have already noted the attention to color in the film, so I will briefly speculate on the meanings of the colors,[13] starting with the beginning of the film. The royal color of the Qin state is black.[14] Some audiences assume that this implies the cold-blooded tyrant's dictatorship and military force. It indicates Ying Zheng's brutality as well as the suffering of the plebs: "Most movie reviewers . . . interpreted this color of black as death or evil."[15] "The main color tone for the fatal meeting is black-and-white to serve as a background of the past for subsequent diversified interpersonal threads replete with color-coded flashbacks, and later to symbolize the final battle between good and evil."[16]

Zhang Yimou's use of the color black indicates his underlying accusation of how ruthless Ying Zheng is; therefore, Zhang Yimou may have a narrow escape from an interrogation by film critics about his cinematic portrayal of Ying Zheng and other cruel totalitarians.[17] At the end of the film, Zhang Yimou allows Ying Zheng only "a power that seems empty, whose value is completely degraded when compared with" the way heroes sacrifice their lives for political ideals are typically portrayed.[18] The use of black may also represent two opposing collective hopes in the film: Nameless in black to assassinate Ying Zheng, and all the people who appear in black at the Qin palace to prevent Ying Zheng from being killed.

The use of red marks Nameless's first version of the story. It serves as a foil for the intense love, jealousy, hatred, remorse, impulse, and violence evident in Long Sky, Flying Snow, Broken Sword, and Moon.[19] The scarlet color also corresponds with Moon's defloration, Broken Sword's blood after Flying Snow stabs him to death,[20] and Moon's blood after her battle with Flying Snow under trees full of crimson leaves.[21] When the ruby color gradually fades away and turns to orange and then yellow, this morphing of colors signifies that Moon is closer and closer to her death.[22]

Accompanying Ying Zheng's version of the story is blue, with which Ying Zheng points out that Broken Sword and Flying Snow are not narrow-minded. The use of sky-blue may also indicate that he highly respects them and praises them "sky-high."

Shades of green exhibit the version of the story that Broken Sword tells Nameless. It may be compared to the growth of the romantic love between Broken Sword and Flying Snow as well as the progress of their initial plans to assassinate Ying Zheng together. The emerald hue also corresponds to Broken Sword's everlasting love for Flying Snow, like evergreen plants that remain green and never fade.

The use of white follows the green, right after Broken Sword's and Flying Snow's failure to kill Ying Zheng and Flying Snow's cold war with Broken Sword. Contrasting with the black color of the Qin army in the battlefield at the beginning of the film, the milky color may serve to emphasize Nameless's dilemma: to assassinate Ying Zheng or not assassinate him. White also serves to mourn those who died in the plan to assassinate Ying Zheng. It corresponds to the white included in the historical fact of *ciqin* during the Warring States era. According to historical records, people who saw the assassin off put on whitish mourning robes and hats.[23]

Zhang Yimou's artistic use of colors constitutes his cinematic, colorful, and multi-layered reassessment of the age-old story of *ciqin*. Compared with the version of the story about *ciqin* in *The Stratagems of the Warring States*,[24] Zhang Yimou's *Hero* displays the unexpected complexity that occurs when different versions of the same story exist, especially the complicated process of the assassin making choices and deciding the history of the warring states. Attention to these different versions evidences Zhang Yimou's re-examination and problematization of the old story of *ciqin*.

Whom in the Warring States Period Do *Hero's* Characters Mirror?

To support my argument for Zhang Yimou's cinematic rethinking of *ciqin*, I will compare the main characters in this film with the four people who, according to historical records of *ciqin* in *The Stratagems of the Warring States*, died in the plan to assassinate Ying Zheng: Tian Guang, Fan Wuqi, Jing Ke, and Gao Jianli. In Zhang Yimou's *Hero*, Long Sky (Zen Zidan/Donnie Zen) represents Fan Wuqi, because they each sacrifice their lives to enable the assassins, whom they support, to be granted an audience in Qin. Nameless represents Jing Ke, because they are both assassins who fail to kill Ying Zheng. Broken Sword represents Tian Guang, because they each die to illustrate that they are trustworthy. Finally, Flying Snow represents Gao Jianli, because they each promise to avenge themselves on Ying Zheng.

According to *The Book of Yan* in *The Stratagems of the Warring States*, Tian Guang dies for his promise.[25] The heir of the Yan state, Prince Dan, seeks an assassin to kill Ying Zheng and consults Tian Guang. Tian Guang recommends

Jing Ke, visits Jing Ke, and asks Jing Ke to help Prince Dan assassinate Ying Zheng. Before Jing Ke sets off to meet Prince Dan at the royal palace of the Yan state, Tian Guang kills himself to demonstrate that he has kept his promise to not disclose Prince Dan's and Jing Ke's secret plan. He dies to show that he deserves Prince Dan's trust:

> Of course, Tian Guang may commit suicide for other reasons. Just like what he says, it is disreputable for a righteous expert of martial arts to be distrusted...In order to encourage Jing Ke, and in order to clarify that he is not afraid of death, he resolutely and determinedly commits suicide[26] (Author's translation).

Tian Guang's death is similar to Broken Sword's death for his promise. In Zhang Yimou's *Hero*, Broken Sword, like Tian Guang, volunteers to die for his promise: the promise to show that he is truly in love with Flying Snow. When Flying Snow complains that Broken Sword bears only the *tianxia*[27] in his mind, Broken Sword volunteers to be killed by her to show that he loves not merely the *tianxia* but also her. When Flying Snow asks Broken Sword why he does not use his sword to defend himself, he confesses that he wants his death to convince her that he will never stop loving her: he wants his death to convince her that he deserves her trust. Even if this is not the only reason for him to die, it is dishonorable for Broken Sword, who identifies himself as a righteous expert of martial arts, to be distrusted by Flying Snow. To show that he is still emotionally attached to Flying Snow, and to clarify that he is still trustworthy, Broken Sword does not defend himself and decides to be killed by Flying Snow.

Fan Wuqi dies to enable the assassin, Jing Ke, to approach Ying Zheng at the royal palace of the Qin state to kill him. According to historical records, Fan Wuqi, a courageous general faithfully working for Prince Dan, kills himself to grant Jing Ke audience in Qin.[28] He requests Jing Ke cut his head off after his suicide and then bring his head to the royal palace of the Qin state so Ying Zheng will allow Jing Ke to approach the throne. Without Fan Wuqi's head after his suicide, Ying Zheng would not be interested in meeting Jing Ke, and Jing Ke would not have had an opportunity to assassinate Ying Zheng. Fan Wuqi's death is similar to Long Sky's sacrifice in Zhang Yimou's *Hero* because it enables Nameless to be granted audience in Qin and to approach the throne of Ying Zheng at the Qin palace. Without Long Sky's sacrifice, Ying Zheng would not meet Nameless and Nameless would not be able to approach the throne to kill Ying Zheng.

The Book of Yan in *The Stratagems of the Warring States* includes a section called "Jing Ke, the Assassin." With Prince Dan's sponsorship, Jing Ke poisons "the sharpest dagger in all the empire,"[29] carries a box containing Fan Wuqi's head, brings "a map of Yan's [Tukang] regions,"[30] and leaves for the royal palace of the Qin state to assassinate Ying Zheng together with Qin Wuyang, a young killer in his teens. In Zhang Yimou's *Hero*, Nameless represents Jing Ke. Both Nameless and Jing Ke are granted audience in Qin, approach the throne, and try to assassinate Ying Zheng.

The Stratagems of the Warring States mentions the famous poem, "Song of the Generous Knight," written to see Jing Ke off along the Yi River.

> Xiao-xiao soughs the wind, oh—
> Cold the waters of the Yi.
> The knight who leaves you now, oh—
> You shall nevermore see.[31]

The musician to sing this poem for Jing Ke is Gao Jianli. He plays his *zhu* (lute) and sings mournfully. All the people join him and sing in a sorrowful key.

Historical records say that Gao Jianli, after Jing Ke's death, seeks revenge by throwing his musical instrument at Ying Zheng in an effort to kill him when serving as Ying Zheng's blind musician at the royal palace of the Qing state. He does not succeed, and Ying Zheng kills him.[32] Gao Jianli's revenge is similar to Flying Snow's determination to take revenge in Zhang Yimou's *Hero*: Both Gao Jianli and Flying Snow take their revenge on Ying Zheng, and both bravely die in the process.

So, Long Sky represents Fan Wuqi, Nameless represents Jing Ke, Broken Sword is Tian Guang, and Flying Snow is Gao Jianli. These parallels and interrelations between Zhang Yimou's *Hero* and historical records about *ciqin* are not coincidental, but carefully planned. They clearly trace how heroic Fan Wuqi, Jing Ke, Tian Guang, Gao Jianli, Long Sky, Broken Sword, Nameless, and Flying Snow appear in both *Hero* and *The Stratagems of the Warring States*. They also illustrate the way in which Zhang Yimou rethinks and problematizes the story of *ciqin*, and they allow us to see the new elements that Zhang Yimou brings to the story of *ciqin* through the film. Zhang Yimou takes advantage of Long Sky, Nameless, Broken Sword, and Flying Snow to problematize the stories of Fan Wuqi, Jing Ke, Tian Guang, and Gao Jianli, which may not be as simple as they are in *The Book of Yan*. In *Hero*, Zhang Yimou engenders his own cinematic version of Fan Wuqi, Jing Ke, Tian Guang, and Gao Jianli as well as his own filmic edition of *The Book of Yan*.

In other words, Zhang Yimou rethinks and engenders various stories about *ciqin*: two fake versions and a true version (Zhang Ziyi's summary), five colorful versions (film critics' analyses of the five colors in the film), and four swordfighters' stories paralleling historical records of the four people who died in the plan to assassinate Ying Zheng (*The Book of Yan*). All the various versions of the same story show that history is probably stories that historians tell, engender, record, and rethink from their viewpoints and standpoints. Different historians and story-tellers engender or produce different versions of the same story. There are not authentic versions. There is not true history. According to Zhang Yimou, history is indeed (en)gender-able, creatable, and rethinkable. *Hero* is Zhang Yimou's engendering, reshaping, and rethinking of the history about *ciqin*—namely, his cinematic version of *The Book of Yan*, *The Stratagems of the War-*

ring States, and even *The Biography of Assassins*.

More evidence that Zhang Yimou wholly rethinks the story of *ciqin* in the film is the calligraphic and philosophical epiphany. The simplest meaning of the character *jian* (sword) is to have a sword in the assassin's hand. The deeper meaning is to have a sword in the assassin's heart. These two meanings appear in historical records of *ciqin*. Jing Ke does have a sword in both his hand and his heart. The deepest and the most philosophical meaning of the character *jian*, however, is to have no sword in hand or heart—namely, to give up both the sword and the plan to assassinate anyone. The reversal of Nameless's and Broken Sword's plan to kill Ying Zheng matches the deepest and the most philosophical meaning of the character. Perhaps the harshest way to take revenge on Ying Zheng is not to assassinate him with any sword, but to force him to exist under the unbearable pressure of nationwide censorship and historians' infinite denunciation of him once he breaks his promise about securing a better future for the *tianxia*. This is why Zhang Yimou wants Nameless to warn Ying Zheng at the end of the film: "Remember the *tianxia*!" Regardless of whether this is convincing to all the audience, this philosophical epiphany about the *tianxia* verifies that Zhang Yimou has rethought the story of *ciqin* and has added his own explanation for the failure to assassinate Ying Zheng.

Hero is Zhang Yimou's first martial arts film. A number of film critics relate it with other martial arts films, such as Akira Kurosawa's *Rashomon* and Lee Ang's *Crouching Tiger Hidden Dragon*, or even dozens of King Hu's works; I would avoid repetition of their views in this article and point out what few martial arts films focus on: the three-tiered philosophical depth of the character *jian*. Aside from the marvelous colors and fantastic practice of martial arts that enthrall the international film industry and viewers all over the world, *Hero* calligraphically enriches the philosophy of Chinese martial arts. This is what other martial arts films seldom achieve. The three-layered meanings of *jian* also echo a Zen Buddhist epiphany: *jian shan shi shan, jian shan bu shi shan, jian shan you shi shan* (Mountains are mountains at the first sight; later on, mountains are not mountains; finally, mountains are mountains again). At the beginning, one sees mountains and thinks that they are mountains because of his or her innocence, purity, straightforwardness, or simplicity. This is like the first meaning of *jian*: to have a sword in hand without complicated thoughts but a simple attempt to kill. Later, one sees mountains but does not regard them as only mountains because of his or her sophistication, shrewdness, or complexity. This is similar to the second meaning of *jian*: to have a sword in both hands and mind, or to sophisticatedly have complicated schemes and swordplay against Ying Zheng. At the end, one sees mountains and thinks them as mountains again because he or she realizes the beauty of simplicity and gives up complexity. This may be compared to the deepest meaning of *jian*: to stop conspicuous plans and complicated battle array, and to leave Ying Zheng to time and future generations under the power of heaven.

Women in Zhang Yimou's Films

If there is a fabled "mirror on the wall,"[33] Zhang Yimou wants us to think that the mirror reflects his hero.[34] As a matter of fact, determining "who the real hero of the movie is"[35] also concerns viewers and film critics. Is it Ying Zheng, the King of the Qin state, who promises to subjugate all the warring states[36] and release the *tianxia* (the plebs under heaven) from endless battles in the film? Is it the martial arts experts such as Long Sky and Namelss who volunteer to sacrifice their lives for their beliefs? Is it Broken Sword, the philosopher who combines calligraphy, swordsmanship, and the endorsement of Ying Zheng's promise to save the *tianxia* from wars? Or is it the head of the calligraphy academy who tenaciously insists that the tyrant of the Qin state is powerless to obliterate the culture of his home country?[37] When considering the word "hero," most audiences think about these men. But what about the heroines, especially when one of them appears to play only a trivial and marginalized role?

With reference to the stories told in his films, Zhang Yimou specializes in telling stories about and through women.[38] In Zhang Jiuying's interview, Zhang Yimou insists that there must be women in his films:

> Some rules must be obeyed. For example, there must be women in films. The image of the female protagonist is vague in Yu Hua's fiction, *To Live*. But in the film, *To Live*, Gong Li is as significant as Ge You. There is not any blind girl in Mo Yan's fiction; however, we insist on adding a blind girl to the film, *Happy Times*[39] (Author's translation).

In Mayfair Mei-hui Yang's interview with Zhang Yimou, he mentions why he uses women to make statements in films:

> All my films come from novels. It just so happens that these novels say things through women. This also fits in with my own sensibilities. Somehow this is in the air. What I want to express is the Chinese people's oppression and confinement, which has been going on for thousands of years. Women express this more clearly on their bodies . . . because they bear a heavier burden than men.[40]

In Li Erwei's interview, Zhang Yimou also talks about women in his films:

> To portray how women face their pressures can better clarify problems that concern me because women tolerate more than men. From a traditional point of view, everything seems easier for men but harder for women. As for why my films focus on women, this is related to the fictions that I choose to base my movies on. People who study literary development and changes realize why I must film women[41] (Author's translation).

A short list of his works illustrates Zhang Yimou's use of unique women in their fascinating stories:

Cui Qiao in *Yellow Earth* (1984)
Jiu'er in *Red Sorghum* (1987)
Ju Dou in *Ju Dou* (1990)
Song Lian in *Raise the Red Lantern* (1991)
Qiu Ju in *The Story of Qiu Ju* (1992)
Jia Zhen in *To Live* (1994)
Xiao Jinbao in *Shanghai Triad* (1995)
An Hong in *Keep Cool* (1996)
Turandot in *Turandot* (1997-1998)
Wei Minzhi in *Not One Less* (1999)
Zhao Di in *The Road Home* (1999)
Wu Yin in *Happy Times* (2000)
Xiaomei in *House of Flying Daggers* (2004)

Some film critics believe that the "flourishing of women's stories . . . demonstrated that, in order to make themselves heard, the filmmakers had no other tools more powerful or more handy than speaking for the women."[42] Zhang Yimou seems to be one of the best examples of speaking for women. If Zhang Yimou is so good at telling stories about women in his films that every one of his female protagonists appears to be unique, significant, meaningful, and attractive, why are the two female characters in *Hero* exceptions?

Flying Snow and Moon are Zhang Yimou's first martial arts ladies.[43] In a feminist point of view, both Flying Snow and Moon are fatherless and thus free from patriarchal pressure. Moon is an orphan, and Flying Snow loses her father. Unlike most ancient Chinese women waiting for matchmakers and candidates for spouses, lamenting or grieving in boudoirs, jailed within extensive family structures, chained by endless housework, and restrained by patriarchal rules, Flying Snow and Moon have no domestic burden. They never silently and patiently wait for matchmakers or future spouses; they carefreely and confidently choose their beloveds and decide their own fates. They develop intimate relations with the men they want and never hesitate about pre-marital physical contact. Even when they encounter the romantic triangle and become rivals competing for the same man, they do not simply wail in bedrooms; they bravely fight against each other. Their kung fu and swordplay show that they have had strong bodies and good physical education since childhood, not the physical fragility that most ancient Chinese women had in common. Their swordsmanship and fighting spirits show that they have good sportsmanship and physical vigor. Even when men do not share the same opinions about *ciqin* with them, they insist on their own standpoints and are seldom obedient only because they are women. The patriarchal tradition of inferior women and superior men does not exist in their value system at all.

Compared to the fact that most ancient Chinese women would not perform kung fu and existed under the patriarchal pressure of polygamy, foot-binding, and domestic burdens, martial arts ladies enjoyed more freedom and gender egalitarianism in the imaginary world of Chinese kung fu. They usually do not have a lot of family chores, housework, and domestic burdens. Seldom are they abused by mothers-in-law or sisters-in-law. Scarcely do they suffer from domestic violence or marital violence like many victims in crisis centers. With strong bodies and personalities, most of them are supposed to be able to fight for themselves, make their own decisions, go where they want to go, and try to do what they want to do. They are often "endowed with knightly virtues . . . [and they are] drastically different from the Confucian archetype of self-effacing, submissive women."[44] They are usually well educated and sometimes ambitious. Romantic love usually concerns them; more often than not, they decide whom they love and choose their partners or spouses.

Both Flying Snow and Moon illustrate these characteristics. Although Moon calls Broken Sword "master," she is not an abused servant bombarded by endless housework, family chores, and domestic burdens. Instead, she is adopted and well educated by Broken Sword. She has a healthy body and strong personality. With the kung fu that Broken Sword teaches her, she uses a pair of curved daggers as her weapons, fights for Broken Sword and herself, makes her own decisions, loves Broken Sword, and generally does what she wants to do. Flying Snow similarly has few problems with family chores or housework. A dead general's daughter, she is well educated. With good kung fu, a strong personality, and her ambition to take revenge for her father, Flying Snow wants her partner, Broken Sword, to join her in assassinating Ying Zheng, and decides to return home with him by dying with him at the end of the story.

Binary Opposites to Highlight the Problematization: Life and Death

Although the title of the film, *Hero*, tends to focus on men rather than women, Zhang Yimou stresses the importance of not underestimating Flying Snow and Moon, the first martial arts ladies in his film. They function as a pair of binary opposites to highlight the problematization of making choices and deciding the history of the warring states—and problematization is exactly what Zhang Yimou needs to add to the passé story of *ciqin*.

Flying Snow and Moon form a pair of binary opposites[45] in many perspectives. For example, Flying Snow appears to be the lady of the household, while Moon is like an abigail. Flying Snow enjoys a lot of privilege, power, resources, and authority in the institution of calligraphy and their house, where Moon does not. Flying Snow's status is obviously higher than Moon's according to the way they interact with each other. From the beginning through the end of the film,

Flying Snow is obviously the female leading role, while Moon plays more of a supporting role. Moon faithfully loves Broken Sword only, yet Flying Snow, as Broken Sword's partner, has a love affair with Long Sky. Flying Snow is truly Broken Sword's beloved, whereas Moon seems to be merely someone of whom Broken Sword takes advantage to test whether Flying Snow still loves him and whether she would be angry with him when she peeps through the door and witnesses his sexual relation. Moon does not win Broken Sword's heart after their sex and is even expelled from Broken Sword's bed. But Flying Snow's agony comforts and pleases Broken Sword because it proves that Flying Snow's love for him has not faded away.

The scene in which Flying Snow and Moon fight each other under the trees in the film supports my argument that Zhang Yimou aims to bring to light their existence as binary opposites. The fighting scene succeeds in turning these two women into dramatic contrasts. Flying Snow's kung fu is apparently better than Moon's. Her sword is by far a more powerful weapon than Moon's two curved daggers, which clearly correspond to the shape of a crescent moon. Further, the crimson, scarlet, ruby, red, carroty, orange, and yellow leaves symbolize dander, hatred, hostility, umbrage, jealousy, and confrontation. At the end of the fight, Flying Snow defeats and kills Moon. With Moon dead and Flying Snow alive, Zhang Yimou presents another set of binary opposites: life and death.

The end of the film strengthens the life-and-death binary because Flying Snow longs for Ying Zheng's death after enabling Nameless to approach the throne but Moon begs Nameless not to kill Ying Zheng. Flying Snow wants Ying Zheng dead, but Moon, following in Broken Sword's footsteps, hopes Ying Zheng to live. The question of whether to assassinate Ying Zheng is the pivot around which the story turns. While these two women solidify their stance as opposites, Long Sky, Broken Sword, and Nameless struggle to make choices and decide Ying Zheng's fate.

In other words, Flying Snow and Moon function as a significant symbol of opposition that serves to intensify how Zhang Yimou problematizes the final decision over Ying Zheng's destiny and the history of the warring states. If "*Hero* displays and deconstructs the [problematic] process of making history,"[46] then Flying Snow and Moon, the two women who form the binary opposite that signifies Ying Zheng's life and death, heighten the complication that Zhang Yimou adds to the story of *ciqin*. Without Flying Snow and Moon, Zhang Yimou would have difficulty emphasizing his problematization of choices and decisions over the history of the warring states in *Hero*. Under these circumstances, Flying Snow and Moon are heroines whose significance should not be underestimated despite the fact that *Hero* focuses primarily on men and at first appears to lack significant attention to women.

Another way to rethink the opposites is to relate life and death with women. On the one hand, women are those who can give birth to future generations, produce new life, and breast-feed and nurture newborns. The two women in this film can better represent life (Ying Zheng's life) and the future (future generations and time as the harshest censors of Ying Zheng) than can men. On the other hand, women in patriarchal societies usually outlive men, bury men, and continue managing everything after the men's deaths. It is, therefore, not out of anticipation that Flying Snow insists on Ying Zheng's death from the beginning to the end and that Moon outlives heroes, buries men, and witnesses whether Ying Zheng's political promise will come true.

Mirror, Mirror on the Wall, Don't Underestimate the Heroines in *Hero*!

The title of the film raises many questions in audiences: Why is the English title "*Hero*" instead of "*Heroes*"? Is there only one hero in the film? If so, who is the hero? Is the hero Nameless, who voluntarily risks his life to assassinate Ying Zheng? Is the hero Long Sky, whose death enables Nameless to approach Ying Zheng at the royal palace of the Qin state? If Long Sky is considered a hero, does it mean that Flying Snow should be as heroic as him because she also sacrifices herself to enable Nameless to approach Ying Zheng? Is the hero Broken Sword, whose calligraphic enlightenment stops Nameless's original plan to assassinate Ying Zheng? If Broken Sword is regarded as a hero, does it imply that Moon should be as heroic as him because she shares Broken Sword's philosophical belief about the *tianxia* and helps persuade Nameless to not assassinate Ying Zheng? If Broken Sword is deemed a hero because of his hope for a more peaceful future for the *tianxia*, does it indicate that Ying Zheng, who shares his political ideal about the *tianxia* and promises to put it into practice regardless of his notoriety, should also be a hero? If calligraphy is the philosophical source of heroic figures' great expectation for the *tianxia*, does it signify that the head of the institute of calligraphy should also be heroic because there would not be any calligraphic enlightenment without his professional nurturance of calligraphy?

Different people have different answers to all these questions. Let me take Li Feng's and Zhang Yimou's answers as examples. In Li Feng's fiction *Hero*, from which Zhang Yimou's film script derives, Long Sky loses only his arm, remains alive, and concludes that Broken Sword, Flying Snow, and Nameless are heroes because they understand one another's pursuits and entrust their lives to one another.[47] This comment reminds readers of a famous sentence in *The Book of Zhao* in *The Stratagems of the Warring States*: *shi wei zhi ji zhe si, nü wei yue ji zhe rong* (literal translation: A gentleman dies for one who knows his heart; a woman makes up her face for the man who wins her heart; my paraphrase according to the literal meaning: A true hero is ready to die a loyal death for those who know his ambition and pursuits; a woman is eager to live a happy life with one who touches her heart). According to Li Feng, Broken Sword, Flying Snow, and Nameless die for those who understand their ambition and beliefs and are, therefore, heroes.

Zhang Yimou's definition of who is a hero seems broader than Li Feng's, however. At the press conference for the film in Taipei on January 11, 2003, Zhang Yimou said, "Whoever participated in *Hero* is a hero." If we view the silver screen as a sort of magic "mirror on the wall" that reflects heroic roles in Zhang Yimou's film, then, according to Zhang Yimou's answer to journalists at the press conference, Nameless, Long Sky, Broken Sword, Ying Zheng, the head of the institute of calligraphy, soldiers of the Qin state, and Zhang Yimou's staff at the film studio are all heroes reflected in this mirror.

Because different people will inevitably have different interpretations about what constitutes a heroic character in a film, I suppose that I can also have a different interpretation. I argue that the magic "mirror on the wall" should reflect not only heroes but also heroines—namely, the two martial arts ladies in the film. Flying Snow is as heroic as Long Sky in the film because, like Long Sky, she volunteers to sacrifice her life for Nameless's plan to assassinate Ying Zheng. Moon is as heroic as Broken Sword because she shares Broken Sword's philosophical ideal about the *tianxia*. I contend that these two heroines are as heroic as the male heroes in the film. While Zhang Yimou intends for his audience to think that the "mirror on the wall" reflects only his hero(es), I propose that the two heroines in *Hero*, Flying Snow and Moon, not be underestimated. They should be in the magic mirror, too.

The Jiangshan and Tianxia

Another reason not to underestimate Flying Snow in the film is her alias. The first time Broken Sword and Flying Snow enter the royal palace of the Qin state, they have a good opportunity to kill Ying Zheng, but Broken Sword stops his plan because of his ideals for the *tianxia*. After their return from the Qin palace, Broken Sword names himself Gaoshan (High Cliff or High Mountain) and Flying Snow calls herself Liushui (Spring Brook or Flowing Water).

The combination of their aliases, "brook and mountain," is, in fact, another way to represent the *tianxia*: The literal meaning of the phrase, *tianxia*, is "under the heaven." It refers to all the plebs and territory under the emperor's control. Coincidentally, the phrase *jiangshan* frequently stands for the territory under the heaven. The character *jiang* signifies rivers or brooks, just like Flying Snow's designation, Liushui (Spring Brook or Flowing Water). The character *shan* refers to mountains or cliffs, exactly like Broken Sword's designation, Gaoshan (High Cliff, or High Mountain).

In Chinese language, both *jiangshan* and *tianxia* symbolize the same thing: the plebs and territory that the ruler is responsible for. From this perspective, *jiangshan* and *tianxia* are interchangeable phrases with the same meaning; *jiangshan* means *tianxia*, and *tianxia* means *jiangshan*. This is perhaps why

Broken Sword and Flying Snow do not have their aliases, the combination of which means the *tianxia*, until the political ideal for the *tianxia* stops their plan to assassinate Ying Zheng. Hence, their aliases double the concern for a brighter future of the *tianxia* in the film. If the *tianxia* or the combination of Flying Snow's and Broken Sword's aliases is the philosophical concern that deeply influences the life and death of Ying Zheng and all the other knights in Zhang Yimou's *Hero*, the significance of Flying Snow is beyond description though heroines, or women, literally speaking, are not what the title of the film signifies.

In addition, the *liushui* (flowing water) that Flying Snow's alternative name literally refers to serves as a political warning for Ying Zheng. In Chinese language, there is a saying: *shui keyi zai zhou yi keyi fu zhou*. Literally, this proverb means that the flowing water can carry the weight of a boat or capsize and sink a boat. Metaphorically speaking, the flowing water symbolizes the plebs under the heaven, while the boat represents the ruler of the *jiangshan* or *tianxia*. According to classics and books written by Xun Zi (313-238 B.C., a philosopher in the Warring States era) and Zhu Xi (1130-1200 A.D., a thinker and educator in the Southern Song Dynasty),[48] Confucius says, "*Jun zhe, zhou ye, shu ren zhe, shui ye; shui ze zaizhou, shui ze fu zhou*" (The monarch is like the boat, the multitude is like the flowing water; the flowing water can carry the boat, yet it can topple it). That is to say, civilians will support the head of state if he or she takes good care of the *jiangshan* or *tianxia*, but the masses will overthrow or depose the leader of the whole empire if he or she fails to do a good job. In this axiom or maxim, the word *fu* can signify not only *fumo* (to topple the boat, which stands for Ying Zheng) but also *fuwang* (the fall of Ying Zheng, or the end of the Qin Dynasty that Ying Zheng aims to establish).

The Moon and Time

After acknowledging that the designations of Flying Snow and Broken Sword refer to the *tianxia* and that their political ideals about the *tianxia* stop Broken Sword and Nameless from assassinating Ying Zheng, new questions arise: Will Ying Zheng faithfully and honestly carry out their political aspirations for the *tianxia*? Will he really take good care of the *jiangshan*? Or will he simply eat his words and forget the plebs? How does one know whether Ying Zheng is truly loyal to the *tianxia* or *jiangshan* after the deaths of Nameless, Broken Sword, Long Sky, and Flying Snow?

Time will tell. Time will be the ultimate test of whether Ying Zheng is a good emperor for the *tianxia*. Even if Ying Zheng lies to Broken Sword and Nameless, over time, he will ultimately meet his judgment. Time will tell regarding Ying Zheng, just like a popular Chinese proverb, *lu yao zhi ma li, ri jiu jian ren xin* (A distant journey tests the strength of a horse, and a long period of time proves the character of a man).

Moon's name denotes "time" because the moon in the sky transcends human life-spans and is infinite; therefore, Moon kneels down and begs Nameless to allow Ying Zheng more time to put the political plan for the *tianxia* into practice. Like most statesmen or politicians, Ying Zheng needs time to realize his political dreams. While Moon represents time in the film, Ying Zheng needs her help to be given more time to bring about his political pursuits before his death.

In Chinese language, there is a phrase: *gu yue zhao jin chen* (The old moon shines on the present). Perhaps it is the case that Moon serves as a metaphor for time in Zhang Yimou's film *Hero* so that Moon survives the problems of how to make choices and decide the history of the warring states. In Li Feng's fiction, *Hero*, the "Moon" in the "Long Sky" represents time so that both Moon and Long Sky remain alive and hold a memorial ceremony for Flying Snow, Broken Sword, and Nameless in front of their graves.

Moon represents time as well as the future. In the film, she is the youngest among all the characters. She represents all the younger and future generations that will live to see whether Ying Zheng treats the plebs well. Future generations, like the moon in the sky and time, will endure in their careful observation of Ying Zheng's true attitude toward the *tianxia* or *jiangshan*. Even thousands of years after the Qin Dynasty was overthrown, all the plebs under heaven have not stopped accusing Ying Zheng of his cruelty. Zhang Yimou himself is an example: He is one of the numerous descendants of the Qin Dynasty; this is why Chen Kaige calls him *qinguo ren*.[49] Zhang Yimou, as a *qinguo ren*, re-examines what Ying Zheng truly does to the plebs in his film. According to the explanation Zhang Yimou now adds to the story of *ciqin*, this kind of endless scrutiny is a far harsher punishment for Ying Zheng than was the plan to assassinate him. The meaning of Moon's name indicates that Zhang Yimou indirectly condemns Ying Zheng to everlasting admonition and reproach.

A *Qinguo Ren*'s Gendered History about *Ciqin*

The heroines, Flying Snow and Moon, are in fact as heroic and significant as the men in *Hero*. Zhang Yimou indirectly proposes not to underestimate Flying Snow and Moon, precisely as Ying Zheng points out that Nameless should not *xiang jiandan* (underestimate) him and as Nameless alerts Ying Zheng not to underestimate Broken Sword in the film. I contend that Flying Snow (who is firmly determined to do whatever she can do to end Ying Zheng's life) and Moon (who kneels down to beg Nameless not to assassinate Ying Zheng) serve as binary opposites who problematize the difficulty in making important choices and deciding the history of the warring states. In addition, with "Flowing Water or Spring Brook" as her designation, Flying Snow accompanies Broken Sword (High Mountains or High Cliff) to represent the *jiangshan* (literally speaking, rivers and mountains), a Chinese phrase that represents the territory and civilians under heaven—that is, the *tianxia* that Ying Zheng aims to conquer and claims to care for. As for Moon, her name signifies time because in Chinese there is a phrase, *gu yue zhao jin chen*, which means the ancient moon can shine on and oversee the present. The moon in the sky transcends time and is infinite; therefore, the moon in the sky is all-knowing as to whether Ying Zheng truly keeps his political promise after the heroes sacrifice their lives, after which they cannot see whether Ying Zheng is honest and faithful to the *tianxia*. On the one hand, time is what Ying Zheng desperately needs to put his political aspirations for the *tianxia* into practice. Ying Zheng, like any statesman or politician, requires time to win the plebs over to his political views, and Moon, with her name that implies infinite time, kneels before Nameless and begs him to allow Ying Zheng more time to carry out his political plans for the *tianxia*. On the other hand, time is the harshest critic for what Ying Zheng actually does to the *tianxia*. Ying Zheng can lie to Nameless and to everyone else in the film by breaking his promise about the *tianxia*, but he cannot lie to the true judges: the moon in the sky, time, and all future generations. When viewed like this, Moon no longer plays simply a trivial supporting role in *Hero*, and Flying Snow, for that matter, is at least as significant as Broken Sword in terms of her significance to the *jiangshan* or *tianxia*. Without Moon and Flying Snow, Zhang Yimou cannot easily problematize the complex endeavor of making choices and deciding the history of the Warring States era.

When viewers, journalists, and film critics wondered who the hero is after the first release of the film, Zhang Yimou indirectly underscored the importance of the heroines and urged caution to those tempted to underestimate the heroines. The various versions of the same historical story that Zhang Yimou rethinks, engenders, and problematizes are actually all gendered history. In *Hero*, the new and surprising elements that Zhang Yimou adds to the old story of *ciqin* are his problematization, rethinking, and engendering of the gendered history related to *ciqin*. As a *qinguo ren*, Zhang Yimou engenders his own version of *qinguo ren*'s filmic *Book of Qin* if people of the Yan state engender *The Book of Yan* and people of the Qin state engender *The Book of Qin* in *The Stratagems of the Warring States*. In this sense, Zhang Yimou also engenders his own edition of a *qinguo ren*'s filmic *Stratagems of the Warring States*. In *Hero*, Zhang Yimou tells audiences stories of gendered history in his *qinguo ren*'s cinematic *Book of Qin* and *qinguo ren*'s filmic *Stratagems of the Warring States*. *Hero* is Zhang Yimou's version of the gendered history about *ciqin* in a *qinguo ren*'s cinematic *Book of Qin* as well as a *qinguo ren*'s filmic *Stratagems of the Warring States* in the twenty-first century.

Conclusion

As most viewers and critics point out, *ciqin* is nothing new. What Zhang Yimou adds to the story of *ciqin* is his cinematic reconsideration of how problematic it is to make choices and decide the history of the Warring States era. Different people have different opinions about who the heroes are in the film. In Li Feng's fiction, Long Sky does not die but believes that Broken Sword, Nameless, and Flying Snow are heroes. If there is a magic "mirror on the wall," Zhang Yimou wants it to reflect his hero(es). In this sense, Broken Sword mirrors Tian Guang, Long Sky mirrors Fan Wuqi, and Nameless mirrors Jing Ke. I argue, however, that the two heroines, Flying Snow and Moon, are as heroic and significant as the male characters in *Hero*. Although the title of the film seems to emphasize heroic men instead of women, Zhang Yimou shows that the two heroines, Flying Snow and Moon, form binary opposites that highlight his problematization of the processes of making choices and deciding the history of the Warring State era. Flying Snow mirrors Gao Jianli. In addition, Flying Snow's alias, accompanied by Broken Sword's designation, represents the *jiangshan*, which signifies the *tianxia*. Moon's name symbolizes time and also refers to the future generations that oversee Ying Zheng and check whether he keeps his promise or simply eats his words after the death of Flying Snow, Broken Sword, Long Sky, and Nameless. Just as Ying Zheng cautions Nameless against underestimating him and Nameless warns Ying Zheng against underestimating Broken Sword, Zhang Yimou indirectly proposes not to underestimate the heroines of *Hero*.[50] As a descendent of the Qin state, Zhang Yimou (en)genders various versions of gendered history about *ciqin*: He (en)genders and films his own edition of a *qinguo ren*'s problematized *Book of Yan*, *Book of Qin*, *The Stratagems of the Warring States*, and even *The Biography of Assassins*.

References

Banh, Meina. "Oh My Hero!" UCLA Asia Institute: *Asian Pacific Arts.* 9/3/2004. www.asiaart.ucla.edu/article.asp?parentid=14301.

Berry, Chris. "Calm in the Eye of the Storm: Salutes to Zhang Yimou." *Cinemaya* 30 (Autumn 1995): p. 116.

Cai, Rong. "Gender Imaginations in *Crouching Tiger, Hidden Dragon* and the Wuxia World." *Positions: East Asian Cultural Critique* 13, no. 2 (Fall 2005): 441–71.

Chai, Ying. *Wenhua shiyu zhong de Zhang Yimou*. Beijing: Zhongguo shehui kexue, 2011.

Chen, Kaige. "Qinguo ren" (The Person with Heritage of the Qin State). *Zhongguo dianying yishujia yenjiu congkan: lun Zhang Yimou* (*The Book Series of Research on Chinese Film Artists: Zhang Yimou*). Beijing: Zhongguo dianying (Chinese Films), 1994.

Chen, Xiaoming and Ming-Yeh Rawnsley. "On '*Tianxia*' (All under the heaven) on Zhang Yimou's *Hero*." *Global Chinese Cinema: the Culture and Politics of Hero*. Gary Rawnsley and Ming-yeh T. Rawnsley edt. London: Routledge, 2010.

Chen, Xihe. "On the Father Figures in Zhang Yimous' Films: From *Red Sorghum* to *Hero*." *Asian Cinema* (Fall/Winter 2004): 133–40.

Cheng, Huizhe. *Dianying dui xiaoshuo de kuayue: Zhang Yimou yingpian yanjiu* (*Filmic*

Strides across Fictions: Research of Zhang Yimou's Films). Beijing: Zhongguo dianying, 2010.
Chiu, Tzu-hsiu (Beryl). "Public Secrets: Geopolitical Aesthetics in Zhang Yimou's *Hero*." *The Electronic Journal of the Asian Studies on the Pacific Coast* (2004/5): mcel.pacificu.edu/easpac/2005/tzuchiu.php3.
Chung, Tsai-chun. *Chuancheng yu chuangxin (Heritage and Originality)*. Taipei: Institute of Chinese Literature and Philology, Academia Sinica, 1999.
Crump, James Irving. *Chan-Kuo Ts'e (The Stratagems of the Warring States)*. Ann Arbor: University of Michigan Press (Center for Chinese Studies), 1996 (Revised Edition).
---. *Intrigues: Studies of the Chan-kuo Ts'e*. Ann Arbor: University of Michigan Press, 1964.
---. "The Assassins." *Legends of the Warring States: Persuasions, Romances, and Stories from Chan-kuo Ts'e*. Ann Arbor: University of Michigan (Center for Chinese Studies), 1998.
Eng, Robert Y. "Is Hero a Paean to Authoritarianism?" UCLA Asian Institute: *Asian Media: Media News Daily* (9/7/2004): http://goo.gl/dLWSN.
Huang, Xiaoyang. *Yingxiang zhongguo: Zhang Yimou zhuan (Impressions on China: Zhang Yimou's Biography)*. Beijing: Huaxia, 2008.
Jia, Leilei. "Yingxiang yüyan de ganxing xingshi yü biaoshu yüjing—Zhang Yimou yingpian zhong de shijue/sinli yiyi" (The Sensational Forms and Expressive Contexts of the Cinematic Language—The Visual/Psychological Meanings in Zhang Yimou's Films). *Zhongguo dianying yishujia yenjiu congkan: lun Zhang Yimou (The Book Series of Research on Chinese Film Artists: Zhang Yimou)*. Beijing: Zhongguo dianying (Chinese Films), 1994.
Kovacsics, Violeta. "Agit Pop: The 52nd San Sebastian International Film Festival." *Senses of Cinema* (December 2004): http://goo.gl/rRkqv.
Kraicer, Shelly. "Absence as Spectacle: Zhang Yimou's *Hero*." *Cinema Scope* 5.1 (2003): 9-11.
Levitin, Jacqueline. "*Crouching Tiger Hidden Dragon, Hero*, and *House of the Flying Daggers*: Interpreting Gender Thematics in the Contemporary Swordplay Film—View from the West." *Asian Cinema* 17:1 (Spring/Summer 2006): 166–182.
Li, Erwei. *Zhi mian Zhang Yimou: Zhang Yimou de dian ying shi jie (Facing Zhang Yimou: Zhang Yimou's Cinematic World)*. (Beijing: Economic Daily Press, 2002), 134-48, 322-29.
Li, Feng. *Ying Xiong (Hero)*. (Hong Kong: Mingchuang / Bright Windows, 2002), 4, 53, 120-56, 334.
Mo Mo. *Zhongguo dianying jiaofu: Zhang Yimou zhuan (Godfather of Chinese Films: Zhang Yimou's Biography)*. Beijing: Zhongguo dianshi guangbo, 2008.
Pang, Laikwan. *Building a New China in Cinema*. (New York: Rowman and Littlefield, 2002), 128.
Rawnsley, Gary D. and Ming-yeh T. Rawnsley. *Global Chinese Cinema: the Culture and Politics of "Hero."* New York: Routledge, 2010.
Sibu congkan (The Four Treasures Series). (Shanghai: Commercial Press, 1921), 9.41b.
Tung, Chi. "To America, With Love: Zhang Yimou's One-Note Rhapsody." UCLA Asian Institute: *Asian Pacific Arts* 9/3/2004. For details, consult http://goo.gl/9OZXP.
Wang Bin. *Zhang Yimou zhege ren (A Biographical Sketch of Zhang Yimou)*. (Beijing: Tuanjie, 1998), 85-90.

Wang, John Ching-yu. "Cung *Cike liezhuan Jing Ke zhuan* kan *Shi Ji* de xüshi tece yu chengjiu" (On the narrative characteristics and achievements of *Records of the Historian* from *The Biography of Jing Ke* in *The Biography of Assassins*). Chung Tsaichun's *Chuancheng yu chuangxin* (*Heritage and Originality*). Taipei: Institute of Chinese Literature and Philology, Academia Sinica, 1999.
Wei, Long. *Mou tian xia* (*Zhang Yimou: from a Man of Northwest China to the Chief Director of the 2008 Beijing Olympic Games*). Beijing: China Pictorial Publishing House, 2009.
Yang, Mayfair Mei-hui. "Of Gender, State, Censorship, and Overseas Capital: An Interview with Chinese Director Zhang Yimou." *Zhang Yimou Interviews*. Frances Gateward, ed. (Jackson: University Press of Mississippi, 2001), 38.
Yu, Sabrina Qiong. "Jet Li: Star Construction and Fan Discourse on the Internet." *Chinese Film Stars*. Mary Farquhar and Yingjin Zhang edt. London: Routledge, 2010.
Zhang, Huijun. *Fengge chuangzao: Zhang Yimou dianying chuangzuo lun* (*Creation of Styles: Analyses of Zhang Yimou's Films*). Beijing: Zhongguo dianying, 2010.
---. *Xingshi zhuisuo yu shijue chuangzao: Zhang Yimou dianying chuangzuo yanjiu* (*Searches for Forms and Creations of Visions*: *Studies of Zhang Yimou's Creative Works*). Beijing: Zhongguo dianying, 2008.
Zhang, Jiuying. *Fanpai Zhang Yimou*. (Beijing: Zhongguo mangwen, 2001), 246–49.
Zhang, Yimou and Li Erwei. "Wei zhongguo dianying zouxiang shijie pulu" (To Pave the Way toward the World for Chinese Films). *Zhang Yimou, di wudai daoyan congshu: wei yi mou buwei daoliang mou* (*Zhang Yimou, the Fifth Generation Filmmaker in Book Series: For Art's Sake, Not For Rice and Sorghum's Sake*). (Changsha: Hunan wenyi, 1997), 389.

Notes

1. Chen Kaige believes that Zhang Yimou has Qin heritage because Zhang Yimou's birthplace, Xi'an, used to be the capital of Qin. He remarks, "Yimou is a true descendent of the Qin." For details, consult Chen Kaige's "Qinguo ren" (The Person with Heritage of the Qin state), 283, 291. Also consult Wei Long's *Mou tian xia* (*Zhang Yimou: from a Man of Northwest China to the Chief Director of the 2008 Beijing Olympic Games*); Huang Xiaoyang's *Yingxiang zhongguo: Zhang Yimou zhuan* (*Impressions on China: Zhang Yimou's Biography*); Chai Ying's *Wenhua shiyu zhong de Zhang Yimou* (*Zhang Yimou in the Cultural Vision*); and Mo Mo's *Zhongguo dianying jiaofu: Zhang Yimou zhuan* (*Godfather of Chinese Films: Zhang Yimou's Biography*).
2. For scholarly research about Jet Li, consult "Jet Li: Star Construction and Fan Discourse on the Internet."
3. The "unison cry of 'Feng! Feng!' [was] chillingly similar to the Nazi salute 'Sieg Heil.'" For details, consult Robert Y. Eng's "Is Hero a Paean to Authoritarianism?" http://www.asiamedia.ucla.edu/article.asp?parentid=14371 (online data accessed in July 2009).
4. See my first note.
5. See my first note.
6. In "*Crouching Tiger Hidden Dragon, Hero,* and *House of the Flying Daggers*: Interpreting Gender Thematics in the Contemporary Swordplay Film—A View from the

West," Jacqueline Levitin seems to believe that Broken Sword "is the highest level hero. . . . It is no surprise that he is male." Different from her, I hope to highlight how heroic, insightful, and significant women and heroines can be in this film. For details, consult page 175 of this article.

7. Ying Zheng established the Qin Dynasty in 221 B.C., but his dynasty did not last long. It ended in 206 B.C..

8. For details, consult Chen Kaige's *The Emperor and the Assassin* (1995). Another film about Ying Zheng is Tony Siu-Tung Ching's *The Terra Cotta Warrior* (1989). Zhang Yimou is the male protagonist, and Gong Li, the female protagonist, in this film. For details, consult pages 291 and 292 of Chen Kaige's *Zhongguo dianying yishujia yenjiu congkan: lun Zhang Yimou* (*The Book Series of Research on Chinese Film Artists: Zhang Yimou*).

Chen Kaige once said that Zhang Yimou looks like a terra-cotta warrior. For details, consult Chen Kaige's "Qinguo ren" (The Person with Heritage of the Qin State).

In addition to these movies, there are other films about *ciqin* or the establishment of the Qin Dynasty. When talking about recent feature films related to Ying Zheng, some film critics and viewers also mention *The Myth* (2005), directed by Stanley Tong.

9. See page 10 in Shelly Kraicer's "Absence as Spectacle: Zhang Yimou's *Hero*." Also consult Gary D. Rawnsley and Ming-yeh T. Rawnsley's *Global Chinese Cinema: the Culture and Politics of "Hero"*; Cheng Huizhe's *Dianying dui xiaoshuo de kuayue: Zhang Yimou yingpian yanjiu* (*Filmic Strides across Fictions: Research of Zhang Yimou's Films*); Zhang Huijun's *Fengge chuangzao: Zhang Yimou dianying chuangzuo lun* (*Creation of Styles: Analyses of Zhang Yimou's Films*); and Zhang Huijun's *Xingshi zhuisuo yu shijue chuangzao: Zhang Yimou dianying chuangzuo yanjiu* (*Searches for Forms and Creations of Visions: Studies of Zhang Yimou's Creative Works*).

10. Chen Kaige reveals that Zhang Yimou sold his blood to have a camera of his own. For details, consult Chen Kaige's "Qinguo ren" (The Person with Heritage of the Qin State).

11. See Chris Berry's "Calm in the Eye of the Storm."

12. Consult Violeta Kovacsics's "The 52nd San Sebastian International Film Festival September 17–25, 2004."

13. Every color may have dozens, hundreds, or even thousands of meanings. Different viewers and film critics have different interpretations, so it is impossible to make a list of everybody's opinions about colors in this film. In this article, my list serves only as a sample of some possible meanings.

14. Consult Li Feng's *Ying Xiong* (*Hero*).

15. For details, see Beryl Tzu-hsiu Chiu's twenty-seventh footnote for "Public Secrets: Geopolitical Aesthetics in Zhang Yimou's *Hero*."

16. Beryl Tzu-hsiu Chiu's "Public Secrets: Geopolitical Aesthetics in Zhang Yimou's *Hero*."

17. "First Emperor Qin was presented as a peacemaker and unity founder. It is on this point that the film caused fierce controversy. Many critics consider First Emperor Qin as a cruel despot, not a peacemaker. For instance, he had buried 400,000 soldiers alive once he took State Zhao." For details, consult Chen Xihe's "On the Father Figures in Zhang Yimous' Films: From *Red Sorghum* to *Hero*."

18. See page 10 in Shelly Kraicer's "Absence as Spectacle: Zhang Yimou's *Hero*."

19. Consult pages 125-156 and 144 in Li Feng's *Ying Xiong* (*Hero*).

20. See pages 140-144 in Li Feng's *Ying Xiong* (*Hero*).

21. Consult pages 147-155 in Li Feng's *Ying Xiong* (*Hero*).

22. From *The Red Sorghum*, *Judo*, *The Story of Qiu Ju*, and *Raise the Red Lantern* to *Hero*, Zhang Yimou displays his expertise in dealing with different shades of red in films. The use of crimson, scarlet, ruby, carroty, and orange in *Hero* is an exhibition of Zhang Yimou's specialization in shades of red. For details, consult pages 25-26 in Jia Leilei's "Yingxiang yüyan de ganxing xingshi yü biaoshu yüjing—Zhang Yimou yingpian zhong de shijue/sinli yiyi" (The Sensational Forms and Expressive Contexts of the Cinematic Language—The Visual/Psychological Meanings in Zhang Yimou's Films).

23. Consult page 508 in James Irving Crump's *Chan-Kuo Ts'e* (*The Stratagems of the Warring States*).

24. *The Stratagems of the Warring States* is one of the English translations of *Zhanguo ce* (*Chan-Kuo Ts'e*). *The Intrigues of the Warring States* is another English translation used by some literary scholars and historians. Consult James Crump's *Intrigues: Studies of the Chan-kuo Ts'e*.

The Book of Yan in *The Stratagems of the Warring States* is the earliest formal source of the story about *ciqin* in Chinese history. In addition to *The Stratagems of the Warring States*, other historical records also include the story of *ciqin*, including *Shiji* (*Records of the Historian*). For instance, John Ching-yu Wang analyzes the biography of Jing Ke in *The Biography of Assassins* and comments on the narrative characteristics and accomplishments of *Records of the Historian* from literary perspectives. For details, consult Chung Tsai-chun's *Chuancheng yu chuangxin* (*Heritage and Originality*).

25. Consult pages 553-555 in James Irving Crump's *Chan-Kuo Ts'e* (*The Stratagems of the Warring States*).

26. For details, consult page 127 in John Ching-yu Wang's "Cung *Cike liezhuan Jing Ke zhuan* kan *Shi Ji* de xüshi tece yu chengjiu" (On the narrative characteristics and achievements of *Records of the Historian* from *The Biography of Jing Ke* in *The Biography of Assassins*).

27. Chen, Xiaoming and Ming-Yeh Rawnsley. "On '*Tianxia*' (All under the heaven) on Zhang Yimou's *Hero*." *Global Chinese Cinema: the Culture and Politics of Hero*. Gary D. Rawnsley and Ming-yeh T. Rawnsley edt. London: Routledge, 2010.

28. Consult pages 506-508 in James Irving Crump's *Chan-Kuo Ts'e* (*The Stratagems of the Warring States*).

29. See page 508 in James Irving Crump's *Chan-Kuo Ts'e* (*The Stratagems of the Warring States*).

30. Consult page 509 in James Irving Crump's *Chan-Kuo Ts'e* (*The Stratagems of the Warring States*).

31. My adoption and minor modification of James I. Crump's translation.

32. Consult page 137 in James Irving Crump's "The Assassins" in *Legends of the Warring States: Persuasions, romances, and Stories from Chan-kuo Ts'e*. Also consult *Sibu congkan* (*The Four Treasures Series*). Shanghai: Commercial Press, 1921, 9.41b.

33. See my first note.

34. Consult Tung Chi's "To America, With Love: Zhang Yimou's One-Note Rhapsody."

35. See Meina Banh's "Oh My Hero!" at http://goo.gl/3tzTu (online data accessed in July 2009).

36. Historians and literary classicists have different opinions about when the War-

ring State era began and ended. Roughly speaking, the Warring States period initiated around 403 B.C. and was over in 221 B.C..

37. See Robert Y. Eng's "Is Hero a Paean to Authoritarianism?" For details, consult www.asiamedia.ucla.edu/article.asp?parentid=14371 (online data accessed in July 2009).

38. Among all the leading actresses in Zhang Yimou's films, the most frequently seen women are Gong Li and Zhang Ziyi. Zhang Yimou remarks that Gong Li is good at playing unyielding and tough women with strong personalities in films he has directed. For details, consult pages 85-90 in Wang Bin's *Zhang Yimou zhege ren* (*A Biographical Sketch of Zhang Yimou*). Also consult pages 134-148 in Zhang Yimou's chat about Gong Li in Li Erwei's *Zhi mian Zhang Yimou: Zhang Yimou de dian ying shi jie* (*Facing Zhang Yimou: Zhang Yimou's Cinematic World*).

39. Consult pages 246-249 in Zhang Jiuying's *Fanpai Zhang Yimou*.

40. See page 38 in Mayfair Mei-hui Yang's "Of Gender, State, Censorship, and Overseas Capital: An Interview with Chinese Director Zhang Yimou."

41. Consult page 389 in Zhang Yimou and Li Erwei's "Wei zhongguo dianying zouxiang shijie pulu" (Paving the Way toward the World for Chinese Films). This part of the interview also appears in *Zhongguo dianying yishujia yenjiu congshu: lun Zhang Yimou* (*The Book Series of Research on Chinese Film Artists: Zhang Yimou*). (Beijing: Zhongguo dianying / Chinese Films, 1994), 296.

42. See page 128 in Pang Laikwan's *Building a New China in Cinema*.

43. Consult pages 322-329 in Li Erwei's *Zhi mian Zhang Yimou: Zhang Yimou de dian ying shi jie* (*Facing Zhang Yimou: Zhang Yimou's Cinematic World*).

44. See page 445 in Cai Rong's "Gender Imaginations in *Crouching Tiger, Hidden Dragon* and the Wuxia World."

45. "To have characters form a pair or pairs of binary opposites is a fundamental way to encode feature films. It derives from the most primitive and the simplest judgment according to human logic: black/white, day/night, cold/hot, and even strong/weak, good/evil." For details, consult page 28 in Jia Leilei's "Yingxiang yüyan de ganxing xingshi yü biaoshu yüjing—Zhang Yimou yingpian zhong de shijue/sinli yiyi" (The Sensational Forms and Expressive Contexts of the Cinematic Language—The Visual/Psychological Meanings in Zhang Yimou's Films).

46. See Robert Y. Eng's "Is Hero a Paean to Authoritarianism?"

47. Consult page 334 in Li Feng's *Ying Xiong* (*Hero*).

48. For details, consult the following books: Xun Zi's *Xun Zi* (*Xun Zi*), Zhu Xi's *Yi li jing zhang tong jie* (*Comprehensive Annotations of The Book of Manners and Decorum*), and Wu Jing's (670-749 A.D., a historian in the Tang Dynasty) *Zhenguang zheng yao* (*The Political Outline of the Zhenguang Period*).

49. See my first note.

50. I would like to thank John Ching-yu Wang for providing the background information about James I. Crump.

Chapter Three
There Is a Beauty in the Door(way) of Flying Daggers

Beifang you jiaren (In the North there is a beautiful woman,)
Jueshi er duli (Unique, unequaled in the world.)
Yigu qing ren cheng (With one glance she conquers a city of men,)
Zaigu qing ren guo (With another glance a country of men)
Ning buzhi qingcheng yü qingguo (Don't you know? A city and country conquering)
Jiaren nanzaide (Beauty cannot be found again.)

Li Yannian[1]

In the summer of 2004, Zhang Yimou's *Shimian maifu* (*House of Flying Daggers*) was shown and released for the first time in Beijing. Most Chinese audience members' interpretations of the film do not closely relate the film and Li Yannian's poem, which is sung at the beginning and the end of the movie. This article begins with my interpretation of possible interrelations between the film and the above-mentioned poem that begins with *beifang you jiaren* (There is a beauty in the North; my own English translation). Li Yannian inadvertently turns the *jiaren* into a scapegoat if the country and citizens are not taken good care of. Zhang Yimou revises the destiny of the *jiaren* by permitting her to speak her mind and decide her fate.

Before my own interpretation, let me briefly summarize some of the anonymous responses that audience members have posted on Chinese websites about the film. Because the English title of the movie is *House of Flying Daggers*, the power struggle between the police and the *feidaomen* (House of Flying Daggers; the English translation of the name of the group of insurgents, which have been adopted as the English title of the whole film) seems to be the story Zhang Yimou promises to tell. The interrelations between the police and *feidaomen* are truly significant parts of the story plot at the beginning and the middle of the film; however, Zhang Yimou ignores them at the end of the film. He seems to break his promise. The love triangle is the only focus at the end of the film. Some Chinese audience members feel that Zhang Yimou traps viewers in the *maifu* (snare or trickery; an important part of the Chinese title of this movie) of the mystery of the fight between the police and House of Flying Daggers.

It may be humorous to think that Zhang Yimou *maifu* (tricks; the same phrase can be used as either a verb or a noun in Chinese language) his audience. But I would like to argue that it is necessary and indispensable for Zhang Yimou to neglect the power struggle between the police and House of Flying Daggers and to focus on the love story of Xiaomei (played by Zhang Ziyi), who is the *jiaren* in this film. Why? The answer lies in the poetic lines, *ning buzhi qingguo yü qingcheng / jiaren nanzaide* ("Don't you know? A city and country conquering / Beauty cannot be found again"; Hans H. Frankel's English translation). In the poetic lines, the Chinese character *ning* indicates the storyteller's preference for the *jiaren* to the terrible political power struggles, which even include *qingguo* ("the country is defeated") and *qingcheng* ("the city or the castle is conquered"). The word *ning* implies that the storyteller would rather ignore or have no idea about *qingguo* and *qingcheng*. The Chinese character *ning* indicates how the storyteller deliberately chooses or decides to pay attention only to the *jiaren* (beauty) because *jiaren nanzaide* (beauty cannot be found again).

The Storyteller's Promise

If the filmmaker is the storyteller who tells the audience the whole story shown in the film, then Li Yannian's poetic lines clearly tell us what Zhang Yimou, as the director of the movie and the storyteller, decides to neglect as well as what he chooses to focus on. On the one hand, Zhang Yimou may seem to break his promise by saying nothing about what he promises to tell his audience in the English title of the film. On the other hand, Zhang Yimou must disclose nothing about what happens to the House of Flying Daggers and the police at the end of the film because he, as the storyteller, prefers knowing nothing about *qingcheng* and *qingguo* to running the risk of losing the beauty that is unique and unequaled according to Li Yannian's promise to readers in the poem. At the end of the film, Zhang Yimou clearly tells his audience how Liu (played by Andy Lau) and Xiaomei use their flying daggers to cope with the love triangle; Zhang, as a matter of fact, is a responsible storyteller because the English title of this film, literally speaking, is directly related to flying daggers.

The Unequaled and Unique Beauty

According to Li Yannian's depiction, the *jiaren* is the most beautiful woman in the whole world. Nobody is prettier than she is. She is unequaled. She is such a unique woman that the storyteller cannot find anybody to replace her once he loses her. In *House of Flying Daggers*, the *jiaren* is also both unique and unequaled.

To Jin (played by Takeshi Kaneshiro whose Chinese name is Jin Chengwu), Xiaomei is different from other women when they meet in the brothel. Although all the other courtesans name themselves after blossoms and hope to be as pretty as blossoms, Xiaomei refuses to name herself after any flowers. She is unique and so different from all the other courtesans that she surprises and impresses Jin.

To Liu, Xiaomei is unequaled and irreplaceable, though there are many *xiaomei* (little sister or young girl) in the House of Flying Daggers. Liu is one of the members in the House of Flying Daggers and knows that there are many *xiaomei* in the House of Flying Daggers even before he serves as a spy for the rebels in the police. But he loves only this Xiaomei. From Liu's point of view, none of the other *xiaomei* can substitute for this Xiaomei because this Xiaomei is the only *jiaren* for him. If Liu loses this Xiaomei, there will no longer be any *jiaren* though the House of Flying Daggers will still have other *xiaomei*. Thus he patiently spends three years waiting for an advanced relationship with Xiaomei.

In addition to how Xiaomei names herself, she is unique and unequaled because of her appearance, temperament, dancing, singing, chivalry, talent, courage, kung fu, and so forth. Because Xiaomei is matchless, the storyteller, Zhang Yimou, cannot miss such an unequaled and unique *jiaren*. He cannot help but neglect the fight between the police and House of Flying Daggers in order to focus only on her when telling the story to the audience.

The Door(way) of Flying Daggers

The *jiaren* in *House of Flying Daggers*, Xiaomei, serves as both a "door" that the House of Flying Daggers opens for the police and a "doorway" that the House of Flying Daggers uses to entice the police to enter. Xiaomei pretends to be a blind courtesan in the brothel, the blind daughter of the ex-head of the House of Flying Daggers, and a fugitive rescued by a policeman who is assigned to follow her to the House of Flying Daggers. She does all of this to seduce Jin and bring him from the police to the House of Flying Daggers.

Because Xiaomei pretends to be a blind courtesan in the brothel, she serves as a "door" that the House of Flying Daggers opens for the police. When Jin visits the blind courtesan that Xiaomei pretends to be, he is actually "knocking at the door of the House of Flying Daggers."

When Xiaomei pretends to be the escaped convict rescued by Jin and the blind daughter of the ex-head of the House of Flying Daggers, she tempts Jin to follow her from the jail to the House of Flying Daggers. She serves as a "doorway" for Jin to enter to reach the House of Flying Daggers.

On the way from the brothel to the police and then to the House of Flying Daggers, Xiaomei's first strategy is to erotically affect and attract Jin. First, Xiaomei offers Jin the opportunity to strip her outfit from her. She entertains him by reciting Li Yannian's poem, singing and dancing. She tempts him to embrace and kiss her. After Jin releases her from the jail, she actively explores his body by touching and feeling his legs, waist, chest, arms,[2] eyes, and nose. She smells the air from his mouth, touches his lips with her own lips, and almost kisses him. The moment when her lips touch Jin's, Xiaomei suddenly terminates her erotic seduction by warning Jin of the arrival of soldiers. This sudden termination of her seduction makes Jin keenly desire to continue following her. Second, she embraces him and sobs on his shoulders as if she were already his girlfriend after their first fight against soldiers. Later on, she deliberately satisfies his voyeurism during her bath time in the woods. She even comes close to allowing him to have sex with her. These erotic games keep Jin interested in continuing the trip with her from the police toward the House of Flying Daggers.

After Jin discovers that the central government has assigned fierce soldiers to kill him and that the government does not know his and Liu's plan to follow Xiaomei to the House of Flying Daggers, Jin realizes that he must risk his own safety and life on the way from the police to the House of Flying Daggers. He loses his interest in this journey and tells Liu that he quits; in reaction, Xiaomei changes her seductive strategies. She ceases her attempts at erotic seduction and beings to remind Jin of his verbal promise of a relationship and requirements for his commitment. For instance, she reminds Jin of the *shanye lanman chu* ("the bright-colored mountainous areas"), echoing Jin's promise to elope with Xiaomei and take her away from the brothel to a romantic place. She questions whether the "wind," which Jin identifies himself with, would stay with her, and she bursts into tears immediately after Jin insists that the "wind" will not stop for her. She smiles at Jin and holds his hand in the bamboo forest after he returns and rejoins her trip toward the House of Flying Daggers as if she were cordially in ecstasy of the "wind's" stop for her and continuation of their romantic comradeship in various fights.

Xiaomei serves as such a successful "door" and "doorway" that Jin follows her all the way from the brothel to the police and from the police to the House of Flying Daggers regardless of the risk he faces. In fact, the Chinese pronunciation of "the House of Flying Daggers," *feidaomen*, clearly indicates the "door(way)" that I highlight. The word, *men*, literally means "door," while *feidao* of the *feidaomen* refers to "flying daggers." In other words, the literal translation of *feidaomen* from Mandarin Chinese to English should be "the door of flying daggers." In addition, this "door" is actually the *jiaren* or the female protagonist in this story—namely, Xiaomei.

The Sexual Indication of "Door(way)"

In addition to why and how Xiaomei functions as the "door(way)" of flying daggers, I would like to point out the sexual indication of this "door(way)" in the romantic triangle. Xiaomei's body or sexual organ is actually the "door(way)" for both Jin and Liu. Her hymen is like a "door" that Jin and Liu compete to open and her vagina is like a "doorway" that enthralls them.

Jin tries to open this "door" and enter this "doorway" on at least three occasions. First, early when Jin visits Xiaomei in the brothel, he almost rapes her. Xiaomei resists, and the pander and other courtesans drag him away from Xiaomei. Liu safeguards this "door(way)" in the brothel and stops Jin from raping Xiaomei. Second, after Jin peeps at Xiaomei during her bath and Xiaomei puts on his clothes, he attempts to open the "door" and enter the "doorway" again. Xiaomei insists that she does not know him well and rejects him. Third, Jin finally opens the "door" and enters the "doorway" with Xiaomei's approval after Xiaomei brings him out of the House of Flying Daggers, releases him, and suggests that he escapes.

Liu also keenly desires to open the "door" and enter the "doorway." In the police headquarters, Liu touches Xiaomei's face, head, shoulders, arms, and legs almost as if he were caressing Xiaomei. When Liu explains the implement for torture to Xiaomei, his lips almost reach Xiaomei's, as if he would kiss her. Xiaomei does not refuse him at all, acting as if she will permit him to do whatever he wants. Liu, therefore, firmly believes the "door(way)" should belong to him, not Jin. He repetitively complains that it is extremely difficult for him to witness how Jin almost opens the "door" and how Xiaomei almost lets Jin into the "doorway" on the way from the brothel to the house of flying daggers because he does everything for Xiaomei and has been waiting for Xiaomei for three years.

He almost rapes Xiaomei after she stops his foreplay and honestly acknowledges that she hesitates because of Jin. Liu emphasizes that Jin's adoration for her is only a play or a sexual game. He stresses that he is her faithful "Prince Charming" and therefore the right person to open the "door" and enter the "doorway." Yet the supervisors in the House of Flying Daggers stop Liu from raping Xiaomei and insist that he should not continue forcing Xiaomei once she says no. After Xiaomei has sex with Jin and tries to elope with Jin, Liu throws two flying daggers and hits Xiaomei's chest[3] because Liu has decided, "If I cannot possess her, nobody should possess her."

If Xiaomei's hymen is like the "door" that both Jin and Liu try hard to open and her vagina is like the "doorway" that they would like to enter at the cost of their friendship, Xiaomei is also the door(way) that brings them into the love triangle. On the way from the police to the prison and then to the House of Flying Daggers, Xiaomei gradually guides, "walks," and brings Jin into the romantic triangle. Xiaomei is the entrance to the love triangle. Her hymen is like the threshold of the physical aspect of the romantic triangle, and her vagina is like the path toward it.

The Door(way)/Exit from the Love Triangle

Jin and Liu compete to open the "door," enter the "doorway," and then become involved in the love triangle. But the "door" can be not only opened but also closed. If Xiaomei closes the "door" and terminates the romantic triangle, she can direct Jin and Liu to the exit of the love triangle. At the end of the film, Xiaomei pulls Liu's dagger out of her chest and sacrifices her life to release Jin and Liu from the romantic triangle. Her death closes the "door," blocks the "entrance," and serves as a "doorway" that brings Jin and Liu away from the love triangle. If the love triangle is like a "lock" that keeps Jin and Liu in captivity, then Xiaomei's death unlocks them. Her death is like an "exit" from the romantic triangle for not only Jin and Liu but also herself.

If the English title of this film can be literally understood as "the door of flying daggers" which Xiaomei represents, then what Zhang Yimou, in English, promises to tell the audience is the story of "the door of flying daggers, Xiaomei." That is to say, it is entirely appropriate for Zhang Yimou to focus on Xiamei, the *jiaren* in this story, and disregard *qingcheng qingguo* and what happens during the fights between the police and House of Flying Daggers. If the "door(way)" that Xiaomei represents is not only the "door(way)" between the police and House of Flying Daggers but also the "door" that Jin and Liu compete to open and the "doorway" that they try to enter at the cost of their friendship, it makes sense for Zhang Yimou to excuse Jin and Liu from everything related to the police and the House of Flying Daggers and to focus solely on the "door(way)" or the *jiaren* at the end of this film.

Cinematic Revision of Li Yannian's *Jiaren* and Narrative Perspective

Although both Li Yannian and Zhang Yimou focus on the *jiaren* in their works of arts, Zhang Yimou revises the *jiaren*'s fate. He compensates the *jiaren* for her lack of freedom by allowing her to speak her mind.

Li Yannian indirectly objectifies the *jiaren* when comparing her with the *guo* (country) and *cheng* (city) in his poetic line: "I'd rather have no idea about the collapse of my city and country and choose the beauty because the irreplaceable beauty cannot be regained once I lose her." He also inadvertently labels the *jiaren* as the *hongyan huoshui* if the *cheng* and *guo* are not taken good care of (literally, "pretty women with rosy cheeks are like a flood disaster"; metaphorically, "pretty women as an excuse or a scapegoat for men who do not dare to be responsible for their failures"). Li Yannian unconsciously turns his younger sister, namely, the *jiaren*, into a Chinese version of Pandora, who is "a beautiful woman manufactured by [Greco-Roman gods] to seduce and bring harm to man."[4] Because of the objectification of the *jiaren*, Li Yannian does not give the *jiaren* equal right to speak her mind. What if the *jiaren* does not like the emperor who patronizes her or the person who chooses her? Or what if the *jiaren* already has a lover? Li Yannian does not take what the *jiaren* prefers into account at all.

Zhang Yimou, in *House of Flying Daggers*, compensates the *jiaren* for what Li Yannian fails to take into consideration: an equal right to decide her own destiny after Jin and Liu choose to love her and disregard everything else. The whole film focuses on how the *jiaren* defines her relationship with Jin and Liu. The woman's right to speak her mind that Zhang Yimou gives to Xiaomei can more or less offset the male-centered or chauvinistic narrative perspective in Li Yannian's poem. Zhang Yimou allows Xiaomei to answer the questions on her own: What if the *jiaren* already has Liu's three-year commitment? How does the *jiaren* choose between the two admirers? What if the *jiaren* is involved in the love triangle? How would the *jiaren* decide her fate?

At the end of this film, Liu and Jin fight against each other from spring or summer through winter. Some Chinese audience members comment that it takes too many seasons for Xaimei to die. Indeed, *House of Flying Daggers* is probably the first Chinese martial arts film to allow so many seasons for the female protagonist to die. But I argue that in *House of Flying Daggers* Zhang Yimou probably allows Xiaomei so much time to speak her mind on purpose to compensate the *jiaren* for her lack of opportunities to decide her destiny in Li Yannian's poem.

The Tang Dynasty

The other way for Zhang Yimou to counterbalance the male-centered or chauvinistic narrative perspective in Li Yannian's poem written in the Han Dynasty[5] is probably to let Xiaomei become a tough career woman with good kung fu in the Tang Dynasty. The Tang Dynasty is one of the most feminist dynasties in Chinese history. Women in the early and mid Tang Dynasty, on average, were given more freedom to define their personal relationships with men and decide their marriages than were women in other dynasties. In the late Tang Dynasty, women enjoyed less freedom; however, compared with women in other dynasties, they were still less restricted by patriarchy.

In the early and mid Tang Dynasty, marriages were not always under men's control only. Women could request to terminate their marriages or get divorced. Women could be remarried after they lost husbands. Twenty-three princesses in the Tang dynasty married second husbands, whom they selected. For instance, four daughters of the first emperor of the Tang Dynasty married twice, and six daughters of the second emperor of the Tang Dynasty married twice.[6] Three princesses married three times in their lives. Wu Zetian, the only female emperor in feudalist China,[7] and a number of princesses even had male concubines or male prostitutes. Although some wealthy people in the Tang Dynasty mistreated female slaves, servants, concubines, prostitutes, or spouses and some women married people whom they did not like because of their parents' or masters' arrangements in the Tang Dynasty, the sexual discrimination against women in the Tang Dynasty was less than that in other dynasties.

Women in the Tang Dynasty were usually given more freedom to socialize with men in public than were women in other dynasties. For instance, Yang Yühuan, a well-known royal concubine, went to dinner and had fun with An Lushan. Bai Jüyi's famous poem, "Pipa xing," is about how a businessman's wife in the Tang Dynasty traveled on her own at midnight, chatted with a male traveler on the same boat, and played her musical instrument for him. Generally speaking, women in the Tang Dynasty usually had more opportunities to socialize with men, compare different men, and reconsider their choices of different kinds of men than those in other dynasties. It is therefore comprehensible for Xiaomei, as a woman in the Tang Dynasty,[8] to rethink and choose whom she prefers in Zhang Yimou's *House of Flying Daggers*.

The early and mid Tang Dynasty did not have strict rules for women's virginity and chastity.[9] For example, widows were not required to give up their sexual life. In 627 A.D., the emperor encouraged widows and girls after the age of fifteen to be married.[10] Premarital sexual behaviors and extramarital love affairs at that time were much more common than in other dynasties. For instance, Yuan Zhen's *Yingying zhuan* (*Biography of Yingying*), a famous literary masterpiece written in the Tang Dynasty, is a love story in which protagonists have premarital sexual gratification. The increasing number of *chuanqi* (legendary stories) and stories about premarital sexual gratification between men of letters and talented women, pretty women, or attractive female ghosts in the Tang Dynasty can also verify the lack of strict regulations for women's virginity or premarital sexual behaviors. Although the government in the late Tang Dynasty gradually started to advocate women's chastity, the overall requirement for women's chastity and virginity was still less than that in dynasties following the Tang Dynasty. For example, according to the historical record of the number of chaste women, whom the central government offered awards to, there were 51 chaste women in the Tang Dynasty, 267 chaste women in the Song Dynasty, 36,000 chaste women in the Ming Dynasty, and 12,000 chaste women in the Qing Dynasty. The Tang Dynasty provided awards to a much smaller number of chaste women than did the Song Dynasty, Ming Dynasty, and Qing Dynasty. Maybe because of the gender ideology in the Tang Dynasty, Liu and Jin, in *House of Flying Daggers*, do not seem to dislike, devalue, or abandon Xiaomei after she has premarital sexual intercourse and loses her virginity.

So far among all the award-winning Chinese martial arts films, *House of Flying Daggers* has probably included the most scenes in which the female protagonist wears sexy dresses, exposes her breastline and shoulders, and has her clothes stripped off. These scenes reflect the most popular kinds of women's dresses in the Tang Dynasty: colorful and sexy dresses that expose the upper part of the chest, high-waisted skirts, and so forth.[11] For example, Ouyang Xun depicts the upper part of women's chests in his poem "Nan xiang zi": *xiongqian ru xue lian ru hua* (the front part of the chest is like snow; the face is as beautiful as a flower).

In addition, Xiaomei puts on Jin's clothes after her bath because she did not bring any clean clothes with her when Jin helped her escape from the prison. But it may not be simply a coincidence for Xiaomei, because some women in the Tang Dynasty did wear men's clothes, do exercise, play ball, ride horses, and even learn martial arts. Wu Zetian and her ambitious daughter, Princess Taiping, for instance, sometimes wore men's clothes in the royal palace and might motivate women in the Tang Dynasty to put on men's clothes more frequently than women in other dynasties. The large non-Han population in the Tang Dynasty also increased women's opportunities to wear clothes that were not traditional dresses for women.

The Tang Dynasty is the dynasty in which the earliest archetype of Chinese martial arts stories occurred. The most famous stories related to Chinese chivalrous spirit and kung fu in the Tang Dynasty include *Nie Yinniang*, *Qiuran ke (The Man with a Curly Beard)*, and *Kunlun nu (The Slave of Kunlun)*. Almost all the Chinese martial arts fictions derive from *chuanqi* about chivalry and kung fu in the Tang Dynasty. Most Chinese martial arts scripts and films can hardly escape from the influence of successful Chinese martial arts fictions. Zhang Yimou's film and Li Feng's script and fiction are no exception. For example, in the script, fiction, and film, Zhang's and Li's female protagonist, just like Nie Yinniang, is the most mysterious and influential woman. Xiaomei and Nie Yinniang are not frail beauties lamenting in boudoirs as in most Chinese *caizi jiaren* (beauty-scholar) romances. They are not "little women" in need of heroes' special protection or companionship as in most Chinese *yingxiong meiren* (hero and beauty) legends, either.

The Tang Dynasty is also the dynasty in which the government formally allowed talented women to become governmental officers, have their careers, and decide their own destinies, especially after Wu Zetian ruled the country. For instance, Song Ruochao was a female *xueshi* (scholar) in the royal palace; Shangguan Wan'er was a female governmental officer; Yü Xuanji was a female poet anthologized in *Quan tang shi (Poetry of the Whole Tang Dynasty)*. Zhang Yimou's choice of the Tang Dynasty foregrounds how and why Xiaomei's career in the *feidaomen* and her destiny are under her own control regardless of what Jin and Liu compel her to do about the love triangle. It compensates the *jiaren* for the lack of her career and opportunities to speak her mind. It also counterbalances the chauvinistic or male-centered narrative perspective in Li Yannian's poem written in the Han Dynasty.

Was Li Yannian aware of the chauvinist or male-centered narrative perspective in his poem? Probably not. Because of the prevalence of Confucian gender ideology at the end of the Zhou Dynasty[12] and the beginning of the Han Dynasty, Li Yannian probably did not notice that the *jiaren* should be given equal right to make her own decision. He probably did not think of what the *jiaren* had except for the skin-deep beauty, such as her talent, potentiality, and career. During the Han Dynasty, Confucianism, including the Confucian definition of women's lower status, was revived. The Han Dynasty is also the dynasty in which two of the most famous books about patriarchal gender ideology were written. These two well-known books about the Confucian definition of women in the Han Dynasty are Liu Xiang's *Lienüzhuan* (*Biography of Chaste Women*) and Ban Zhao's *Nüjie* (*Admonitions for Women*).[13] For example, Ban Zhao in *Nüjie* warns that women should *beirou xiaren* (not to think about [themselves] until the end of all the concerns for others in every situation). Although Li Yannian wrote the poem about the *jiaren* before Ban Zhao wrote *Nüjie*, the emperor, whom Li Yannian wrote the poem for, was the emperor who started to revive and advocate Confucianism in the Han Dynasty. In Li Yannian's poem, the *jiaren* truly does what Ban Zhao admonishes: not thinking about herself even after the emperor or the male storyteller finishes making his decision and selecting what he prefers. Although emperors of the late Tang Dynasty began to make chauvinist laws that decreased women's freedom in terms of second or third marriages, chastity, virginity, choices of husbands, and so on, the Tang Dynasty, especially the early and mid Tang Dynasty, is still the era more feministic than other dynasties in feudalist China. Zhang Yimou chooses the Tang Dynasty probably because it can serve as a contrast to the Han Dynasty, in which Li Yannian wrote the poem about the *jiaren*. Thus, he can compensate the *jiaren* for the lack of freedom to speak her mind and counterbalance the chauvinistic or male-centered narrative perspective in Li Yannian's poem.

The *Jiaren*'s Balance: The Game of *Xianren zhilu*

If Zhang Yimou does compensate the *jiaren* and offers her the freedom to speak her mind and make her choice, then whom or what Xiaomei selects at the end of *House of Flying Daggers* is inevitably worth investigation. Between *qingcheng qingguo* and the *jiaren*, the storyteller chooses the *jiaren* and disregards everything else. But Xiaomei attempts strongly to balance between Jin and Liu, instead of making a choice between Jin and Liu at the end of the film, though both Jin and Liu force her to select one of them.

Hwanhee Lee, in "House of Flying Daggers: A Reappraisal," included in *Senses of Cinema*, directly examines Xiaomei's predicament with Jin and Liu. After close readings of (1) Xiaomei's threat to pull the dagger from her chest to prevent Liu from killing Jin, (2) Jin's willingness to sacrifice his own life in order to let the dagger remain in Xiaomei's chest and to save Xiaomei's life, and (3) Liu's attempt to die with Xiaomei (by moving as if he has thrown out another dagger to kill Jin in order to compel Xiaomei to pull the dagger from her chest to kill him), Hwanhee Lee points out that Xiaomei decides to "die for both Jin *and* [Liu], given that she chooses to save Jin *and* let [Liu] live."[14] Xiaomei deals with the love triangle at the end of the film by not choosing between Jin and Liu but finding balance between them. For example, when Liu intended to have sex with Xiaomei, she hesitated because of Jin, and when Jin invited Xiaomei to run away with him, Xiaomei hesitated because of Liu. Xiaomei honestly admits her hesitation in front of both Jin and Liu. After Liu throws two flying daggers, one of which hits Xiaomei, to stop Xiaomei from choosing Jin and riding her horse to elope with Jin, Xiaomei frankly confesses her relationships with Liu and Jin. In the following paragraphs, I explore the interrelation between the game of *xianren zhilu* and the way Xiaomei balances between Jin and Liu.

The game of *xianren zhilu* (namely, Liu throws beans to reach some drums, and then she hits those drums), which is the game she played with Liu before the House of Flying Daggers assigned him as a spy in the police, is always how Xiaomei greets Liu and defines her relationship with him. In the film, Xiaomei and Liu play this game on at least three occasions: first, in the brothel after Jin kisses Xiaomei; second, in the private meeting with Liu after Jin arrives at the House of Flying Daggers; third, in the moment when Xiaomei pulls the dagger from her chest and throws it to prevent Liu from killing Jin. This special aspect of her relationship with Liu repeats itself whenever the relationship between her and Jin becomes closer. In other words, Xiaomei always thinks of her relationship with Liu whenever her relationship with Jin advances. For instance, Xiaomei and Liu play the game of *xianren zhilu* right after Jin kisses and tries to rape Xiaomei in the brothel. They play the same game again right after Jin agrees to marry Xiaomei after his arrival at the house of flying daggers. They play the same game for the third time right after Jin demonstrates his true love for Xiaomei by volunteering to be killed by Liu to save her life.

Why do Xiaomei and Liu play this game whenever the relationship between Jin and Xiaomei advances? This is not a coincidence. Literally speaking, *xianren zhilu* refers to fairies who would guide someone on which path to take. The phrase, *xianren*, means "fairies." *Zhi* means to point out something or make something clear. The Chinese character, *lu*, is a pun in the story plot. It literally refers to "the road or the way taken" but indicates "the way Xiaomei decides to cope with the love triangle." Xiaomei knows that Liu loves her early on before Jin develops the relationship with her. If Jin did not exist, Liu would have been Xiaomei's only choice and she would not be so confused by the two choices. But Jin enters Xiaomei's personal life and thus establishes the love triangle. Whenever the relationship between Jin and Xiaomei advances, Xiaomei is torn between the two men, becomes perplexed and pained, and subconsciously wishes *xianren* (fairies) to *zhilu* (to show which road/way to be taken / to show the way she should cope with the tension between Jin and Liu because of the love triangle) for her. This is probably why Xiaomei and Liu play the game of *xianren zhilu* and look to fairies to show them which way to take in dealing with their predicament.

It is apparent that from the beginning to the end Xiaomei does not know which path she should take or whom to choose as her "Prince Charming" because she still plays *xianren zhilu* and subconsciously asks the fairies to show her what she should do at the end of the film. Xiaomei balances between Jin and Liu by dying for both of them, stopping them from killing each other, releasing them from the love triangle, and therefore choosing neither of them.

If it makes sense to regard Xiaomei as the *jiaren* who serves as a "door" in this story, then she is a "door" that balances between the two male protagonists, Jin and Liu. Xiaomei is like a door between the *shanye lanman chu* (the brightcolored mountainous areas / the romantic and ideal place) that Jin promises her and the *shanye lanman chu* that Liu prepares for her. She is like a door between Jin's three-day romantic companionship and Liu's three-year commitment. She plays the game of *xianren zhilu* on three occasions, but what the fairies show her is probably the path between Jin's and Liu's *shanye lanman chu*. On the one hand, she is like a door, a material object, and the object of Zhang Yimou's filmic gaze. On the other hand, she is an active, thinking subject; she decides to choose neither of them in the love triangle and to serve as a door(way) that brings Jin and Liu away from the predicament. At the beginning of the film, in the brothel, Xiaomei chooses not to be named after any flowers; at the end of the film, she also decides not to be a blossom in anyone's *shanye lanman chu*. As Li Yannian's poem says, this kind of *jiaren* "cannot be found again"[15]; this unique and unequaled Xaimei cannot be found again after her death though there are many *xiaomei* in the House of Flying Daggers.[16]

Blindness in the "Blind" Alley of Romantic Triangle

Let me return to Xiaomei's blindness. Is Xiaomei really blind? My answer is yes and no. On the one hand, Xiaomei can clearly see everything. She is not physically blind. She pretends to be blind. She only pretends to be the blind daughter of the ex-head of the *feidaomen*. On the other hand, Xiaomei cannot clearly see her future. She is "blind" when facing Jin's and Liu's strong desires to have her romantic love. She is blind in terms of how to tackle the problem of her romantic triangle. She is so blind and helpless spiritually that she asks for *xianren zhilu* (fairies to point out her way) on three occasions from the beginning to the end of the film.

Xiaomei's blindness is not physical blindness but emotional blindness, especially at the moment when she is compelled to decide her romantic love between Jin and Liu as well as life and death for them. Xiaomei is not a blind martial arts lady, but she is a "blind" girl when Jin and Liu force her to decisively make a quick choice between them. She is a "blind" girl in the game of *xianren zhilu*. She is the "blind" girl whom fairies point out the way for: the "blind" alley toward her suicide and the deadend or tragic closure of her love story to rescue both Jin's and Liu's lives and lead them away from the deadlock of the romantic triangle.

Conclusion

Li Yannian is famous for his vivid description of how beautiful the *jiaren* is. Because of his poem, *qingguo qingcheng* has become an idiom in Chinese language to specify how nice-looking a woman can be. But Li Yannian inadvertently adopted a chauvinistic or male-centered narrative perspective, objectified the *jiaren,* labeled the *jiaren* as a scapegoat when the *guo* and *cheng* are not taken good care of, and "muffled" the *jiaren* by neglecting her equal right to speak her mind.

Zhang Yimou shares what Li Yannian's poem focuses on: the *jiaren,* yet he compensates the *jiaren* for what Li Yannian fails to take into account, and revises her fate in *House of Flying Daggers.* Xiaomei, like the *jiaren* in Li Yannian's poem, is still the object of the storyteller's gaze, but she is given plenty of time to respond to people who choose to focus on her and ignore everything else. With the woman's right to decide her destiny, the *jiaren* becomes an active, thinking subject in *House of Flying Daggers.*

References

Chen, Dongyuan. *Zhongguo funü shenghuo shi (History of Chinese Women's Life).* Shanghai: Shanghai Bookstore, 1984, p. 118.
Chen, Jingliang and Zou Jianwen. *Bainian zhongguo dianying jingxuan (The Best of Centennial Chinese Cinema).* Beijing: Zhongguo shehui kexue, 2005, p. 608.
Frankel, Hans H. "The Development of Han and Wei *Yüeh-fu* as a High Literary Genre." *The Vitality of the Lyric Voice: Shih Poetry from the Late Han to the Tang.* Lin Shuen-fu and Stephen Owen edt. Princeton: Princeton University Press, 1986.
Lee, Hwanhee. "House of Flying Daggers: A Reappraisal." *Senses of Cinema* 35 (April-June 2005): www.sensesofcinema.com.
Mulvey, Laura. "The Myth of Pandora: A Psychoanalytical Approach." *Feminisms in the Cinema.* Laura Pietropaolo and Ada Testaferri edt. Bloomington: Indiana University Press, 1995, p. 3.
Quan tang shu (The Whole Book of the Tang Dynasty). Beijing: Zhonghua, 1982.
Zhenguan zhengyao (Significant Policies During the Zhenguan Era). Chengdu: Sichuan renmin, 1987.
Zhou, Feng. *Zhongguo gudai fuzhuang cankao ziliao (Reference for Clothes in Ancient China).* Beijing: Yanshan, 1988.
Zhu, Xi. *Zhuzi yülei (Categories of Zhuzi's Words).* Beijing: Zhonghua, 1986.

Notes

1. Hans H. Frankel translated Li Yannian's poem into English. For details, consult Hans H. Frankel's "The Development of Han and Wei *Yüeh-fu* as a High Literary Genre." In *The Vitality of the Lyric Voice: Shih Poetry from the Late Han to the Tang.* Lin Shuen-fu and Stephen Owen edt. Princeton: Princeton University Press, 1986.
2. Some Chinese audience members complained that Xiaomei's description of Jin's left arm does not match how Jin truly shoots arrows in the first fight against soldiers. When Xiaomei touches and feels Jin's left arm, she comments that Jin uses his left hand for archery. But when Jin attacks soldiers, he uses his right hand to shoot arrows.
3. Several Chinese audience members criticized the inconsistency of which part of

Xiaomei's chest Liu's dagger hits. It seems to hit the left side of Xiaomei's chest while Xiaomei is still on her horse, yet it looks to be on the right side of Xiaomei's chest when Jin runs back, finds Xiaomei on the grass, and holds her. At the end of the film, the injury that Liu's dagger causes seems to be on the left side of Xiaomei's chest when Xiaomei dies in Jin's arms.

4. Laura Mulvey, "The Myth of Pandora: A Psychoanalytical Approach." *Feminisms in the Cinema*. eds. Laura Pietropaolo and Ada Testaferri. (Bloomington: Indiana University Press, 1995), 3.

The Han Dynasty started in 206 B.C. and was terminated in 220 A.D..

6. Dongyuan Chen, *Zhongguo funü shenghuo shi (History of Chinese Women's Life)*. (Shanghai: Shanghai Bookstore, 1984), 118.

7. Wu Zetian was born in 624 A.D. and died in 705 A.D.. She named her dynasty "Da Zhou."

8. Although the aristocracy and wealthy men in the Tang Dynasty usually bought and sold female slaves, concubines, or prostitutes, Xiaomei is free from this kind of sexual discrimination because the House of Flying Daggers enables her to be a tough career woman with good kung fu and chivalrous backgrounds.

9. For details, consult the following publication:

Xi Zhu, *Zhuzi yülei (Categories of Zhuzi's Words)*. Beijing: Zhonghua, 1986.

10. For details, consult the following books:

Quan tang shu (The Whole Book of the Tang Dynasty). Beijing: Zhonghua, 1982.

Zhenguan zhengyao (Significant Policies During the Zhenguan Era). Chengdu: Sichuan renmin, 1987.

11. Feng Zhou, *Zhongguo gudai fuzhuang cankao ziliao (Reference for Clothes in Ancient China)*. (Beijing: Yanshan, 1988). Women in the Tang Dynasty loved red peonies. The sex workers, female musicians, singers, and dancers in the brothel in *House of Flying Daggers* may have some ornaments with pictures of red peonies. Some of them may name themselves after peonies or red flowers. The name of the brothel is exactly "*mu dan fang*," which means "the workshop of peonies." The floor of the brothel also has peonies as its decorations. For details, consult Chen Jingliang's and Zou Jianwen's *Bainian zhongguo dianying jingxuan (The Best of Centennial Chinese Cinema)*. (Beijing: Zhongguo shehui kexue, 2005), 608. Except for the prostitutes in the brothel, however, Xiaomei and other women in the House of Flying Daggers do not show their preference for red peonies.

12. The Zhou Dynasty began in 1066 B.C. and ended in 206 B.C. Confucius (around 551-479 B.C.) defined women's social status in the patriarchal society.

13. Ban Zhao was born in 42 A.D. and died in 120 A.D. She was Ban Zhao's younger sister. As a widow, she wrote this book for her daughter, but this book turned out to be one of the most famous books about the Confucian code of proper female conduct.

14. Consult Hwanhee Lee's journal article "House of Flying Daggers: A Reappraisal" in *Senses of Cinema*.

15. Li Yannian's poetic line is *jiaren nanzaide*. Hans H. Frankel's translation of this poetic line is "Beauty cannot be found again."

16. I would like to thank Megan Ferry and Daniel Hsieh for their reading responses and bibliographical information.

Chapter Four
Women Who Do Not Practice Martial Arts in *Seven Swords*

In martial arts films, the most impressive characters are usually people who use weapons, and the most attractive scenes are usually combat scenes; for instance, Chris Berry and Mary Ann Farquhar comment that the "main attraction [of *Crouching Tiger Hidden Dragon*, the first Chinese martial arts film to win an Oscar Award][1] . . . is the combat scenes."[2] I contend, however, that women without martial arts backgrounds should neither be neglected nor ignored in martial arts films. I aim to use *Seven Swords*[3] for an example, focus on the two women who do not practice martial arts, Liu Yüfang and Lüzhu, in the film, and propose that they contribute as much as all the knights and martial arts ladies in the film. Compared with all the people who practice martial arts, Liu Yüfang and Lüzhu seem weak, fragile, and unable to make significant achievements; however, Liu Yüfang risks her life to help Wu Yüanying and Han Zhibang rescue Fu Qingzhu and enables Fu Qingzhu to ask for the swordsmen's help in Tianshan. She is also the only adult to fight against the enemy agent, Qiu Dongluo, and save all the children in the village. Also important, Lüzhu tells Chu Zhaonan the secret about the military budget in order to help the seven swordsmen win their battle against Fenghuo Liancheng. She also deepens the fighting scenes in *Seven Swords* and extends them to not just physical exhibition of martial arts but also invisible contests of wit and secret service behind the enemy line.

In addition to watching the survival of the village, the film includes love stories of Liu Yüfang and Lüzhu. For instance, Lüzhu has two male admirers, Fenghuo Liancheng and Chu Zhaonan, and the woman fighter among Fenghuo Liancheng's twelve troopers also illustrates her obsession with Lüzhu. Liu Yüfang loves both Han Zhibang and Chu Zhaonan and decides to stick to Han Zhibang after she realizes that Chu Zhaonan and Lüzhu love each other. The love triangles and lesbianism enrich the film and support my argument that even people who do not practice martial arts are important in martial arts films. Women who do not do weapon practice in martial arts films are not simply decorative and trivial roles; they are as significant as all the other characters that practice martial arts in the film.

Two Contributions: Fights and Gender Issues

In *Seven Swords*, Liu Yüfang and Lüzhu make two important contributions: first, fights against Fenghuo Liancheng and his spy, Qiu Dongluo; second, gender issues. None of the characters who practice martial arts can make more important contributions to the fights against Fenghuo Liancheng's servile followers and the gender issues in this film than can Liu Yüfang and Lüzhu. Except for the children in the village, Liu Yüfang and Lüzhu are the only two characters who do not have any martial arts backgrounds and seem to be easily overpowered and the less significant people because of their femininity and lack of kung fu, yet theirs are the toughest and the most contributive roles within the entire story plot of the film.[4]

Liu Yüfang and Lüzhu in the Fights

Since the story about Huang Feihong (Wong Fei Hung; played by Kwan Tak Hing) hit theaters and became a jumpstart in Hong Kong cinema in 1949,[5] King Hu began the tradition for filmmakers to have martial arts directors. Combat scenes and marvelous kung fu are usually "the main spectacle-attraction"[6] of martial arts films in the late 1960s and early 1970s. Tsui Hark "secured a place . . . in the Hong Kong cinema and gained cult status in the West with films such as *Peking Opera Blues* and *Once upon a Time in China*."[7] *Crouching Tiger, Hidden Dragon* turned out to be "the highest-grossing Chinese-language film in the West"[8] in 2000. Fights are usually the most indispensable and enthralling elements in Chinese martial arts films. Hong Kong cinema is famous for its emphasis on "the concreteness and clarity of each [kung fu] gesture. Doubtless, traditions of martial arts . . . have been central to this aesthetic."[9] *Seven Swords* is no exception. The fantastic effects in fighting scenes need

> revitalized martial arts styles, costumes, realistic performances . . . film editing, bodily spectacles in which movement, costume, and stylized combat converge as dance and poetry. Editing [and high-tech visual effects add] surprises and speed, stretching cinematic time, space, and performance to the outer bounds of credibility . . . narrative heartbeat, bodily display, and the choreographed rhythm of stillness and motion.[10]

In *Seven Swords*, Fenghuo Liancheng aims to defeat the village, and the villagers try to defend themselves and fight against Fenghuo Liancheng. Although one of the most dramatic turning points for the villagers to save themselves and protect their own village in the fights undoubtedly is winning the seven swordsmen's help, the seven swordsmen will not travel from Tianshan to assist the villagers if Liu Yüfang does not enable Han Zhibang and Wu Yüanying to bring Fu Qingzhu to Tianshan. There will not be any villagers for the seven swordsmen to rescue if Liu Yüfang does not fight against the traitor in the village and Fenghuo Liancheng's spy, Qiu Dongluo.

That is to say, Liu Yüfang makes almost everything possible; Liu Yüfang herself is an important turning point in this film, too. Without her self-sacrifice, Han Zhibang and Wu Yüanying would not be able to bring the severely injured village head, Fu Qingzhu, to Tianshan. If Han Zhibang and Wu Yüanying could not bring Fu Qingzhu to Tianshan, Master Huiming could not cure Fu Qingzhu, and he could not assign his four disciples, Chu Zhaonan, Yang Yüncong, Xin Longzi, and Mu Lang, to rescue the village and give them the seven swords:

1. *Mowen* Sword (Sword of No Questions): This sword symbolizes wisdom, and Fu Qingzhu, the leader of the seven swordsmen, is the owner of it.
2. *Youlong* Sword (Sword of Swimming Dragon): This sword represents attack and Chu Zhaonan, Master Huiming's first disciple, is the user of it.
3. *Qinggan* Sword (Sword of Green and Interference): This sword indicates defense. It serves as the *youlong* sword's counterpart. Yang Yüncong possesses this sword. The *youlong* sword and *qinggan* sword are two of the most significant swords among all the seven swords.
4. *Shesheng* Sword (Sword of Spirit): Han Zhibang uses this sword.
5. *Tianpu* Sword (Sword of Heavenly Waterfall): This is Wu Yüanying's sword.
6. *Riyue* Sword (Sword of the Sun and Moon): Mulang is the user. He secretly loves Wu Yüanying.
7. *Jingxing* Sword (Sword of Competitive Stars): Xin Longzi is the possessor of this sword.

Without Liu Yüfang's contributions, none of the seven swords and knights would play a role in the survival of the villagers and village. Weapons and experts with kung fu would not be useful or helpful without this lady who lacks a martial arts background and does not practice martial arts. In this film, Liu Yüfang overthrows the frequent misconceptions that the most eye-catching and important components of martial arts films are martial arts, fights, and powerful weapons and that the most impressive and influential characters in martial arts films are people who do weapon practice. Trinh Minh-ha once remarked that there is a margin in the center and a center in the margin;[11] Liu Yüfang, a woman who does not know martial arts, thus seems marginalized in such a martial arts film but is the most important key point to bringing the most influential seven swords into the center of the storyline.

In addition to Liu Yüfang, Lüzhu is another example of a woman who is important despite not doing weapon practice. She also dispels the popular belief that martial arts, unequaled weapons, fights, and knights should be the only focus of martial arts films and that people who do not practice any kung fu should be marginalized, not deserving of equal attention from the audience. Lüzhu knows the secret about where Fenghuo Liancheng hides his military budget, and she discloses it to Chu Zhaonan to help Chu Zhaonan defeat Fenghuo Liancheng and rescue the villagers. In this sense, she volunteers to function as Chu Zhaonan's sleuth or information division and offer secret information to assist the village in Chu Zhaonan's fight against Fenghuo Liancheng. When Fenghuo Liancheng brandishes his weapon and almost kills Chu Zhaonan, Lüzhu grasps his hands and swords to stop him from killing Chu Zhaonan. At that moment, she saves Chu Zhaonan's life.

By providing secret information to Chu Zhaonan, serving as his intelligence agent, and saving his life, Lüzhu hence repeatedly reminds Fenghuo Liancheng of his partner, Duan Yüzhu, who collected intelligence data for Fenghuo Liancheng before her death. Although Fenghuo Liancheng is motivated to transfer his love for Duan Yüzhu to his desire for and possession of Lüzhu because of the women's similarities (both women are Korean, love their partners, disclose enemies' top secrets to their partners, and die in front of their partners), Duan Yüzhu and Lüzhu are entirely opposite in many ways. For instance, Duan Yüzhu has professional training in scouting out intelligence information, and thus, being an intelligencer is her job, but Lüzhu has neither a martial arts background nor formal training in working behind enemy lines and her job is to be a military prostitute or comfort woman, not a professional detective or secret agent. In other words, Lüzhu is a counterpart to Duan Yüzhu.

Furthermore, Lüzhu is also a counterpart to Qiu Dongluo, who disguises as one of the innocent villagers and acts as Fenghuo Liancheng's stool pigeon in the village. Qiu Dongluo shares similar—or even the same—biological heritage, living experiences and linguistic and sociocultural backgrounds with all the villagers, while Lüzhu, as an alien from Korea, does not have any Chinese biological heritage, language ability, or lifestyle. Qiu Dongluo does not cause all the villagers' distrust until he shows that he is a traitor in the village; however, some of the villagers suspect that Lüzhu poisoned Liu Yüfang, and even Chu Zhaonan does not believe Lüzhu until he finishes double checking if she understands Chinese language and if she is a secret spy working for Fenghuo Liancheng like Duan Yüzhu. Qiu Dongluo is not treated as a suspect but does not truly deserve all the villagers' spiritual brotherhood and reliance, yet Lüzhu is mistaken as an espionage agent but undoubtedly deserves Chu Zhaonan's and all the villagers' trust. In Qiu Dongluo's plan, he wants all the villagers to lose their lives, but Lüzhu loses her life because she tries to save Chu Zhaonan's life.

In terms of the fights in *Seven Swords*, Lüzhu functions as a counterpart to Fenghuo Liancheng's two spies, Duan Yüzhu and Qiu Dongluo, and serves as a perfect measure of trust and distrust among Chu Zhaonan, Fenghuo Liancheng, and the villagers. Lüzhu is a skillful and successful foil to Duan Yüzhu and Qiu Dongluo. She sets off the contest of wits between Fenghuo Liancheng and the seven knights, especially Chu Zhaonan, by contrast. Without Lüzhu, Qiu Dongluo's secret scheme to betray all his fellow villagers would not be understood. Without Lüzhu, Fenghuo Liancheng's memory of and affection for his former emissary would not be revived and doubled. That is to say, thanks to

Lüzhu, the fights in *Seven Swords* include not only the frequently seen physical fights but also spiritual fights or severe contests of wit regarding trust, distrust, belief, and disbelief. Lüzhu deepens the originally shallow meaning of fights and extends the meaning from mere physical displays of good kung fu to collaborative strategizations and secret service behind physical fights and the enemy line. Without Lüzhu and her contributions, the fights, which are usually deemed one of the most significant and indispensable parts of martial arts films, would not be as spiritually deepened and cinematically elaborated as they are in *Seven Swords*.

Love Stories to Clinch the Point

In addition to the fighting scenes and the survival of the village, the love stories of Liu Yüfang and Lüzhu also contribute significantly to *Seven Swords*. Romantic love and sexuality are "posited as an untouched force of energy"[12] in the film:

> Romantic love [is] always already romanesque. Its power, sweeping lovers to their deaths, [is] the power of a literary language that gradually refine[s] itself and that [finds] its full aesthetic form in romantic texts ... Romantic love draws its vitality from the unnegatable separation between real life and verbal hallucination, [and] between real relationships and emotional rapture.[13]

Although critics may regard the scenes of women's faces, bodies, and sexual gratification as cinematic reinforcement of the patriarchal interests for which women are merely sex objects, excessive sexist exchanges motivated by male desire, or polarization of the male gaze,[14] this chapter aims to undo the phallocracy and turn Lüzhu and Liu Yüfang into central and significant starting points of love stories and love triangles, which *Seven Swords* cannot go without to maintain its luster and attraction. For instance, Lüzhu has two male admirers, Fenghuo Liancheng and Chu Zhaonan, and the female fighter among Fenghuo Liancheng's twelve troopers, who also shows her obsession with Lüzhu. Liu Yüfang loves both Han Zhibang and Chu Zhaonan and decides to stick to Han Zhibang after she realizes that Chu Zhaonan and Lüzhu love each other. Compared with Wu Yüanying's clear-cut attitude toward her ex-boyfriend, Han Zhibang, and decisive initiation of her romantic relationship with Yang Yüncong, Liu Yüfang's and Lüzhu's love stories include more tension and intensify conflicts that correspond to the fights. Although the importance of romantic love and women who do not do weapon practice are usually minimized to be trivial decoration in martial arts films, Liu Yüfang's and Lüzhu's love stories successfully contribute to the little-recognized importance of romantic love to martial arts films, highlight the emotional clashes hidden inside of the acrobatic combats, expand the fights to spiritual power struggles and complicated frictions, and therefore enliven endless battlefields and enrich the emptiness of repetitive physical confrontations. They add a word for women without good kung fu to clinch the point. If the film *Seven Swords* is compared to a painted dragon, then Liu Yüfang's and Lüzhu's love stories are like the pupils of the dragon's eyes.

Lüzhu's Romantic Love

Without Lüzhu's romantic love, the emotional fracas and invisible hostility between Chu Zhaonan and Fenghuo Liancheng would not be embodied, represented, and cinematized well. Without Lüzhu's romantic love, what is between Chu Zhaonan and Fenghuo Liancheng will become nothing but meager physical fights and scanty competitions of kung fu without any amplitude in extent or compass. Without Lüzhu, Fenghuo Liancheng's strong love for Duan Yüzhu and emotional scars resulting from Duan Yüzhu's death would not be well depicted. Without this in-depth cinematic portrait of Fenghuo Liancheng's true love for Duan Yüzhu and abysmal remorse for her death, Fenghuo Liancheng would be only a plain and boring "flat character" who is a bad guy and a beast-like war monster from the beginning to the end of the film rather than an enriched and multi-faceted "round character."

What Duan Yüzhu means to Fenghuo Liancheng is mirrored in Lüzhu's impacts on Chu Zhaonan. While Fenghuo Liancheng confesses his love for Duan Yüzhu and laments for her death, Chu Zhaonan has equal love for Lüzhu and contrition for her death. While Fenghuo Liancheng feels hurt by the sad truth of Duan Yüzhu's death, Chu Zhaonan is also emotionally injured by the cruel fact that Lüzhu dies. Lüzhu's romantic love clearly reflects that Chu Zhaonan and Fenghuo Liancheng share the death of beloved women, loss of romantic love, profound regret, and psychological trauma. Fenghuo Liancheng's final words before his death illustrate this: "You and I are the same kind of persons." Without Lüzhu and her romantic love, Chu Zhaonan and Fenghuo Liancheng will not be so parallel in this film.

Lüzhu also turns Chu Zhaonan into an interesting round character by underscoring that suspicion or misgiving is Chu Zhaonan's "harmartia,"[15] which refers to the tragic flaw or character weakness that ultimately brings about unavoidable downfall in a life story. When Chu Zhaonan uses Mandarin Chinese to tell Lüzhu that he believes her, Lüzhu immediately unveils the irony of Chu Zhaonan's so-called belief and frankly reveals the fact that Chu Zhaonan distrusts her and hence tests whether she, like Duan Yüzhu, understands Mandarin Chinese. Chu Zhaonan's lack of trust kills Lüzhu's romantic love for him and deeply harrows her; in return, Lüzhu's unexpected death, like a punishment leaves a psychological wound and bottomless grief for Chu Zhaonan. Without Lüzhu and her romantic love, Chu Zhaonan would not be an attention-grabbing round character worthy of the audience's note. Instead, he would be only a good but tedious guy without any character flaw from the beginning to the end of the whole film—in other words, a dull flat character.

Liu Yüfang's Romantic Love

If the love triangle formed by Chu Zhaonan, Fenghuo Liancheng, and Lüzhu is the first love triangle in *Seven Swords*, Liu Yüfang is involved in the second and third love triangles: the second one formed by Chu Zhaonan, Liu Yüfang, and Han Zhibang, and the third formed by Lüzhu, Liu Yüfang, and Chu Zhaonan. Liu Yüfang is originally in love with Han Zhibang, Wu Yüanying's ex-boyfriend; however, Chu Zhaonan enchants her. Because of Chu Zhaonan, Liu Yüfang feels uncertain about her love for Han Zhibang. She and Lüzhu also discover that both of them have fallen in love with Chu Zhaonan.

Within these two love triangles, one of Liu Yüfang's largest contributions is to set off different attitudes toward rivals in love by contrast. Han Zhibang's attitude toward his rival in love is to kill him if he knows who this person is. It is exactly the same hostility as that between Chu Zhaonan and Fenghuo Liancheng. Under this circumstance, it may not be illogical to induce that the attitude of men in this film, or at least these three men, toward rivals in love is enmity. In contrast, Liu Yüfang's attitude toward her rival in love is entirely different from these men's attitudes toward their rivals. From the beginning to the end, Liu Yüfang tries her best to bridge the linguistic obstacle, observe, communicate, and understand her rival in love, Lüzhu. For example, on the riverside, Liu Yüfang pays special attention to how Lüzhu cherishes and washes Chu Zhaonan's scarf, and makes efforts to see whether Lüzhu is in love with Chu Zhaonan. When Lüzhu misunderstands her and thinks that she would like to take the scarf away, Liu Yüfang immediately clarifies and explains that she is just using the scarf as a tool to help her express herself and move across the Sino-Korean linguistic boundary. Later on, when Lüzhu returns from Fenghuo Liancheng's military base, Liu Yüfang carefully checks her physical injuries, listens to her, and demonstrates her eagerness to understand her. She is even the final person who asks her questions, speaks with her, and tries to decode her Korean before her death. That is to say, Liu Yüfang seems to have a special kind of spiritual sympathy or sisterhood with Lüzhu after she discovers that they share the same romantic love for the same man.

This sort of emotional compassion or spiritual sisterhood is what men, such as Fenghuo Liancheng, Chu Zhaonan, and Han Zhibang, do not share with one another. It problematizes the oversimplified antagonism that these three men have in common for their rivals in love. The men's rage and strong yearning to kill their rivals in love mainly result from their loss of possession of their beloved women. This type of wish to kill rivals in love is similar to their death penalty for robbers or thieves after properties or belongings are stolen or robbed. It is similar to men's ownership of their properties or legal right to the possession of their belongings, so that they seem to unconsciously turn their beloved women into something like their properties or belongings. In other words, they seem to unconsciously objectify their girlfriends. If Lüzhu and Liu Yüfang were truly objects without their own critical thoughts, the right to explore what or whom they love more, and the freedom to make decisions, it would have been acceptable for their owners to punish chiselers or burglars to force them to return the stolen goods. In the Qing Dynasty, when the death penalty was not prohibited, it is understandable that some plunderers were really put to death, though owners were usually neither the judges nor the executors of the criminals' death penalties. But Lüzhu and Liu Yüfang are not objects. They are human beings who deserve as much right and freedom as these three men. They should be given the same opportunities to make decisions about their own lives, and their choices or uncertainties also deserve as much understanding as these three men's. If Han Zhibang could have avoided objectifying Liu Yüfang, respected her as a person who deserves understanding and respect, been understanding about her uncertainty and chagrin about her choice between him and his rival in love, and, furthermore, appreciated her honesty to confess this truth to him, he might not have been so angry and experienced such spleen.

On the contrary, Liu Yüfang is not as vexed by her rival in love as Han Zhibang is. She respects both Chu Zhaonan and Lüzhu, and she also understands Han Zhibang's fury. Why can she respect Chu Zhaonan's decision to love Lüzhu and Lüzhu's determination to love Chu Zhaonan? It is because she respects them as human beings who should be given freedom and the right to decide whom they love and what kind of destiny they will have. She allows them as much freedom and right as herself. Why does she not hate Chu Zhaonan for not loving her? Because she does not regard Chu Zhaonan as her property or an object that she possesses. Liu Yüfang clearly knows that Chu Zhaonan is not something that she owns. She does not objectify Chu Zhaonan at all. She fully understands that Chu Zhaonan should have the freedom and right to decide whom he loves and whom he does not love. Hence, she is not as irritated by her rival in love as Han Zhibang is. Why does she not attempt to kill Lüzhu after she realizes the romantic relation between Lüzhu and Chu Zhaonan? Because she never regards Lüzhu as someone who robs Chu Zhaonan from her. Liu Yüfang has no reason to put her to death because she does not deem Lüzhu a thief and thus her attitude toward her rival in love is different from Han Zhibang's.

Moreover, Liu Yüfang's spiritual sisterhood for her rival in love serves as a foil to Han Zhibang's possession and irritation. Without Liu Yüfang and her connection with Lüzhu, all the romantic triangles would have been full of oversimplified aversion and would not have been deepened and enriched enough to deserve the audience's further thoughts.

Liu Yüfang's and Lüzhu's Multiple Choices in Love Triangles

In love triangles, both Liu Yüfang and Lüzhu are given plenty of time and opportunity to meet with different kinds of men, get to know them, interact with them, and rethink and compare them before they decide their lives and fate. They are given many choices of men.

In Liu Yüfang's case, she likes both Han Zhibang and Chu Zhaonan, and she is given the freedom and right to make her own choice between these two men. In Lüzhu's case, she has physical contacts with Fenghuo Liancheng and Chu Zhaonan. They both love her. She is given at least these two men as her choices.

In contemporary China, it is nothing new for women to have different men to choose from. However, in ancient China, women under severe parental or Confucian sociocultural control and the system of arranged marriage could seldom enjoy the freedom and right to interact with different men and select their favorite ones from many candidates. Because of "the 2000 years of largely unchallenged Confucian family structure,"[16]

> Chinese women were embedded in perhaps the oldest, most highly developed, male-dominated kinship system in history.[17]

In ancient Chinese gender ideology, it was even forbidden for women to have premarital sexual relationships with men, not to mention that Lüzhu has physical intimacy with both of the men who love her. Liu Yüfang's and Lüzhu's choices in love show that the imaginary world of martial arts in film compensates ancient Chinese women by giving them the freedom and right to rethink their romantic love, decide their own lives, and dominate their fate. Without Liu Yüfang, Lüzhu, and their love triangles, ancient Chinese women in *Seven Swords* would not have been recompensed for their lack of rights.

Same-Sex Love out of the Cinematic Closet

In addition to heterosexuality, *Seven Swords* to some extent includes same-sex love. The woman fighter among Fenghuo Liancheng's twelve troopers clearly shows her obsession with Lüzhu. Although from the beginning to the end of *Seven Swords* this woman fighter's name is not apparently revealed to the audience, she and Lüzhu collaboratively add the most diversified gender orientation and gender concerns to the story plot. For example, she calmly watches the physical intimacy between Lüzhu and Fenghuo Liancheng and later asks Lüzhu for exactly the same physical contact. In other words, she brings gender concerns regarding heterosexuality, lesbianism, and bisexuality to *Seven Swords*, though Lüzhu immediately rejects her request for their same-sex love and denies the possible bisexual relationship with both Fenghuo Liancheng and her. Without Lüzhu and this woman fighter, *Seven Swords* would have been a film with only heterosexual romantic love,[18] would not have included diverse sexual orientation and gender issues, and would not have been one of the rarely seen Chinese martial arts films that extend romantic love and love triangles beyond heterosexuality. Without Lüzhu and this woman fighter, *Seven Swords* would not be one of the few Chinese martial arts films in which same-sex love and lesbian desire come out of the cinematic closet. The only pity is that the film does not provide viewers more details about this same-sex love.

Conclusion

Chinese martial arts films usually focus on kung fu, gallantry, overpowering weapons, and amazing skills in physical fighting scenes, and *Seven Swords* is no exception. It includes excellent showcases of good martial arts, enthralling master-strokes, physical strength, seven wonderful swords, and chivalry. This is perhaps why the village is named Wu Zhuang, which refers to "the village of martial arts." In addition, from the beginning to the end of the film, the fight among the village, the government, and Fenghuo Liancheng is the same fight for the legitimacy of martial arts or kung fu. However, I contend that the women who do not practice martial arts are actually as significant and contributive to the whole film as are kung fu, swordsmanship, weapons, and acrobatic combats. For instance, the village is called the village of martial arts, and it is full of experts of kung fu and unequaled swords; however, ironically it is Liu Yüfang, a woman who does not have any background in martial arts, who kills the traitor, protects all the children, and rescues the future generations of the village. The other woman who also has no training in martial arts, Lüzhu, points out the significance of strategization and the secret agent hidden in all the fighting scenes. Moreover, the love triangles of these two women underscore the spiritual battles that deeply influence the acrobatic combats, broaden the fights, and add invisible power struggles and multilayered conflicts behind heterosexuality, and therefore dampen the aridity of combat zones and enrich the emptiness of repetitive physical clashes. Liu Yüfang and Lüzhu are so much more than simply romantic and nice-looking decorations attached to the martial arts world in *Seven Swords*. Without these two women who do not practice martial arts, the film would have already lost its radiance and attraction.

References

Berry, Chris and Mary Farquhar. *China on Screen: Cinema and Nation*. New York: Columbia University Press, 2006, pp. 54, 70.

Berry, Michael. "Introduction: Speaking in Images." *Speaking in Images: Interviews with Contemporary Chinese Filmmakers*. New York: Columbia University Press, 2005, pp. 10-18.
Bordwell, David. "Aesthetics in Action: Kungfu, Gunplay, and Cinematic Expressivity." *At Full Speed: Hong Kong Cinema in a Borderless World*. Esther C. M. Yau edt. Minneapolis: University of Minnesota Press, 2001, pp. 78-79.
Browne, Nick, Paul G. Pickowicz, Vivian Sobchack, and Esther Yau. *New Chinese Cinemas: Forms, Identities, Politics*. Cambridge: Cambridge University Press, 1994.
Chow, Rey. *Primitive Passions: Visuality, Sexuality, Ethnography, and Contemporary Chinese Cinema*. New York: Columbia University Press, 1995, pp. 151-152.
Cornelius, Sheila. *New Chinese Cinema: Challenging Representations*. London Wallflower: 2004, p. 71.
Fu, Poshek. *Between Shanghai and Hong Kong: The Politics of Chinese Cinemas.* Stanford: Stanford University Press, 2003, p. 91.
Johnson, Kay A. *Women, the Family and Peasant Revolution in China*. Chicago: University of Chicago Press, 1983, p. 24.
Li, Shaohong. "Wo de nüxing juewu" (My Feminist Awakening). *Jiushi niandai de "di wu dai"* (*The 5th Generation of Chinese filmmakers in the 1990s*). Yang Yüanying, Pan Hua, Zhang Zhuan, and Shen Yun edt. Beijing: Beijing Broadcast Academy Press, 2000, p. 54.
Lo, Kwai-cheung. *Chinese Face/Off: The Transnational Popular Culture of Hong Kong*. Urbana: University of Illinois Press, 2005, pp. 21, 247.
Teo, Stephen. "Tsui Hark: National Style and Polemic." *At Full Speed: Hong Kong Cinema in a Borderless World*. Esther C. M. Yau edt. Minneapolis: University of Minnesota Press, 2001, p. 143.
Thornham, Sue. "Women and Film: A Discussion of Feminist Aesthetics." *Feminist Film Theory: A Reader*. New York: New York University Press, 1999, p. 117.
Treut, Monika. "Female Misbehavior." *Feminisms in the Cinema*. Laura Pietropaolo and Ada Testaferri edt. Bloomington: Indiana University Press, 1995, p. 115.
Trinh, Minh-ha. "Who Is Speaking: Of Nation, Community, and First Person Interview." *Feminisms in the Cinema*. Laura Pietropado and Ada Testaferri edt. Bloomington: Indiana University Press, 1995.
Yang, Jeff. *Once Upon a Time in China: A Guide to Hong Kong, Taiwanese, and Mainland Chinese Cinema*. New York: Atria, 2003, p. 41.
Zhang, Yingjin. "The Transnational Imaginary, 1990-2002." *Chinese National Cinema*. New York: Routledge, 2004, p. 296.

Notes

1. Lo Kwai-cheung has made a short list of some significant awards that Ang Lee's *Crouching Tiger Hidden Dragon* won. Consult Lo's *Chinese Face/Off: The Transnational Popular Culture of Hong Kong*. (Urbana: University of Illinois Press, 2005), 247.

2. Chris Berry and Mary Farquhar, *China on Screen: Cinema and Nation*. (New York: Columbia University Press, 2006), 70.

3. The story plot of *Seven Swords* derives in part from Liang Yüsheng's fiction entitled *Seven Swords*. I base my textual analysis on Tsui Hark's film, *Seven Swords*, instead of Liang Yüsheng's martial arts novel of the same name.

4. Li Shaohong, a female Chinese filmmaker, has once questioned: "If one day women truly step from the margin to the center, what kind of miracle will happen? Will it be a brand new century or a matriarchal society?" For details, consult Li Shaohong's "Wo de nüxing juewu" (My Feminist Awakening) in *Jiushi niandai de "di wu dai"* (*The 5th Generation of Chinese filmmakers in the 1990s*). (Beijing: Beijing Broadcast Academy Press, 2000), 54.

In this chapter, I would like the most marginalized women, namely, women who do not practice martial arts in martial arts films, to move from the margin to the center of the discursive course. I do not think that the imaginary world of martial arts will become a matriarchal society, but I do think of the "new millennium" that Zhang Yingjin mentions at the end of his book, *Chinese National Cinema*. For details, consult Zhang Yingjin's "The Transnational Imaginary, 1990-2002." *Chinese National Cinema*. (New York: Routledge, 2004), 296.

I hope that the "new millennium" that belongs to the so-called marginalized, unimportant, and decorative women in martial arts films can come and change male-centered, patriarchal, or fundamentalist viewers' gazes and viewpoints.

5. Jeff Yang, *Once upon a Time in China: A Guide to Hong Kong, Taiwanese, and Mainland Chinese Cinema*. (New York: Atria, 2003), 41.

6. Chris Berry and Mary Farquhar, *China on Screen: Cinema and Nation*. (New York: Columbia University Press, 2006), 54.

7. Stephen Teo, "Tsui Hark: National Style and Polemic" in *At Full Speed: Hong Kong Cinema in a Borderless World*, ed Esther C. M. Yau. (Minneapolis: University of Minnesota Press, 2001), 143. In *Senses of Cinema*, Tsui Hark is compared to Steven Spielberg and named "The Steven Spielberg of Asia." For more information about the status of Tsui Hark in Hong Kong film industry, also consult the following publications:

Nick Browne, Paul G. Pickowicz, Vivian Sobchack, and Esther Yau, eds. *New Chinese Cinemas: Forms, Identities, Politics*. (Cambridge: Cambridge University Press, 1994).

Grandy Hendrix, "Tsui Hark." *Senses of Cinema* (June 2003): http://goo.gl/NjocR.

Michael Berry, "Introduction: Speaking in Images." *Speaking in Images: Interviews with Contemporary Chinese Filmmakers*. (New York: Columbia University Press, 2005), 10-18.

8. Kwai-cheung Lo, *Chinese Face/Off: The Transnational Popular Culture of Hong Kong*. (Urbana: University of Illinois Press, 2005), 21.

9. David Bordwell, "Aesthetics in Action: Kungfu, Gunplay, and Cinematic Expressivity" in *At Full Speed: Hong Kong Cinema in a Borderless World*, eds. Esther C. M. Yau. (Minneapolis: University of Minnesota Press, 2001), 78-79.

10. See footnote 7.

11. Minh-ha Trinh, "Who Is Speaking: Of Nation, Community, and First Person Interview" in *Feminisms in the Cinema*, eds. Laura Pietropado and Ada Testaferri. (Bloomington: Indiana University Press, 1995). Also consult Poshek Fu's *Between Shanghai and Hong Kong: The Politics of Chinese Cinemas*. (Stanford: Stanford University Press, 2003), 91.

12. Sue Thornham, "Women and Film: A Discussion of Feminist Aesthetics." *Feminist Film Theory: A Reader*. (New York: New York University Press, 1999), 117.

13. Monika Treut, "Female Misbehavior." *Feminisms in the Cinema*, eds. Laura Pietropaolo and Ada Testaferri. (Bloomington: Indiana University Press, 1995), 115.

14 . Rey Chow, *Primitive Passions: Visuality, Sexuality, Ethnography, and Contemporary Chinese Cinema*. (New York: Columbia University Press, 1995), 151-152.
15. This term derives from the Greek word, *hamartanein*. The literal meaning of the Greek word is "to miss the mark."
16. Sheila Cornelius, *New Chinese Cinema: Challenging Representations*. (London Wallflower: 2004), 71.
17. Kay A. Johnson, *Women, the Family and Peasant Revolution in China*. (Chicago: University of Chicago Press, 1983), 24.
18. It is a pity that there are not more details about this woman and her lesbian desire in the film. I cannot deepen my textual analysis because of this limitation.

Chapter Five
Cinderella, Sleeping Beauty, and Snow White in *The Promise*

In *The Promise*, Chen Kaige digests, combines, sinicizes,[1] enriches, problematizes, and rewrites love stories of Cinderella, Snow White, and Sleeping Beauty.[2] Goddess Manshen (played by Chen Hong) turns Qingcheng (played by Cecilia Po-chi Cheung) into a beauty. This is the Cinderella motif. When Qingcheng is doomed to find no true love in men, Kunlun (played by Jang Don-gun) plays her "Prince Charming" who travels faster than the speed of light to rescue her. This includes the motifs of Snow White and Sleeping Beauty. In addition, Chen Kaige problematizes the archetypal patterns of Cinderella, Snow White, and Sleeping Beauty by adding to it the complex love "triangle" that Qingcheng, Kunlun, Duke Wuhuan (played by Nicolas Ting-Fung Tse), and General Guangming (played by Sanada Hiroyuki) form.

Qingcheng is the Chinese version of Cinderella, Sleeping Beauty, and Snow White whose beauty conquers the city in Chen Kaige's cinematic creation. Her name also reminds Chinese viewers of Lady Li's appearance and her love story with Emperor Wu in Li Yannian's poem. While the stories of Sleeping Beauty, Cinderella, and Lady Li in Li Yannian's poem do not appear to give women enough opportunities to interact with more men, or to compare them, rethink their romantic love, and select one of them as their "Prince Charming," I argue that the stories of Snow White and *The Promise* seem to give women more freedom to interact with different men, to compare and contrast them, and to choose their "Prince Charming." In terms of comparing and contrasting different men, I contend that in the story of Snow White, the seven dwarfs are not merely physically shorter than Prince Charming but also "defeated" and thus "dwarfed" by him in the competition for Snow White, while Wuhuan and Guangming are not simply physically "killed" or "dead" but also "defeated" by Kunlun and thus "die" in their competition with Kunlun for Qingcheng. Kunlun "wins" and therefore is "alive" at the end of the competition for Qingcheng with Wuhuan and Guangming. At the end of the film, Kunlun, as Guangming's slave, is the only winner, but Duke Wuhuan and General Guangming are both losers in the competition for Qingcheng. I regard this as Chen Kaige's cinematic problematization and "proletarian revolution" of the archetype that the stories of Cinderella, Sleeping Beauty, Snow White, and Lady Li share: the archetype that aristocrats or men with higher social status always win the women they want.

Qingcheng: The Chinese Cinderella Who Conquers the City

In *The Promise*, Qingcheng is Chen Kaige's Chinese version of Cinderella: a poor girl turned into a pretty woman.[3] Qingcheng is originally a poor and starved girl in the battlefield. She fights with Wuhuan for a bun. When she helplessly weeps over her hunger, Goddess Manshen tells her that she can turn Qingcheng into a beauty. Qingcheng happily agrees and becomes an attractive lady. This moment vividly reminds viewers of the plot of Cinderella when Cinderella's godmother "touches [Cinderella] with her wand, and, at the same instant, [Cinderella's] clothes turn into cloth of gold and silver, all beset with jewels. This done, she gives [Cinderella] a pair of glass slippers, the prettiest in the whole world."[4]

Qingcheng is a Chinese version of Cinderella.[5] Her name, Qingcheng, denotes how glamorous and alluring she is. Literally speaking, *qingcheng* means "to defeat the city"; metaphorically speaking, in this context, it refers to a pretty woman whose beauty conquers the whole city.

The name Qingchen derives from a famous *yüefu* poem by Li Yannian in the Han Dynasty (206 B.C.-220 A.D.) as well as a well-known love story of the Emperor Wu and Lady Li. Li Yannian, as the Emperor Wu's royal musician, wrote a poem about his beautiful sister and matched the poem with music.

> *Beifang you jiaren*
> *Jueshi er duli*
> *Yigu qing ren cheng*
> *Zaigu qing ren guo*
> *Ning bu zhi qingcheng yu qingguo*
> *Jiaren nan zai de*

According to Hans H. Frankel's English translation, this poem describes how Li Yannian's sister is so attractive that one would prefer the beauty of Li Yannian's sister to a city or country of men.

> In the North there is a beautiful woman,
> Unique, Unequal in the world.
> With one glance she conquers a city of men,
> With another glance a country of men.
> Don't you know? A city and a country conquering
> Beauty cannot be found again.[6]

Because of this poem, the Emperor Wu of the Han Dynasty fell in love with Li Yannian's sister and turned her into a royal concubine. Q*ingcheng qingguo*, the phrase in the poem that describes how beautiful Lady Li is, gradually became a popular phrase in Chinese-speaking areas to emphasize how attractive a woman can be in Chinese-speaking areas.

Qingcheng, the name of the female protagonist in *The Promise*, is exactly the *qingcheng* of the phrase *qingcheng qingguo*. It is a name to immediately remind the Chinese-speaking audience that Qingcheng in *The Promise* is as alluring and enticing to men as Li Yannian's sister was. In addition, the name Qingcheng indirectly equates Goddess Manshen's sorcery with the magic power of Cinderella's godmother. It relates Goddess Manshen with Cinderella's godmother because Goddess Manshen in *The Promise* turns the poor, starved, and dirty girl in the battlefield into such a pretty woman whose beauty defeats a city or country of men and Cinderella's godmother transforms Cinderella from a poor and mistreated girl in her stepmother's house to an extraordinarily enchanting and adorable princess wearing glass slippers who dances with her "Prince Charming" in a luxurious ballroom of the royal palace.

> [Cinderella's] godmother only just touched her with her wand, and, at the same instant, her clothes were turned into cloth of gold and silver, all beset with jewels. This done, she gave her a pair of glass slippers, the prettiest in the whole world.[7]

The name Qingcheng in *The Promise* also relates Goddess Manshen's promise about Qingcheng's future appearance to Li Yannian's promise as well as the promise of Cinderella's godmother's promise. Cinderella's godmother enables Cinderella to meet her Mr. Right in the royal party and become the hostess of the royal palace. Similarly, Goddess Manshen's promise enables Qingcheng to be the king's beloved woman in the royal palace, and Li Yannian's promise about his sister's beauty enables his sister to enter and live in the royal palace. Qingcheng in *The Promise* is therefore truly a Chinese version of Cinderella from this point of view. Chen Kaige chooses a "style that looks international but has deep Chinese roots,"[8] "Westernized allegories,"[9] and "the spread of popular culture."[10] In *The Promise*, he negotiates the past of both China and the West.[11] As a Chinese filmmaker, he mediates stories "between the repressive and ideal order of the myth that is familiar to all Chinese and the problematic 'real' world onscreen so as to criticize, modernize, and revitalize the myth ... through some sort of narrative resolution."[12]

Cinderella and Sleeping Beauty

Qingcheng and Cinderella have another thing in common: the warning of the negative outcomes and limits of sorcery. Cinderella's godmother warns her that all the sorcery will be invalid and that she will no longer be a pretty princess after midnight. Cinderella panics and leaves the ballroom around midnight; therefore, her glass slippers left behind are the only clue for the prince to find her:

> [Cinderella's] godmother . . . commanded her not to stay till after midnight, telling her, at the same time, that if she stayed one moment longer, the coach would be a pumpkin again, her horses mice, her coachman a rat, her footmen lizards, and her clothes become just as they were before. She promised her godmother she would not fail to leave the ball before midnight.[13]

In *The Promise*, Goddess Manshen also warns Qingcheng that she will not find true love unless time goes backward. Hence, Qingcheng does not dare to believe in true love even after the man in the crimson armor advises her to continue her life, discourages her from suicide, and jumps off the cliff for her. She also panics after Guangming claims his love for her and asks for her love, and Kunlun keeps the gate of the castle open for her.

This kind of warning about the negative outcomes or limitations of sorcery also reminds the audience of the story of Sleeping Beauty[14]:

> At the christening of a long-wished-for princess, a wicked fairy places the princess under an enchantment as her gift, saying that, on reaching adulthood, she would prick her finger on spindle and die. A good Fairy alters the effect of the curse so that the princess, instead of dying, will fall asleep for one hundred years, until awakened by the kiss of a prince.[15]

Sleeping Beauty pricks her finger on a spindle. She falls asleep for a long time, and does not wake up until the prince, who truly loves her, kisses her.

None of the heroines—Cinderella, Sleeping Beauty, or Qingcheng—escape from the prophecy about the negative outcomes or limitations of sorcery. Sleeping Beauty's father tries his best to protect her, but she still only narrowly escapes from her fate. She still needs the prince to rescue her from the enchantment:

> The prince approached her trembling, and fell on his knees before her. The enchantment was over; the princess woke . . . . "Is it you, my prince?" she said. "You have kept me waiting for a long time."[16]

Cinderella also only narrowly escapes from her godmother's sorcery. She returns to her original status and resumes the endless housework in her stepmother's house. Her destiny is not changed until the prince finds her. In *The Promise*, Qingcheng does not escape from Goddess Manshen's prophecy about her fate, either. Although Guangming claims his love for Qingcheng and Wuhuan is also cordially concerned about Qingcheng since his childhood, Guangming and Wuhuan kill each other in front of Qingcheng. They also severely injure Kunlun. At the end of the film, Qingcheng cannot help but depend on Kunlun, who puts on the dark cloak to run faster than the light and let time move backward; otherwise, Qingcheng has no opportunity to escape her destiny. This is probably why the Chinese title of this film is *Wu ji*.

"Wu ji" can be deemed a container that includes destiny. Or it can be regarded as something that writes our destiny. However, according to the legendary story, you can peep into the changes of fate in the container through "wu ji," and you can also read the changeful fate through "wu ji." However, "wu ji" can be read only. It cannot be revised.[17]

Cinderella, Sleeping Beauty, and Qingcheng share the same archetypal pattern: female protagonists waiting for their boyfriends or lovers to arrive and attempt to rescue them from prophecies and advance their romantic relationships. It is therefore reasonable to compare Qingcheng in *The Promise* to Cinderella and Sleeping Beauty.[18]

Qingcheng as a Chinese Version of Snow White

In addition to the Chinese version of Cinderella and Sleeping Beauty, Qingcheng is also the Chinese version of Snow White. First, as I have already mentioned about the interrelation between Qingcheng's appearance in *The Promise* and Lady Li's beauty in Li Yannian's poem, the name Qingcheng indicates that her beauty conquers the entire city:

> In *The Promise*, Chen Kaige names the role that Cecilia Po-chi Cheung plays "Qingcheng." It is anticipatable that he will have some cinematic elaboration of her beauty.[19] (author's translation)

At the beginning of the film, every man in the castle listens to Qingcheng and does what she wants him to do because of his strong desire to know what is under Qingcheng's clothes and because of his obsession with Qingcheng's unequalled attractiveness. Without any weapons in her hands, Qingcheng easily controls every man in the castle because of her appearance. In *The Promise*, this scene eloquently argues that Qingcheng is the fairest of all. It also indirectly reminds the audience of Princess Snow White, who is the fairest of all according to the mirror on the wall:

"Mirror, Mirror on the wall, who's the fairest of all? Snow White is the fairest far to see."

Just like Snow White, Qingcheng is "the fairest far to see" in the castle, judging by every man's reaction to her question about what is under her cloak and outfit. Goddess Manshen promises and gives her the most alluring appearance. Qingcheng, as the fairest of all in the castle, matches the historical meaning of the phrase *qingcheng* in Li Yannian's poem.

Second, both Qingcheng and Snow White share the same need of true love from men. In the fairytale, Snow White needs Prince Charming's true love to undo the sorcery attached to her stepmother's poisonous apple. In *The Promise*, Qingcheng also needs true love from her "Prince Charming," which will not be possible until time flies backward according to Goddess Manshen's sorcery. Before they find true love with men, Snow White and Qingcheng are both helpless; neither of them can escape destiny.

More than Cinderella, Sleeping Beauty, and Snow White

So far, Chen Kaige seems to combine Cinderella, Sleeping Beauty, and Snow White and turn his own cinematic mixture of them into Qingcheng in *The Promise*. What else does he do with Cinderella, Sleeping Beauty, and Snow White? He rethinks and problematizes their romantic love in *The Promise*. Chen Kaige adds to the love stories of Cinderella, Sleeping Beauty, and Snow White how they determine who their true "Prince Charming" should be.

In the story of Cinderella, the prince can choose his princess from many aristocratic or wealthy ladies in the ballroom. He has many choices. It is the prince who seeks out and finds Cinderella. Cinderella, however, does not have many men to choose from. Except for the prince, Cinderella does not have other choices. At the moment when the prince realizes that Cinderella is the pretty woman with the glass shoes, Cinderella does not have any other choices. She is not given any opportunity to determine whether the prince is really her Mr. Right. She does not have any opportunity to figure out who her true "Prince Charming" is.

In the story of Sleeping Beauty, she is not given many choices, either. During her one-hundred-year slumber, Sleeping Beauty neither knows nor meets any men. Like Cinderella, Sleeping Beauty is not offered an opportunity to figure out who she truly loves, who her true "Prince Charming" is, and why she loves the prince. It is not clear what Sleeping Beauty wants from her Mr. Right, and how she makes sure that the prince is exactly her Mr. Right. Just like the story of Cinderella, it is the prince who looks for, finds, kisses, wakens, and rescues the heroine.

Yet the story of Snow White is not exactly the same as those of Cinderella and Sleeping Beauty in terms of the prince's search for her and her choices of who her Mr. Right should be. In the story of Snow White, she is provided an opportunity to meet, know, and interact with different men: the seven men living in the woods.[20] After Snow White leaves the palace where her father and stepmother live, the seven men shelter and accommodate her in the woods. She meets, knows, and interacts with them in the woods:

> Mirror, Mirror on the wall, who's the fairest of all? Snow White is the fairest far to see. Over the hills and far away, she dwells with seven dwarfs today.

She is therefore given an opportunity to figure out what she wants from her Mr. Right, which kind of man or which man her Mr. Right should be, and why she loves or dislikes different men. She must know why she does not fall in love with any of the seven men who know, interact with, shelter, and accommodate her in the woods. She must know why none of the seven men is her Mr. Right. At the moment when Prince Charming kisses her, she must also know why she is sure that she loves him. Although it is still the prince who finds, kisses, and rescues Snow White, Snow White has more men to choose from and is given an opportunity to recognize and figure out who her true Mr. Right is.

In *The Promise*, Chen Kaige turns Qingcheng into a Chinese version of Cinderella, Sleeping Beauty, and Snow White who knows what she wants from her Mr. Right: true love that Kunlun proves to her by jumping off the cliff to save her life. She is given opportunities to know, meet, and interact with different men. She is given many men to choose from. She is given opportunities to rethink, recognize, figure out, search, and find who her true "Prince Charming" is.

In terms of gender egalitarianism, Chen Kaige awards more freedom and abilities of critical thinking to Qingcheng in *The Promise* than Cinderella and Sleeping Beauty have. Cinderella and Sleeping Beauty do not seem to have a chance to compare their interactions with different men and rethink why one man is more attractive than any other. They do not have enough opportunities to know different men, interact with them, evaluate them, compare them, and critically think about whether they will be truly happier with one man for whatever reasons. After the princes find them, select them, and declare their love, Cinderella and Sleeping Beauty are not given the opportunity to decide whether they would like to choose the princes or other men. In contrast, Snow White and Qingcheng are both given enough freedom to meet, know, interact with, compare, and even live with different men before they determine who their "Prince Charming" should be while their "Prince Charming" and other men enjoy the male privilege to choose their beloved women among all the women they can meet, know, interact with, evaluate, and compare in ancient male-centered societies and gender ideologies. From this perspective, Qingcheng and Snow White enjoy more gender equalitarianism than do Cinderella and Sleeping Beauty. From this standpoint, Chen Kaige deeply rethinks the gender inequality in the stories of Cinderella and Sleeping Beauty, problematizes it, and compensates Qingcheng and Snow White by rewarding them equal rights and the capabilities of critical thinking. Although Qingcheng is indeed Chen Kaige's cinematic creation of a Chinese version of Cinderella, Sleeping Beauty, and Snow White, she is more than simply a Cinderella-and-Sleeping-Beauty who "revolves around . . . physical attraction and the mating games . . . with male characters"[21] in fairytales. She is a Chinese Snow White who enjoys equal rights, unlocks herself from "the legacy of Confucian ethics [that limits women to domestic] position at the bottom of the hierarchy of authority,"[22] dares to discard the patriarchal restriction of women's sexual experiences, enjoys sexual experience with the man she decides to love,[23] and has abilities of critical thinking to figure out who her true Mr. Right is.

Comparisons and Contrasts According to What Women Truly Want

With reference to the equal rights that Chen Kaige gives to Qingcheng and Snow White to evaluate and compare different men according to their own criteria in order to make sure which men would become their true "Prince Charming," he successfully cinematizes Qingcheng's comparing and contrasting of different men. In *The Promise*, Guangming and Wuhuan are not compatible with Kunlun in Qingcheng's point of view and are thus treated as "defeated and dead" in terms of their competition with Kunlun for Qingcheng. Kunlun is the chosen one among the three male protagonists; therefore, he is the only "living" man in terms of his competition for Qingcheng with Guangming and Wuhuan at the end of the film. His final possession of the crimson armor symbolizes his triumph in the competition for Qingcheng. The crimson armor is like his reward for winning the competition.

The final scene of the film highlights the contrast and comparison of Guangming, Wuhuan, and Kunlun in a more eye-catching way. Guangming and Wuhuan die because they kill each other to win Qingcheng back, not really because they are willing to sacrifice themselves to rescue Qingcheng from her dearth of true love. They more or less unconsciously objectify Qingcheng as if she were simply a war trophy to glorify the winner of the competition. To objectify a person and treat him or her as a war trophy to glorify oneself in a competition for love is not the definition of "true love." Under this circumstance, Guangming and Wuhuan do not seem to be the men who truly love Qingcheng.

The correct meaning of "true love" is to try one's best to understand the beloved person and to sincerely take good care of him or her regardless of one's sacrifice. Guangming does not fully understand how much the lack of true love hurts Qingcheng. Except for his possession of Qingcheng, Guangming does not appear to try his best to solve Qingcheng's problem and to save her from her dearth of true love. When Qingcheng forces him to make a choice between her and his return to his original military position and workplace, he chooses to return to his original position, leaving Qingcheng alone at home. This choice between his job and Qingcheng underscores Guangming's interest in his possession of Qingcheng, not exactly what Qingcheng needs. To possess Qingcheng, Guangming even lies to her and pretends to be the man in the crimson armor. This is not true love at all. His dishonesty also evidences that he does not deserve Qingcheng's love. In fact, what Guangming truly loves is not Qingcheng but his possession of her.

Wuhuan also does not help Qingcheng, though he realizes and keeps an eye on how much Qingcheng desires true love. Instead, he enjoys witnessing how Qingcheng suffers from the lack of true love and regards this as a way for him to avenge himself for Qingcheng cheating him and stealing his bun in childhood. On the one hand, he deeply cares about Qingcheng and is obsessed with Qingcheng's suffering. On the other hand, he loves being a voyeur to her suffering from the lack of true love. To Wuhuan, Qingcheng is like a helpless bird or slave under his careful control and is jailed in the cage of the dearth of true love. His love and hatred for Qingcheng is so complicated that he himself cannot have a narrow escape from his pathetic affection for Qingcheng. In fact, the name Wuhuan conveys his unhappiness and impossibility of a happy ending in his story with Qingcheng. In Mandarin Chinese, *wu* means "no" or "lack," while *huan* refers to happiness. Wuhuan's name foretells his lack of happiness in this film. What Wuhuan truly loves is not Qingcheng but his own psychological satisfaction and balance, which may lead him to emotional balance and spiritual happiness. Unfortunately, he does not gain any psychological satisfaction or balance from the beginning to the end of the film.

Kunlun, however, knows exactly what Qingcheng wants the most: true love and the opportunity to escape from her fate. From the beginning to the end of the film, the colorful butterfly on Qingcheng's dark cloak and the feather from her feathery outfit signify her desire to escape her destiny and gain true love from a man who deserves her love. She almost becomes free at the moment when she is like a kite flying after Kunlun in the sky. Unfortunately, the fact that Qingcheng is neither a butterfly, a kite, nor a free bird emphasizes how disappointed and helpless she is. Kunlun tries his best to decrease Qingcheng's emotional hurt. He is willing to do everything to take good care of her regardless of his own sacrifice. Although he is wounded, his true love for Qingcheng drives him to put on Snow Wolf's black feathery cloak, which enables him to run or fly faster than the speed of light to save Qingcheng from the lack of true love. The black feathery cloak also keeps him alive as long as he wears it.

That is to say, how much Guangming, Wuhuan, and Kunlun desire to rescue Qingcheng from her lack of true love determines whether they would put on the black feathery cloak before their death in the final scene of the film. To put on the cloak is to keep them alive in terms of not merely their own lives but also their competition for Qingcheng. To put on the black feathery cloak, run faster than time, enable time to go backward, and save Qingcheng from her dearth of true love is to truly love Qingcheng at the same time; therefore, the person who truly cares about and loves Qingcheng, puts on the dark cloak regardless of his own wounds or death, and rescues her from the lack of true love is the winner in the competition for Qingcheng. According to this definition, Kunlun is the only winner. Guangming and Wuhuan are "defeated" by Kunlun and "dead" in the competition for Qingcheng, while the black feathery cloak and true love for Qingcheng keep Kunlun "alive" at the end of the film.

The lives and deaths of Kunlun, Guangming, and Wuhuan show Chen Kaige's cinematic emphasis on Qingcheng's consideration about who her "Prince Charming" should be as well as her comparison and contrasting of them in *The Promise*. As a matter of fact, Snow White also indirectly discloses her thoughts about who her Mr. Right should be, as well as her comparison and contrasting of different men. According to the criterion of what Snow White wants from her Mr. Right, none of the seven men in the woods are chosen by Snow White as her Mr. Right, and they are thus regarded as "dwarfs" in terms of their competition for Snow White with Prince Charming. In other words, the seven men in the woods are physically "dwarfs" on the one hand and "dwarfs without enough compatibility" in the competition for Snow White's love on the other hand. The seven men in the woods are "dwarfs" in terms of not merely their physical size but also their competition for Snow White with Prince Charming.

Complicated Love Triangle

Chen Kaige problematizes the archetypal patterns in the love stories of Cinderella, Snow White, and Sleeping Beauty by adding the complex love "triangle" that Qingcheng, Kunlun, Wuhuan, and Guangming form, to the love story in *The Promise*. As I have previously mentioned, Sleeping Beauty is not given any opportunity to choose her Mr. Right from different men. There are only one female protagonist and one male protagonist in the whole story; there is no love triangle. The story of Cinderella offers the prince a lot of ladies to choose but not many men for Cinderella to choose from. Cinderella's case is closer to that of Li Yannian's poem because Lady Li is not given any opportunity to select her boyfriend or spouse, according to the poem and historical records. Although in Cinderella's and Lady Li's cases, the male protagonists enjoy the male privilege of being surrounded by many pretty women and selecting one or more than one of them, the women are too objectified or oversimplified to show what they think about or how they go about making decisions about their love; thus there is no apparent or palpable love triangle.[24] The story of Snow White allows Snow White to interact with different men, compare them, rethink who she loves, highlight the differences between the seven men in the woods and Prince Charming, and decide who her Mr. Right should be. It includes a romantic triangle formed by Snow White, the seven men in the woods, and Prince Charming; however, the love triangle in the story of Snow White is not as clear as that in *The Promise*.

Although both the story of Snow White and *The Promise* include comparisons and contrasts of different men, the love "triangle" in *The Promise* draws more attention from the audience because Kunlun, Guangming, and Wuhuan obviously compete for Qingcheng and thus have noticeable conflicts when they interact with one another whereas the seven men in the woods and Prince Charming do not have any direct or palpable conflict in the story of Snow White. For example, at the beginning of the film, Wuhuan asks his Snow Wolf to assassinate Guangming for him before he goes to the Imperial City and tries to kill the king in order to bring Qingcheng to him from the king. Wuhuan confesses to the king that he even gave up his wish to kill Guangming on his own in order to win Qingcheng back. According to Wuhuan's statement, Qingcheng is apparently what causes the conflicts among Wuhuan, Guangming, and the King. Kunlun cherishes the feather from Qingcheng's white feathery outfit after Wuhuan keeps Qingcheng in his cage. The feather clearly symbolizes the conflicts among Kunlun, Wuhuan, and Guangming.

The most eye-catching foil to underscore the problematics between Kunlun and Guangming is Kunlun's magic phrase at the edge of the cliff: "You must not die. You must go on living." It appears at least four times throughout the movie. First, Kunlun in the crimson armor says this to Qingcheng and jumps off the cliff, disregarding his own safety and life to rescue her. Second, Qingcheng mentions this phrase and regards it as what Guangming says to her after she mistakes Guangming for the man in the crimson armor and makes love with him. Third, in the trial, Kunlun corrects Qingcheng and tells her that what he says to her at the edge of the cliff was actually "You must not die. You must go on living" and not "Don't be sad." At that moment, Qingcheng discovers that Guangming is pretending to be the man in the crimson armor and is lying to her; she slaps him on his face and leaves him. Fourth, before the moment of Guangming's death, Qingcheng says the first half of the magic password to Guangming: "You must not die."

If this magic phrase is the phrase to Qingcheng's true love, this first half of the magic phrase before Guangming's death coincidentally implies that Guangming almost becomes Qingcheng's true love and that he had Qingcheng's love and was Qingcheng's boyfriend only at the front part of the film. The incomplete half of the magic password signifies that Guangming does not completely win Qingcheng's heart in the final half of the film and that Qingcheng's romantic dream to gain true love from Guangming can neither be completed nor come true at the end of the story.

Contrary to Guangming's case related to the first half of the magic phrase, Qingcheng says the last half of the magic phrase to Kunlun though she deliberately changes the beginning part of it in the trial. This final half of the magic phrase foreshadows that Kunlun turns out to be Qingcheng's true love at the end of the film and enjoys a happy ending to their romantic story. It suggests the completion of Qingcheng's wish to gain true love and the whole process of how Kunlun wins Qingcheng's heart at the end of the story.

Social Status of the Winner

Chen Kaige's film also adds to the story of Snow White, intensifying the conflicts and problematics between Kunlun and Guangming, the conflicts of social status between the winner and losers in the competition for Qingcheng. In the story of Snow White, the man who wins Snow White is Prince Charming, an aristocrat, while the losers are seven laborers in the woods; however, in *The Promise*, the winner in the competition for Qingcheng is Kunlun, a slave, while the losers are his master, General Guangming, and another aristocrat, Duke Wuhuan. There is an incredible gap between Guangming's and Wuhuan's social status and Kunlun's, just like Prince Charming's social status and the seven dwarfs'. The storyteller lets the aristocrat defeat the seven dwarf laborers in the competition for Snow White, yet Chen Kaige switches the preference for aristocrats by letting the slave outshine his master and Duke Wuhuan in *The Promise*. At the beginning of the film, Guangming easily dominates, conquers, and possesses Kunlun as his slave by feeding him meat, but at the end of the story he loses everything, including his own life, in the competition with Kunlun for Qingcheng. If the fact that Qingcheng says the initial half of the magic phrase to General Guangming denotes that the man with higher social status is almost the winner of the competition for Qingcheng and that the story of Qingcheng derives from the story of Snow White, the fact that she says the final half of it to Kunlun, Guangming's slave, shows Chen Kaige's "proletarian revolution" of the archetypal pattern that the stories of Cinderella, Sleeping Beauty, Lady Li in Li Yannian's poem, and Snow White have in common: the archetype that aristocrats or men with higher social status always defeat men with lower social status and win the hands of the female protagonists in their love stories.

Conclusion

Chen Kaige has said that he grew up thinking that film is like a dream, and that his cinematic works are stamped with his filmic digests of both dreams and reality.[25] In *The Promise*, he rethinks, problematizes, revises, and cinematizes the fairytales of Cinderella, Sleeping Beauty, and Snow White by surprising viewers with the heroicness of a slave named Kunlun. He revises the clichéd motifs of a hero saving a beauty and a prince winning his princess at the same time.[26] He also frees Qingcheng from the male-centeredness in ancient China, compensates ancient Chinese women such as Qingcheng by offering them more opportunities to explore possibilities to be with different men, and deprives male aristocrats of the privilege to limitlessly enjoy being surrounded by countless pretty women or always win their competitions for the women who attract or obsess them in patriarchal societies.[27] *The Promise* is a sort of "Chinese Western" film in terms of Chen Kaige's combination of Chinese and Western cultural elements in the same film.[28] In this film, Chen Kaige's reconsideration of the Western hackneyed motif of how a rich or aristocratic hero rescues, wins, and marries a fragile and helpless beauty is his Chinese response to the frequently seen paradigm from Western cultures. The processes Chen Kaige uses to reassess the past and interrogate the present[29] do include a variety of acceptance, adaptation, appropriation, application, revision, resistance, rejection, and acculturation[30] in terms of how he rationalizes, processes, develops, and rewrites Cinderella, Sleeping Beauty, and Snow White "on the threshold of different worlds and destinies."[31] While storytellers of fairytales breathe "life into human cultures,"[32] Chen Kaige adds his own critical annotation to the breath.

References

Ashliman, D. L. "Cinderella" or "The Little Glass Slipper" in "Folklore and Mythology Electronic Texts.": http://www.pitt.edu/~dash/type0510a.html#perrault.

Berry, Chris and Mary Farquhar. *China on Screen: Cinema and Nation*. New York: Columbia University Press, 2006, p. 139.

Berry, Michael. "Chen Kaige: Historical Revolution and Cinematic Rebellion." *Speaking in Images: Interviews with Contemporary Chinese Filmmakers*. New York: Columbia University Press, 2005, p. 87.

Browne, Nick and Paul G. Pickowicz and Vivian Sobchack and Easter Yao. *New Chinese Cinemas: Forms, Identities, Politics*. Cambridge: Cambridge University Press, 1994, p. 5.

Chow, Rey. *Primitive Passions: Visuality, Sexuality, Ethnography, and Contemporary Chinese Cinema*. New York: Columbia University Press, 1995, p. 39.

Clark, Paul. *Chinese Cinema: Culture and Politics Since 1949*. Cambridge: Cambridge University Press, 1987, p. 180.

---. *Reinventing China: A Generation and Its Films*. Hong Kong: Chinese University Press, 2005, p. 140.

Cornelius, Sheila. *New Chinese Cinema: Challenging Representations*. London: Wallflower, 2002, p. 71.

Curtin, Michael. "The Future of Chinese Cinema: Some Lessons from Hong Kong and Taiwan." *Chinese Media, Global Contexts*. Chin-Chuan Lee edt. New York: Routledge, 2003, p. 237.

Frankel, Hans H. "The Development of Han and Wei *Yüeh-fu* as a High Literary Genre." *The Vitality of the Lyric Voice: Shih Poetry from the Late Han to the Tang*. Lin Shuen-fu and Stephen Owen edt. Princeton: Princeton University Press, 1986, p. 256.

Gallehugh, D. Sue and Allen Gallehugh. *Bedtime Stories for Grown-ups: Fairy-Tale Psychology*. Deerfield Beach, Florida: Health Communication, 1995, pp. 17-24.

Grimm, Jacob and Wilhelm. "Snow White." *Folk & Fairy Tales*. Martin Hallett and Barbara Karasek edt. Second Edition. New York: Broadview Press, 2000, p. 68.

Guo, Jingming. *Wu ji (The Promise)*. Bejing: Renmin wenxue, 2006, p. 152.

Harries, Elizabeth Wanning. *Twice upon a Time: Women Writers and the History of the Fairy Tale*. Princeton, N.J.: Princeton University Press, 2001, p. 13.

Harris, Kristine. "The Romance of the Western Chamber and the Classical Subject Film

in 1920s Shanghai." *Cinema and Urban Culture in Shanghai, 1922-1943*. Yingjin Zhang edt. Stanford: Stanford University Press, 1999, p. 56.
Jameson, R.D. "Cinderella in China." *Cinderella: A Folklore Casebook*. Alan Dundes edt. New York: Garland, 1982, p. 74.
Kuang, Shi. *Tianxia wuji Chen Kaige*. Beijing: Zhongguo guangbo dianshi, 2005, p. 132.
Lang, Andrew. *The Blue Fairy Book*. New York: Random House, 1959, pp. 96-104.
Lu, Sheldon H. *Transnational Chinese Cinemas: Identity, Nationhood, Gender*. Honolulu: University of Hawaii Press, 1997, p. 10.
---. *China, Transnational Visuality, Global Postmodernity*. Stanford: Stanford University Press, 2001, p. 50.
Pang, Laikwan. *Building a New China in Cinema*. New York: Rowman and Littlefield, 2002, p. 128.
Perrault, Charles. "Cinderella, or the Little Glass Slipper." *Cinderella: A Folklore Casebook*. Alan Dundes edt. New York: Garland, 1982, p. 18.
---. "The Sleeping Beauty in the Wood." *Folk & Fairy Tales*. Martin Hallett and Barbara Karasek edt. Second Edition. New York: Broadview Press, 2000, p. 44.
Silbergeld, Jerome. *China into Film: Frames of Reference in Contemporary Chinese Cinema*. London: Reaktion Books, 1999, p. 9.
Smith, Sharon. "The Image of Women in Film: Some Suggestions for Future Research." *Feminist Film Theory: A Reader*. Sue Thornham edt. New York: New York University Press, 1999, p. 14.
Stone, Judy. *Eye on the World: Conversations with International Filmmakers*. Los Angeles: Silman-James Press, 1997, p. 93.
Yolen, Jane. *Favorite Folktales from Around the World*. New York: Pantheon Books, 1986, p. 1.
Zhang, Yingjin. *Chinese National Cinema*. New York: Routledge, 2004, p. 287.
Zhang, Zhen. *"An Amorous History of the Silver Screen*: The Actress as Vernacular Embodiment in Early Chinese Film Culture." *A Feminist Reader in Early Cinema*. Jennifer M. Bean and Diane Negra edt. Durham: Duke University Press, 2002, p. 524.
Zhu, Ying. "A Culture and an Economy in Disarray." *Chinese Cinema During the Era of Reform*. Westport, Connecticut: Praeger, 2003, p. 17.
Zipes, Jack. "Setting Standards for Civilization through Fairy Tales: Charles Perrault and His Associates." *Fairy Tales and the Art of Subversion: The Classical Genre for Children and the Process of Civilization*. New York: Wildman Press, 1983, p. 14.

Notes

1. I agree with Rey Chow on her statement:

Chen Kaige confirms O'Brien's judgment: "In China the east is mountainous, the west is flat; the west is poor, and the east is rich . . . In this spirit . . . recent graduates of the Beijing Film Academy . . . have chosen this yellow earth—poor, barren, and yet full of possibilities—to begin our artistic careers."

For details, consult Rey Chow's *Primitive Passions: Visuality, Sexuality, Ethnography, and Contemporary Chinese Cinema*. (New York: Columbia University Press, 1995) 39.

2. Although Chen Kaige seemed to pollute the environment because of this film, the box office of *The Promise* reached 1.8 billions RMB in China within only twenty days after the first release on December 14, 2005. One of the possible reasons for this film to successfully enthrall its audience is probably Chen Kaige's cinematic digest of love stories of Cinderella, Snow White, and Sleeping Beauty.

3. Although Kristine Harris comments that classical subjects tracked an erratic and even controversial course in Chinese filmmaking and had been a staple of experiments with cinema, I contend that Western classical subjects in the well-known fairytales of Cinderella, Snow White, and Sleeping Beauty also track their own course in this Chinese film, *The Promise*. For details, consult Kristine Harris's "The Romance of the Western Chamber and the Classical Subject Film in 1920s Shanghai" in *Cinema and Urban Culture in Shanghai, 1922-1943*. ed. Yingjin Zhang. (Stanford: Stanford University Press, 1999), 56.

4. For details, see "Cinderella" or "The Little Glass Slipper" in D. L. Ashliman's "Folklore and Mythology Electronic Texts." http://goo.gl/7SkH7 (July 2009).

5. Because the story of Cinderella is a fairytale and legendary story, there are various versions of the same story. According to R. D. Jameson, the oldest written European version is Des Periers' *Nouvelles Récréations et Ioyeux Devis*, published at Lyon in 1558. For details, consult R. D. Jameson's "Cinderella in China" in *Cinderella: A Folklore Casebook*. ed. Alan Dundes. (New York: Garland, 1982), 74. The single most popular version of the story of Cinderella is told by Charles Perrault and translated into English and included in *The Blue Fairy Book* edited by Andrew Lang. For details, consult Andrew Lang's *The Blue Fairy Book*. (New York: Random House, 1959), 96-104. I base my argument on the most popular version, which includes Cinderella's godmother, instead of revised or more modernized version of the same story. For instance, D. Sue Gallehugh and Allen Gallehugh created their own version of Cinderella. In their version of the story, Cinderella does not have a godmother. For details, see D. Sue Gallehugh and Allen Gallehugh's *Bedtime Stories for Grown-ups: Fairy-Tale Psychology*. (Deerfield Beach, Florida: Health Communication, 1995), 17-24.

6. For details, consult Hans H. Frankel's "The Development of Han and Wei *Yüeh-fu* as a High Literary Genre." *The Vitality of the Lyric Voice: Shih Poetry from the Late Han to the Tang*. eds. Lin Shuen-fu and Stephen Owen. (Princeton: Princeton University Press, 1986).

7. Charles Perrault, "Cinderella, or the Little Glass Slipper" in *Cinderella: A Folklore Casebook*. ed. Alan Dundes. (New York: Garland, 1982), 18.

8. Clark, Paul. *Chinese Cinema: Culture and Politics since 1949*. Cambridge: Cambridge University Press, 1987, p. 180.

9. Ying Zhu, "A Culture and an Economy in Disarray" in *Chinese Cinema During the Era of Reform*. (Westport, Connecticut: Praeger, 2003), 17.

10. Sheldon H. Lu remarks, "In the post-Tiananmen era (1989 to the present), or what Chinese intellectual historians call the "post-New Era" (*hou xin shiqi*), Chinese society is characterized by the expansion of consumerism, the spread of popular culture, the commercialization of cultural production, and the advent of postmodern formations." For details, consult Sheldon H. Lu's *Transnational Chinese Cinemas: Identity, Nationhood, Gender*. (Honolulu: University of Hawaii Press, 1997), 10.

11. Michael Berry, "Chen Kaige: Historical Revolution and Cinematic Rebellion" in *Speaking in Images: Interviews with Contemporary Chinese Filmmakers*. (New York: Columbia University Press, 2005), 87.

12. Chris Berry and Mary Farquhar, *China on Screen: Cinema and Nation*. (New York: Columbia University Press, 2006), 139.

13. See note 7.

14. In 1696, Charles Perrault "issued a separate edition of [fairytale entitled] *Sleeping Beauty*." For details, consult Jack Zipes's "Setting Standards for Civilization through Fairy Tales: Charles Perrault and His Associates" in *Fairy Tales and the Art of Subversion: The Classical Genre for Children and the Process of Civilization*. (New York: Wildman Press, 1983), 14.

15. Consult Charles Perrault's *Sleeping Beauty* in *Contes de ma Mère l'Oye* (*Mother Goose Tales*). Eds. Martin hallett and Barbara Karasek. Second Edition. (New York: Garland, 1982), 44.

16. Charles Perrault, "The Sleeping Beauty in the Wood" in *Folk & Fairy Tales*. eds. Martin Hallett and Barbara Karasek. Second Edition. (New York: Broadview Press, 2000), 44.

17. Jingming Guo, *Wu ji* (*The Promise*). (Bejing: Renmin wenxue, 2006), 152.

18. Some feminist literary critics regard the female protagonists' waiting for their men's arrival as a pattern for "feminine passivity and martyrdom." For details, consult Elizabeth Wanning Harries's *Twice upon a Time: Women Writers and the History of the Fairy Tale*. (Princeton: Princeton University Press, 2001), 13. However, I would like to defend Chen Kaige. In *The Promise*, Qingcheng's strong refusal to be with any men after the king is assassinated and before Kunlun jumps off the cliff is probably Chen Kaige's cinematic rejection of this sort of "feminine passivity and martyrdom" in the fairytales.

19. Shi Kuang, *Tianxia wuji Chen Kaige*. (Beijing: Zhongguo guangbo dianshi, 2005), 132.

20. Jacob and Wilhelm Grimm, "Snow White." *Folk & Fairy Tales*. eds. Martin Hallett and Barbara Karasek. Second Edition. (New York: Broadview Press, 2000), 68.

21. Sharon Smith, "The Image of Women in Film: Some Suggestions for Future Research." *Feminist Film Theory: A Reader*. ed. Sue Thornham. (New York: New York University Press, 1999), 14.

22. Sheila Cornelius, *New Chinese Cinema: Challenging Representations*. (London: Wallflower, 2002), 71.

23. Zhang Yingjin states, "[A]fter *The Woman from the Lake of Scented Souls* (Xianghun nu, dir. Xie Fei, 1992) was co-winner of the Golden Bear with *The Wedding Banquet* at the 1993 Berlin Film Festival, the subject of sexuality seemed no longer a taboo" for Chinese filmmakers. For details, consult his *Chinese National Cinema*. (New York: Routledge, 2004), 287.

24. In "Women's Stories On-screen versus Off-screen" in *Building a New China in Cinema*, Pang Laikwan has a paragraph about the cinematic objectification of women.

> Cinema is most revealing in illuminating this power dynamic. When the visual and illusionary nature of the medium conincides with the vulnerability of female representation, it becomes most seductive to male's confiscation. But this sheer vulnerability, as discussed in Chow's and Zizek's analyses, can also exert power back to such seizure, ultimately invalidating this appropriation mechanism. Cinema is able to protect its subjects within its frame...when the objectification of woman is intensified to the degree that little space is left between the characters and the spectators, the latter is made to confront the former directly, bypassing the ideological mediation of the patriarchy. While

female representation is invested with various interests of different parties, the direct visual portrayal of hers also facilitates a head-on collision between the viewer and the viewed, allowing her a certain autonomy not available in the public discourse.

25. Judy Stone, *Eye on the World: Conversations with International Filmmakers.* (Los Angeles: Silman-James Press, 1997), 93.

26. A large number of Hollywood films repeat the archetype of Cinderella's love story, such as *Pretty Woman* (directed by Gary Marshall in 1990), *The King and Me* (directed by Pamela Dresser in 1999), and *Maid in Manhattan* (directed by Wayne Wang in 2002). Chen Kaige's cinematic revision of Cinderella's story in *The Promise* seems to coincidentally stage a filmic dialogue with them and question whether aristocrats or wealthy men always win their "Cinderella" easily and smoothly on the silver screen. After Michael Curtin questions whether Chinese filmmakers survive direct competition from Hollywood in his article entitled "The Future of Chinese Cinema," *The Promise* indirectly shows Chen Kaige's ambition to face and survive direct competition from Hollywood from the viewpoint of Qingcheng as his Chinese cinematic version of Cinderella.

27. Jerome Silbergeld mentions that "artistic production presented by Chinese male filmmakers as 'gender liberation' has sometimes been understood as nothing more than 'female appropriation,' a display of 'male desire' and nationalist hegemonism." For details, consult Jerome Silbergeld's *China into Film: Frames of Reference in Contemporary Chinese Cinema*. (London: Reaktion Books, 1999), 9. I do not claim that Chen Kaige is a feminist or someone perfectly free from oversights about gender egalitarianism because Qingcheng is really in need of Kunlun's help in order to gain true love in *The Promise*. However, Chen Kaige does more or less release Qingcheng from rigid male-centeredness or ancient Chinese patriarchy because she enjoys interactions and even sexual relations with different men, which are absolutely forbidden in ancient Chinese gender ideology.

28. Paul Clark, *Reinventing China: A Generation and Its Films.* (Hong Kong: Chinese University Press, 2005), 140.

29. Nick Browne and Paul G. Pickowicz and Vivian Sobchack and Easter Yao, *New Chinese Cinemas: Forms, Identities, Politics.* (Cambridge: Cambridge University Press, 1994), 5.

30. Sheldon H. Lu, *China, Transnational Visuality, Global Postmodernity.* (Stanford: Stanford University Press, 2001), 50.

31. Zhen Zhang, "*An Amorous History of the Silver Screen*: The Actress as Vernacular Embodiment in Early Chinese Film Culture" in *A Feminist Reader in Early Cinema*. eds. Jennifer M. Bean and Diane Negra. (Durham: Duke University Press, 2002), 524.

32. Jane Yolen, *Favorite Folktales from Around the World*. (New York: Pantheon Books, 1986), 1.

Chapter Six
The Chinese Hamlet's Two Women and Shakespeare's Chinese Sisters: Qing Nü and Wan'er in *The Banquet*

The Banquet, released in September 2006, is the first martial arts film and cinematic adaptation of William Shakespeare's *Hamlet* by Feng Xiaogang, who directed commercial comedies in China. In this film, Prince Wuluan (played by Daniel Yen-tzu Wu) is apparently modeled after Hamlet; Qing Nü (played by Zhou Xün), Ophelia; Emperor Li (played by Ge You), Hamlet's uncle; Empress Wan'er (played by Zhang Ziyi), the queen in the Shakespearian drama. Both Prince Wuluan in *The Banquet* and Prince Hamlet in the Shakespearean drama suffer from melancholy. Emperor Li's murder of Prince Wuluan's father resembles Hamlet's uncle poisoning of his own brother, Hamlet's father. Prince Wuluan's stage or theater is so similar to Shakespeare's Elizabethan stage that viewers cannot but recognize Feng Xiaogang's adaptation of Shakespeare's most famous tragedy in his film.[1] The swordsmen's helmets in *The Banquet* look like Western knights' helmets, not like the kind worn by ancient Chinese warriors on the battlefield. The white masks that Wuluan's performing troops wear on their faces in *The Banquet* remind the audience of the masks in Western drama, such as in *The Phantom of the Opera*, not stereotypical Chinese masks. "To be, or not to be" is the question in not merely *Hamlet* but also *The Banquet*. Whereas most viewers of this film rarely miss this parallel between *Hamlet* and *The Banquet*, the Chinese traditions behind Prince Wuluan's two women, Qing Nü and Empress Wan'er, elude many of these viewers. Although it is obvious that Qing Nü and Empress Wan'er both love Prince Wuluan, most viewers, especially Western viewers without a background in sinology or Chinese history, probably miss the Chinese traditions behind Qing Nü and Empress Wan'er. In this article, I would like to focus on the Chinese literary, historical, and sociocultural traditions behind Qing Nü and Wan'er.

Qing Nü and *Yüeren ge*

Qing Nü's romantic love for Prince Wuluan draws on a romantic poem in the Chinese literary tradition. This poem about a female rower's secret love for Prince Zixi is included in the story that Zhuang Xin tells Prince Xiangcheng of the Chu State during the spring and autumn era (around 770-403 B.C.) in the Eastern Zhou Dynasty (771-221 B.C.). The romantic poem, *Yüeren ge* (A Song from Yüe), was recorded in the eleventh roll, *Shan shuo* (Good Words), of *Shuo yüan* (*Collection of Words*) authored by Liu Xiang (77-6 B.C.) in the Western Han Dynasty (206-9 B.C.).[2] It is a poem translated from the language spoken in the Yüe State to the language spoken in the Chu State. This poem is usually regarded as the first translated poem in Chinese literary history. It also reappeared as the second poem in the ninth roll of Xü Ling's *Yütai xinyong* (*New Songs from a Jade Terrace*) in the Southern Dynasty (420-589 A.D.).

> *Jinxi he xi xi?* (What blessed night is this?)
> *Jianzhou zhong liu.* (Drifting down the River Jian.)
> *Jinri he ri xi?* (What auspicious day is this?)
> *De yü wangzi tong zhou.* (Dreaming beside my Prince.)
> *Meng xiu pei hao xi,* (Too bashful to stare,)[3]
> *Bu zi gou chi.* (A secret I cannot share.)
> *Xin ji fan er bu jue xi,* (My heart fills with longing,)
> *De zhi wangzi.* (To know you, dear my Prince.)
> *Shan you mu xi mu you zhi,* (Trees live on mountains and branches live on trees.)
> *Xin yue jun xi jun bu zhi.* (My heart lives for you, but you do not see me.)[4]

According to Liu Xiang's book, Zhuang Xin, a governmental official of the Chu State, hopes to shake hands with Prince Xiangcheng, but Prince Xiangcheng rejects him. Zhuang Xin then tells Prince Xiangcheng a story of how Prince Zixi reacted to a female rower's secret love for him: When Prince Zixi took a boat, he overheard his female rower[5] sing a song in the language spoken in the Yüe State. Because he spoke only the language of the Chu State and thus did not understand the meaning of his rower's song, he asked his interpreter to translate the song from the language of the Yüe State to the language of the Chu State. Through the translation, he realized the rower's secret love for him, gave her a hug, and covered her with his embroidered sleeves or fabric. By telling this story, Zhuang Xin compares his own social status with that of the female rower, points out that his social status is higher than that of the female rower, and persuasively argues that he deserves Prince Xiangcheng's handshake. After listening to Zhuang Xin's story of Prince Zixi hugging the rower, who loved him, Prince Xiangcheng apologizes to Zhuang Xin and shakes hands with him.[6]

In *The Banquet*, the character of Qing Nü recalls Prince Zixi's female rower, especially when she sings the poem of *Yüeren ge*. Qing Nü expressing her love for Prince Wuluan in her love song is exactly the same as the rower divulging love for Prince Zixi in her song. Qing Nü's desire for Prince Wuluan's romantic love directly parallels Zhuang Xin's desire for a handshake with Prince Xiangcheng and the rower's hope for romantic love from Prince Zixi. Prince Wuluan's original indifference to Qing Nü's love is similar to Prince Zixi's unawareness of his rower's love and Prince Xiangcheng's rejection of shaking hands with Zhuang Xin. The moment that Prince Wuluan realizes that the masked singer is Qing Nü parallels the moment that Prince Zixi realizes that his female rower loves him. Prince Wuluan's embrace of Qing Nü parallels Prince Zixi's hug of his female rower.

Furthermore, in the romantic triangle formed by Qing Nü, Wuluan, and Wan'er, *yüeren ge* is the love poem that Qing Nü sings to Wuluan, Wuluan desires but fails to sing to Wan'er, and Wan'er wants but cannot sing to Wuluan because of various political concerns about her and Wuluan's safety. Wuluan clearly points out that both Qing Nü and Wan'er hope for him to enter their embraces after he shows *yüeren ge* to Qing Nü.

Wan'er and Wu Zetian

The character of Empress Wan'er in *The Banquet* is probably modeled on Wu Zetian (624-705 A.D.), the only female ruler in imperial Chinese history. Wu Zetian was originally a low-ranked concubine of Li Shimin, the Emperor Taizong of the Tang Dynasty (599-649 A.D.), and became a nun after Li Shimin's death. Yet her beauty amazed Li Shimin's son, Li Zhi, the Emperor Gaozong of the Tang Dynasty (628-683 A.D.), when he visited the temple where she was a nun. Li Zhi fell in love with her and brought her back from the temple to the royal palace. He turned her into his concubine and, later on, promoted her to be his queen in 655 A.D..[7] Wu Zetian gave birth to two emperors who inherited Li Zhi's royal throne, Li Xian and Li Dan. After her degradation of Li Dan, she proclaimed herself a female ruler and named her short-lived dynasty "Da Zhou," "Wu Zhou," or "Nan Zhou" in 690 A.D.

Empress Wan'er in *The Banquet* parallels Wu Zetian in several ways. First, Wu Zetian was Li Shimin's spouse; Wan'er is also the first emperor's spouse. Second, both Li Shimin and his son fell in love with Wu Zetian; in *The Banquet* the first emperor and his son, Prince Wuluan, also love Wan'er. Third, Wu Zetian was a wife of Li Shimin and Li Zhi, the second emperor, who followed Li Shimin; Wan'er is also married to both the first emperor and Emperor Li, the second emperor. Fourth, Wu Zetian turned herself from a queen into a female ruler; Wan'er also changes herself from a queen to a female ruler.

Political and Administrative Insistence on Gender Equalitarianism

During Wu Zetian's reign as the female ruler of China, she named herself Zhao. There are two ways to write this special Chinese character. The first way to write this special Chinese character includes the characters of the sun, the moon, and the sky: 曌. Because the sun usually refers to men or masculinity and the moon usually stands for women or femininity, this special character means that men and women can equally prop up the universe, sky, or heaven. From this perspective, Wu Zetian clearly indicated that her political power and accomplishment should deserve as much applause as all the other male emperors' power and accomplishments. The other way to write this special Chinese character is to include two characters that represent eyes and the character of the sky: 瞾. In this case, this special character signifies her two eyes to watch or look after the universe or her empire. Although there is rarely perfection in almost anything in the human world, including sexual equality, the name Wu Zetian gave to herself demonstrated her political and administrative insistence on gender equalitarianism, which is exactly what Wan'er displays after she becomes the female ruler in *The Banquet*.

Oedipal Princes: Wuluan, Li Zhi, and Hamlet

Both Wan'er's life story in *The Banquet* and Wu Zetian's life story include their beloveds' Freudian complexes: both Prince Wuluan and Li Zhi display an Oedipus complex,[8] which reminds the audience of the famous research on Shakespeare's *Hamlet* and Oedipus. Specifically, in *The Banquet*, Wuluan loves his father's woman, Wan'er; similarly, Chinese historical records show that Li Zhi loved his father's woman, Wu Zetian. As sons and crown princes, both Wuluan and Li Zhi compete with their fathers for their beloved women. Psychoanalytically speaking, this psychological complex is called an Oedipus complex, and almost every son or little boy experiences it. According to Freudian psychoanalytic theory, "castration fear" or "castration anxiety" usually starts when sons or little boys witness the fact that their sexual organs are smaller than their fathers' and they unconsciously interpret the smaller size of their genitals as either their ethical inferiority to their fathers or a sort of sociocultural punishment for their immoral desires to possess their fathers' women. Nevertheless, they usually accept the sociocultural norms regarding their fathers' higher priority in possessing their beloved women. Thus their fathers usually win the psychological competitions with their sons for their mutually desired women. In *The Banquet*, Prince Wuluan's departure from the royal palace following his father's wedding to Wan'er clearly illustrates Wuluan's acceptance of his father's victory and his own loss of the competition for Wan'er, now his stepmother. Likewise, in the Tang Dynasty, Li Zhi lost the competition with his father for Wu Zetian; he had to wait until his father's death to make Wu Zetian his wife.[9]

The Beauty that Conquers the Country and Territory

Moreover, at the moment when Wan'er sees herself wearing the new red dress in the mirror, Emperor Li recites the final two lines of Li Yannian's poem: *ning buzhi qingguo yü qingcheng, jiaren nan zaide* (I'd rather have no idea about the loss of my nation and castle. The beauty cannot be regained).[10]

> *Beifang you jiaren* (In the North there is a beautiful woman,)
> *Jueshi er duli* (Unique, unequaled in the world.)
> *Yigu qing ren cheng* (With one glance she conquers a city of men,)
> *Zaigu qing ren guo* (With another glance a country of men.)
> *Ning buzhi qingcheng yü qingguo* (Don't you know? A city and country conquering)
> *Jiaren nanzaide (*Beauty cannot be found again.)[11]

Emperor Li compares Wan'er to the beautiful woman in the poem. Although Li Yannian and his beautiful sister, who married the Emperor Wu of the Han Dynasty (156-87 B.C.), lived during the Han Dynasty (202 B.C.-220 A.D.), these two poetic lines connect Wan'er to Wu Zetian because Wu Zetian's actions resulted in the Li royal family's *qingguo* (loss of the country) and *qingcheng* (loss of the territory or city) between 690 A.D. and 705 A.D..[12]

Wan'er in *The Banquet*, Wu Zetian of the Tang Dynasty, and Lady Li of the Han Dynasty—all share the unequaled and irreplaceable beauty that can *qingcheng qingguo* (conquer both the nation and city). Lady Li's beauty wins Li Yannian's poetic praise during the Han Dynasty; Wan'er's beauty is rewarded with Emperor Li's recitation of Li Yannian's poem in *The Banquet*. Finally, Wu Zetian's beauty attracted Emperor Taizong during the Tang Dynasty. Emperor Taizong named her Meiniang because the character, *mei*, refers to the irresistible fascination of women's beauty. The character, *mei*, is also one of the words that General Yin and Qing Nü use to describe the attractive eyes of Empress Wan'er while discussing how Qing Nü should embroider the eyes of the phoenix on her red fabric in *The Banquet*.

Both Wan'er and Wu Zetian are round characters in terms of their life stories. They experience emotional ups and downs as well as dramatic psychological change over time from innocent childhood, romantic girlhood, different kinds of marital lives, traumatic widowhood, power struggles in royal palaces, to their own reign. Ye Jintian (Tim Yip), the art director of *The Banquet*, mentions that Renaissance paintings, especially Caravaggio's works, inspired him to design Wan'er's dresses and hairstyles to show the dramatic complexity of this round character in the film:

> I had to push [her] age and make her look more powerful but still have innocence in that power . . . I wanted to go somewhere deep in the human mind. Humans betray; they have desires. They are not constant. I needed a contrast so I reached for Western elements . . . The Western element is mixing in the dark parts of people.[13]

According to the official website of *The Banquet*, red and black are the two colors Ye Jintian uses to highlight Wan'er's interpersonal conflicts and power struggles in the royal palace. In *The Banquet*, Wan'er explains that the red represents desires and lust: desires to succeed and lust for romantic love or sexuality. Feng Xiaogang, as the filmmaker, regards the story of Wan'er as a story about desires. He says,

> The most attractive thing about it is that "crime" is not premeditated but is often the result of self-preservation. Take the Empress for instance. Her first move is to protect herself. Her second move is to protect the Crown Prince. When she discovers that the Prince can no longer be protected, she needs to take things in her own hands . . . . This kind of set-up is more human: as the characters get lost in their desire, the situation becomes uncontrollable, and everything starts changing and developing rapidly.[14]

The red represents victory over disorder. For instance, it is no coincidence that Wan'er wears red dresses in ceremonies, in which she is confirmed as the new queen or female ruler; namely, the red implies the smooth advancement of her royal status and political success. Nor is it coincidental that she puts on the red sportswear,[15] thereby clarifying that Wuluan will not threaten Emperor Li, because the red signifies her political power and administrative capability to comfort Emperor Li, protect Wuluan, and benefit from her balance between Emperor Li and Wuluan. The red curtain around the royal bed, the red panties, the red skirt, the red bra, the red *dudou* (undergarment for the belly), and the red tattoo on the back likewise indicate the sexuality and physical intimacy between Wan'er and Emperor Li as well as Emperor Li's sexual desires and lust for Wan'er. Wan'er keeps the red fabric that she had originally planned to give to Qing Nü as a wedding gift; this denotes the impossibility for Qing Nü to marry Wuluan and have any physical contact or sexual relationship with him. Before Wan'er's death, the red fabric suddenly becomes uncontrollable in her hands and falls to the floor before she can catch it or secure it within her palms; this depicts Wan'er's inability to continue or secure her political advancement, successful career, ambitious plans, and romantic relationship at the end of the film.

The black is emblematic of all that is opposite to red. For example, Emperor Li wears black when he overhears Wan'er say that people expect Prince Wuluan, not him, to take the royal responsibility of leading the empire. He is also in black when he learns that Wan'er plans to poison him. Ethically speaking, he formally admits that he is an immoral thief who stole his older brother's and nephew's royal throne. He also suspects that his dead brother's spirit[16] sends Wuluan to right this wrong; black marks his larceny, failure, crime, guilt, suicide, and lack of political correctness to maintain his royal leadership.[17] In his relationship with Wan'er, Emperor Li misinterprets her warning of his impending death; instead, thinking that her whispered warning implies their future sexual pleasure following the banquet. Interestingly, Wan'er whispering the warning directly into his ear mirrors him blowing the poison into his older brother's ear. When Wan'er warns him of his death, black represents the color of mourning. The black visible at Wan'er's death and her stealthy notification of Wuluan concerning the death of his father fulfill the same function. When Wan'er notifies Qing Nü that the red fabric is no longer her wedding gift, Wan'er's black dress mourns the doomed "death" of the love between Qing Nü and Wuluan. That is to say, black is emblematic not only of Wuluan's father's, Emperor Li's, and Wan'er's death but also of the death of the love between Qing Nü and Wuluan.

Another color of symbolic importance in *The Banquet* is green. Even the green that signifies Wan'er's memory of her past romantic relationship with Wuluan is not an eye-catching and energetic green, however, but of a more depressing hue. The only exception to the dull greens in most of the movie is probably the livening green of the duckweed in the fish glob. It is common in Chinese to compare sexual pleasure to *yüshui zhi huan* (the joy of fish in water); hence, the green of the duckweed symbolizes Wan'er's and Wuluan's romantic dream for their happy union in the future. Unfortunately, the lethal weapon that Wan'er pulls out of her body is thrown into the fish glob and consequently represents the tragic ending of the romantic relationship of Wan'er and Wuluan.

In an interview with CCTV6's on May 10, 2006, Zhang Ziyi explained Wan'er's psychological changes and emotional ups and downs:

> I think my character goes through a lot of emotional struggle and sacrifice. You think she didn't love her husband, the late king? Or even the new Emperor, played by Ge You? She has feelings, too. Ge You's character gives her many things she has never enjoyed or experienced before. What Wuluan brings out of her is childhood innocence, her deep-buried self.

Moreover, historical records demonstrate that one of the most talented female poets and governmental officials during Wu Zetian's reign in the Tang Dynasty was named Wan'er: the same name for the Empress Wan'er in *The Banquet*. The full name of this female poet and governmental official is Shangguang Wan'er (664-710 A.D.). It is not a coincidence that Wan'er in *The Banquet* and Shangguang Wan'er of the Tang Dynasty share their given name. The name, Wan'er, functions as a bridge that points to the cinematic connection between the *bildungsroman* (a literary term for stories about protagonists' growth and life experience) of Wan'er in *The Banquet* and Wu Zetian's political ambition in her biography.

Yüenü jian

Yüenü jian (the sword of women in the Yüe State), which demonstrates the harmonious swordplay of both Wan'er and Wuluan to the audience, also indirectly connects Wan'er in *The Banquet* with Wu Zetian or other women in the Tang Dynasty. In comparison to women in most other dynasties in ancient China, women in the Tang Dynasty were much more encouraged and allowed to learn martial arts and do physical exercise.[18] For example, Wan'er puts on her sportswear, rides her horse, and plays ball with Emperor Li. She is not merely a beautiful "dutch wife" or sex toy in Emperor Li's bedroom but also a martial arts lady whose excellent kung fu can defeat enemies and rescue her Mr. Right, Prince Wuluan. This kind of women's power to influence men's destinies is exactly what Wu Zetian possessed, her political strength allowing her to make significant decisions about several crown princes' fates during the Tang Dynasty.

In *The Banquet*, Wan'er's and Wuluan's swordplay of *yüenü jian* looks as marvelously harmonious as a *pas de deux*. Well-paralleled in the swordplay of *yüenü jian* are not only their ballet-like physical gestures but also the common feeling about their future safety and their shared political predicament. This concern for safety and difficult situations in the royal palace parallels Wu Zetian's feeling when she lived in the royal palace as spouse to both Li Shimin and Li Zhi.

Yüenü jian and *Yüewang jian*

Rooted in Chinese history, *yüenü jian* draws a triangular connection between Prince Wuluan's wish to avenge his dead father and Prince Hamlet's plans of retaliation through King Gou Jian's revenge of the Yüe State in the spring and autumn era (around 770-403 B.C.) during the Eastern Zhou Dynasty (771-221 B.C.).

According to the film's website, a young woman in the Yüe State met a mysterious old man and was given a sword. An ape in the forest fought with her and taught her the skills of swordplay. Later on, this young woman passed on her knowledge about swordplay to King Gou Jian of the Yüe State. After being amazed by this young woman, Gou Jian named the sword *yüenü jian*.

In Chinese history, Gou Jian is famous for his political quest for vengeance. Having lost his nation in 494 B.C., he struggled for more than two decades to force Fuchai, the king of the Wu State, to commit suicide, defeat the Wu State (473 B.C.) in order to then resume his own reign (around 496-494 B.C. and 473-469 B.C.) in the Yüe State.[19] Similarly, Prince Wuluan goes to the Wu and Yüe areas and returns from there to his royal palace for his political counterblow in *The Banquet*. Although current historical records do not clearly show the connection between the legend of *yüenü jian* and Gou Jian's struggle to repossess his country, anthropologists have evidence that Gou Jian and his people owned excellent weapons, especially a sword named *yüewang jian* (the sword of the King of the Yüe State; length: 55.7 cm; width: 4.6 cm) excavated in Hubei, China, in December 1965. Even twenty-five hundred years after Gou Jian's reign, the sword, which was discovered in an ancient grave, is neither rusty nor eroded. It is surprisingly sharp.[20] In *The Banquet*, Prince Wuluan's revenge and the *yüenü jian* remind the audience of Gou Jian's revenge and *yüewang jian* as well as Prince Hamlet's retaliation for his dead father.

The Banquet in Hongmen

Furthermore, *The Banquet* draws on another even in Chinese history, the *hongmen yan* (the banquet in Hongmen) in 206 B.C.. At the end of the Qin Dynasty (221-206 B.C.), Liu Bang (247-195 B.C.) and Xiang Yü (232-202 B.C.) were two of the most influential military generals. Ziying (?-206 B.C.) acted as the third king of the Qin State for only forty-six days, and gave way to Liu Bang, who had previously won control of Guangzhong. Subsequently, Xiang Yü defeated the main army force of the Qin State in the war of Julu. He had learned from Cao Wushang (?-206 B.C.), a governmental official whom Liu Bang hired to deal with military strategies, of Liu Bang's secret plan to proclaim himself the king of Guangzhong. Xiang Yü's schemer, Fan Zen (275-204 B.C.),[21] claimed to discern Liu Bang's ambition to be the future emperor of the whole of China, not only the king of Guangzhong. He therefore advised Xiang Yü to kill Liu Bang as early as possible. Xiang's and Fan's plan was to host a banquet for Liu Bang in Hongmen, ask someone to entertain Liu Bang with swordplay in the banquet, and kill Liu Bang during the swordplay. Xiang Yü's uncle, Xiang Bo (?-192 B. C.), divulged the plan of the banquet in Hongmen to Zhang Liang (?-186 B.C.), Liu Bang's staff officer, and hoped Zhang Liang would escape from Liu Bang's military camps to secure his life because of his special friendship with Zhang Liang. Zhang Liang decided not to leave Liu Bang and told Liu Bang about the banquet. At that time, Liu Bang had around 100,000 soldiers, but Xiang Yü had around 400,000 soldiers. In other words, Xiang Yü's military force was four times stronger than Liu Bang's. Owing to his inferior military force, Liu Bang showed special respect for Xiang Bo, asked Zhang Liang to consult Xiang Bo, and politely attended the banquet that Xiang Yü hosted in Hongmen. Historians called this famous banquet *hongmen yan* (banquet in Hongmen).

During the banquet, Xiang Yü claimed that Cao Wushang had spread incorrect information or rumor about Liu Bang's political ambition and caused their misunderstanding, but he did not seem to be strongly determined to kill Liu Bang. Although Fan Zen arranged for Xiang Zhuang, Xiang Yü's cousin, to entertain Liu Bang with swordplay, Xiang Bo joined the swordplay to stop

Xiang Zhuang from killing Liu Bang. Zhang Liang realized Xiang Bo's intention to protect Liu Bang, left the banquet, and notified Fan Kuai (?-204 or 189 B.C.), a military staff officer who worked for Liu Bang and married the younger sister of Liu Bang's wife. Then, Fan Kuai entered the dining room. He told Xiang Yü that Liu Bang was actually waiting for Xiang Yü's arrival because he could have already proclaimed himself the political leader right after he conquered the area of Guanzhong. By doing so, he tried to stop Xiang Yü from killing Liu Bang. Xiang Yü rewarded Fan Kuai with wine and pork, yet he did not respond to Fan Kuai's request to not assassinate Liu Bang. Under these circumstances, Liu Bang could not but lie that he needed to use the bathroom. He escaped from the dining room with Fan Kuai and other staff people in order to guarantee their safety. Although Xiang Yü sent Chen Ping (?-178 B.C.) as a messenger to the bathroom to invite Liu Bang to return to the dining room, Fan Kuai persuaded Liu Bang not to go from the restroom to the dining hall. At the moment of Liu Bang's escape, Fan Kuai had an extremely famous sentence recorded by historians: *Ren wei daozu wo wei yü rou* (All the other people, such as Xiang Yü, are like the knife and the chopping board, but we are like the fish to be cut by them).[22]

In *The Banquet*, Empress Wan'er's interruption of the swordplay to protect Prince Wuluan parallels the actions of Xiang Bo, Fan Kuai, and Zhang Liang, who tried to protect Liu Bang. Emperor Li's arrangement of the swordplay in *The Banquet* parallels Xiang Yü's and Fan Zen's plan of the swordplay in the banquet located in Hongmen. The swordsmen who worked for Emperor Li to assassinate Prince Wuluan in *The Banquet* are modeled after Xiang Zhuan, Xiang Yü's cousin whom Fan Zen summoned to kill Liu Bang in the swordplay. Prince Wuluan in *The Banquet* is like Liu Bang, because both of them narrowly escape from murderous swordplays during political banquets. Historically speaking, the banquet in Hongmen indirectly resulted in Xiang Yü's failure and Liu Bang's establishment of his own dynasty. The banquet in *The Banquet* also indirectly results in Emperor Li's death and Wan'er's political success to initiate her reign. Wan'er's success is like Liu Bang's success. Because of this emblematic connection between these two banquets, Wan'er becomes Shakespeare's Chinese sister, as she similarly enjoys political power and a successful career as Liu Bang, the initiator of the Han Dynasty, which is one of the greatest dynasties in ancient China. In this sense, the cinematic applause for Wan'er in *The Banquet* is beyond verbal description.

Shakespeare's Chinese Sisters: Qing Nü and Wan'er

Virginia Woolf (1882-1941 A.D.) in *A Room of One's Own* questions whether society appreciates women's talents and ambitions by hypothesizing that William Shakespeare had a talented and ambitious sister named Judith

Shakespeare. She firmly believed that Judith Shakespeare died a miserable death because of her talent and ambition.

> Let me imagine, since the facts are so hard to come by, what would have happened had Shakespeare had a wonderfully gifted sister, called Judith, let us say.... She could get no training in her craft ... she found herself with child by that gentleman and so—who shall measure the heat and violence of the poet's heart when caught and tangled in a woman's body?—killed herself one winter's night and lies buried at some crossroads where the omnibuses now stop outside the Elephant and Castle.[23]

However, in *The Banquet*, Shakespeare's Chinese sisters—Qing Nü, who has profound artistic talents, and Wan'er, whose ambition is as great as that of male politicians and Emperor Li—do not necessarily die because their talent and ambitions fail to be appreciated or accepted. Emperor Li, Queen Wan'er, Prince Wuluan, and the rest of the audience deeply appreciate Qing Nü's literary, singing, and performing talents. Emperor Li even awards her a cup of royal wine after her successful performance on stage. Her talents do not kill her at all. Rather, she dies because Emperor Li is unaware of the poison that Empress Wan'er has added to the wine to murder him, and Queen Wan'er is unable to immediately stop Qing Nü from drinking the wine from the royal cup. Wan'er's ambition does not seem to be a big problem, either. She successfully assumes political power after Emperor Li's and Prince Wuluan's deaths and becomes the female ruler. She is not killed by her ambition. What kills her is the *yüenü jian* thrown into her back by an unknown assassin or someone who is jealous of her achievement.

Death of the Young Girl Wan'er

Metaphorically speaking, this death is not the death of ambitious Empress Wan'er but the death of the young girl Wan'er, who grew up with Prince Wuluan, enjoyed the romantic and unchangeable boyfriend-girlfriend relationship with him from childhood, became his beloved in adulthood, and tried her best to protect him behind the scenes from death. The ambitious Empress Wan'er never dies; her ambitious spirit is everlasting and will remain forever alive regardless of the limit of her lifetime. The young girl Wan'er, however, whose romantic love for Prince Wuluan is as deep as the female rower's adoration for Prince Zixi, "withers" and "dies" after the death of her love object or "Prince Charming," namely, her beloved Wuluan. After Prince Wuluan's death, the young girl Wan'er's romantic love will never be reciprocated. That is to say, Wan'er will never enjoy the same happy ending that the female rower and Prince Zixi enjoy in Zhuang Xin's story. Prince Wuluan's reaction to Wan'er's love will never be like Prince Zixi's reaction to that of the rower. The final scene of death shows the impossibility that the young girl

Wan'er's and Prince Wuluan's love story can be like that of the rower and Prince Zixi. This is probably why the weapon that kills the young girl Wan'er after Prince Wuluan's death is the *yüenü jian*, instead of some other weapon. It is also for this reason that Wan'er "dies" immediately after she sentimentally recalls Prince Wuluan's affection and love for her since childhood. Wan'er identifies herself with a helpless woman who has sacrificed too much for Prince Wuluan and his father. After sacrificing the possibility of a happy ending for her love story with Wuluan, Wan'er's life becomes blank, empty, dry, and meaningless; therefore, the young girl Wan'er spiritually dies. This is perhaps also why Tan Dun, the music director of *The Banquet*, has the song "wo yong suoyou baoda ai" (I reward my love with everything) follow Wan'er's "death." The young girl Wan'er rewards her romantic love for Prince Wuluan with everything, including her "death."

Conclusion

In *The Banquet*, Feng Xiaogang rewrites the destiny of the Chinese Hamlet's two women and William Shakespeare's two Chinese sisters: Qing Nü, who has amazing literary and performing talents, and Wan'er, whose ambition is as great as that of male politicians and Emperor Li. Qing Nü is much more talented than Ophelia. Wan'er is much more ambitious than the queen in *Hamlet*. But Qing Nü and Wan'er are more fortunate than Judith Shakespeare, whom Virginia Woolf believed to die a miserable death, because their talents and ambitions do not kill them in a Chinese context. In *The Banquet*, Shakespeare's Chinese sisters and Chinese Hamlet's two women relive their lives, which are different from those in Shakespeare's drama and Virginia Woolf's "room of her own." These are what most viewers may not immediately notice, though most of them may be aware of Feng Xiaogang's adaptation of *Hamlet* in *The Banquet*.[24]

References

Adelman, Janet. *Suffocating Mothers: Fantasies of Maternal Origin in Shakespeare's Plays, Hamlet to the Tempest*. London: Routledge, 1992.
Alexander, Peter. *Hamlet: Father and Son*. Oxford: Clarendon Press, 1955.
Banke, Cécile De. *Shakespeare Stage Production Then and Now*. London: Hutchinson, 1954.
Bate, Jonathan and Russell Jackson. *The Oxford Illustrated History of Shakespeare on Stage*. Oxford: Oxford University Press, 2001, pp. 11, 13, 102, 118, 145, 152, 153, 155.
Birrell, Anne. *New Songs from A Jade Terrace: An Anthology of Early Chinese Love Poetry*. New York: Penguin Books, 1986, p. 231.
---. *Erotic Decor: A Study of Love Imagery in the Sixth Century A. D. Anthology*. New York: S. N., 1979.

---. *The Classic of Mountains and Seas*. New York: Penguin, 1999.
Chen, Dongyuan. *Zhongguo funü shenghuo shi* (*History of Chinese Women's Life*). Shanghai: Shanghai Bookstore, 1984, p. 118.
Davison, Peter. *Hamlet: Text and Performance*. London: Macmillan, 1983, p. 44.
Donaldson, Peter S. "Oliver, Hamlet, and Freud." *Shakespeare on Film: New Casebooks*. R. Shaughnessy edt. London: Macmillan, 1998.
Draper, John W. "The Elder Hamlet and the Ghost." *The Hamlet of Shakespeare's Audience*. New York: Octagon Books, 1970, pp. 97-108.
Erlich, Avi. *Hamlet's Absent Father*. Princeton: Princeton University Press, 1977.
Fitzgerald, C. P. *The Empress Wu*. London: Cresset, 1968.
Frankel, Hans H. "The Development of Han and Wei *Yüeh-fu* as a High Literary Genre." *The Vitality of the Lyric Voice: Shih Poetry from the Late Han to the Tang*. Lin Shuen-fu and Stephen Owen edt. Princeton: Princeton University Press, 1986.
Freud, Sigmund. *The Interpretation of Dreams*. James Strachey trans. New York: Avon, 1965. p.298.
---. "Some psychopathic Characters on the Stage." *The Penguin Freud Library: Volume 14: Art and Literature*. James Strachey edt. Harmondswoth: Penguin, 1985, p. 126.
Frye, Roland Mushat. "The 'Questionable' Ghost." *The Renaissance Hamlet: Issues and Responses in 1600*. Princeton: Princeton University Press, 1984, pp. 14-29.
Goddard, Harold. "Hamlet: His Own Falstaff." *William Shakespeare's Hamlet*. Harold Bloom edt. New York: Chelsea House, 1986, pp. 11.
Gurr, Andrew. *The Shakespearian Playing Companies*. Oxford: Clarendon, 2003.
---. *The Shakespeare Stage*. Cambridge: Cambridge University Press, 1992.
---. *The Shakespeare Company, 1594-1642*. Cambridge: Cambridge University Press, 2004, pp. 48, 60, 61.
Guilford, Gwynn. "All in the Thread." *That's Beijing* (April 29, 2006): http://goo.gl/Q1LZc (online data retrieved in April 2011).
Hans H. Frankel's "The Development of Han and Wei *Yüeh-fu* as a High Literary Genre." *The Vitality of the Lyric Voice: Shih Poetry from the Late Han to the Tang*. Lin Shuen-fu and Stephen Owen edt. Princeton: Princeton University Press, 1986.
Huang, Alexander C. Y. *Chinese Shakespeares: Two Centuries of Cultural Exchange*. New York: Columbia University Press, 2008.
Hutchuel, Sarah. *Shakespeare, From Stage to Screen*. Cambridge: Cambridge University Press, 2004.
Jones, Ernest. *Hamlet and Oedipus*. New York: Norton, 1976, p. 22.
Kang, Zhengguo. *Congshen fengyüe jian— xing yü zhongguo gudian wenxue* (*Aspects of Sexuality and Literature in Ancient China*). Shenyang: Liaoning, 1998, pp. 124-127.
Kennedy, Dennis and Li Lan Young. *Shakespeare in Asia: Contemporary Performance*. Cambridge: Cambridge University Press, 2010.
Levith, Murray J. *Shakespeare in China*. London and New York: Con-tinnum, 2004.
Li, Ruru. *Shashibiya: Staging Shakespeare in China*. Hong Kong: Hong Kong University Press, 2003.
Lu, Yüan-chun. *Shuo yüan jinzhu jinyi* (*Current Annotation and Translation of Collections of Words*). Taipei: Sanmin, 1991, pp. 348-385.
Prosser, Eleanor. "Enter Ghost." *Hamlet and Revenge*. Second Edition. Stanford: Stanford University Press, 1971, pp. 101-117.
Serban, George. *The Tyranny of Magical Thinking*. New York: E. P. Dutton, 1982.

Sima, Qian. *Shi ji (Records of the Grand Historian of China)*. Original Version Published in the Han Dynasty. Shanghai: Hanyü da cidian, 2004.
Styan, J. L. *The English Stage: A History of Drama and Performance*. Cambridge: Cambridge University Press, 1996.
Sun, Lin and Shi Feng. *Yüwen yanjiu conglun (A Series of Studies on Languages and Literature)*. 7 (1997): 57-65.
Thomson, Peter. *Shakespeare's Theatre*. Second Edition. New York: Routledge, 1992.
Vardac, Nicholas. *Stage to Screen*. Cambridge: Harvard University Press, 1949.
Wei, Qingwen. "*Yüeren ge* yü zhuangyü de guangxi shiyi" (Explanations of the Relations between *A Song from Yüe* and the Language of the Zhuang Tribe). *Minzu yüwen lunji (Anthology of Critical Essays on People's Languages and Literatures)*. Beijing: Shehui kexue, 1981, p. 23-46.
---. "Shi lun baiyüe minzu de yüyan" (On the Languages of Hundreds of Tribes of the Yüe State). *Baiyüe minzushi lunji (Anthology of Essays on Hundreds of Tribes of the Yüe State)*. Beijing: Shehui kexue, 1982, pp. 276-288.
Woolf, Virginia. *A Room of One's Own*. San Diego: Harcourt Brace Jovanovich, 1989.
Wright, Elizabeth. *Psychoanalytic Criticism: A Reappraisal*. Second Edition. Cambridge: Polity Press, 1998.
Zheng, Zhang Shangfang. "Decipherment of *Yüeren ge*." *Chaiers de Linguistique Asie Orientale*. Centre de Recherches Linguistiques sur l'Asie Orientale (Paris). Vol. 2. 20. No.1, 1991, pp. 159-168.
Zhou, Feng. *Zhongguo gudai fuzhuang cankao ziliao (Reference for Clothes in Ancient China)*. Beijing: Yanshan, 1988.
Zhuo, Qiuming. *Zuozhuan (Zuo's Commentary)*. Changsha, Hunan: yüelu shushe, 2001.
---. *Guo yü*. Jinan: Qilu shushe, 2000.

Notes

1. Shakespeare's company provided four kinds of theaters: "the Globe (outside); the Blackfrairs (indoors); the Court, and on tour." For details, consult Peter Davison's *Hamlet: Text and Performance*. (London: Macmillan, 1983), 44. Also see Andrew Gurr's *The Shakespearian Playing Companies* and *The Shakespeare Stage*, Cécile De Banke's *Shakespeare Stage Production Then and Now*, Nicholas Vardac's *Stage to Screen*, Michale W. Shurgot's *Stages of Play*, Peter Thomson's *Shakespeare's Theatre*, J. L. Styan's *The English Stage*, Sarah Hatchuel's *Shakespeare, From Stage to Screen*, Richard Proudfoot's *Shakespeare: Text, Stage, and Canon*, etc. For illustrations of stages and theaters, see Jonathan Bate and Russell Jackson's *The Oxford Illustrated History of Shakespeare on Stage*. (Oxford: Oxford University Press, 2001), 11, 13, 102, 118, 145, 152, 153, 155. Also see Andrew Gurr's *The Shakespeare Company, 1594-1642*. (Cambridge: Cambridge University Press, 2004), 48, 60, 61. As for scholarly research about Shakespeare in Asia or Chinese-speaking areas, consult Dennis Kennedy and Li Lan Yong's *Shakespeare in Asia: Contemporary Performance*; Li Ruru's *Sahshibiya: Staging Shakespeare in China*; Murray J. Levith's *Shakespeare in China*; and Alexander C. Y. Huang's *Chinese Shakespeares*.

2. For recent scholars' annotation, consult Lu Yüan-chun's *Shuo yüan jinzhu jinyi* (*Current Annotation and Translation of Collections of Words*). (Taipei: Sanmin, 1991), 348-385.

3. The Chinese character *pei* may indicate the passive form. For instance, a Western linguist, Anne Birrell, translates these two lines as "Though ashamed, I am loved. Don't think of slander or disgrace. My heart will never fall, for I have known my lord" to show the passive form that the female rower uses to express her mood. In patriarchal and Confucian traditions, women are expected to show their romantic love for men in a more indirect or passive way or to take a passive role when interacting with men so men can take the initiative and active role. This is perhaps also why the words "bashful" and "ashamed" are usually included in the English translation of the lyric. For details, consult Anne Birrell's *New Songs from A Jade Terrace: An Anthology of Early Chinese Love Poetry*. (New York: Penguin Books, 1986), 231. Also see her *Erotic Decor: A Study of Love Imagery in the Sixth Century A. D. Anthology* and *The Classic of Mountains and Seas*.

4. This is the translation used for the English subtitles of the film. I respect the translator who works for Feng Xiaogang. Some other publications about the translation, annotation, or explanations of this poem: Lu Yüan-chun's *Shuo yüan jinzhu jinyi* (*Current Annotation and Translation of Collections of Words*); Wei Qingwen's "*Yüeren ge* yü zhuangyü de guangxi shiyi" (Explanations of the Relations between *A Song from Yüe* and the Language of the Zhuang Tribe) in *Minzu yüwen lunji* (*Anthology of Critical Essays on People's Languages and Literatures*) and "Shi lun baiyüe minzu de yüyan" (On the Languages of Hundreds of Tribes of the Yüe State) in *Baiyüe minzushi lunji* (*Anthology of Essays on Hundreds of Tribes of the Yüe State*); Zheng Zhang Shangfang's "Decipherment of *Yüeren ge*" in *Chaiers de Linguistique Asie Orientale*. Centre de Recherches Linguistiques sur l'Asie Orientale (Paris); Sun Lin and Shi Feng's *Yüwen yanjiu conglun* (*A Series of Studies on Languages and Literature*); Anne Birrell's *New Songs from A Jade Terrace: An Anthology of Early Chinese Love Poetry*; *Erotic Decor: A Study of Love Imagery in the Sixth Century A. D. Anthology* ; *Erotic Decor: A Study of Love Imagery in the Sixth Century A. D. Anthology*; and *The Classic of Mountains and Seas*.

5. I base my textual analysis on the filmmaker's and screenwriter's belief that the rower is female though I fully understand that some scholars, such as Zhu Xi and Anne Birrell, think that the rower is male. I am aware that other researchers share the filmmaker and screenwriter's belief. They regard the rower as a woman or a girl. Their opinion is different from Zhu Xi and Anne Birrell's. Also see my next footnote about Zhu Xi, Anne Birrell, and Kang Zhengguo.

6. Some scholars, such as Zhu Xi (1130-1120 A.D.) in the Song Dynasty (960-1127 A.D.), Anne Birrell, and Kang Zhengguo wonder whether this love poem is also a gay poem. This reminds the audience of some literary critics' doubts about whether some of Shakespeare's love poems are written for a man. The suspicion of the nonheterosexuality hidden in poems happens to be a Sino-Western parallel in the Chinese case and the Shakespearean case regardless of whether the queer readings are correct. For details, consult Anne Birrell's *New Songs from a Jade Terrace* or Kang Zhengguo's *Congshen fengyüe jian*.

7. For details, consult C. P. Fitzgerald's *The Empress Wu*. (London: Cresset, 1968).

8. It is not coincidental for *The Banquet* and *Hamlet* to share the absence of the prince's biological father. Consult the following publications: Henk de Berg's *Freud's*

Theory and Its Use in Literary and Cultural Studies. (Rochester, NY: Camden Press, 2003); Paul Rosefeldt's *The Absent Father in Modern Drama.* (New York: Peter Lang, 1995); Julia R. Lupton's *After Oedipus: Shakespeare in Psychoanalysis.* (New York: Cornell University Press, 1993); Ernest Jones's *Hamlet and Oedipus.* (New York: Norton, 1976), 22.

9. For details about the father-son discourses related to Shakespeare's *Hamlet*, also consult Peter Alexander's *Hamlet: Father and Son* and Avi Erlich's *Hamlet's Absent Father.* Following is a brief list of other publications related to the father-son complex: Stephen Greenblat's *Hamlet in Purgatory.* (Princeton: Princeton University Press, 2001); Mark Mirsky's *The Absent Shakespeare.* (Rutherford, MJ: Fairleigh Dickens University Press, 1994); Avi Erlich's *Hamlet's Absent Father.* (Princeton: Princeton University Press, 1977); Peter Alexander's *Hamlet: Father and Son.* (Oxford: Clarendon Press, 1955).

In addition, Harold Goddard mentions Shakespeare's dead son, Hamnet, who died not long before Shakespeare's enthusiasm for the Hamlet story, in "Hamlet: His Own Falstaff" in *William Shakespeare's Hamlet.* ed. Harold Bloom. (New York: Chelsea House, 1986), 11. Before Virginia Woolf imagines that William Shakespeare's sister, Judith Shakespeare, dies a miserable death in *A Room of One's Own*, William Shakespeare did have a daughter named Judith Shakespeare. She was Hamnet's twin sister. Both Judith and Hamnet were baptized on February 2, 1585. When William Shakespeare was young, he had a young female neighbor named Ophelia. She fell into a brook and drowned. Hamlet's girlfriend, Ophelia, also dies in the same way in *Hamlet*.

10. This is my translation.

11. This is Hans H. Frankel's translation. For details, consult Hans H. Frankel's "The Development of Han and Wei *Yüeh-fu* as a High Literary Genre." *The Vitality of the Lyric Voice: Shih Poetry from the Late Han to the Tang.* eds. Lin Shuen-fu and Stephen Owen. (Princeton: Princeton University Press, 1986).

12. The Tang Dynasty was established in 618 A.D., and terminated in 907 A.D.

13. Gwynn Guilford, "All in the Thread." *That's Beijing* (April 29, 2006): http://goo.gl/Q1LZc (online data accessed in April 2006).

14. http://www.helloziyi.us/Movies/night-banquet.htm (online data accessed in July 2009). The original source of this information was available at the film's official English website in May 2006.

15. Feng Zhou, *Zhongguo gudai fuzhuang cankao ziliao (Reference for Clothes in Ancient China).* (Beijing: Yanshan, 1988).

16. The spirit of Emperor Li's dead brother reminds the audience of the ghost in Shakespeare's *Hamlet*. For details, consult Eleanor Prosser's "Enter Ghost" in *Hamlet and Revenge.* Second Edition. (Stanford: Stanford University Press, 1971), 101-117. Also see Roland Mushat Frye's "The 'Questionable' Ghost" in *The Renaissance Hamlet: Issues and Responses in 1600* and John W. Draper's "The Elder Hamlet and the Ghost" in *The Hamlet of Shakespeare's Audience.*

17. It is also possible that Emperor Li is simply trying to win citizens' sympathy and forgiveness. However, he still decides to drink the wine by using the poisonous cup and then die on the laps of Empress Wan'er regardless of whether he sincerely apologizes to his dead brother and Prince Wuluan or whether he cordially wants to return his royal throne to the Crown Prince. In *The Banquet,* Emperor Li's decision to suicide saves Sigmund Freud's, Ernest Jones's, and other psychologists' analytical work on the Shakespearean Hamlet's psychological problems about his revenge. For details, consult

the following publications: Sigmund Freud's *The Interpretation of Dream* and "Some psychopathic Characters on the Stage"; Earnest Jones's *Hamlet and Oedipus*; Jacquest Lacan's "Desire and the Interpretation of Desire in *Hamlet*"; George Serban's *The Tyranny of Magical Thinking*; Peter S. Donaldson's "Olivier, Hamlet, and Freud" in *Shakespeare on Film: New Casebooks*; Elizabeth Wright's *Psychoanalytic Criticism: A Reappraisal*; Janet Adelman's *Suffocating Mothers: Fantasies of Maternal Origin in Shakespeare's Plays, Hamlet to the Tempest*.

18. Chen, Dongyuan. *Zhongguo funü shenghuo shi* (*History of Chinese Women's Life*). (Shanghai: Shanghai Bookstore, 1984), 118.

19. Consult the "Yüewang Gou Jian shijia" (The Royal Family of Gou Jian, the King of the Yüe State) in *Shi ji* (*Records of the Grand Historian of China*) by Sima Qian. Shanghai: Hanyü da cidian, 2004. Also see Zhuo Qiuming's *Zuozhuan* (*Zuo's Commentary*). (Changsha, Hunan: yüelu shushe, 2001), and his *Guo yü*. (Jinan: Qilu shushe, 2000).

20. For details, consult *Beijing Daily News* issued on June 22, 2006. This sword is now treasured in the Hubei Museum. "Yüewang Gou Jian, zi zuo yong jian," the characters engraved on the sword, clearly show that this sword was used by Gou Jian, the king of the Yüe State.

21. Xiang Yü highly respected him and called him his *yafu*, secondary father.

22 . For details, consult the seventh chapter of *Xiang Yü ben ji* (the biography of Xiang Yü) in Siman Qian's *Shiji* (*Records of the Grand Historian of China*).

23. Virginia Woolf, *A Room of One's Own*. (San Diego: Harcourt Brace Jovanovich, 1989).

24. I would like to thank Mark Eriksen and Susan Krage for their bibliographical information and search for books.

Chapter Seven
Traffic of Madwomen in the Chinese Royal Attic: Gender Concerns in *Curse of the Golden Flower*

When Zhang Yimou's *Curse of the Golden Flower* was released in December 2006, most Chinese viewers immediately recognized that this film is modeled on Cao Yü's *Thunderstorm*.[1] The queen in *Curse of the Golden Flower* is the cinematic version of Fanyi in *Thunderstorm*. The king in the film parallels Zhou Puyüan, the household head of the Zhou family, in *Thunderstorm*. Doctor Jiang, who, in the film, takes care of the king's health, mirrors Lu Qui in Cao Yü's work. The king's first wife in *Curse of the Golden Flower* is He Shiping in *Thunderstorm*. Crown Prince Han Yüanxiang in the film parallels Zhou Ping in Cao's fiction. The second prince, Han Yüanjie, in the film resembles Zhou Chong, the second son in the Zhou family in *Thunderstorm*. Finally, Jiang Chan in *Curse of the Golden Flower* is modeled on Lu Sifong in the novel. Other comparative parallels, however, may elude the audience. Tracing several of these potentially elusive parallels, I will focus on gender concerns regarding the three female protagonists in *Curse of the Golden Flower*. Specifically, I will rely on the following gender theories: Gayle Rubin's article, "traffic in women"; Betty Friedan's theoretical concept of "the problem that has no name" or "the 'no problem' problem"; Susan Gubar's and Sandra Gilbert's literary critical term, "the madwoman in the attic"; the biological theory of imprinting, and Edward Westermarck's anthropological theory of the Westermarck Effect. Furthermore, I will rely on several comparative literary intertextual links[2] in this film, including Charlotte Perkins Gilman's "The Yellow Wallpaper," Maxine Hong Kingston's "No Name Woman," Huang Chao's poetic line, "*Mancheng jindai huangjin jia*," from which the Chinese title of this film derives, and Mencius's literary work, "The Man of the Qi State Has a Wife and a Concubine," which depicts wives' or concubines' hatred of or dissatisfaction with their shared husbands as well as the mutual understanding and spiritual sisterhood resulting from ancient Chinese polygamy and gender inequality.

Traffic in Women

In *Curse of the Golden Flower*, there are three female protagonists: the queen, the king's first wife, and Jiang Chan, the daughter of Doctor Jiang and the king's first wife. I contend that all of these women are victims of what Gayle Rubin calls traffic in women.[3]

The queen is the daughter of the King of Liang—namely, the princess of Liang. The king marries her only because of royal pedigree and because her father, as the king of Liang, can help him obtain the political leadership of the state. She seems to be nothing but a tool of which he takes advantage to advance politically or exchange for his political status. The king's further political authority and his reign of the state resemble the contents of the queen's bottom drawer on her wedding day. To marry her and turn her into his queen, from the king's standpoint, is like buying a woman and winning political power as a type of dowry. This marriage is entirely a political business deal. In reality, the King does not truly marry the queen; instead, the king marries the political benefits that result from this marriage. Whether the king truly loves the queen is therefore questionable in the film; according to the queen, the king loves only his first wife.

Even the king's first wife, however, does not think that the king really loves her because he betrays and cheats on her over and over again. She had married the king when he was merely a military lieutenant under the leadership of the king of Liang. To become the ruler of the state, he betrays her, abandons her, and marries the princess of Liang. Although he always has a painting of her in his royal bedroom and claims his everlasting love for her in front of his queen, his first son, and others, he does this only to project a positive image of himself in front of his subjects and to deceive his first son and others.

The king's first wife, after being abandoned, falls severely ill and is rescued by Doctor Jiang. She marries Doctor Jiang and becomes his wife after he saves her life. Later, she sneaks into the royal palace to tell the queen what kind of poison the king had added to her hourly medicine and to request that the queen take revenge for her. Before she leaves the royal palace, however, she catches an accidental glimpse of the crown prince and spends some extra time gazing into the window of his bedroom; consequently, the guards of the palace catch her. This provides an opportunity for the king to see her again. Unfortunately, when the king reencounters his first wife, his selfishness overshadows the positive but fake image that he had maintained in the past years. Although the king tells her that he will compensate her, promote Doctor Jiang to governor, and send them from the royal palace to the area he wants Doctor Jiang to govern, he asks his people to assassinate her, Doctor Jiang, and their daughter to cover up his faults and guarantee that others will never know of his irresponsibility toward his first wife or of the dark side of his past. In the royal family's celebration of the Double Ninth Festival, the first wife bravely condemns the king and directly accuses him of lying to her over and over again.

From the king's viewpoint, both his queen and first wife are nothing but business deals allowing him to gain more power and higher political status. They are like immediately disposable objects and purchasable products that, through his abandonment of or accessibility to them, can politically benefit him. Regardless of his awareness of his objectification, and hence, degradation of these two women, he does not think that he does wrong in his "traffic in [these two] women"[4] throughout the film. He also does not take these two women's anger and revenge into consideration at all. He simply enjoys the male privilege of selfishly exchanging women with other men for his own benefit in the patriarchal society.

Even Jiang Chan is no exception. In *Curse of the Golden Flower*, Doctor Jiang knows of his daughter's romantic relation with the crown prince. He indirectly encourages her to deepen this romantic relationship to benefit the Jiang family in the royal palace. He probably hopes to marry Jiang Chan to the crown prince, turn her into the future queen when the current crown prince becomes the new king, and enable himself to be a royal father-in-law. Doctor Jiang's ideal is therefore to "sell" Jiang Chan to the crown prince in exchange for a higher political status and more royal honor for his whole family in the future. If the Queen is viewed as the object that the king "buys" from the king of Liang, then Jiang Chan is like the queen. She is also a sexy and seductive product that Doctor Jiang tries to "trade" with the crown prince for political benefits and that the crown prince hopes to "purchase" from Doctor Jiang. In this sense, Jiang Chan also amounts to nothing but a business deal between these two men. For Doctor Jiang, his daughter is only a comfort woman or female sex worker whom he sends to the crown prince, while the price that the crown prince pays for her sexual entertainment or service is a better future and political privilege of the Jiang family. Neither Doctor Jiang nor the crown prince feel that their objectification of Jiang Chan or this kind of traffic or trade in woman is wrong.

This kind of trade and traffic reminds viewers of Gayle Rubin's "The Traffic in Women." Marriages in patriarchal societies are actually like exchanges or business deals between men, who are usually the women victims' fathers, brothers, husbands, or patrons trading in women, comfort women, or even female sex workers. Sometimes, women in difficult situations, such as the king's first wife, who suffers from not only her husband's abandonment but also illness, family disasters, and poverty, reward men, who can rescue, help, love, or sympathize with them, with their bodies or marriages. Their marital lives and free sexual services become the only payments that they can afford. For example, when the king asks his first wife why she married Doctor Jiang, she angrily replies by shouting and talking back to the king, "Under those circumstances, whom do you want me to marry?" Basically, this kind of trade is similar to what Gayle Rubin means by traffic in women. Almost all the gender problems in this film originate from business deals concerning the three female protagonists: the queen, the king's first wife, and Jiang Chan.

Imprinting

In addition to the traffic in women, another gender problem in *Curse of the Golden Flower* is imprinting. I would like to use this concept to explain why the crown prince and Jiang Chan will naturally fall in love as a result of their ignorance that they share the same biological mother.

Imprinting is a joint psychological and unconscious process that a mother and her baby experience during the first eighteen months after birth. The baby unconsciously introjects or shares the mother's emotions, including pleasure, displeasure, and sexual emotions. Although the baby may have his or her own sexual emotions, he or she is unable to distinguish the mother's sexual emotions from his or her own sexual emotions. Usually, the mother's sexual emotions will be stronger than the baby's, and thus, the baby is more influenced by the mother's sexual emotions than by his or her own. Because of this circumstance, the mother's sexual feelings and attitudes become the signposts and boundaries that direct the baby's exploration of sexuality. In this way, the mother establishes the pattern by which her baby forms his or her own sexual feelings and attitudes. The baby's acceptance of the mother's pattern of sexuality will become his or her sexual feelings and attitudes. The baby's desirable mate will be those who look, sound, or act like his or her mother.

When the crown prince is a baby, he is influenced by his biological mother's sexual feelings, attitudes, and emotions more than his own. Although later, the king expels the crown prince's biological mother from their home to marry the princess of Liang, his former wife has already guided her baby son's sexual emotions and preference. She has already served as her baby son's signposts and boundaries for his future exploration of sexuality. In other words, the characteristics of the king's first wife are what the crown prince will look for when he searches for his mate.

Jiang Chan has exactly the same characteristics as the king's first wife. She has biologically inherited the characteristics of the king's first wife because she is her daughter. It is not surprising that Jiang Chan looks, sounds, acts, and behaves like the king's first wife. She resembles the king's first wife. She perhaps even unconsciously reminds the crown prince of his biological mother. Another way to explain why Jiang Chan shares the characteristics of the king's first wife is the theory of filial imprinting. Douglas Spalding (1840-1877 A.D.),[5] Oskar Heinroth (1871-1945 A.D.), and Konrad Lorenz (1903-1989 A.D.) discovered that animals, including domestic chickens, ducks, greyleg geese, and human beings, imprint on caretakers who are intimately with them during the critical period of time before and after their births. For instance, Konrad Lorenz proved that greyleg geese imprinted on him after the greyleg geese hatched and spent the critical period of time with him after they were born. This theory of imprinting can explain why babies resemble their parents and can be applied to explain why Jiang Chan imprints on her mother as well as why the crown prince falls for Jiang Chan, who has inherited his biological mother's characteristics and is thus a younger copy of his biological mother, before he knows that Jiang Chan is his biological mother's daughter.

The theory of imprinting can also explain why Jiang Chan loves the crown prince so much that she disregards her mother's disagreement with her love and runs away from home to meet with her beloved in the royal palace. The crown prince is the son of the king and his first wife. Because of filial imprinting, he resembles them and has their characterisics. Jiang Chan has introjected and accepted her mother's sexual emotions, feelings, and attitudes in her infancy. Therefore, it is not unlikely that Jiang Chan prefers the characteristics of her mother and of the man her mother had loved and married. The crown prince has the characteristics of her mother and her mother's first husband. It is thus not surprising that Jiang Chan falls in love with the crown prince before she learns that her biological mother is also the crown prince's biological mother.

The theory of imprinting explains why sons tend to unconsciously love and marry women who resemble their mothers and why daughters seem to choose men as their spouses who remind them of their fathers or their mothers' husbands. The crown prince in *Curse of the Golden Flower* is no exception. His love affair with the queen is probably because of his imprinting on his father's selection, preference, or love for this specific kind of woman, though the king believes that it results from the queen's seduction. The theory of imprinting seems to offer an additional explanation that is more scientific and more convincing than the king's belief, because it also explains why the crown prince does not make a stronger effort to reject the queen and why he cannot resist the queen's seduction, especially when he, as an adult, absolutely knows that it is immoral and illegal to violate the incest taboo.

Moreover, the theory of imprinting may explain why Jiang Chan immediately replaces the queen and turns out to be the crown prince's true beloved woman right after she meets him, gets to know him, and interacts with him and before she realizes that they share the same biological mother. Although the crown prince's imprinting of his father may have caused his preference for the kind of woman that his father chooses to be with—and, thus, his agreement about, or at least his lack of rejection of, the romantic relationship with the queen—Jiang Chan shares even more characteristics with his parents— especially his biological mother, whom the crown prince's father had also selected as his spouse. Specifically, Jiang Chan resembles his biological mother, but the queen does not. Imprinting, hence, offers a scientific and reasonable explanation for why Jiang Chan replaces the queen and wins more romantic love from the crown prince and why the queen cannot win the crown prince back from Jiang Chan except through announcing that Jiang Chan and the crown prince share the same biological mother and have committed the crime of incest.

Although the theory of imprinting seems to indirectly suggest the possibility of familial incest, which also resonates in Freudians' belief that members of the same family—especially Oedipal sons' love for their mothers and daughters' Electra Complexes, or love for their fathers—tend to sexually love each other, Edward Westermark (1862-1939 A.D.) argues the reverse. The theory of the Westermarck Effect explains that siblings' shared living experiences in childhood in the same family invalidates their sexual attraction to one another.[6] Together with the incest taboo, the Westermarck Effect explains why the crown prince points to their nominal mother-son relationship and shared living experience in the same family to refuse the queen's request to resume their broken romantic relationship and why the queen says that she is not his mother when she tries to win him back. In addition, the Westermarck Effect helps explain why the Freudian theory of the sexual attraction between or among siblings is not invalid in the case of the crown prince and his half sister, Jiang Chan—namely, the lack of shared living experience since childhood in the same family environment.

"No Problem" Problem: Women's Problems That Have No Name

Except for the second prince's sympathy for the queen, whom the king is slowly poisoning, men in this film rarely understand the three female protagonists, seldom take their predicaments into serious consideration, and never really make any effort to solve these women's gender problems. For instance, the King does not care about how his first wife feels when he abandons her; he also does not care about how the queen feels about his indifference to her. The crown prince does not care about how the queen feels after he initiates his physical contacts with Jiang Chan; nor does he attempt to comfort Jiang Chan after the queen reveals the shocking truth that Jiang Chan and he share the same biological mother. The third prince does not solve any gender problems and focuses only on his power struggles to succeed to the royal throne. These selfish men are so indifferent to women's predicaments and gender problems that it is as if these women's gender problems had no name and were thus "no problem" problems.

The fact that both the queen and the king's first wife are not given names indicates how little they concern the self-centered and chauvinist male dominators, especially the king, in the film. This offers a comparative parallel to the feminist concept that Betty Friedan (1921-2006 A.D.) calls "the problem that has no name" or "the 'no problem' problem" for chauvinists in patriarchal societies. In *Feminine Mystique*, Betty Friedan thinks that American women's inability to grow to their full human capacities takes a far greater toll on the physical and mental health of their country than any known disease. She underscores chauvinists' ignorance of or indifference to women's lack of possibilities to fully develop their capacities, emphasizes how the ignorance and indifference worsen this gender problem and turn it into the problem that has no name, and names this kind of women's gender problem a "'no problem' problem":

> The problem lay buried, unspoken for many years in the minds of . . . women. It was a strange stirring, a sense of dissatisfaction, a yearning that women suffered . . . . Each suburban housewife struggled with it alone. As she made the beds, shopped for groceries, matched slipcover material, ate . . . with her children . . . lay beside her husband at night, she was afraid to ask even of herself the silent question: Is this all?[7]

Although Betty Friedan blames men for their ignorance and misinterpretation of this problem as "no problem," she sympathizes with them because they also suffer from this "'no problem' problem" together with women. As Friedan writes, "Man is not the enemy here, but the fellow victim." Friedan's statement also holds true for men in *Curse of the Golden Flower*. For example, the king in this film loses all his family members and suffers from the psychological hurt caused by the queen's adultery, the two kinds of incest between the queen and the crown prince and between the crown prince and his half-sister, family disasters, his youngest son's assassination of the crown prince and his intention to overthrow him, his second son's suicide, and later on the death of his third son because of his ignorance of and indifference to his first wife's and his queen's gender concerns, his misinterpretation of these two women's gender "problems that have no name," and his minimizing of their gender problems as no problem. The crown prince suffers from the same psychological hurt because of his indifference to the queen's hatred for the king and him—the two men who do not give her the spiritual warmth that she desires. Doctor Jiang loses his life because of his encouragement of Jiang Chan to advance the romantic relationship with the crown prince and his unconscious attempt to marry or trade his daughter into the royal family. Even though the second prince, Han Yüanjie, realizes his mother's gender problems because of the king's plan to poison her, he also suffers because he fails to rescue his mother and free her from her gender problems. Similar can be said concerning the case of the youngest prince. He also comprehends the queen's gender problems and her relationship with the crown prince, but he simply takes advantage of these gender problems that have no name and uses them as tools for him to become the next king. Therefore, just as Betty Friedan argues in *Feminine Mystique*, then, men also suffer from the problems women suffer from. The king, the crown prince, the second prince, the youngest prince, and Doctor Jiang suffer and are indeed fellow victims in *Curse of the Golden Flower*, though the king seems to be the enemy that his first wife and the queen share. Although chauvinists may still cruelly regard women's gender problems as "no problem" problems in this film, these men's suffering is the best proof that women's gender problems are true problems, not "no problem" problems.

No Name Women

The fact that the queen and the king's first wife have no name in *Curse of the Golden Flower* also signifies the king's lack of understanding of his two women, his intentional decision to ignore or be indifferent to the concerns of these two women, or even his deliberate hostility toward and severe punishment of them. These two women's lack of names may remind the audience of the "no name woman" in Maxine Hong Kingston's *The Woman Warrior*. In this story, Kingston's aunt has no name and is thus forever expunged because of her extramarital affair after her husband travels to America. This is considered a kind of communal retribution for and familial hostility toward the "no name woman."[8]

In *Curse of the Golden Flower*, nobody mentions the queen's name. The queen is like a no-name woman. The royal family's collective removal of the queen's name is similar to the Kingston family's collaborative erasure of the aunt's name, especially when both the queen in the film and the no-name woman in the Kingston family commit adultery. As a matter of fact, the king's pressure and all the princes' requests indirectly compel the queen to drink all the poison in her cup; this fact parallels the villagers' and the family's cooperative pressure that indirectly forces the no-name woman to commit suicide by jumping into the family's well and thus disappearing from the family tree or family history.

The other no-name woman in *Curse of the Golden Flower* is the king's first wife. From the beginning to the end of the film, nobody mentions her name, making her another a no-name woman. Just like the no-name woman in the Kingston family, she happens to be also the woman who has sex with two different men and has children with different men. In the ancient Chinese patriarchal tradition, a woman was supposed to stick to only one man for her entire life and should not have sexual relationships with different men. It is therefore possible that this film's refusal to give her a name is no coincidence. It probably indicates a punishment similar to that of the no-name woman thus constituting an allegorical or metaphorical way to show the patriarchal intention of eliminating the no-name woman from the family history. This is perhaps also why the king aims to kill his first wife and delete the existence of her—and everybody related to her—from his royal family history and records of his own past.

The Yellow Wallpaper

In Kingston's "No Name Woman," the communal pressure causing this no-name woman to jump into the family well and commit suicide is the way by which the villagers indirectly put her to death. In *Curse of the Golden Flower*, however, the king's deliberate erroneous diagnoses of his two wives are his way of indirectly putting them to death. For instance, the king lies to his son, his second wife, and others by telling them that his first wife is already dead. Unaware of his first wife's survival, the king makes an erroneous diagnosis by declaring that she had died. The queen's so-called anemia is also the king's deliberate erroneous diagnosis. It serves as an excuse for the king to add poisonous fungus to the queen's hourly medicine to gradually cause her mental retardation or even insanity. In the final family meeting on the chrysanthemum terrace, the queen clearly refutes the King's assertion about her disease; she insists that she is healthy and refuses the medication that the king gives to her.

The king's incorrect treatment for the queen in *Curse of the Golden Flower* may remind the audience of Charlotte Perkins Gilman's "The Yellow Wallpaper,"[9] which is a story of how a physician husband's erroneous diagnosis of and mistaken remedy for his wife's postpartum depression drive his wife crazy. In *Curse of the Golden Flower* and "The Yellow Wallpaper," both of these two husbands claim that they are confident in their medical and pharmaceutical knowledge. Their diagnoses of and treatments for their wives' "illnesses" are both erroneous because they both exacerbate their wives' mental retardation or insanity. Both of these two husbands are their wives' largest obstacles as the female protagonist in "The Yellow Wallpaper" says: "I am getting angry enough to do something desperate."[10]

The Madwoman in the Royal Attic

In addition to the deletion of names and the intentional erroneous diagnoses in *Curse of the Golden Flower*, the males' refusal to understand their women or the meaning of their existence results in the claim that the women are mad. By determining that someone is mad, one does not make any efforts to understand this person, rejects any attempts to make sense of this person's thoughts and behaviors, and thus quarantines this person from the ordinary world, emotionally crucifying this person, and mentally assassinating this person.

In *Curse of the Golden Flower*, the queen is considered mad. Both the crown prince and the king allege that the queen is a madwoman. Their assertion shows that they will not make any more efforts to justify, figure out, or understand the meaning of the queen's predicaments, gender problems, thoughts, decisions, reprisals, and actions. Their assumption blackens the queen's name and discredits her. Their declaration separates and quarantines the queen from ordinary people and the ordinary world. Their misleading conclusion of the so-called madness indirectly sentences the queen to the lunatic asylum, locating and locking her in the madhouse. It negates the meaning of the queen's existence, and the meaninglessness of her existence equates to their emotional crucifixion and mental assassination of her. Their verbal accusation of the queen's madness spiritually sentences her to death, while the poison in the hourly medicine physically damages her body.

The queen's so-called madness in the film may remind viewers of Sandra Gilbert's and Susan Gubar's feminist literary critical term, "the madwoman in the attic."[11] Because the feminist theory of the madwoman in the attic derives from Charlotte Brontë's *Jane Eyre* and Jean Rhys's *Wide Sargasso Sea*, there are also intertextual connections among *Curse of the Golden Flower*, *Jane Eyre*, and *Wide Sargasso Sea*, especially when these three works address the madwomen in their storylines.

In *Jane Eyre*, Bertha, the woman who does not receive any spiritual warmth, understanding, or sympathy, is labeled as a madwoman and locked in the attic by her husband and other male or patriarchal dominators[12]; however, she is given no opportunity to speak for herself in the book. Readers have no other option but to believe her husband's conclusion about her madness. The problem caused by the muted woman in *Jane Eyre* is remedied by Jean Rhys.

In *Wide Sargasso Sea*, readers can finally know the life story of Bertha, the name her husband, Rochester, gives to Antoinette Cosway. Bertha, her husband, and other people offer readers an (auto)biographical narration of what happened, ranging from her childhood to her adulthood and the end of her life.[13]

Similarly, in *Curse of the Golden Flower*, the queen is given opportunities to tell her life story, express her irritation, and explain her reasons and motivations to plan the coup with her favorite son's cooperation. Even though the king's first wife is not denigrated as a madwoman, she is provided with opportunities for autobiographical narration to explain what happens to her after the king abandoned her, release her rage, and justify her decisions to remarry and expose the impossibility of the romantic relationship between her daughter and the crown prince.

In *Curse of the Golden Flower*, the queen's irritation and the rage of the king's first wife serve as an intertextual link between this film, *Jane Eyre*, *Wide Sargasso Sea*, and the feminist critical idea of the madwoman in the attic. Bertha in *Jane Eyre*, Antoinette in *Wide Sargasso Sea*, and the queen in *Curse of the Golden Flower* are all angry women. They are all madwomen because they are all mad at or furious with their husbands. The word "mad" has two meanings here—it denotes anger as well as insanity. Susan Gubar and Sandra Gilbert recover this pun, "mad," out of the attic, a reference to Bertha's upstairs madhouse in *Jane Eyre*, and outline feminist justifications of women's unhappiness, dissatisfaction, frustration, and dander for these victims in patriarchal societies. Antoinette in *Wide Sargasso Sea* and the king's two wives in *Curse of the Golden Flower* share Bertha's ire. They are all what Sandra Gilbert and Susan Gubar call "madwomen."

Mencius's "The Man of the Qi State Has a Wife and a Concubine"

In *Curse of the Golden Flower*, the king's two wives share the same hatred for the king. Although the king's two wives may compete for the same man's love, become enemies of love, and feel jealous of each other, there is a special kind of mutual understanding, emotional alliance, or even spiritual sisterhood between them because of their shared animosity for the king. For example, the queen's people protect the king's first wife when the king's people kill Doctor Jiang. After the king's first wife runs into Jiang Chan in the royal palace and tells her that the king wants to kill their whole family, the queen sends a eunuch to keep them safe. Except for the queen, nobody in the film helps or protects the king's first wife. If the queen had not sent her people and the eunuch to rescue the king's first wife, she would have already been dead. Throughout the film, the queen is the only person who completely understands how much the king hurts his first wife, how keenly the king's first wife desires to take revenge on the king, and how similar the king's plan to poison her is to his abandonment of his first wife.

While the queen is the only person to give a hand to the king's first wife, the king's first wife is also the only person to secretly tell the queen about the king's plan to poison her. The king adds poison to the queen's hourly medicine to mentally put the Queen to "death" and abandon her. This is the same goal that the king had pursued concerning his first wife: abandoning her and wanting her death. It is because of the parallel between the king's relationships with the two women that the king's first wife is the only person who understands the danger for the queen; she thus reveals the king's secret attempt to poison the queen and warns the queen of her forthcoming mental retardation or insanity. Except for the king's first wife, nobody in the film discloses anything about this poison. If the king's first wife were not friendly enough to tell the queen about the poison and about her own intention of taking revenge, the queen would have remained ignorant of what is happening around her, what has been added to the medicine she is taking hourly, why the king insists that she must finish every drop of this medicine, and how this medicine will cause her to become mentally retarded or insane in a few days.

Women's shared anger at or hatred for the same men was not unusual in ancient polygamous China, especially when two or more women shared the same husband and suffered from the same or similar psychological hurt in interactions with their husband. For instance, Mencius (372-289 B.C.) wrote a story about a man of the Qi State who has a wife and a concubine:

> The man of the Qi State has a wife and a concubine living in the same household with him. Whenver the husband leaves home, he eats meat, drinks wine, and enjoys good meals. When his wife asks him who eats and drinks with him, he always tells her that he shares his meals with billionaires and powerful people. The wife talks with the concubine, "Our husband never returns without eating meat, drinking wine, and enjoying good meals whenever he leaves home. Whenever he is asked about who eats and drinks with him, he answers that he dines with wealthy people or people of an extremely high social status. However, no important visitors have ever come to our home. I will follow him and go where he goes in order to see what happens." The next morning, the wife gets up early, follows her husband, and goes where he goes. But nobody converses with her husband while he traverses almost the whole city. Finally, her husband reaches people who clean their ancestors' graveyards in the eastern suburbs of the city. He begs for the rest of the food and wine that they use to honor their ancestors in front of the tombs. If the food is not enough, he looks elsewhere, goes to other graveyards, and begs other people for more food and wine. This is how he eats meat, drinks wine, and enjoys good meals before returning home. The wife goes back home and tells the concubine, "Our husband is the person on whom we both rely until the end of our lives. Now, see what kind of person he is!" The wife and the concubine condemn their husband, hug each other, and cry in their yard. Their husband does not realize that they have discovered what he does in the graveyards and proudly boasts about his supposedly good connections with the rich and powerful in front of them after returning home. From the righteous gentleman's point of view, few wives and concubines of men who beg for more wealth, authority, and power, would not weep out of shame for their husbands' behaviors.[14]

Although a frequently used phrase, *qiren zhi fu* (men who have two spouses or double sexual pleasure), in Chinese language originates from this story writtten by Mencius and his disciples, I highlight this story because it also explains why and how the wife and the concubine can engage in and share the same displeasure with their shared husband. It supports my argument that women who shared the same husband in polygamous China experienced the same or similar anger in their interactions with their husband which allowed them to establish mutual understanding, emotional coalitions, and even spiritual sisterhood; nevertheless, Mencius's work and my argument do not preclude the possibility that wives and concubines who share the same husband might still be jealous of each other because of the polygamous system which rests on women's inequality. Furthermore, this story also suggests why and how the king's first wife and the queen in *Curse of the Golden Flower* help each other, understand each other, and unite to fight against the king.

This spiritual sisterhood, resulting from women's shared psychological hurts in patriarchal societies and shared goals in their fight against oppressive husbands, closely resembles the spiritual sisterhood among current feminists; namely, the feminists' spiritual sisterhood also results from women's shared experience in patriarchal societies and their shared aim to counteract and end chauvinism as much as possible. Importantly, this spiritual sisterhood is perhaps what Bertha in *Jane Eyre*, Antoinette in *Wide Sargasso Sea*, the nameless female protagonist in "The Yellow Wallpaper," the king's two nameless wives in *Curse of the Golden Flower*, and the wife and concubine in "The Man of the Qi State Has a Wife and a Concubine" share across cultural, chronical, and linguistic borders. It provides a strong feminist intertextual bond that tightly coalesces all the above-mentioned women, who are victims of their husbands' psychological hurt and emotional crucifixion.

Huang Chao's Coup to Overthrow Emperor Xi of the Tang Dynasty

In *Curse of the Golden Flower*, the queen plans to take revenge by staging a coup to overthrow the king and replace the king with the second prince. The queen's embroidery of the golden blossoms of chrysanthumums signifies her coup. This representative totem of golden flowers relates the queen in this film to Huang Chao (?-884 A.D.); specifically, one of Huang Chao's poems about chrysanthemum blossoms reveals his intentional use of these blossoms as a representative totem of his coup to overthrow the Emperor Xi (lived 862-888 A.D.; reigned 873-888 A.D.) of the Tang Dynasty. In fact, the Chinese title of *Curse of the Golden Flower* is *Mancheng jin dai huangjin jia*, which is a direct quote from the following poem written by Huang Chao.

> Daidao qiulai jiu yüe ba
> Wohua kai hou baihua sha
> Chongtian xiangzhen tou Changan
> Mancheng jin dai huangjin jia

> When the autumn comes after the eighth day of the ninth month [the day of the Double Ninth Festival in the Chinese lunar calendar],
> My [golden chrysanthemum] blossoms will outshine and defeat [the beauty of] all the other hundreds of flowers.
> The fragrance, which is strong enough to reach the heavens, is like the battle array to permeate or conquer all of [the capital City of] Changan.
> At that time, people in all of [the capital] city [of Changan] will be wearing golden [chrysanthemum blossoms that are like golden] suits of armor.[15]

Huang Chao was a man of letters, but he repeatedly failed in nationwide exams and became dissatisfied and angry with the central government and the emperor. From 875 to 881 A.D., Huang Chao joined peasants' riots against the government and led his own army troops to occupy Shandong, Henan, Guangzhou, Lingnan, and the capital city of Changan. He called himself *Chongtian jianjün* (the Heaven-Reaching General) and proclaimed his political reign Da Qi. The title that he bestows upon himself, *Chongtian*, signifies his intention to stage an ambitious coup to overthrow the emperor, defeat the Tang central government, and conquer the capital city of Changan; he demonstrates this intention in the poem about the golden chrysanthemum blossoms because the phrase, *chongtian*, appears in the third lyric line of his poem and refers to the fragrance of the golden chrysanthemum blossoms, which is strong enough to reach the heavens.

In 884 A.D., Huang Chao and his troops were defeated by the army that fought to resume the political reign of Emperor Xi of the Tang Dynasty. Some historians claim that Huang Chao committed suicide, while other historians suggest that he was killed by his staff officer, Lin Yan. In *Curse of the Golden Flower*, the failed coup of the queen and her favorite son parallels Huang Chao's unsuccessful coup, a parallel that also exists on a symbolic level. In both the movie and Huang Chao's poem, golden chrysanthemums are emblematic of the coup. Moreover, the suicide of the second prince, Yüanjie, and the impending death of the queen caused by the king's poison added to her hourly medicine immediately following the failed coup parallel Huang Chao's death directly after his futile attempt to overthrow the emperor.

Women's Ambitions and Careers in the Late Tang

Although Huang Chao and the queen fail in their attempts to seize power, it is obvious that the queen's ambition in *Curse of the Golden Flower* is modeled on that of Huang Chao in the Tang Dynasty (618-907 A.D.). Despite the futile nature of their respective revolts, the film text of *Curse of the Golden Flower* affirms that women are as ambitious and politically skillful in initiating their political careers by staging coups as men are. In the imaginary world of *Curse of the Golden Flower*, women enter politics as actively as men. Even Jiang Chan and her mother, the king's first wife, are people of abilities, equaling those of men in their workplaces. Jiang Chan is also a certified pharmacist and thus a career woman. Her mother possesses professional pharmaceutical knowledge, too. In addition, she is courageous enough to disclose the king's attempt to poison the queen. The king's first wife is even more courageous than men because Doctor Jiang, who also knows about the king's plan, lacks the necessary courage to defy the king and righteously alert the queen to the poison.

One of the historical models for these three ambitious and professional female protagonists is the Tang Dynasty. It is one of the most feminist dynasties in the history of imperial China. It is also a dynasty in which a queen, Wu Zetian (624-705 A.D.), successfully replaced the original crown princes and emperors with people she preferred. Wu Zetian even proclaimed herself the female ruler of China and named her reign Da Zhou. The queen in *Curse of the Golden Flower*, therefore, resembles Wu Zetian because they both have the political ambition to replace the king with their favorite candidates for the new king. Deviating from the historical model, however, the queen in the film fails to achieve her goals.

Generally speaking, women in the Tang dynasty were given more freedom and rights than women in other dynasties,[16] though gender inequality continued to exist and gender problems began to worsen in the late Tang Dynasty. For instance, in *Curse of the Golden Flower*, almost every woman feels free to expose her body, including her breast line.[17] The king's first wife can marry another man after the king abandons her because of the Tang people's open-mindedness and the Tang government's lack of emphasis on women's chastity and virginity.[18] Jiang Chan and her mother can put on sportswear, ride horses, defeat male knights whose kung fu is worse than theirs, move around freely, do what they desire to do, and select the men they truly love, because that is what most women in the Tang Dynasty did.[19]

Conclusion

Because almost all the Chinese viewers can easily recognize that *Curse of the Golden Flower* mirrors Cao Yü's *Thunderstorm*, I refrain from discussing the intertextual explorations between these two texts in this space. Instead, I have pointed out gender problems in the film from different theoretical perspectives, focusing on traffic in women, filial and sexual imprinting, the Westermarck Effect, "the madwoman in the attic," and "the problem that has no name." I also comparatively read the film text of *Curse of the Golden Flower* and other literary texts, including "The Yellow Wallpaper," *Jane Eyre*, *Wide Sargasso Sea*, "No Name Woman," Huang Chao's poem about chrysanthemum blossoms, and Mencius's "The Man of the Qi State Has a Wife and a Concubine." Regardless of the three female protagonists' gender problems in the patriarchal society and their deaths at the end of *Curse of the Golden Flower*, they are ambitious and professional women whose versatile abilities equal those of the men in the film. The imaginary martial arts world of *Curse of the Golden Flower* is still a "room of [these women's] own,"[20] which allows these three female protagonists to be as ambitious and professional as men, though "'no problem' problems" resulting from patriarchal husbands' or chauvinists' ignorance of gender egalitarianism continue to exist.

References

Brontë, Charlotte. *Jane Eyre*. New York: Norton, 2001.
Cao, Yü. *Lei yü* (*Thunderstorm*). Wang Zuoliang and Barnes trans. Beijing: Foreign Language Press, 2003.
Chen, Dongyuan. *Zhongguo funü shenghuo shi* (*History of Chinese Women's Life*). Shanghai: Shanghai Bookstore, 1984, p. 118.
Culler, Jonathan. *The Pursuit of Signs—Semiotics, Literature, Deconstruction*. Ithaca, New York: Cornell University Press, 1981, p. 105.
Friedan, Betty. *The Feminine Mystique*. NY: Dell, 1974, p. 50.
Gilbert, Sandra and Susan Gubar. *The Madwoman in the Attic: The Woman Writer and the Nineteenth-Century Literary Imagination*. New Haven: Yale University Press, 2000.
Gilman, Charlotte Perkins. *The Yellow Wallpaper and Other Writings*. New York: Modern Library, 2000.
Kingston, Maxine Hong. "No Name Woman." *The Woman Warrior: China Men*. New York: Everyman's Library, 2005, pp. 1-16.
Kristeva, Julia. *Desire in Language: A Semiotic Approach to Literature and Art*. New York: Columbia University Press, 1980, p. 13.
Mencius. *The Book of Mencius*. Lionel Giles trans. J. L. Cranmer-Byng edt. London: Butler & Tanner, 1949, pp. 79-80.
---. D. C. Lau trans. London: Penguin Books, 2004, pp. 97-80.
Rubin, Gayle. "The Traffic in Women." *Toward an Anthropology of Women*. Rayna R. Reiter edt. New York: Monthly Review, 1975. pp. 157-210.
Spalding, Douglas A. "Instinct: With Original Observations on Young Animals." *Macmillan's Magazine* 27 (1837): 282-297.
---. "On Instinct." *Nature* 6 (1972): 485-486.
Wang, Xiaoxin. *Ciyü yüanliu manbi* (*Scripts on the Origins of Words and Phrases*). Guangzhou: Guangdong Education, 1990, p. 75.
Westermarck, Edward Alexander. *The History of Human Marriage*, 5th edn. London: Macmillan, 1921.
---. *Marriage Ceremonies in Morocco* (microfilm). Woodbridge, Conn.: Research Publications, 1977. Also consult Edward Westermarck's *The History of Human Marriage* (microfilm). Woodbridge, Conn.: Research Publications, 1977.
Woolf, Virginia. *A Room of One's Own*. New York: Harcourt, Brace, and Company, 1929.
Xü, Shiyi. "Explanations on Some Words in History about the Han, Wei, Jin, Northern and Southern Dynasties." *Journal of Nanyang Normal University* 5.7 (2006): 32-38.
Zhou, Feng. *Zhongguo gudai fuzhuang cankao ziliao* (*Reference for Clothes in Ancient China*). Beijing: Yanshan, 1988.

Notes

1. Cao, Yü. *Lei yü* (*Thunderstorm*). trans. Wang Zuoliang and Barnes. (Beijing: Foreign Language Press, 2003).
2. With reference to intertextuality, Julia Kristeva mentions two axes: first, a horizontal axis that links the author and reader of a text; second, a vertical axis that relates the text to other texts. For details, consult Julia Kristeva's *Desire in Language: A Semiotic Approach to Literature and Art*. (New York: Columbia University Press, 1980), 13. Also consult Jonathan Culler's citation of Kristeva: "Every text is from the outset under the jurisdiction of other discourses which impose a universe on it." For details, see Jonathan Culler's *The Pursuit of Signs—Semiotics, Literature, Deconstruction*. (Ithaca, New York: Cornell University Press, 1981), 105.
3. Gayle Rubin, "The Traffic in Women" in *Toward an Anthropology of Women*. ed. Rayna R. Reiter. (New York: Monthly Review, 1975), 157-210.
4. See my footnote about Gayle Rubin's article about the traffic in women.
5. Douglas A. Spalding, "Instinct: With Original Observations on Young Animals" in *Macmillan's Magazine* 27 (1837): 282-297. Also consult his "On Instinct" in *Nature* 6 (1972): 485-486.
6. Edward Alexander Westermarck, *The History of Human Marriage*, 5th ed. (London: Macmillan, 1921).
---. *Marriage Ceremonies in Morocco* (microfilm). Woodbridge, Conn.: Research Publications, 1977. Also consult Edward Westermarck's *The History of Human Marriage* (microfilm). (Woodbridge, Conn.: Research Publications, 1977).
7. Betty Friedan, *The Feminine Mystique*. (New York: Dell, 1974), 50.
8. Maxine Hong Kingston, "No Name Woman" in *The Woman Warrior: China Men*. (New York: Everyman's Library, 2005), 1-16.
9. Charlotte Perkins Gilman, *The Yellow Wallpaper and Other Writings*. (New York: Modern Library, 2000).
10. Charlotte Perkins Gilman, *The Yellow Wallpepr and Other Writings*. (New York: Modern Library, 2000), 19.
11. Sandra Gilbert and Susan Gubar, *The Madwoman in the Attic: The Woman Writer and the Nineteenth-Century Literary Imagination*. (New Haven: Yale University Press, 2000).
12. Charlotte Brontë, *Jane Eyre*. (New York: Norton, 2001).
13. Antoinette's biological father is a white master of black slaves but dies after the legislative release of slaves. Her mother, Annette, marries Mr. Mason and becomes insane after her brother, Pierre, dies in a conflagration during Annette's honeymoon trip. Mr. Mason and his son, Richard Mason, marry Antoinette to Rochester. Rochester thinks that Antoinette gradually goes insane after their honeymoon. According to him, she has violent quarrels with him and screams to stop him from calling her Bertha. Later on, Rochester locks Antoinette in an upstairs room under the watch of a servant. After repetitvely dreaming that she leaves the locked room, carries a candle to explore the downstairs quarters of Rochester's house, and burns the whole house, Antoinette decides to put this dream into practice. She is carrying her candle and walking downstairs from her upstairs madhouse at the end of Jean Rhys's *Wide Sargasso Sea*.

14. This is my English translation. Lionel Giles's English translation of this story is available in *The Book of Mencius*. ed. J. L. Cranmer-Byng. (London: Butler & Tanner, 1949), 79-80. D. C. Lau's translation is included in *The Book of Mencius*. (London: Penguin Books, 2004), 97-98. The original Chinese text comes from the thirty-third chapter of the second volume of Mencius's *Li lou (Sagaciousness)*. As for the translation of what *Li lou* means, consult Wang Xiaoxin's *Ciyü yüanliu manbi (Scripts on the Origins of Words and Phrases)*. (Guangzhou: Guangdong Education, 1990), 75. Also see Xü Shiyi's "Explanations on Some Words in History about the Han, Wei, Jin, Northern and Southern Dynasties." *Journal of Nanyang Normal University* 5.7 (2006): 32-38.

15. This is my English translation of Huang Chao's Chinese poem. The words in the parentheses are my explanations to facilitate readers' comprehension of the poetic lines.

16. For more details, consult my critical analysis of women in the Tang Dynasty in *House of Flying Daggers*.

17. Feng Zhou, *Zhongguo gudai fuzhuang cankao ziliao (Reference for Clothes in Ancient China)*. (Beijing: Yanshan, 1988).

18. It is a pity that the name of the king's first wife is so unclear that audience members can barely vividly remember her name. In this sense, she is as nameless as the no-name woman in Kingston's story though she does marry twice.

19. Dongyuan Chen, *Zhongguo funü shenghuo shi (History of Chinese Women's Life)*. (Shanghai: Shanghai Bookstore, 1984), 118.

20. Virginia Woolf, *A Room of One's Own*. (New York: Harcourt, Brace, and Company, 1929).

PART 2

INTEGRATED ANALYSES ABOUT THE LIMITATION OF FEMINIST EMANCIPATION

Chapter Eight
Let's Make a Wish: Women's Wishes under the Cinematic Pen(is) from *A Touch of Zen* to *Crouching Tiger Hidden Dragon*, *Hero*, *House of Flying Daggers*, and *The Promise*

Ang Lee's *Crouching Tiger Hidden Dragon* amazes viewers and recalls worldwide audience's attention to Chinese martial arts films that it had not had since King Hu's award-winning film, *A Touch of Zen*. However, the ending of this film perplexes viewers (see my survey of viewers' feedback in Appendix 9-0).

Luo Xiaohu:	We have a legend. Anyone who dares to jump from the mountain, God will grant his wish. Long [time] ago, a young man's parents were ill. So he jumped. He didn't die. He wasn't even hurt. He floated away, far away, never to return. He knows his wish had come true. If you believe, it will happen. The elders say, "A faithful heart makes wishes come true"...
Yü Jiaolong:	Do you remember the legend of the young man?
Luo Xiaohu:	"A faithful heart makes wishes come true."
Yü Jiaolong:	Make a wish.
Luo Xiaohu:	To go back to Xinjiang together.

(Yü Jiaolong jumps into the abyss right after Luo Xiaohu's wish.)

If the ill parents in the legend truly recover after the son jumps into the abyss, why does Luo Xiaohu not ask his dear girlfriend to make her wish, leap into the abyss, and make her wish come true? Why does Luo Xiaohu not sacrifice himself to realize Yü Jiaolong's wish? Why should the person who jumps into the abyss be Yü Jiaolong and not her boyfriend? Why does Luo Xiaohu's wish to go home deserve Yü Jiaolong's risk of losing her life and leap into the abyss?

Luo Xiaohu and Yü Jiaolong have entirely opposite wishes about their homes. Luo Xiaohu wants to return to his home, yet Yü Jiaolong makes efforts to leave her home. Luo Xiaohu persuades Yü Jiaolong to return to her home even though he knows that her wish is to leave her home.

Luo Xiaohu:	Your father's men are looking for you. They're still out there, circling closer.
Yü Jiaolong:	Let them look.
Luo Xiaohu:	It is trouble for me.
Yü Jiaolong:	Don't send me back.
Luo Xiaohu:	You must decide. You might get tired of this life. You might begin to miss your family. If it were our daughter, we'd look for her, too. She would miss us.

But Yü Jiaolong jumps into the abyss to fulfill Luo Xiaohu's dream to return his home. Why is Yü Jiaolong's wish less significant than Luo Xiaohu's wish when their wishes about their homes are contradictory? Why do Luo Xiaohu and Yü Jiaolong not both leap into the abyss to double the possibility for God to grant the wish of their return to Xinjiang together? Why should the film be concluded with Yü Jiaolong's sacrifice, instead of Luo Xiaohu's sacrifice? Does it make sense for Yü Jiaolong to sacrifice herself so selflessly after she keenly desires liberation, freedom, selfhood, and autonomy? If Yü Jiaolong were not a character in the film text but a truly living woman who had the power to make her own wish, would she really wish for what Luo Xiaohu wishes so much that she would volunteer to immediately risk her own life for his wish?

In addition to the end of *Crouching Tiger Hidden Dragon*, a number of wishes made by women in Chinese martial arts films of the new millennium are equally perplexing: first, in *A Touch of Zen*, Yang Huizhen's wish to discard morality, have premarital sex, become pregnant, give birth to Gu Shengzhai's child, and turn herself into a free birth machine for the Gu family without any marital relation with Gu Shengzhai for no other reason than to make the wish of Gu Shengzhai's mother come true; second, in *Hero*, Moon's suicidal wish to sacrifice her life to revenge Broken Sword's death after his sexual irresponsibility; third, in *House of Flying Daggers*, Xiaomei's suicidal decision to pull out the dagger from her chest to rescue Jin. Even in *The Promise*, Qingcheng, who does not die for a man, ends up being only a dependent, heavily relying on Kunlun's running skills, help, and love. Why do these women in film texts share the same—or at least similar—sacrifice of themselves for men, suicidal decision making for men, subordination to men, or reliance on salvation by men, which may repetitively imply female inferiority and male superiority? Why is the ratio of women's sacrifice of themselves, suicide for men, or subordination to men so eye-catching in these films? Do these women truly volunteer or keenly desire to be so self-sacrificial, selfless, suicidal, subordinate, dependent, and inferior?

In other words, what puzzles viewers is the women's sacrifice of themselves or their lives in these film texts. This chapter aims to provide a possible answer: women's wishes under male filmmakers' cinematic pen(is). In ancient China, most women could hardly make decisions of their own, and it was even more of a luxury for their wishes to come true because they were under patriarchal control. In the martial arts films, directors compensate them by letting them make wishes; however, there is a strong self-destructive, self-sacrificing, or suicidal tendency in their wishes. In *A Touch of Zen*, Yang Huizhen voluntarily offers herself as a birth machine without any extensive romance with Gu Shengzhai; in *Crouching Tiger Hidden Dragon*, Yü Jiaolong struggles to leave the restrictions of home but ironically leaps into the abyss to make Luo Xiaoju's dream to return home come true; in *Crouching Tiger Hidden Dragon*, Jade Fox and Yü Jiaolong seduce Jiang Nanhe and Li Mubai to fulfill their strong desire to learn the secret kung fu of Wudang; in *Hero*, Flying Snow sacrifices her life to help Nameless assassinate the king; in *Hero*, Moon insists on her suicidal fight against Flying Snow to avenge her dead master at the cost of her life; in *House of Flying Daggers*, Xiaomei chooses no man, committing suicide to stop Jin and Liu from killing each other; and so on. Even though Qingcheng's wish is to access true love in *The Promise*, she is eventually doomed to depend on her male savior, Kunlun, to change her fate.

Academic Approaches and Research Strategies

I begin this chapter with questions about the lack of sufficient feminism in the storylines of the above-mentioned martial arts films, then move from the diegetic and narrative aspects to the politics of representation, such as who creates and decides on the films, the industry that supports the production of these films, the determining roles of directors, screenwriters, etc. The research strategies included in this article can be divided into two parts. The first part focuses on the phallocentrism of male filmmakers' cinematic pen(is). I will highlight the disproportion of award-winning male filmmakers and female filmmakers to illustrate the overempowerment of the phallocentric pen(is) in terms of the production of successful films. Empirically speaking, I will investigate the number of award-winning male filmmakers and compare it with the number of award-winning female filmmakers. The unbalanced ratio of award-winning male filmmakers to award-winning female filmmakers will evidence my problematization of the cinematic pen(is).

The second part of my research strategy centers on the disproportionate anthologization of women writers and my metaphor of the pen(is) in patriarchal social systems. Fewer women writers' dreams to be anthologized or award-winning come true than do male writers'. The selective criteria in the overall phallocentric social system inadvertently underestimate the value of women writers' works and thus comprehend, appreciate, respect, treasure, realize, or support women's literature less enthusiastically than men's. Compared with male writers' or filmmakers' wishes to be anthologized or award-winning, the same wish of women writers or female filmmakers has fewer opportunities to be accepted, endorsed, supported, realized, and valued. Women's wishes, generally speaking, have fewer opportunities to be understood, appreciated, respected, treasured, realized, or supported than men's wishes by the overall male-centered tradition. It is also likely that women's wishes are ignored, misinterpreted or replaced by what men want women to wish. Women writers' wish to be anthologized and the probability for their wish to come true are probably as disappointing to feminists as are women filmmakers' wish to be award-winning and the ratio of their success on the job market in the film industry.

Award-Winning Filmmakers

According to the list of Oscar Award winners, there were, in total, sixty-four best directors from 1929 to 2009 (see Appendix 9-1). Among these sixty-four filmmakers, John Ford is a four-time winner, and William Wyler is a three-time winner. Elia Kazan, Joseph Mankiewicz, Frank Borzag, Frank Lloyd, Frank Capra, Leo McCarey, and Billy Wilder won the same award twice in their lives. Except for Katherine Ann Bigelow, all of the recipients are male filmmakers. In addition to the disproportionate ratio of male and female winners, the most unbelievably dramatic facts are that worldwide female filmmakers waited for 82 years in order to win the first Oscar award and that Western female directors overpower Chinese female filmmakers in terms of the possibility to win the award.

From 1962 to 2008, the Golden Horse Film Festival gave awards to thirty-five filmmakers (see Appendix 9-2). Li Han-hsiang, Wang Tung, and Johnnie Kei-fung To were awarded twice. Ang Lee and Li Xing were awarded three times. Among these thirty-five award-winning filmmakers, thirty-three were male. Joan Chen and Ann Hui were the only two female award-winning filmmakers.

The same ratio of only two female winners applied to best directors who won the Hong Kong Film Awards from 1982 to 2008 (see Appendix 9-3). Johnnie Kei-fung To and Allen Yuk-ping Feng were awarded three times. Wong Kar-wai, Peter Ho-Sun Chen, Derek Tung-Sing Yee and Ann Hui were awarded twice. Among these thirteen award-winning filmmakers, only two were female. The only two exceptions were Ann Hui and Mabel Cheung.

In the ceremonies of Golden Rooster Film Awards from 1981 to 2008, twenty-seven filmmakers were announced as best directors (see Appendix 9-4).[1] Wu Tianming and Yang Yazhou were awarded twice. Zhang Yimou was awarded three times. Among these twenty-seven award-winning filmmakers, only three are female: Xiao Guiyun, Peng Xiaolian, and Ma Liwen. One of the three female filmmakers, Xiao Guiyun, won the award because of her collaboration with her husband, not purely her own work. This Chinese phenomenon echoes the Western tendency for women who co-work with male filmmakers to have a better chance at becoming award-winning though "Mao Zedong saw women as a necessary part of China's economic transformation even before liberation."[2] Two important examples of how much more successful husband-and-wife teams are than independent women may be the collected awards for Earl W. Wallace's and Pamela Wallace's screenplay of *Witness* (1985) and Muriel Box's and Sydney Box's screenplay of *The Seventh Veil* (1946). The collaboration with men to increase the chance to win film awards also shows the unbalanced opportunities for women and men to win significant awards, public recognition and professional affirmation.

Generally speaking, the ratio of female-to-male filmmakers of highly ranked and well-anthologized Chinese martial arts films is as low as that of female-to-male filmmakers in lists of Oscar Award winners, Golden Horse Award winners, Hong Kong Film Award winners and Golden Rooster Film Award winners. *Women on Top*, a documentary film about American film classics, silhouettes prominent women in the recent motion picture industry, including female writer-directors such as Callie Khouri, but concludes everything with an unhappy statement that the overwhelming majority of motion picture professionals are male, with a limited proportion of women. In Julie James Bailey's article "Women's History in Film," one of her most striking comments is that "[t]here were few women cinematographers."[3] Take the Academy Awards for example; there has been no female best filmmaker since 1927. The first American woman to receive three Oscar nominations is Sofia Coppola. She was nominated for best film, best picture, and best screenplay, but the possibility for her to win an Oscar is still limited. Martha M. Lauzen, Professor of Communications at San Diego State University, satirically entitles her annual research on this disproportion "The Celluloid Ceiling."[4] Her "celluloid ceiling" is the feminist scholars' theorem of the "glass ceiling":

> Each year, Lauzen tracks female employment in the entertainment industry, examining the top 250 films released. The numbers for 2002 . . . come in . . . . According to the study, the percentage of women hired as directors, executive producers, producers, writers, cinematographers or editors dropped from 19% in 2001 to 17% in 2002. A total of 22% of the films released during the time studied employed no women at all in any of those positions.[5]

The Chicago Area Partnerships (CAPS), an organizational model encompassing community, government, and corporate representatives, coincidentally footnotes Martha M. Lauzen's argument: "Women/minorities have to work twice as hard for the same recognition,"[6] though most men may "uphold the dominant stratification ideology . . . by emphasizing that success and economic reward come from individual talent and effort."[7] Patricia W. Lunneborg questions whether men who co-work with women can be reshaped;[8] my questions are whether the unbalanced ratio is mistaken as a sort of stereotype, whether differences are treated as weaknesses,[9] and whether it is possible for film studios to be true "women-friendly districts."[10] Although affirmative-action policies did increase employment opportunities for women[11] in the past, the disproportion of well-known male and female cinematographers remains the same. There are countless reasons to explain why the number of award-winning and prominent female filmmakers is so obviously smaller than that of male directors in the worldwide film industry. During filming periods, most directors work extremely long hours every working day in various locales, which may be unbelievably far away from their homes, children, spouses, and other family members. Women filmmakers' physical limitations, compared with men's, may be also a factor. Female directors in their twenties, thirties, and forties face more difficulties in terms of pregnancy, marital life, childbirth, and child-raising than do male filmmakers at the same age. This is "role overload."[12] Regardless of which explanation is the most convincing in most female directors' cases, the disproportion turns women into an underrepresented and marginalized minority while men jockey and occupy the mainstream position of power in the global film industry. Rebecca Shambaugh identifies some cases of women's self-restriction and self-doubt in terms of the balance between their careers and lives, but still reminds women of the existence of the limitation: "[O]nce women free themselves from the sticky floors, there [may be] no glass ceiling. Instead, the sky is the limit."[13]

> When women lack . . . access to resources . . . or face other constraints to mobility, it is not realistic to assume that they can participate in, and benefit equally . . . . Specific arrangements should be made for them. These should include directing some activities and resources of the mainstream programme exclusively to the intended women beneficiaries, or instituting positive or affirmative action to help women . . . overcome their initial handicaps and bring them up to a level where they can be equal partners with men, and where mainstreaming can then effectively take place.[14]

Cinematic Pen

If female protagonists in Chinese martial arts films truly volunteer or keenly desire to be so self-sacrificial, selfless, suicidal, subordinate, and inferior in films, it does not make sense for them to be so determinative, tactful, independent, strong-willed, and feminist at the beginning of their stories. If these women do not really volunteer or desire to selflessly sacrifice and lower themselves, why are their wishes so different from their selfhood? Who made these women's wishes so contrary to their feminist autonomy? The possible explanation is that filmmakers created, decided, or preferred these women's selfless and self-sacrificial wishes for men on the silver screen. All these films are products of male filmmakers and hence "male-dominated." All of the stories about women in these "male-dominated" films are "written" and controlled by male filmmakers. Male filmmakers possess and use their "cinematic pen" or "camera pen" to make up and write down these women's stories.

Theoretically speaking, the metaphorical phrases of "cinematic pen" and "camera pen" also appear in other academic publications about film studies. For instance, in a 1948 *L'Écran français*, Alexander Astruc proposes the idea that filmmakers write with their cameras the way writers write with their pens. His professional term is "caméra-stylo." According to his belief, motion pictures are filmmakers' writing in their audiovisual languages.[15] In *Letter from Siberia* (1958), Chris Marker begins his film with the metaphor of his "cinematic pen" or "camera pen" and says to his audience: "I am writing you from a distant land." In addition, numerous filmmakers present their feature films or documentary films in the form of written records such as diaries, letters, meditations or even essays. For example, Abbas Kiarostami

> describes the digital (dv) camera as a "cinematic pen," which offers "a very firm and valid invitation to return the auteur to the scene." Although not explicitly stated, this metaphor denotes a (digital) revival of Alexander Astruc's caméra-stylo (or camera pen) which consolidated auteur theory and fuelled the productivity of the French New Wave. In the . . . clip, Kiarostami stands atop the hilly outskirts of Tehran, looking down over its bustling streets, and reconfirms his preference for a cinema of recording. This provokes the idea that if stories surround Kiarostami then his digital cinematic gaze has increased his access to these.[16]

Cinematic Pen(is)

If gender scholars are allowed to add feminist critical readings to the theoretical framework of caméra-stylo, "cinematic pen," or "camera pen," I contend that the overpowering number of award-winning male filmmakers probably turns the "cinematic pen" or "camera pen" into "cinematic pen(is)" or "camera pen(is)" because the pen(is) a male one. If the argument of cinematic pen(is) is not too incomprehensible, the lack of a well-balanced ratio of award-winning female-to-male filmmakers may be a symptom of "cinematic castration fear." In the motion picture industry the tendency for husband-wife teams and women who co-work with men to become more successful and award-winning than women who do not make films with men may be a warning sign of "cinematic penis envy." Laura Mulvey's analysis of the "male gaze" happens to echo my arguments of camera pen(is), cinematic castration fear, and cinematic penis envy.[17] Luce Irigaray's theoretical tease at the penis and its "one-ness," compared with the multiplicity of women's sexual zones that the theoretical pun, "two lips," indicates in *This Sex Which Is Not One* or *Speculum of the Other Woman* also indirectly seconds my arguments.[18] Jacques Lacan's notion of "The Law of Father,"[19] Jacques Derrida's concept of logocentrism,[20] and Hélène Cixous's advocacy of *écriture féminine* (feminine mode of writing) in "The Laugh of the Medusa"[21] also indirectly support my critical ideas of cinematic pen(is), cinematic castration fear, cinematic syndrome of small penis, and cinematic penis envy.

King Hu's *A Touch of Zen*, Ang Lee's *Crouching Tiger Hidden Dragon*, Zhang Yimou's *Hero* and *House of Flying Daggers*, Chen Kaige's *The Promise*, Tsui Hark's *Seven Swords*, Feng Xiaogang's *The Banquet*, and Zhang Yimou's *Curse of the Golden Flower*—all of these well accepted Chinese martial arts films happen to share the same characteristic: male filmmakers. Their cinematic pen(is) a male one.

The wishes that women make in these Chinese martial arts films are not wishes of these ancient Chinese ladies' own but wishes under the male filmmakers' cinematic pen(is). They are wishes under the control of male filmmakers' cinematic pen(is) because the pen(is) is a male one. What these wishes under male directors' cinematic pen(is) lead to is the phallocentrism or male pride that indirectly or directly highlights women's sacrifice for, need of, or dependence on men. It is probably not a coincidence for male filmmakers to favor women's sacrifices for men, especially martial arts ladies', strong-willed women's or feminists' submission or compromise at the ends of their stories. Disappointingly, these wishes at the ends of their stories seem to offset all the feminist ambitions and potentiality, which these ancient Chinese women disclose throughout the films, and reduce the gender egalitarianism that these Chinese martial arts films could really include.

Award-Winning Screenplays, Playwrights and Screenwriters

If there are feminist cracks on the cinematic glass ceiling in the motion picture industry, they might be from the proportion of women's award-winning screenplays. Although the number is still smaller (and worse) than that of men's award-winning screenplays, it is a little bit better than female filmmakers' chance to be awarded as best directors in noteworthy film festivals.

Before male filmmakers enjoy the phallocentric power to decide ancient Chinese women's fate and their wishes in film studios, female or feminist playwrights may be the most forceful power to rescue these women from self-destruction and provide a narrow escape for them on the silver screen. Unfortunately, the ratio of award-winning and well-anthologized female screenwriters is still limited.

Take the Academy Awards for Writing Original Screenplays for example. From 1940 to 2007, there were only eight female award-winning screenwriters or storywriters: Sydney Box, Pamela Wallace, Jane Compion, Callie Khouri, Nancy Dowd, Sonya Levien, Sofia Coppola and Diablo Cody (Brook Busey). Except for these few women, all the other award-winning screenwriters or storywriters were male (see Appendix 9-5).

According to the list of winners of Academy Awards for Writing Adapted Screenplays from 1927 to 2007, there were merely three female award-winning adapters: Ruth Prawer Jhabvala, Emma Thompson and Diana Ossana. Except for these three women, all the other award-winning adapters were male (see Appendix 9-6).

In the forty-four-year history of the Golden Globe Awards from 1965 to 2008, of fifty-three winners, only five were female award-winning screenwriters: Naomi Foner (1988), Callie Khouri (1991), Emma Thompson (1995), Sofia Coppola (2003), and Diana Ossana (2005). In the forty-four years, there were fifty-three winners. Forty-eight of them were male and only five were female. The percentage of female award-winning screenwriters is less than ten (see Appendix 9-7).

From 1962 to 2008, the Golden Horse International Film Festival in Taiwan has included only sixteen female award-winning screenwriters: Chin I-fu, Ge Rui-fen, Hsu Shu-chen, Hsiao Sa, Wang Hsiao-li, Chang Wan-ting, Teng Bi-yen, Chu Tien-wen, Liao Hui-ying, Chen Chong, Yan Geling, Ivy Ho, Ning Dai, Hu An, Kate Raisz, and Wang Hui-ling. Chang Wan-ting won the same award twice: the first time in 1988 and the second time in 1998. Chin I-fu is a two-time award-winning screenwriter: first in 1962 and again in 1967. Chu Tian-wen won the same award three times: first in 1983, and again in 1985 and 1995. Except for them, all the award-winning screenwriters are male (see Appendix 9-8).

With reference to the Hong Kong Film Critics Society Awards from 1994 to 2008, only four women won awards for screenwriting or adaptation: Chow Hin-yan (1998), Chin Siu-wai (2000), Ge Goo-Bi (2001), and Ivy Ho (2008). This means that, of twenty-one award-winning screenwriters or adapters, seventeen of them are male. The number of male winners is four times greater than that of female winners (see Appendix 9-9).

Screenwriters, Writers and Literary Anthologization

Films, screenplays, stories, literary works, and literary anthologization are all interlocked. Numerous award-winning films derive from outstanding writing or literary pieces of excellent adapters, screenwriters, and fictionists. Ang Lee's *Lust Caution* (2007), for example, depends on Wang Hui-ling's adaptation of Eileen Chang's novelette. *Crouching Tiger Hidden Dragon* (2000) comes from Wang Hui-ling's adaptation of Wang Dulu's fiction. Zhang Yimou attributes the success of his film *Red Sorgham* (1987) to Mo Yan's novel. Thanks to Ni Zheng's adaptation of Su Tong's fiction *Qiqie cheng qun* (*Groups of Wives and Concubines*), Zhang Yimou's film *Raise the Red Lantern* (1991) won the Silver Lion Award at the forty-fourth Venice International Film Festival (Mostra Internazionale d'Arte Cinematografica di Venezia).

Good screenwriters are usually good storytellers and writers. For instance, Paddy Chayefsky is not only an award-winning screenwriter but also a good playwright and adapter of screenplays. Wang Hsiao-li (b. 1953) is a Taiwanese female filmmaker who won the Golden Horse Award for best screenwriter in 1987. Zhang Yimou identifies himself as a good storyteller. In 2005 City University of Hong Kong awarded the honorary doctoral degree in literature to Zhang Yimou. In the ceremony, Li Jinquan, the first president of the Chinese Communication Association and professor of communication at the City University of Hong Kong, praised Zhang Yimou and mentioned him as the "filmmaker that is the best at storytelling."

Chu Tien-wen (b. 1956) is another illustration. She is not merely an award-winning screenwriter and adapter of screenplays but also an award-winning fictionist in Taiwanese literature. Her screenplays and adapted screenplays began in 1982 and 1983. Most of them are significant parts of award-winning Taiwanese films.

Table 9.1. Chu Tien-wen's screenplays

Year	Chinese Title	English Title
1983	風櫃來的人	The Boys from Fengkuei
1983	小畢的故事	Growing up
1984	冬冬的假期	A Summer at Grandpas
1984	小爸爸的天空	Out of the Blue
1985	青梅竹馬	Taipei Story
1985	童年往事	The Time to Live and the Time to Die
1985	最想念的季節	My Favorite Season
1985	結婚	His Matrimony
1986	戀戀風塵	Dust in the Wind
1987	尼羅河的女兒	Daughter of the Nile
1988	悲情城市	A City of Sadness
1988	外婆家的暑假	(lack of English translation)
1993	戲夢人生	The Puppetmaster
1995	好男好女	Good Men, Good Women
1996	南國再見,南國	Goodbye South, Goodbye
1998	海上花	Flower of Shanghai
2001	千禧曼波	Millennium Mambo
2003	珈琲時光	Café Lumière
2005	最好的時光	The Best of Our Times

Table 9.2. Some of Chu Tien-wen's publications about her screenplays

Year	Chinese Title	English Title
1983	小畢的故事	Growing up
1987	戀戀風塵	Dust in the Wind
1989	悲情城市	A City of Sadness
1993	侯孝賢分鏡劇本《戲夢人生》	The Puppetmaster
1995	好男好女	Good Men, Good Women
1998	極上之夢—《海上花》電影全紀錄	Flower of Shanghai
2001	《千禧曼波》電影原著中英文劇本	Millennium Mambo

Chu Tien-wen and her sister, Chu Tien-hsin, are both famous novelists. According to David Der-wei Wang,[22] the Chu family sheltered Hu Lancheng (1906-1981), the ex-spouse of a more renowned Chinese woman writer Eileen Chang (1920-1995); therefore, Chu Tien-wen and Chu Tien-hsin indirectly inherited the literary legacy from the reputable writer, Eileen Chang, through Hu Lancheng.[23] Chu Tien-wen and Chu Tien-hsin's father is Chu Hsi-ning; he is also an eminent writer in Taiwan. In 1993, Chu Tien-wen won the *China Times* Novel Prize for her novel, *Huangren shouji* (*Notes of a Desolate Man*). Howard Goldblatt[24] and Sylvia Li-chun Lin[25] collaboratively translated Chu Tien-wen's award-winning literary work from Mandarin Chinese into English and received the 1999 Translation of the Year Award from the American Translators Association.

Many talented filmmakers and screenwriters have deep collaborative connections with writers. For example, King Hu's ex-wife, Chung Ling,[26] is a well-known writer and scholar in Taiwan and Hong Kong. Chung Ling helped King Hu plan his films, wrote stories for his motion pictures, and accompanied him to prepare for his location shooting.[27] King Hu's film *The Legend of the Mountain* is a story created by Chung Ling. Another example is the co-working relationship between Chu Tien-wen and Hou Hsiao-hsien. Hou Hsiao-hsien (b. 1947) is one of the most influential filmmakers in the Taiwanese history of filmmography. He has been co-working with Chu Tien-wen since 1982.[28] He confessed that the book *Sheng Chongwen's Biography*, which Chu gave to him, inspired him and initiated his career as a filmmaker.

The Pen(is) to Write

Although films, screenplays, stories, creative writing, literature, and literary anthologization are deeply interlocked, the pen to write masterpieces is still male-dominated in the overall history of literary anthologization. Well-anthologized women writers are like small decorations compared with the mainstream male writers, though the ratio of female writers has grown gradually through the nineteenth, twentieth and twenty-first centuries. That is to say, the pen(is) is male-dominated in the mainstream and overall literary history. The writing instrument for mainstream literary history in patriarchal societies is still the male-centered or phallo-centric pen(is) even when the limited number of anthologized women writers is taken into consideration.

Literary Pen(is)

Take the Nobel Prize Laureates in literature, for instance. From 1901 to 2008, there were more than one hundred winners. There were merely ten women Laureates, however: Doris Lessing (2007), Elfreide Jelinek (2004), Wislawa Szymborska (1996), Toni Morrison (1993), Nadine Gordimer (1991), Nelly Sachs (1966), Pearl Buck (1938), Sigrid Undset (1928), Grazia Deledda (1926), and Selma O. L. Lagerlof (1909). The proportion of women winners is less than one tenth (see Appendix 9-10).

George Eliot deliberately chose a man's name as her pen name so readers do not easily discover whether she was male or female. Sandra Gilbert and Susan Gubar utilize "the madwomen in the attic" as a metaphor to symbolize the overall publication market's attitude toward women writers. The lack of women writers also results in Norton Anthology releasing a separate anthology of women's literature.

The underrepresentation of women writers and women's literature also appears in anthologies of Chinese literature. Because screenplays are closer to fictions, I will take the section of fictions in *The Columbia Anthology of Modern Chinese Literature* for instance. Joseph S. M. Lau and Howard Goldbatt anthologize forty-one fictionists: twelve female novelists and twenty-nine male fictionists. There are four female and ten male novelists in the era from 1918 to 1949; one female and five male writers in the period from 1949 to 1976; eight female and thirteen male novelists after 1976 (see Appendix 9-11). In other words, the ratio of anthologized women fictionists is less than one in four.

Traditional Chinese literature's inclusion of women writers is even more limited than modern Chinese literature's. Take the *Shorter Columbia Anthology of Traditional Chinese Literature*, for example. The proportion of women writers in this anthology is smaller than that in the above-mentioned anthology. The insufficient inclusion of women writers in the mainstream anthology of classical Chinese literature finally brings about Chang Sun Kang-I's and Huan Saussy's co-editorial work on *Women Writers of Traditional China: An Anthology of Poetry and Criticism*.

The Cinematic Pen(is) That Overpowers Women Writers' Literary Pen

Even though some award-winning filmmakers co-work with women writers, playwrights and screenwriters, the director's cinematic pen(is) overpowers the female writer's literary pen. Filmmakers still use their cinematic pen(is) to reshape or rewrite the stories that female writers create with their literary pen.

Ang Lee's *Lust Caution*, for instance, evidences how a male filmmaker's cinematic power elongates Eileen Chang's short story. Wang Hui-ling, the female adapter who turns Eileen Chang's literary piece into a shooting screenplay, reveals,

> If Eileen Chang's short story is like a starting point, Ang Lee, [as a male filmmaker, uses the power of his cinematic pen(is) to] lengthen everything . . . A lot of scenes of sexuality and lust do not even appear in the original version of [my] shooting script . . . Eileen Chang likes to use metaphors. Whatever is hidden between lines depends on Ang Lee to visualize it.[29]

The adaptation of Wang Dulu's novel for Ang Lee's *Crouching Tiger Hidden Dragon* doubles the evidence. In the whole process of adaptation, Wang Hui-ling is the only female participant. Except for her, there are four male participants: Ang Lee, Hsu Ligong (the producer of the film), James Schamus (the producer of the English version of the screenplay), and A Cheng (a Mainland Chinese writer). Ang Lee started the whole process with his request for James Schamus's English version of the screenplay for the film in the hopes that it might bring in global or Western funding. Because there was no English translation of Wang Dulu's original story, Ang Lee provided an English outline for James Schamus, discussed it with him many times, and revised the English screenplay at least twice. He did not speak with Wang Hui-ling about *Crouching Tiger Hidden Dragon* in Vancouver until she had finished the screenplay for a soap opera entitled *Renjian siyuetian (April in the Human World)*.[30]

> Wang humbly remarks that her job is simply to add the hidden connection between Li Mubai and Yü Jiaolong as well as the tension and balance to the parallels of two original pairs of lovers: Li Mubai and Yü Xiulian; and Luo Xiaohu and Yü Jiaolong . . . . Although Ang Lee and Wang Hui-ling believe in each other's professional opinions, they argued with each other—even to the extent that both of them color up to temples. Sometimes Hsu Li-gong was worried about their disagreement with each other during the collaborative process and had to serve as an intermediator. In Hsu's viewpoint, Wang is more humanistic and thus against some commercial concerns in the mainstream Hollywood and American culture . . . . Yet Ang Lee attached more importance to James Scha-

mus's concerns and asked A Cheng's help to adjust the lines in the screenplay.[31]

Chung Ling's collaboration with King Hu doubles the evidence of the fact that the cinematic pen(is) overpowers women writers' literary pen. In a journalist's interview with her, Chung Ling says,

> As a matter of course, writing some scripts [for King Hu, in my case,] was actually a part of what a wife does for her husband . . . . I had never learned how to write scripts. I simply discussed the story with King Hu and then wrote it. However, I did not know filmmographical elements such as shooting and scenes . . . . Those were taken care of by others . . . . At that time, I was simply helping King Hu. If someone asks me to write scripts now, no excuse can convince me to do so . . . . After giving my script to [King Hu], I did not worry about what kind of film he would turn my script into. He was the filmmaker. This is his film. I could only write stories and focus on the story plot and human nature. The film *The Legend of the Mountain* should be King Hu's.[32]

Male filmmakers' cinematic pen(is) overpowers women writers' or screenwriters' wishes for how everything is (re)presented on the silver screen. Probably because of the overpowering male filmmakers' cinematic pen(is), the feminism and women's rights that traditional Chinese women enjoy in martial arts films on the silver screen may be still filtered, gatekept, censored, and restricted though the wish of female screenwriters, playwrights, or writers is perhaps for women's entirely unlimited freedom.

This may answer the questions that I list at the beginning of this article: Why does Luo Xiaohu not sacrifice himself to realize Yü Jiaolong's wish in Ang Lee's *Crouching Tiger Hidden Dragon*? Why does Wang Hui-ling, as a female adapter of Wang Dulu's literary work, not stand out to request more feminism and women's rights for the female protagonist Yü Jiaolong in the film directed by Ang Lee? Wang Hui-ling's answer might be similar to what she herself mentions: the script or literary work as only a starting point for Ang Lee's cinematic pen(is) to extend everything.

The same answer may work for questions about other Chinese martial arts films that I included in the beginning section of this chapter: Why do these women in film texts share the same or at least similar sacrifice of themselves for men, suicidal decisions for men, subordination to men, or reliance on salvation from men, which may repetitively imply female inferiority and male superiority? Why is the representation of women's sacrifice of themselves, suicide for men, or subordination to men so eye-catching in these films? Do these women truly volunteer or keenly desire to be so self-sacrificial, selfless, suicidal, subordinate, dependent, and inferior? Female screenwriters, writers, adapters of original stories, and actresses may not cordially wish this kind of women's sacrifice to repetitively happen on the silver screen. Award-winning male filmmakers' cinematic pen(is) may overpower them, however. Even though female filmmakers may disagree with the tragic endings of traditional Chinese women in these Chinese martial arts films, it is an undeniable fact that these films directed by well-known male filmmakers are award-winning and that women directors are not as award-winning as the male filmmakers.

Narrative Analyses in a Counter-Example

It is obvious that female directors' Chinese martial arts films can support my argument; however, the number of award-winning female filmmakers who have directed well-accepted martial arts films is incredibly tiny. Wang Hsiao-li, for instance, has not directed any Chinese martial arts film. Ann Hui (b. 1947) is one of the few award-winning female directors of a martial arts film. She directed two parts of a martial arts film, *The Romance of the Book and the Sword* (Part One, 1987) and *Princess Fragrance* (Part Two, 1987), which are derived from Jin Yong's martial arts novel, *The Book and the Sword*.[33] In this section, I present part two as an example.

The female protagonist, Huo Qingtong, leads a group of male warriors, executes the man who disobeys her, defeats enemies, and successfully safeguards her hometown. She does not share the same tragic death with female protagonists in male filmmakers' martial arts film; she suffers from diseases but the film does not include any scene of her death. Her sister, Princess Fragrance (played by Ke Siluo), breaks the traditional Chinese behavioral code for women and shows her love for the male protagonist, Chen Jialuo, in public. She explains the meaning of the lyric in the local song, points out the respect and honor for the heroine who serves as a spy and saves her people in the song, and shows her intention to do the same thing. Princess Fragrance discovers Emperor Qianlong's villainous scheme and lie to Chen Jialuo and stops Qianlong from turning her into his concubine by committing suicide. Her expression of love for Chen Jialuo and her rejection of Qianlong's tender feeling violates ancient Chinese social rules: first, the impossibility for most ancient Chinese women to select their spouses and show their romantic love in public, and second, the impossibility for most ancient Chinese women to refuse the emperor. This martial arts film of Ann Hui's is far more feminist than almost all the above-mentioned male filmmakers' kung fu movies. Her highlighting of female protagonists' leadership, heroicness, and violation against Chinese patriarchy is out of question. Even Princess Fragrance's suicide symbolizes her unequaled courage and strong objection to the most powerful man in her country, which is entirely different from female protagonists' sacrifice and suicides for men in male filmmakers' works.

The Deciding Power of the Cinematic Pen(is)

Most support for my argument about the deciding power of the filmmakers' cinematic pen(is) originates from Anna May Wong's experience in the film industry. Wong (1905-1961) was a third-generation Chinese-American. She was born and brought up in the US and wished to have a successful acting career. Unfortunately, what welcomed her was racism. At that time, filmmakers hired only Caucasian actresses to play the roles of Asian female protagonists on the silver screen. The Asian female protagonists in these motion pictures were not true Asians but Caucasian male filmmakers' ideals. The filmmakers' cinematic pen(is), which was obviously racially discriminatory, decided that Wong did not fit a Caucasian's imagined perfect appearance for an Asian woman. Regardless of how illogical it was to disallow true Asian women to play Asian female protagonists, Wong had no power over the filmmakers' cinematic pen(is). The cinematic discrimination against her and other Asian actresses in the US finally drove her to leave America. She worked as an actress in British and German motion pictures after her departure from the Hollywood film industry.

Nowadays, we can find endless reasons to disagree with the filmmakers who refused to acknowledge Anna May Wong's talent and potentiality to play the roles of Asian female protagonists, but the deciding power of filmmakers' cinematic pen(is) remains the same even after this kind of ridiculous discrimination stopped decades ago. This power is probably still as strong as it was, or even more forceful. Women's wishes to shatter the glass ceiling still do not come true, according to the ending of the Chinese martial arts films that I have analyzed. In this sense, the male filmmakers' screen lenses[34] are exactly like the glass ceiling that women's heads bump.

References

Adair, Carole K. Cracking the Glass Ceiling: Factors Influencing Women's Attainment of Senior Executive Positions (Ph.D. Dissertation). Colorado State University, 1994, p. 32.
Andrew, Geoff. *10*. London: British Film Institute, 2005.
Astruc, Alexander. "The Birth of a New Avant-garde: La caméra stylo." *The New Wave: Critical Landmarks*. Peter Graham. New York: Doubleday, 1968, pp. 17-23.
Bailey, Julie James. "Women's History in Film." *Reel Women Working in Film and Television*. New South Wales, Australia: Australian Film Television & Radio School, 1999, p. viii.
Baskin, Ellen. "Cracking the Glass Ceiling in the Film Industry." *Los Angels Times*. June 2, 2003.
Chang Sun, Kang-I and Huan Saussy. *Women Writers of Traditional China: An Anthology of Poetry and Criticism*. Stanford: Stanford University Press, 1999.
Chung, Ling. *Dadi chunyu: Chung Ling zixuanji* (*Spring Rain on the Earth: Self-Selected Collections by Chung Ling*). Hong Kong: Tiandi tushu, 2004, pp. 11-16.

Cixous, Hélène. "The Laugh of the Medusa." Keith Cohen and Paula Cohen trans. *Signs* 1, no. 4 (1976): 875-893.
Clark, S & M. Corcoran. "Perspectives on the Professional Socialization of Women Faculty." *Journal of Higher Education* 57 (1): 21-43.
Davies-Netzley, Sally Ann. "Women above the Glass Ceiling: Perceptions on Corporate Mobility and Strategies for Success." *Understanding Inequality: The Intersection of Race/Ethnicity, Class and Gender*. Barbara A. Arrighi edt. Lanham: Rowman & Littlefield, 2007, p. 210.
Fang, Shouchu. *Muoxue yuanliu (The Origin of the Mohist Studies)*. Shanghai: Zhonghua shuju, 1937.
Feng, Youlan. *Zhongguo zhexue shi (History of Chinese Philosophy)*. Hong Kong: Zhongguo tushu, 1959.
---. *History of Chinese Philosophy*. Derk Bodde trans. Princeton: Princeton University Press, 1959.
Grigg, Russell. *Lacan, Language, and Philosophy*. Albany: SUNY Press, 2008.
Gubar, Susan. *Rooms of Our Own*. Urbana: University of Illinois Press, 2006.
Gubar, Suan and Sandra Gilbert. *The Madwomen in the Attic: Women Writers and the Nineteenth Century Literary Imagination*. New Haven: Yale University Press, 1979.
---. Shakespeare's Sisters: Feminist Essays on Women Poets. Bloomington: Indiana University Press, 1979.
Hideki, Mori. *Bokkou*. Sakemi Kenichi (Chinese translation) edt. Taipei: Tongli, 2006.
Hill, John and Pamela Church Gibson. *The Oxford Guide to Film Studies*. Oxford: Oxford University Press, 1998.
Hsu, Li-gong and Ling-i Kung. *Rang women zai ai yi ci—Hsu Li-gong de dianying shijie (Let's Fall in Love Again—Hsu Li-gong's Cinematic World)*. Taipei: Tianxia yuanjian, 2006, p. 263.
Irigaray, Luce. *This Sex Which Is Not One*. Ithaca: Cornell University Press, 1985.
---. *Speculum of the Other Women*. Ithaca: Cornell University Press, 1985.
---. *An Ethics of Sexual Difference*. Ithaca: Cornell University Press, 1993.
---. *Luce Irigaray: Key Writings*. London and New York: Continuum, 2004.
---. *Luce Irigaray: Teaching*. London and New York: Continuum, 2008.
Jin, Yong (Cha, Louis). *The Book and the Sword*. Graham Earnshaw trans. Oxford: Oxford University Press, 2005.
Johnson, Michael J. "Perspectives on Tranformational Leadership and the Modern Glass Ceiling." *Dancing on the Glass Ceiling: Women, Leadership and Technology*. Don Olcott, Jr. and Darcy W. Hardy edt. Madison, WI: Atwood, 2006, p. 43.
Kiarostami, Abbas. *10 on Ten* (DVD). 2004.
Lunneborg, Patricia W. *Women Changing Work*. New York: Greenwood, 1990, p. 187.
Lau, Joseph M. S. and Howard Goldblatt. *The Columbia Anthology of Modern Chinese Literature*. New York: Columbia University Press, 2007.
Lauzen, Martha M. *The Celluloid Ceiling: Behind-the-Scenes Employment of Women on the Top 250 Films of 2006*. San Diego: San Diego State University, 2007.
Lim, Lin Lean. *More and Better Jobs for Women: An Action Guide*. Geneva: International Labor Organization,1996, p. 39.
Mair, Victor. *The Shorter Columbia Anthology of Traditional Chinese Literature*. New York: Columbia University Press, 2000.
Menasche, Ann. "Women Need Affirmative Action to Overcome Discrimination." *Working Women: Opposing Viewpoints*. San Diego: Greenhaven Press, 1998, p. 89.

Michaeldfelder, Diane P. and Richard E. Palmer. *Dialogue and Deconstruction: The Gadmar-Derrida Encounter*. Albany: SUNY Press, 1989.
Mulvey, Laura. "Visual Pleasure and Narrative Cinema." *Screen* 16.3(Autumn 1975): 6-18.
---. *Visual and Other Pleasures*. Basingstoke: Palgrave MacMillan, 2008.
Munt, Alex. "Digital Kiarostami and The Open Screenplay." *Scan: Journal of Media Arts Culture* 3:2 (2006): hdl.handle.net/1959.14/11067.
Neipris, Janet. "A Small Delegation." *Plays by Janet Neipris*. New York: Broadway Play Publishing, 2000, pp. 1-60.
Palmer, Barbara and Dennis Simon. *Breaking the Political Glass Ceiling: Women and Congressional Elections*. New York: Routledge, 2008, p. 177.
Petroff, Jane and Bob Morris. *Women on Top*. New York: WNET TV Station (S.l.: s.n.), 1985.
Rosenman, Ellen Bayuk. *A Room of One's Own: Women Writers and the Politics of Creativity*. New York: Twayne Publishers, 1995.
Samimy, Keiko Komiya. "Multiple Mentors in My Career as a University Faculty." *"Strangers" on the Academy: Asian Women Scholars in Higher Education*. Guofang Li and Gulbahar H. Beckett edt. Sterling, VA: Stylus, 2006, p. 112.
The Chicago Area Partnerships (CAPS). *Pathways and Progress: Corporate Best Practices to Shatter the Glass Ceiling*. Chicago: the Chicago Area Partnerships, 1996, p. 11.
Wang, Lingzhen. *Chinese Women's Cinema: Transnational Contexts*. New York: Columbia University Press, 2011.
Wolf, Margery. "The People's Republic of China." *Women Workers in Fifteen Countries*. Jennie Farley edt. Ithaca: ILR Press, Cornell University, 1985, p. 33.

Notes

1. In the main text and notes of this chapter, most East Asians or Chinese people's names start with surnames, such as Zhang Yimou, Gong Li, or Chen Kaige. Exceptions are King Hu and Ang Lee. This chapter also appears in my co-edited book *Women and Gender in Contemporary Chinese Societies: Beyond Han Patriarchy*. As for the Golden Rooster Award, it has been a bi-annual event, no longer annual film festival from 2005 on.

2. Margery Wolf, "The People's Republic of China" in *Women Workers in Fifteen Countries*. ed. Jennie Farley. (Ithaca: ILR Press, Cornell University, 1985), 33.

3. Julie James Bailey, "Women's History in Film" in *Reel Women Working in Film and Television*. (New South Wales, Australia: Australian Film Television & Radio School, 1999), viii.

4. Martha M. Lauzen, *The Celluloid Ceiling: Behind-the-Scenes Employment of Women on the Top 250 Films of 2006*. (San Diego: San Diego State University, 2007). Also consult *Chinese Women's Cinema: Transnational Contexts*; *The Oxford Guide to Film Studies*.

5. Ellen Baskin, "Cracking the Glass Ceiling in the Film Industry." *Los Angels Times*, June 2, 2003.

6. The Chicago Area Partnerships (CAPS). *Pathways and Progress: Corporate Best Practices to Shatter the Glass Ceiling.* (Chicago: the Chicago Area Partnerships, 1996), 11.

7. Sally Ann Davies-Netzley, "Women above the Glass Ceiling: Perceptions on Corporate Mobility and Strategies for Success" in *Understanding Inequality: The Intersection of Race/Ethnicity, Class and Gender.* ed. Barbara A. Arrighi. (Lanham: Rowman & Littlefield, 2007), 210.

8. Patricia W. Lunneborg, *Women Changing Work.* (New York: Greenwood, 1990), 187. Michael J. Johnson remarks that "there are many of us men who have come to experience and believe that the more women are substantially involved in leading this world—the much better off this world will be." For details, consult his article "Perspectives on Transformational Leadership and the Modern Glass Ceiling" in *Dancing on the Glass Ceiling: Women, Leadership and Technology.* eds. Don Olcott, Jr. and Darcy W. Hardy. (Madison, WI: Atwood, 2006), 43.

9. Carole K. Adair, "Cracking the Glass Ceiling: Factors Influencing Women's Attainment of Senior Executive Positions" (Ph.D. dissertation, Colorado State University, 1994), 32.

10. Barbara Palmer and Dennis Simon, *Breaking the Political Glass Ceiling: Women and Congressional Elections.* (New York: Routledge, 2008), 177.

11. Ann Menasche, "Women Need Affirmative Action to Overcome Discrimination" in *Working Women: Opposing Viewpoints.* (San Diego: Greenhaven Press, 1998), 89.

12. S & M. Corcoran Clark, "Perspectives on the Professional Socialization of Women Faculty." *Journal of Higher Education* 57. I: 21-43. Also consult Keiko Komiya Samimy's "Multiple Mentors in My Career as a University Faculty" in *"Strangers" on the Academy: Asian Women Scholars in Higher Education.* eds. Guofang Li and Gulbahar H. Beckett. (Sterling, VA: Stylus, 2006), 112.

13. Rebecca Shambaugh, *It's Not A Glass Ceiling. It's A Sticky Floor.* (New York: McGraw-Hill, 2008), xvi.

14. Lin Lean Lim, *More and Better Jobs for Women: An Action Guide.* (Geneva: International Labor Organization,1996), 39.

15. Alexander Astruc, "The Birth of a New Avant-garde: La caméra stylo" in *L'Écran Français.* March 30, 1948. This article also appears in *The New Wave: Critical Landmarks.* ed. Peter Graham. (New York: Doubleday, 1968), 17-23.

16. Alex Munt, "Digital Kiarostami and The Open Screenplay" in *Scan: Journal of Media Arts Culture* 3:2 (2006): hdl.handle.net/1959.14/11067 (online data accessed in July 2009). Also consult Abbas Kiarostami's DVD: *10 on Ten* and Geoff Andrew's *10.*

17. Laura Mulvey, "Visual Pleasure and Narrative Cinema" in *Screen* 16.3(Autumn 1975): 6-18. Also consult her *Visual and Other Pleasures.* (Basingstoke: Palgrave MacMillan), 2008.

18. Luce Irigaray, *This Sex Which Is Not One.* (Ithaca: Cornell University Press, 1985). Also consult the following books by her:
Speculum of the Other Women. (Ithaca: Cornell University Press, 1985).
An Ethics of Sexual Difference. (Ithaca: Cornell University Press, 1993).
Luce Irigaray: Key Writings. (London and New York: Continuum, 2004).
Luce Irigaray: Teaching. (London and New York: Continuum, 2008).

19. Grigg, Russell. *Lacan, Language, and Philosophy.* (Albany: SUNY Press, 2008).

20. Diane P. Michaeldfelder and Richard E. Palmer, *Dialogue and Deconstruction: The Gadmar-Derrida Encounter*. (Albany: SUNY Press, 1989).

21. Hélène Cixous, "The Laugh of the Medusa." trans. Keith Cohen and Paula Cohen. *Signs* 1, no. 4 (1976): 875-893.

22. David Der-wei Wang is Edward C. Henderson Professor of Chinese Literature at Harvard University and Director of the Chiang Ching-kuo Foundation Inter-University Center for Sinological Studies.

23. This is a part of David Der-wei Wang's teaching contents when he taught modern Chinese literary courses at Columbia University.

24. Howard Goldblatt finished his B.A. degree at the Long Beach State College in 1961, his M.A. degree at San Francisco State University in 1971, and then his Ph.D. degree from Indiana University in 1974. He is currently a research professor of Chinese at the University of Notre Dame. He has translated a number of Chinese fictions into English.

25. Sylvia Li-chun Lin completed her B.A. and first M.A. degrees at Tamkang University, Taiwan. She also received an M.A. from St. John's University, an M.A. from University of Oregon, and her Ph.D. degree from the University of California in Berkeley. Wife of Howard Goldblatt, she is currently an associate professor of Chinese literature at the University of Notre Dame. In 2007, Columbia University Press published her first monograph, *Representing Atrocity in Taiwan: The 2/28 Incident and White Terror in Fiction and Film.*

26. Chung Ling was born in Chongqing in 1945 and raised in Taiwan. She received her B.A. from Tung Hai University and Ph.D. from the University of Wisconsin in Madison. She taught at the State University of New York in Albany, Hong Kong University, National Sun Yat-sen University, and National Kaohsiung University. She is currently the Dean of Humanities at Baptist University in Hong Kong.

27. Consult Chung Ling's *Dadi chunyu: Chung Ling zixuanji* (*Spring Rain on the Earth: Self-Selected Collections by Chung Ling*). (Hong Kong: Tiandi tushu, 2004), 11-16.

28. Sometimes there are even news reports about their intimate relationship. On March 3 and 4, 2005, the *Liberty Times* and *Epoch Times* reported a picture of Hou Hsiao-hsien and Chu Tien-wen, interpreting the photo as visual proof of Hou's extramarital love affairs and indicating that Chu became Hou's underground mistress after their co-working relationship for more than two decades.

29. This information comes from a news report in *The United Times* on September 25, 2007.

30. Li-gong Hsu and Ling-i Kung, *Rang women zai ai yi ci—Hsu Li-gong de dianying shijie* (*Let's Fall in Love Again—Hsu Li-gong's Cinematic World*). (Taipei: Tianxia yuanjian, 2006), 263. The title of this soap opera comes from Lin Huiyin's poem. Wang Hui-ling regards the soap opera as Lin's description of Xu Zhimou's poetry, though Lin's family members disagree. The director of this soap opera is Ding Yah-min (b. 1958). Like Chu Tien-wen and Chu Tien-hsin, he is influenced by Eileen Chang and Hu Lan-cheng.

31. See *Rang women zai ai yi ci—Hsu Li-gong de dianying shijie* (*Let's Fall in Love Again—Hsu Li-gong's Cinematic World*). (Taipei: Tianxia yuanjian, 2006), 263.

32. Jiahui Zeng, "Chung Ling yu Hu Jinquan shanzhong de rizi" (Chung Ling and King Hu's Days in the Mountains). *Xianggang wenhui bao (Hong Kong Wenhui News)*. August 31, 2005.

33. Yong Jin (Louis Cha), *The Book and the Sword.* trans. Graham Earnshaw. (Oxford: Oxford University Press, 2005).

34. I thank Natasha Gordon-Chipembere's inspiration.

Chapter Nine
Phallocentric Teacher-Student Complex: From *Legend of the Mountain, Crouching Tiger Hidden Dragon*, and *Hero* to *Seven Swords*

King Hu's *Legend of the Mountain* (1979), Ang Lee's *Crouching Tiger Hidden Dragon* (2000), and Zhang Yimou's *Hero* (2003) share a motif: a phallocentric teacher-student complex—specifically, the problematic relationship between male teachers and female students. This chapter aims to problemize educational stories of teacher-student interactions as well as the gender differences of teachers and students in *Legend of the Mountain, Crouching Tiger Hidden Dragon, Hero,* and *Seven Swords*. All these films cinematically draw attention to well-reputed male teachers' cultivation of power over female students and increase of the cost of their female students' careers by indirectly compelling them to sacrifice sexuality or life. [1] For example, the teacher-student relationships in both *Legend of the Mountain* and *Crouching Tiger Hidden Dragon* even include female students volunteering to scapegoat themselves by taking the unjust blame for being seductive "fox-spirit" initiators of their sexual relationships. Yüenian in *Legend of the Mountain* is a ghost-like fox spirit, and Jade Fox's name in *Crouching Tiger Hidden Dragon* clearly associates her with legends of fox spirits. In *Hero*, Moon, Broken Sword's disciple since childhood, has sex with her teacher without hesitation even though he sleeps with her not to show his love for her but to irritate Flying Snow and test whether Flying Snow becomes jealous because of love. Moon also engages in a suicidal combat with Flying Snow and sacrifices her own life to avenge her teacher, Broken Sword.

The portrayal of female teachers and their students in *Crouching Tiger Hidden Dragon* and *Seven Swords* runs counter to the highly honored or successful male teachers in *Legend of the Mountain, Crouching Tiger Hidden Dragon,* and *Hero*. Both lack the narrative focus on student sacrifice for female teachers. Female students reward male teachers in these movies; male students do not react in the same way toward female teachers. This phallocentric teacher-student complex reflects gender inequality. It is not a coincidence for all the successful teachers in the films to be male and the less successful teachers to be female. The patriarchal gender ideology favors men to occupy teaching positions at a high social status and women to be located near the students' relatively lower status. Neither is it an accident for highly respected teachers to have female students who seduce them, have sex with them, or take care of trivial details in their everyday lives in the films, because the male-centered social trends tend to take male privilege for granted by turning women into scapegoats for men's sexuality and portraying them as assistant-like caretakers, again, at a lower status to help men deal with trivialities.

In terms of the highly respected positions of educational enthronement in Confucian traditions, men are portrayed as more successful at attaining teaching positions than women. There is a disproportionate number of male teachers compared to female teachers as well as a marked difference in the status given to different portrayals of male teachers compared to female teachers in cinematic images. Comparing and contrasting male teachers' power over women students and female teachers' power over their students also gives evidence to men's access to positions of power in the films. I argue that the cinematic emphasis on male teachers' power over female students may provide an unconscious relief from castration fears. In patriarchal beliefs, penises and the male privileges that penises may represent secure men's superiority over women. Men's fears of losing their male pride and prestigious position of power, which penises represent in patriarchal systems, are actually castration fears. In this argument, male teachers' power over the female sex represents the phallocentric fears of losing their power or their positions of power in regard to the female sex, and it is predicated on the existence of the penis to ensure male teachers' conquest of the female sex.

Ancient Chinese Educational Systems

Before the establishment of the Western-style schooling system in 1902, China did not have a nation-wide consistent system of elementary schools, middle schools, high schools, colleges, or graduate institutions.[2] Before the popularity of Western-style schooling systems in China and the Chinese governmental rules of compulsory education for every child, countless Chinese women were not educated at all, though there were truly some educated women.

How was ancient Chinese academic education for children, teenagers, and adults? There were nuances in different dynasties, but the most frequently seen form of basic academic education included tutors hired to teach a few children. Wealthy and large families, including royal families, could afford to hire scholars to teach their own next generations; teachers and students used studies, rooms, or inner chambers at their houses or ancestral temples as classrooms.

These educational systems were usually named *sishu* (private tutorial systems, or private schools). Some scholars recruited their own students in order to live on teaching. Poor families sometimes collaboratively hired tutors to teach children in the same or nearby villages. Students who could not afford to pay their tuition could go to *yixue* (free schools), but many of them remained illiterate. Textbooks and reading assignments for pupils at the beginning level were usually *Sanzijing (The Trimetric Classics)*. Calligraphy was also inevitable. The school of calligraphy in Zhang Yimou's film *Hero* is an example. Writing abilities and skills were significant. *Sishu (Four Books)*, *Wujing (Five Classics)*, *Lunyü (Confucius Analects)*, *Mengzi (Mencius)*, *Yijing (Book of Changes)*, chronicles or history of every previous dynasty, literary masterpieces, diverse literary genres, and sages' and philosophers' publications—these were also possible teaching subjects.

After students became adolescents or adults, they usually studied at home by themselves. Most adolescent and adult scholars were male. Daughters in rich or royal families could continue to study by themselves; however, they were at most defined as talented women but never regarded as well-established scholars. Although different dynasties did not share the same curriculum, teaching methods, or divisions of schooling, there was an ideal of nationwide academic evaluation, beginning in the Han Dynasty (206 B.C.-220 A.D.). The experimental stage of academic evaluation was like the election of governmental officers from scholarly candidates in the emperors' academic viewpoints. Emperor Yang of the Sui Dynasty (605 A.D.) put it into practice. From then on, scholars traveled from everywhere to administrative centers of their provinces or to the capital city of the whole country to take examinations. The student who got the top grade in the capital examination was ranked as *zhuangyuan*; second and third, *tanhua* and *bangyan*. Below these three ranks, there were *jinshi*, *juren*, and *xiucai*. *Xiucai* was compared to a bachelor's degree; *juren* to a master's degree; and *jinshi* to a doctoral degree. The Tang Dynasty (618-907) strengthened the foundation of this academic evaluation and had a brief session of it for women scholars during the reign of Empress Wu Zetian (lived: 624-705; reigned: 690-705). The Song Dynasty (960-1279) turned it into a complete system. The whole academic assessment system lasted for more than 1300 years and prospered in the Ming (1368-1644) and Qing (1644-1911) Dynasties. It was abolished in the early 1900s and replaced with Western-style schooling systems.[3]

There were no systematic or reliable census data about the female student population, male student population, and the ratio of female teachers and male teachers; however, it is undoubtable that male students outnumbered female students and male educators outnumbered female teachers. In reality, it was unlikely for male teachers to encounter so many impressively beautiful female students and have so many romantic relationships overlapping with teacher-student relationships as movies portray. The unbelievably high ratio of love stories and sexual relations between male educators and female students in the above-mentioned Chinese martial arts films is not loyal to historical facts. Academic parent-child relationship between male teachers and male students, just like the teacher-student pair of Jiang Nanhe and Li Mubai in Ang Lee's *Crouching Tiger Hidden Dragon*, would be closer to historical facts.

Martial arts education before Republican China did not usually belong to formal academic educational systems, though the nationwide athletic evaluation in the Tang Dynasty started to include the governmental assessment of kung fu and ranks of examinees, such as "martial arts *zhuangyuan*" as the title for examinees who earned the top grades. Disciples usually learned kung fu skills with masters for years and then became knights, swords(wo)men, or other specialists of martial arts. Some of them were Buddhist monks in Shaolin Temple, Taoist monks in Wudang Mountain, or nuns in Emei Mountain. After Chinese educational systems were Westernized, Chinese martial arts education became a part of the overall physical education. Martial arts summer camps, short-term and long-term training centers, cram schools, and college-level kung fu classes began to be gradually institutionalized. Some of the trainings resulted in on-stage performances, such as Peking opera, opera of other provinces, kung fu shows, TV shows, or martial arts films. The kung fu shows of Bruce Lee (1940-1973), Jackie Chan (b. 1954), Jet Li (b. 1963), and Dennie Yen (b. 1963) are globally well-known examples.

Confucianism has been a major influence on East Asian and Southeast Asian educational systems. It was derived from Confucius's educational beliefs and teacher-student ethics in the Zhou Dynasty (1100-221 B.C.) of China. The Confucian ethic systems enthrone educators and turn teachers into god-like holy beings deserving of unlimited respect, high honor, and academic worship from everybody. Li Mubai's respect and revenge for his teacher, Jiang Nanhe, at the unexpected price of his own life can be one of the best proofs. Even today, educators—including K-12 teachers and university professors—in Confucian societies that have never experienced the Cultural Revolution (1967-1976)[4] enjoy better social status and salaries than those in countries without Confucian impacts.

Confucius (551-479 B.C.) is one of the greatest Chinese educators and philosophers in history, though current scholars in the research field of education may not entirely accept every part of his teaching philosophy and educational belief. For instance, gender egalitarianism was probably Confucius's oversight. The ratio of male educators and female educators did not seem to concern Confucius. Neither did the disproportion of the female student population to the male student population. What current academies adopt to decide educators' professional destiny, such as students' teaching evaluations or the tenure-review processes, was illogical to ancient Confucians because it would not make sense to grade, promote, or fire gods or goddesses, which teachers were compared to.

The Interrelation between Castration Fears and Penis Envy

In fact, teachers are not truly omnipotent and flawless deities but ordinary human beings. I argue that castration fears and penis envy impact them in the teacher-student relationships that the film narratives include.

Male sexual organs, especially the penis, in patriarchal societies signify male pride, privilege, and superiority so strongly that Sigmund Freud (1856-1939) proposed his beliefs in "castration fears" and "penis envy." He even advocated males' "small penis syndrome." Briefly speaking, I regard penis envy as women's recognition and acceptance of their lack of the prestige that the penis represents—namely, their so-called inferiority to men and unqualifiedness to deserve equal rights according to patriarchal social norms—and patriarchal societies' sexual discrimination against the female gender. Freudians indirectly associate little girls' penis envy with their Electra Complex (little girls' unconscious love for their fathers). The realization of women's lack of the penis and everything that the penis stands for in patriarchal social rules results in the unconscious equation of women with "castrated" creatures and in men fearing the loss of their male sexual organs—castration fears. Freudians believe that castration fears stop the Oedipus Complex (little boys' unconscious competitions with their fathers for intimate relations with their mothers), dilute little boys' childhood intimacy with mothers, make possible their identification with fathers and the patriarchal world, and transfer their original desires for mothers to romantic love for spouses or women who share similar characteristics with their mothers. The ineffectiveness of the Oedipus Complex is associated with "small penis syndrome" because, as Freud points out, the smaller size of little boys' penises and the larger size of their fathers' penises determine the little boys' losses in the competitions with fathers for mothers. Freudians also think that little girls who suffer from the "masculinity complex" reject the patriarchal definition of them as castrated creatures, refuse to give up their childhood intimacy with mothers or women who share similar characteristics with their mothers, and become lesbians.

After Freud, numerous psychologists, psychoanalysts, and psychiatrists developed their own research related to the above-mentioned Freudian theories.[5] What I adopt for my narrative analyses of the martial arts films is the interrelation between men's castration fears and women's penis envy. I argue that castration fears indirectly result in the cinematic highlight of women's penis envy because women's penis envy indicates their inferiority and impossibility of them jockeying into positions of power, thus helping safeguard male empowerment and superiority.

> The castration complex in the girl is started by the sight of the genital organs of the other sex. She immediately notices the difference and, it must be admitted, its significance. She feels herself at a great disadvantage, and often declares that she would like to have something like that too and falls a victim to penis envy, which leaves ineradicable traces on her development and character-formation, and even in the most favorable instances, is not overcome without a great expenditure of mental energy That the girl recognizes the fact that she lacks a penis does not mean that she accepts its absence lightly. On the contrary, she clings for a long time to the desire to get something like it, and believes in that possibility for an extraordinary number of years and even at a time when her knowledge of reality has long since led her to abandon the fulfillment of this desire as being quite unattainable, analysis proves that it still persists in the unconscious, and retains a considerable charge of energy. The desire after all to obtain the penis for which she so much longs may even contribute to the motives that impel a grown-up woman to come to analysis, and what she quite reasonably expects to get from analysis, such as the capacity to pursue an intellectual career, can often be recognized as a sublimated modification of this repressed wish.[6]

Dramatizing women's inferiority or lower status alleviates castration fears. Therefore, showing women sacrificing themselves, dying for men, or mistreating themselves for the sake of men's best interests releases the male teachers from castration fears and brings them joy. I contend that this joy, psychologically speaking, may be similar to a sort of unconscious masochist ecstasy at the sight of women's sexual self-mistreatment or death for men. My evidence lies in the female teachers' dearth of experiencing either similar self-sacrifice by male students or the empowerment overwhelmingly connected to male teachers in the films. If there were truly unlimited women's rights and gender egalitarianism and no glass ceiling for ancient Chinese women in the films, the teacher-student complex should have already applied to not only male teachers but also female teachers.

Jockeying the Position of Educational or Confucian Enthronement

In the films that this article analyzes, there are at least five male teachers or masters: He Yünqing in *Legend of the Mountain*, Jiang Nanhe and Li Mubai in *Crouching Tiger Hidden Dragon*, and Broken Sword and the head of the calligraphy school in *Hero*. In the same films, the number of female teachers is smaller than half the number of male teachers: only Jade Fox in *Crouching Tiger Hidden Dragon* and Liu Yüfang in *Seven Swords*. Regardless of whether this ratio results merely from a random sample, the unbalanced proportion of men and women in teaching positions reflects the ancient Chinese fact that women's opportunities to occupy teaching positions were more limited than men's. It signifies the patriarchal socio-cultural disbelief in women's professional capacities. It denotes the ancient Chinese presumption and systematic endorsement of men's superiority regarding teaching abilities. It matches the truth that Confucianism, the tradition to respect and worship educators, more obviously enthroned male teachers than female teachers in ancient China although it did not block all the possibilities for women to work as teachers. It grants ancient Chinese women teachers a professional place in either private chambers or institutionalized organizations, and offers them some working and career opportunities, as Dorothy Ko describes in her book on the women teachers in inner chambers.[7] However, the disproportion of male teachers to female teachers still indicates the maximum limitation that patriarchy sets up for women and feminism. On the one hand, ancient Chinese women teachers are lucky because they have their career.[8] However, on the other hand, ancient Chinese women teachers are not fully free from patriarchal societies' expectation for women's self-sacrifice, miserable deaths or even suicides. Liu Yüfang's sacrifice of herself and insistence to be the only adult staying in the village to protect the children irrespective of her lack of martial arts training in *Seven Swords* and Jade Fox's miserable death in *Crouching Tiger Hidden Dragon* are illustrations. The different styles used to cinematically portray male teachers and female teachers in the films also serve to undergird my argument. In the following paragraphs, I will compare and contrast the different cinematic portraits of male teachers and female teachers in the films.

In *Legend of the Mountain*, He Yünqing is also given a perfect cinematic image as a male tutor, too. He does not go through an agonizing job-hunting process. Nor does he experience any bottlenecks in the competitive job market. He even does not actively start to search for a teaching position; on the contrary, the teaching position comes to him entirely unexpectedly. The age of his student is also higher than he originally expected. His initial assumption of teaching a child is transformed by the fact that his student is already an adult woman. The student's higher age indicates that his teaching abilities are at the adults' level. It prevents him from being only a caretaker-like or nanny-like teacher of pupils. It upgrades his teaching status to professor-like teachers of adults in higher education. He Yünqing's drawback is that he does not actively refuse physical intimacy with his female student. Except for this, He Yünqing is portrayed as a good male tutor.

The filmic portrayal of Li Mubai as Yü Jiaolong's martial arts mentor in *Crouching Tiger Hidden Dragon* is even better than that of He Yünqing in *Legend of the Mountain* from the standpoint of gender equality to avoid objectifying nice-looking women students; he rejects Yü Jiaolong's sexual seduction. In other words, Li Mubai's image as a male teacher does not cause the same feminist criticism with which women viewers may react to He Yünqing.

Broken Sword's image as a male teacher in *Hero* is not limited only to the teaching level. It extends to Moon's everyday life because he adopts, raises, supports, and educates her since her childhood. He not only teaches but also parents Moon. Although it is not fair for him to sleep with Moon only to revenge Flying Snow's previous romantic relationship with Long Sky, Moon's attitude toward Broken Sword is reflected in the Chinese proverb: "Once he is a teacher for a day, he is regarded as a father for the rest of the whole life."

The head of the calligraphy school in *Hero* is represented as a patriotic teacher whose art of hand-writing spiritually defends his country and guides his teenage or adult students toward the same patriotic path. His immortal patriotism outlives his physical death. His teaching abilities exceed his profession of calligraphy and include his everlasting love and endless passions for his country. His motionless sitting posture and tranquil writing gestures are in fact the loudest shouts and the most dynamic reactions to impact his students. He teaches not only during his regular teaching hours but also every minute before his death as an indisputable patriotic role model.

Jiang Nanhe's cinematic image as a male teacher in *Crouching Tiger Hidden Dragon* is probably the only disputed part deserving viewers' severe critique (See my audience research in Appendix 9-1). However, his attitude toward male students is without problems. Li Mubai safeguards Jiang Nanhe's respectful image as a male teacher regardless of Jade Fox's accusation that Jiang Nanhe tricks her by "bed[ding] her but not teach[ing] her kung fu."[9] In terms of professional martial arts knowledge and skills, he is still portrayed as a highly respected master and advances Li Mubai's kung fu. He still wins the unquestionable respect from his student, Li Mubai. He is still rewarded by Li Mubai's avenge of his death at the cost of Li Mubai's life. Although Jiang Nanhe's sexual relationship with Jade Fox may irritate feminist viewers, the cinematic image of Jiang Nanhe as a male teacher is undoubtedly protected by men, such as Li Mubai.

Crouching Tiger Hidden Dragon includes one more teacher: Jade Fox. She initiates Yü Jiaolong's learning of kung fu as her personal tutor but pretends to be her servant. She also initiates Yü Jiaolong's dreams about the martial arts world. Jade Fox stands out from most ancient Chinese women who lack martial arts training, career, freedom, and adventures. She also differs from most ancient Chinese women because of her courage to expose her unhappy cohabitation with

Jiang Nanhe, disclose how Jiang Nanhe sleeps with and lies to her, and explain why she kills Jiang Nanhe and steals his secret manual of martial arts. Unfortunately, the overall cinematic image of Jade Fox is rather that of a she-devil who misleads and poisons her student than that of a female educator who deserves as much Confucian respect and gratitude as all the above-mentioned male teachers. Professionally speaking, the film clearly shows the limitation of Jade Fox's martial arts knowledge because she is illiterate. Her dependence on Yü Jiaolong's reading comprehension of advanced kung fu disqualifies Jade Fox to be an adequate teacher for Yü Jiaolong. This kind of cinematic image is definitely not ideal. Moreover, she dies a miserable death. The way she crawls on the ground and the physical gesture at the moment of her death turn her almost into a dying animal, which is opposite to the way Li Mubai meditates and sits on the ground at the moment of his death as if he were a Buddha or a highly respected sage. Different from Li Mubai's revenge for Jiang Nanhe's death, Yü Jiaolong does not avenge Jade Fox's death; on the contrary, she tries to rescue the life of Li Mubai, who kills Jade Fox.

Liu Yüfang in *Seven Swords* does not have a negative image as a female teacher. However, from the beginning to the end of the film, the most significant part of her job seems to be her protection of pupils, not her teaching. Throughout the film, her most important instructions for the children are tips or reminders about how to shelter themselves and save their own lives. Although at the end of the film Liu Yüfang and her students read Wen Tianxiang's "Zhengqi ge" (Extol of Integrity), the scene does not include her as a reader. Her teaching contents, teaching methods, teaching philosophy, teaching materials, teaching experience, educational background, and professional credentials are indicative of a relatively minor social status throughout the film. The priority of her profession and teaching career is not as high as that of her protection of and care for the children's safety. Her students are so young that the level of her teaching seems lower than the level of the above-mentioned male teachers. She is more a nanny-like caretaker than a Confucius-like educator enthroned at the Confucian temple:

> Occupationally, effective teachers are trained to be caring towards students, and personally, many are inclined as well to be nurturing to others . . . . Women, more so than men, are socialized to assume these nurturing roles.[10]

Even though she successfully defeats the traitor and rescues the children, she is portrayed not as a heroine who enjoys the villagers' esteem but as a hysterical, posttraumatic, pathetic madwoman who crazily waves a sword in the air and cannot tell the past from the present until her boyfriend helps her return from the past to the present. Although Liu Yüfang's teaching position looks more institutionalized because of the village school's endorsement than does Jade Fox's, neither female teachers' cinematic image is as reputable as the above-mentioned male teachers'.

In a comparison of the male teachers and female teachers, the male teachers seem to be sheltered and revered by the defensive style of cinematic portrayals; both female teachers are portrayed as disqualified, negative, evil, lower-leveled or irrational educators. None of the female teachers' students volunteer to reward them while many male teachers' students do, suggesting that female teachers deserve less reputation, gratitude, or honor than male teachers. The glass ceiling against which female teachers' heads bump, the limitations on feminism, and the restrictions of gender equality show not merely the disproportionate ratio of male teachers and female teachers but also the cinematic images of male teachers and female teachers.

Educational Sculpting Power over Women: The Penis-Like Chalk and Swords as a Relief from Castration Fears

In addition to their status as educators, Yünqing in *Legend of the Mountain* and Jiang Nanhe in *Crouching Tiger Hidden Dragon* both seem to enjoy the beauty of female students during teaching hours. From a feminist viewpoint, this appreciation of women's appearance is a type of objectification of women. The same sort of male-centered appreciation for female students' appearances occurs in the cases of Jiang Nanhe and Li Mubai as male mentors in *Crouching Tiger Hidden Dragon*. Jiang's and Li's female students, Jade Fox and Yü Jiaolong, are beautiful, too. Although Li Mubai's response to Yü Jiaolong's seduction is ambiguous and thus not obviously chauvinistic, Jiang Nanhe takes advantage of Jade Fox's wish to learn his kung fu and feels free to have a sexual relationship with her. In *Hero*, Broken Sword also has an exceptionally beautiful student, Moon, whom he sleeps with. The only exception from all these male teachers is probably the head of the calligraphy school in *Hero*. The film does not explicitly depict the appearance of his female students.

If there were truly gender egalitarianism, female teachers should have also had equally nice-looking male students even though feminist viewers would not like female teachers to repeat male teachers' objectification of students or the male sex. Unfortunately, the films do not provide details on the appearance of female teachers' male students. In *Crouching Tiger Hidden Dragon*, Jade Fox does not have any male students. In *Seven Swords*, there is not any elaboration on the appearance of Liu Yüfang's pupils, and they are all children at the levels lower than high school and middle school. Liu Yüfang, as a female teacher, does not show any special interest in her male students' appearances. The patriarchal society in ancient China did not encourage female teachers to be interested in male students' appearances though a number of male teachers seem to enjoy female students' appearances in the films.

There is a similar lack of detailed depiction of teachers' appreciation of students' appearance in pairs of female teachers and female students or male teachers and male students. For instance, in *Crouching Tiger Hidden Dragon*, Jade Fox and Yü Jiaolong are a teacher-student pair who are both female. The female student's appearance does not have much to do with the female teacher. In the same film, Jiang Nanhe and Li Mubai are a pair of teacher and student who are both male. The male student's appearance does not seem to influence the male teacher, either. Judging from these two cases, students' appearances do not impact teachers of the same sex.

Because most students admitted to ancient Chinese educational institutions were not female but male,[11] the large percentage of male teachers' appreciation of female students' appearance in the films does not match the historical facts, the issue deserves academic exploration and begs rational explanations because the female teachers seem to lack strong interest in male students' appearances and the heterosexual teachers have no interest in students of the same sex.

One of the possible explanations is that men of a higher status tend to enjoy the ecstasy of possessing women, especially nice-looking women, of a lower status in patriarchal China. Psychoanalytically speaking, the phallocentric value system regards men as owners of penises, which represent power, authority, and higher status, while women lack penises, possess less privilege than men, and thus depend on their appearance to please men or people of a higher status. Owners of penises, therefore, feel more certain about their possession of power, authority, or high status when they view what women lack and compare themselves with women. Female students of a relatively inferior status imbue male teachers' higher status and provide male teachers with the sense of authoritative superiority, psychological comfort, and security or a guarantee of empowerment. The existence of penises, psychologically speaking, precludes the need to worry about the absence of penises and hence is a relief from castration fears. Female students' attractive appearances, in the male-centered psychological perception, function to compensate for women's lack of penises and male privilege in patriarchal China and indirectly strengthens and certifies male teachers' possession of penises, authority, power, and high status as well as their sense of superiority and confidence.

In this sense, women or female students in the films are like mirrors that reflect what men unconsciously want. In *Crouching Tiger Hidden Dragon*, Jade Fox is like a mirror, showing that Jiang Nanhe, regardless of the historical fact that the Wudang martial arts school in ancient China seldom admitted female students, wants to feel his higher status and possession of power signified by his penis in the patriarchal sociocultural system through a female student's appearance, body, sexuality, and sexual service as rewards for his instruction.

Only a female student's lack of penis can serve as a contrast to the existence of his penis and whatever power and privilege that his penis stands for; therefore, the student that he really wants must be female though it is abnormal and unusual for Wudang kung fu teachers to have female students. Only a female student's attractive appearance and sexual companionship can multiply the confirmation of his high status, power, authority, and superiority. The same is true of He Yünqing's relationship with his female student in *Legend of the Mountain*. The more afraid of castration they are, the more comfort they unconsciously need from their female students.

Broken Sword in *Hero* needs more than Jiang Nanhe in *Crouching Tiger Hidden Dragon*. What he wants is not merely to prove himself through his female student but also to prove that he is as powerful as Long Sky, the man who competes with him for his girlfriend. His is not merely a psychological battle between a male teacher and a female student in terms of differences of gender and status but also a psychological war between two men who share a romantic relationship with the same woman. The war between Broken Sword and Long Sky is a sort of psychological competition for which a man can find and win the most satisfaction from the female sex. Under such a circumstance, only a woman whose vagina accommodates Broken Sword's penis whenever and wherever he wants, regardless of his purpose, can release him from the failure of losing the war with Long Sky and contrast his stronger power to Long Sky's. Flying Snow is not the woman forever standing by to satisfy him but the female student forever ready to serve him in whichever aspects he needs. Because his psychological scar resulted from his loss of Flying Snow to Long Sky, he keenly desires to show that the immediate and convenient satisfaction, which his female student offers to him but Flying Snow cannot provide, not only compensates for his loss and lack but also brings him the wanted sense of triumph and superiority over Long Sky.

Broken Sword's psychological need to feel the existence of penis, power, superiority, authority, and high status also deserves the audience's cautious scrutiny. The best proof is that his female student takes care of his affairs of everyday life as if she were a housekeeper or housewife to take care of his affairs. This seems to confirm his need for a woman—someone inferior and less significant because of the lack of the organ that signifies the same power he possesses—to deal with trivialities and less important matters, thus creating a contrast to his superiority and importance. High-level matters deserve his own attention and efforts; low-ranked matters deserve his secretary's or housekeeper's attention. Psychologically speaking, only a woman, especially an assistant-like woman, who keeps track of small and less important details for him, can be low enough to contrast his elevated statement.

I argue that the penis-like chalk and swords in linguistic or martial arts courses embody the metaphorical existence of the above-mentioned male teachers' penises—that is, power, privilege, authority, superiority, and high status—and rescue them from the psychological hurt of castration fears. My argument is supported not simply by my analyses of Broken Sword, He Yünqing, and Jiang Nanhe in the previous paragraphs but also the fact that the same penis-like chalk and swords do not produce the same psychological effects in female teachers' hearts based on Jade Fox's and Liu Yüfang's interactions with students. The penis-like chalk and swords do not release female teachers from any castration complex. Female teachers do not need male students to rescue them or certify the existence of anything that denotes male privilege. This is perhaps one of the best explanations of why the films tend to elaborate male teachers' educational patronization or romantic relations with attractive female students more than female teachers' interactions with male students.

Teacher-student pairs of the same sex also support my argument. Male students possess the same sexual organs that indicate the same male privilege as male teachers. Male students do not lack penises and, therefore, cannot contrast their male teachers' possession of more powerful organs. In terms of the phallocentric psychological meanings of penises, male students and male teachers are all owners of penises and male pride. Male teachers cannot show off by using anything penis-like in front of male students, and the status of male students, who have as much male pride as male teachers in the patriarchal value system, is not low enough from a chauvinistic viewpoint to contrast male teachers' superiority. This may be why male teachers need female students, not male students, to subconsciously comfort themselves in the films. With reference to female teachers and female students, they share the same lack of organs that imply the male privilege; therefore, the psychological meaning of the penis-like chalk and swords between male teachers and female teachers does not appear in the interactions between female teachers and female students.

Unconscious Sadomasochist Ecstasy: Female Students' Sacrifice for Male Teachers and Penis Envy

Beyond the penis-like chalk and swords to alleviate castration fears, male teachers in the films tend to have female students' sacrifice of their lives for them in order to please them and fulfill their wishes. The students' sacrifice does not occur in female teachers' cases. The contrasts between female students' sacrifice for male teachers and the students' lack of sacrifice for female teachers deserve scholars' feminist scrutiny.

I contend that male teachers' superiority and satisfaction partially derives from female students' acceptance of their lack of everything penises represent in the patriarchal socio-cultural evaluation system. From a male-centered standpoint, one of the deepest kinds of women's acceptance of their lack is probably their exhibition of penis envy, and one of the ways for women to show and confirm their penis envy is to do whatever they can or even to sacrifice and mistreat themselves in order to favor or please owners of penises and male pride. Women students' display of penis envy contrasts male teachers' possession of penises and everything superior that their sexual organs refer to in phallocentric social contexts. It also highlights the unconscious delights that male teachers may experience but are not aware of. The delights resemble the abusive or sadomasochist ecstasy of seeing people sexually mistreat themselves in order to demonstrate how low their status is, how high the viewers' status is, and how much the viewers' high status is what people at a lower status envy. That is to say, women's penis envy is also envy of higher status, male pride, and whatever more powerful and superior in the patriarchal value system. To ask women students for as much envy of penises and male privilege as possible is to ask women students to lower themselves as much as possible—namely, to request female students to look down upon themselves, sacrifice or ignore their self-esteem and dignity, and psychologically mistreat themselves as much as possible. The more penis envy male teachers unconsciously need to see from their female students, the more sacrifice and self-mistreatment they need from their female teachers, and the more sadomasochist and abusive they unconsciously are at the moment of their female students' sacrifice, self-mistreatment, and even suicide.

In *Legend of the Mountain*, Yüenian should have been given enough feminist awareness and related support to say no to, strongly reject, and escape from He Yünqing if there were really unlimited gender egalitarianism and if he were truly what she describes: the male initiator of their sexual relationship or even the drunken male teacher who intends to rape his female student. It is questionable why everybody else in the banquet mysteriously does nothing or even disappears at the moment when He Yünqing and Yüenian have sex regardless of whether Yüenian seduces her male teacher or whether He Yünqing forces himself on his female student to the extent that she cannot resist him. The film, after all, still does not clarify this sexually scandalous teacher-student incident; it simply moves on to the seemingly doomed or already well-prescheduled morning-after scene, in which the male teacher and everybody else takes for granted Yüenian's lack of strong enough support structure to refuse him as well as her sacrifice of body and sexuality as the price paid for her failure to show her rejection. At the end of the film, the storyline even strongly implies that Yüenian volunteers to seductively initiate the sexual relationship with He Yünqing in exchange for his Buddhist scripts as if He Yünqing were entirely innocent and had no responsibility for initiating their sexual relationship. Their original teacher-student relationship would have already sufficed for her to steal or gain his religious scripts and their husband-wife relationship after their teacher-student relationship is unnecessary and in fact redundant if her goal is only to gain his scripts. The indication that Yüenian volunteers to discard and sacrifice her rights to say no to her male teacher, obey her teacher's request for their sexual relationship, or even self-mistreatingly take the blame for being the seductive initiator responsible for her male teacher's so-called "innocent premarital sex" in this film slays her feminist awareness, and puts her in a predicament in which she is cinematically portrayed as self-mistreating.

The blame that Jade Fox bears in *Crouching Tiger Hidden Dragon* is almost the same as the blame which Yüenian takes in *Legend of the Mountain*. Although Jade Fox in *Crouching Tiger Hidden Dragon* tries to defend and justify herself, the ending scenes that imply Yüenian is not a human being in *Legend of the Mountain* and that Jade Fox is as evil as a dying fox, which is also not a human being, crawling on the ground, mistreatingly denigrate these two women students, degrade them to animal-like or devil-like non-human creatures, and "butcher" their original self-identity as good and hard-studying students and social status as educators' wives or partners who also share the Confucian respect for teachers.

Yü Jiaolong is also a woman who volunteers to sacrifice herself for men in *Crouching Tiger Hidden Dragon*. She is portrayed as Li Mubai's female student who seductively unbuttons her dress, sexily exposes her neck, underwear, and shoulders, soaks her pants and outfit in the pond water so that the white and light-colored fabrics turn almost transparent and her body is almost visible under her wet clothes. In this sense, she bears the same blame as Jade Fox and Yüenian. In addition, she volunteers to make an almost suicidal decision, sacrifice herself, and jump into the bottomless abyss after Xiao Hu makes his wish to return home. She tries to make his wish come true regardless of her original wish to leave home, which is entirely contrary to his wish to go back home.

In *Hero*, Moon is a female student who sacrifices herself for her male teacher, Broken Sword. Although she does not bear the same seductive blame of initiating her sexual relationship with her male teacher as all the abovementioned female students, she is innocently used and taken advantage of by Broken Sword at the moment when she sleeps with him. He does not tell her in advance that he is using her as a tool to indirectly compete with Long Sky and test whether Flying Snow is jealous. Right after their sexual gratification, Broken Sword immediately kicks his female student off him regardless of the tears on her face and how she feels. His sexual irresponsibility in *Hero*, strictly speaking, is similar to Jiang Nanhe's sexual irresponsibility in *Crouching Tiger Hidden Dragon*. However, Broken Sword's actions do not result in any negative outcome; nor do they cause Moon's hatred of him. Moon does not accuse her male teacher in the way Jade Fox does. On the contrary, Moon advances her nearly self-mistreatingly sacrifice and volunteers to die for him by insisting on engaging in suicidal combats with Flying Snow to avenge his death. Broken Sword's escape from the blame for his sexual irresponsibility "slaughters" the gender equality that Moon deserves to enjoy as well as the feminist compensation for ancient Chinese women that feminist viewers hope to see in the film.

All the above-mentioned female students sacrifice themselves for their male teachers in stark contrast to the male students' lack of the same self-mistreating sacrifice for their teachers. For example, different from Moon in *Hero*, Li Mubai in *Crouching Tiger Hidden Dragon* does not intentionally decide to do anything suicidal in order to avenge his teacher. Contrary to Moon's understanding of Flying Snow's excellent kung fu and Flying Snow's statement of warning to Moon, it is entirely out of Li Mubai's original anticipation that he would be poisoned by Jade Fox at the moment when he attacks Jade Fox for his teacher. So Li Mubai does not plan or pre-schedule to be as self-mistreating as Moon to the extent of giving his life up though he shares the same wish to avenge the dead teacher with Moon. Neither do male pupils do anything suicidal to rescue Liu Yüfang in *Seven Swords*. All these male students' lack of the same sacrifice for their teachers in the films are not a coincidence but a collective representation and proof of the fact that the unconscious sadomasochist ecstasy of students' sacrifice works for male teachers but not for female teachers or pairs of teachers and students of the same sex.

Conclusion

Analytically comparing and critically reading King Hu's *Legend of the Mountain*, Ang Lee's *Crouching Tiger Hidden Dragon*, and Zhang Yimou's *Hero*, I conclude that there is a specially phallocentric kind of teacher-student complexes in these films. These grow out of the psychological subtleties hidden in the interactions between male teachers and female students in the patriarchal value system. Male teachers jockey the power position of educational or Chinese Confucian enthronement though female teachers are given some teaching opportunities but are limited by the glass ceiling. Male teachers' overall cinematic images are better than female teachers' as if they were standing upon the glass ceiling, against which female teachers' heads bump. Male teachers' penis-like chalk and swords in linguistic and martial arts courses increase their cultivating power and superiority over female students and signify their psychological need to be released from castration fears even though the same chalk, swords, educational sculpting power, and superior teaching status do not apply to female teachers or pairs of teachers and students of the same sex. Female students' determination to self-mistreatingly sacrifice themselves for male teachers may be a sort of unconscious sadomasochist ecstasy in the Sino-Western patriarchal socio-cultural trends that the films include.

References

Aguirre, Adalberto. *Women and Minority Faculty in the Academic Workplace: Recruitment, Retention, and Academic Culture.* San Francisco: Jossey-Bass, 2000, p. 61.
Clark, William. *Academic Charisma and the Origin of the Research University.* Chicago: University of Chicago Press, 2006.
Fennema, Elizabeth and Penelope Peterson. "Autonomous Learning Behavior: A Possible Explanation of Gender-Related Differences in Mathematics." *Gender Influences in Classroom Interaction.* Louise Cherry Wilkinson and Cora B. Marrett edt. New York: Academic Press, 1985, p. 26.
Ko, Dorothy. *Teachers of the Inner Chambers: Women and Culture in Seventeenth-Century China.* Stanford: Stanford University Press, 1994.
Macfarlane, Bruce. *The Academic Citizen: the Virtue of Service in University Life.* London and New York: Routledge, 2007.
Perna, Laura. "The Relationship between Family and Employment Outcomes." *The Challenge of Balancing Faculty Careers and Family Work.* John W. Curtis edt. San Francisco: Jossey-Bass, 2005, p. 17.
Poole, Gregory S. and Ya-chen Chen. *Ethnographies of the Professoriate in East Asia: The Cultural Translation of Faculty Tradition in the Face of Globalizing Reforms.* Rotterdam, the Netherlands: Sense Publishers, forthcoming.
Rance, PTJ. *Martial Arts.* London: Virgin Books, 2005, p. 128.
Rosser, Sue V. *The Science Glass Ceiling: Academic Women Scientists and the Struggle to Succeed.* New York: Routledge, 2004, p. 54.
Tsouluhas, Litsa. "The Cost of Caring: Female Beginning Teachers, Occupational Stress and Coping" (Ph.D. Dissertation). Department of Curriculum, Teaching and Learning, University of Toronto, 2005.
Woolf, Virginia. *A Room of One's Own.* Orlando, FL: Harcourt, 2005.

Notes

1. Although her return to Henry Hoggins may result from their newly established romantic relationship, it does not make sense for her to give up her ambition and career for their love while Henry Hoggins sacrifices nothing for their love. "Research suggests that some women who want marriage and children settle for lower-status positions . . . [For instance] . . . several structural and social forces contribute to the notion that family commitments come at the expense of career attainment among college and university faculty." For details, consult Laura Perna's "The Relationship between Family and

Employment Outcomes." *The Challenge of Balancing Faculty Careers and Family Work.* edt. John W. Curtis. (San Francisco: Jossey-Bass, 2005), 17.

Take the discovery of the American Association of University Professors (AAUP) for instance, the U.S. faculty "salary gap between men and women faculty has not narrowed and . . . in fact, has expanded at the assistant professor level." Consult Adalberto Aguirre's *Women and Minority Faculty in the Academic Workplace: Recruitment, Retention, and Academic Culture.* (San Francisco: Jossey-Bass, 2000), 61. In Sue Rosser's research, one of her interviewees confessed that "there is still a level of discrimination against women—can she really do . . . work as well as a man?" For details, see Sue V. Rosser's *The Science Glass Ceiling: Academic Women Scientists and the Struggle to Succeed.* (New York: Routledge, 2004), 54.

2. For Western-style education systems in China, consult the Chinese part of the beginning chapter in Gregory S. Poole and Ya-chen Chen's *Ethnographies of the Professoriate in East Asia: The Cultural Translation of Faculty Tradition in the Face of Globalizing Reforms.* Rotterdam, the Netherlands: Sense Publishers, forthcoming. For Western-style education systems in the West, consult William Clark's *Academic Charisma and the Origin of Research University* and Bruce Macfarlane's *The Academic Citizen: the Virtue of Service in University Life.*

3. For details about the initiation of Western-style schooling systems in China, consult Gregory S. Poole and Ya-chen Chen's *Ethnographies of the Professoriate in East Asia*: *the Cultural Translation of Faculty Tradition in the Face of Globalizing Reforms.* Rotterdam, Netherlands: Sense Publishers, forthcoming.

4. The Chinese Communist Party had the Cultural Revolution in Mainland China from 1967-1976. During this period, the whole educational systems were entirely changed. Students' power struggles against teachers were frequently seen, and numerous educators and elites were sent down. The Cultural Revolution resulted in the overall Mainland Chinese academic decline. Its damage cannot even be erased in the early twenty-first century.

5. Carl Jung, Anna Freud, Ernest Jones, Melanie Klein, Heinz Kohut, Otto Rank, Harry Stack Sullivan, Susan Sutherland, Isaacs, and Erich Fromm are all influenced by Sigmund Freud. Other scholars who digest Freudian studies include Karen Horney, Jacques Lacan, Jacques Derrida, Luce Irigaray, Julia Kristeva, Hélène Cixous, Nancy Chodorow, etc. For details, consult their academic publications.

6. Betty Friedan, "The Sexual Solipsism of Sigmund Freud." *The Feminine Mystique.* (New York: W.W. Norton, 2001), 103-104.

7. Dorothy Ko, *Teachers of the Inner Chambers: Women and Culture in Seventeenth-Century China.* (Stanford: Stanford University Press, 1994).

8. For example, Virginia Woolf complains about women's difficulties in having their own career or space. For details, consult her *A Room of One's Own.* (Orlando, FL: Harcourt, 2005).

9. Rance, PTJ. *Martial Arts.* (London: Virgin Books, 2005), 128.

10. Litsa Tsouluhas, "The Cost of Caring: Female Beginning Teachers, Occupational Stress and Coping" (Ph.D. Dissertation). (Department of Curriculum, Teaching and Learning, University of Toronto, 2005), 80.

11. Even if schools admit both male and female students, it is still possible that "teachers do not treat girls and boys the same in classrooms." For details, consult

Elizabeth Fennema and Penelope Peterson's "Autonomous Learning Behavior: A Possible Explanation of Gender-Related Differences in Mathematics." *Gender Influences in Classroom Interaction*. eds. Louise Cherry Wilkinson and Cora B. Marrett. (New York: Academic Press, 1985), 26.

Chapter Ten
A Chinese Cinematic Martial Arts Room of Pygmalion's Own

This chapter offers Sino-Western comparative supports for my arguments in previous chapters reading the glass ceiling for the unlimited advancement of feminism and the incompleteness of "Chinese cinematic martial arts feminism." I combine Plato's "cave theory" in *The Republic*, Virginia Woolf's insistence on a room of women's own in *A Room of One's Own*, the gender theorem of the "glass ceiling," and literary textual analyses of film texts. Intertextuality brings and mixes these elements. So far there has not been the same academic combination of theoretical explorations to investigate women's roles and test filmmakers' feminist revisions of gender ideology in martial arts films.

> And now, I said, let me show in a figure how far our nature is enlightened or unenlightened—Behold! Human beings living in an underground den, which has a mouth open towards the light and reaching all along the den; here they have been from their childhood, and have their legs and necks chained so that they cannot move, and can only see before them, being prevented by the chains from turning round their heads. Above and behind them a fire is blazing at a distance, and between the fire and the prisoners there is a raised way; and you will see, if you look, a low wall built along the way, like the screen which marionette players have in front of them, over which they show the puppets.
> Plato *The Republic Book VII*

One of Plato's most famous books records how Socrates illustrates the philosophical epiphany of the truth to a young man called Glaucon. It is the well-known allegory of the cave. Inside of the cave, prisoners are chained, and their necks and legs cannot move. They are forced to face the wall in front of them. Behind them, directors control marionettes or puppets with distant flames as the source of light to project the images of dummies or dolls onto the front wall of the cave.[1] In this cave, detainees view the images projected onto the wall, just like people in movie theaters see motion pictures on the silver screen. The allegorical cave is like a movie theater. The front wall of the cave is like the theatrical screen that shows Chinese martial arts films of the new millennium: *Crouching Tiger Hidden Dragon* (2000), *Hero* (2002), *House of Flying Daggers* (2003), *Seven Swords* (2005), *The Promise* (2005), *The Banquet* (2006), and *Curse of the Golden Flower* (2007). The directors of the puppet shows in the cave parallel filmmakers: Ang Lee (b. 1954), Zhang Yimou (b. 1951), Chen Kaige (b. 1952), Tsui Hark (b. 1952), and Feng Xiaogang (b. 1958). With their feet tied since childhood and the freedom to go wherever they want simply a dream, most ancient Chinese women were like the prisoners whose feet are chained and physical movements restricted in the cave. The mannequins under the directors' control mirror actresses who play the roles of ancient Chinese women in kung fu movies. They are ancient Chinese ladies cinematically sculpted by kung fu filmmakers, just like Galatea, who is the ivory beauty sculpted by Pygmalion in the Greco-Roman myth. In other words, filmmakers of these martial arts movies are the cinematic Pygmalion. This chapter will articulate and theorize the epiphany of truth that the cinematic martial arts world created by directors, including King Hu (1932-1997)[2] and current Chinese award-winning directors, is a Chinese cinematic martial arts room of Pygmalion's own. In this room, ancient Chinese women win the freedom that filmmakers provide on the one hand, but they can rise little beyond the "glass ceiling" on the other hand. I argue that this is due to what I term the "Chinese cinematic martial arts world of Pygmalion's own," one which is not necessarily the women's own.

A Touch of Zen, Crouching Tiger Hidden Dragon, Hero, House of Flying Daggers, Seven Swords, The Promise, The Banquet, and *Curse of the Golden Flower*[3] can be viewed as a sort of martial arts "room," in which filmmakers create, sculpt, and portray the images of ancient Chinese women that they imagine. It is like a martial arts "room" where gender egalitarianism attempts to compensate ancient Chinese women for past inequality. Virginia Woolf (1882-1941) recognized that "a woman must have money and a room of her own," in a renowned statement from her book, *A Room of One's Own*. This fact holds true for ancient Chinese women included in martial arts films of the new millennium. If ancient Chinese women want to rewrite their life stories or autobiographies, they must be financially independent and possess a "room of their own." If current filmmakers want to revise biographies or *Bildungsroman* (literary works or fictions about protagonists' growth or psychological changes over time) of ancient Chinese women cinematically, they still have to grant them a more spacious "room" than the ancient Chinese reality. The "room of women's own," however, is not exactly the same as the "room of the cinematic Pygmalion's own" where filmmakers scribe ancient Chinese women's biographies. I contend that the martial arts films of the new millennium are a "room of the cinematic Pygmalion's own" for filmmakers' rewriting of ancient women's biographies only, not yet the place where ancient Chinese women interpret their expectations. As in the Platonic cave, the controllers who arrange puppets and stuffed animals are the filmmakers and not the ancient Chinese women themselves.

There Is Truly a Room

Generally speaking, ancient Chinese women enjoyed fewer rights than men. The martial arts world serves as an imaginary space to compensate them. It enables ancient Chinese women to gain more freedom and control their fate. It highlights the variety of women's choices that ancient patriarchal society usually disallowed, releases women from the patriarchal oversimplification of women's capability and thoughts, and problematizes how they deal with romantic love.

The imaginary world of martial arts, to some extent, releases ancient Chinese women from foot-binding and rewards them with the fantasy of the space to develop themselves, protect themselves, and even defeat or conquer men. It also unbinds them in terms of education, critical thinking, talent, ambition, job market, career, financial difficulties, ceaseless housework, opportunities to socialize and interact with different men, and the freedom or right to choose their spouses and decide their fates. Accordingly, Yang Huizhen in *A Touch of Zen*; Yü Jiaolong, Jade Fox, and Yü Xiulian in *Crouching Tiger Hidden Dragon*; Flying Snow and Moon in *Hero*; Xiaomei in *House of Flying Daggers*; Liu Yüfang and Lüzhu in *Seven Swords*; Qingcheng in *The Promise*; and Qing Nü and Wan'er in *The Banquet*; the queen, the king's first wife, and Jiang Chan in *Curse of the Golden Flower* do not suffer from foot-binding, financial difficulties, household chores, child care, or illiteracy. They have talent, ambition, and plans for their lives.

Ancient Chinese women in the films do gain some freedom and compensation. For instance, women in the films are concerned with romantic love, and most of their love triangles in the cinematic martial arts films involve one woman and two men to contrast with the male-centered polygamous marital system that usually included one man and multiple women. Zhang Yimou's *House of Flying Daggers* offers two men, Jin and Liu, for Xiaomei to choose from. Ang Lee's *Crouching Tiger Hidden Dragon* gives Yü Jiaolong choices: the fiancé arranged by her parents or Xiao Hu. Yü Xiulian also clearly discloses that her fiancé and Li Mubai are the two men in her mind, though her fiancé is dead. Flying Snow in Zhang Yimou's *Hero* has two men, Long Sky and Broken Sword, competing for her love. In Tsui Hark's *Seven Swords*, Liu Yüfang loves both Chu Zhaonan and Han Zhibang at the same time. In Chen Kaige's *The Promise*, both General Guangming and Kunlun love Qingcheng. Wan'er in Feng Xiaogang's *The Banquet* marries the former king and the new king but loves Prince Wuluan. The Queen in *Curse of the Golden Flower* marries the king but has an extramarital relationship with his firstborn. Each one of the seven kung fu films of the new millennium has at least one romantic triangle that is composed of two men and one woman. It is not merely coincidence that so many martial arts films share the non-patriarchal archetype of love triangles. These filmmakers seem to hold a common view: to challenge the ancient Chinese male-centered polygamous system with the cinematic presentation of the one-woman-and-two-men romantic triangle. Even though Yang Huizhen in *A Touch of Zen* and Jade Fox in *Crouching Tiger Hidden Dragon*[4] do not have any explicit experience in love triangles, their premarital sexual relationships with men without traditional Chinese social constraints are a dramatic and sarcastic contrast to the ancient Chinese double standards that required women's but not men's virginity and chastity. That is to say, in these films, there is truly a "room" reserved for women's rights and a feminist dialogue questioning phallocentrism. Thus Rey Chow's implication that these filmmakers' "wish to 'liberate' women" is true.[5]

Kung fu enables Yang Huizhen, Yü Jiaolong, Yü Xiulian, Jade Fox, Flying Snow, Moon, Xiaomei, Wan'er, Jiang Chan and Jiang Chan's mother to participate in physical exercise and sportsmanship.[6] This access to sports grants them the capability to travel where they want and favors their ability to control their lives. For example, in *Hero*, Moon travels to beg Nameless to join Broken Sword and to prevent Nameless from assassinating Ying Zheng; furthermore, she journeys to fight Flying Snow. Additionally, kung fu endows these martial arts ladies with the capacity to protect themselves and even defeat men, who are usually deemed stronger than and superior to women in the stereotypical Chinese patriarchal society. For instance, in *The Banquet*, Wan'er exceeds Prince Wuluan's skill at swordplay. She clearly demonstrates her capability to use the *yüenü jian* (the sword of women in the Yüe State) to defeat him, although they learned martial arts at the same time during childhood. In these films, female protagonists gain opportunities to develop their talent and ambition in their contemporary societies. They are also given the energy and capability to have their own careers, which result in their independence and advance their social status and self-esteem. All of the female protagonists are women with financial independence, professional credentials, and confidence. They make important contributions to society as well as to the films that include them.

The imaginary martial arts world or room of martial arts is originally called *jianghu*, whose literal meaning is "rivers and lakes" but whose metaphorical meaning is "fighting fair, respecting your opponent, and celebrating the shared bond that comes of living in the fraternity of the rivers and lakes. It is a recipe for a kind of honor among renegades; guideposts for living life the 'martial way.'"[7] With reference to the stereotypical room of kung fu fights, they usually happen in green bamboo forests, such as those in which Yang Huizhen in *A Touch of Zen*, Yü Jiaolong in *Crouching Tiger Hidden Dragon*, and Xaomei in *House of Flying Daggers* fight or exhibit their martial arts skills. Zhuo Boshang's detailed analysis of the 115 fighting scenes in the bamboo forest that King Hu's *A Touch of Zen* includes is probably the best evidence.[8] Taverns or

inns are also stereotypical locations of kung fu displays in martial arts films. According to King Hu, "I always feel that ancient taverns—especially inns in deserted and wild fields—are indeed the most dramatic locations. Seldom can a location include all the conflicts, time, and space."[9] King Hu also stated,
> Chinese opera favors public locations like a bustling tavern or an isolated inn. They became the stages for my movies. There is no place like these that concentrates the time, space, and conflict.[10]

Women's Sacrifices and Suffering

While the cinematic martial arts world does, to varying degrees, compensate ancient Chinese women, it is a mystery why many of these women end up suffering, sacrificing themselves, or losing their lives. For example, in *A Touch of Zen*, Yang Huizhen turns herself into an emotionless[11] birthing machine for a man she does not want to marry, simply because she would like to make this man's mother's wish come true. Xiaomei makes a fatal decision to pull the dagger out of her chest in exchange for Jin's life at the cost of her own after the blood bursts out of her body in *House of Flying Daggers*. In *Hero*, Flying Snow is determined to sacrifice her life for Nameless's assassination of the King, and Moon also willingly enters the fatal battle against Flying Snow for Broken Sword. Wan'er is assassinated when she becomes the ruler of the whole of China in *The Banquet*, whereas the king of Qin in *Hero* remains alive even as he becomes the ruler; the former's death provides an ironic contrast to the latter's survival. Both Wan'er's death in *The Banquet* and the death of the poisoned Queen in *Curse of the Golden Flower* signify the failure of these two ancient Chinese women to fulfill their dreams about the dynasties that they establish or support. The most puzzling case, however, is Yü Jiaolong's leap into the abyss only to make Xiao Hu's wishes come true in *Crouching Tiger Hidden Dragon*.

> Even though some martial arts films, such as *A Touch of Zen*, . . . focus on women, . . . most of them end up being "martyrs" of some value systems . . . the audience's "object of desires," . . . different kinds of men's unconscious imagination about women.[12]

If the martial arts room were truly a "room of ancient Chinese women's own," it should have been Xiao Hu's leap into the abyss for either his own wish or Yü Jiaolong's wish at the end of *Crouching Tiger Hidden Dragon*. It should not have been Yang Huizhen's pregnancy and childbirth that fulfilled Gu Shengzhai's mother's dream in *A Touch of Zen*. Wan'er in *The Banquet* and the queen in *Curse of the Golden Flower* should have succeeded in having their dreams come true and creating their own dynasties. If the cinematic martial arts room were truly a room of ancient Chinese women's own, all of their wishes should have come true to fully compensate them for the gender inequality they suffer in reality. The ending of *Crouching Tiger Hidden Dragon* should have been about how Yü Jiaolong's wish to get rid of familial restrictions comes true, not how she jumps into the valley between precipices for Xiao Hu's wish to return home, because her original struggle to leave home is entirely opposite to Xiao Hu's.

The same is true with Xiaomei in *House of Flying Daggers*. If there were truly a room of ancient Chinese women's own, she should not suffer guilt over who she likes less nor feel responsible for rescuing the two men from the love triangle. She should choose whomever she prefers regardless of the burden to save the men's lives at the end of *House of Flying Daggers*. Because men in the ancient Chinese polygamous system seldom felt guilty about their preference for favorite wives or concubines and seldom committed suicide to prevent their wives' or concubines' jealousy and fights with one another, the freedom and compensation for ancient Chinese women in the martial arts films should be choices equal to those of men, instead of their suicide and sacrifices for men up to the moment of their death.

A Room with a "Glass Ceiling" and "Job Ceiling"

One reasonable interpretation for the cause of the "ceiling" is that the freedom and compensation for ancient Chinese women in the films must be kept within and cannot exceed what filmmakers, or whoever dominates the storyline, allow. On the one hand, in films there is truly a "room" in which women benefit from what ancient Chinese society granted to them. On the other hand, the room provides only slightly more freedom than the reality in ancient China, not the limitless improvement one would hope for.[13] For instance, Gu Long (1938-1985) confessed that women in the martial arts stories that he and Zhang Che (1922-2002) created never really participate in the order of the male world. He says, "Women should be women. I share exactly the same viewpoint with Zhang Che. My [martial arts] fictions are entirely male-centered."[14] Chen Mo points out that Zhang Yimou is not perfect when portraying women's problems in films.[15] He criticizes that women in Zhang Yimou's films are only "a sort of 'path' [toward Zhang Yimou's own cinematic world]" due to Zhang Yimou's lack of personal experience, unique feeling, and practical thoughts about how women feel.[16] Kwok-kan Tam and Wimal Dissanayake seem to share similar opinions with Chen Mo:

> Women are central to the work of Zhang in a way that they are not in Chen [Kaige]'s films, but despite their strong wills and strength of character, women in Zhang's films are victimized and subject to numerous indignities. They are

chained to a highly repressive system...[17]

Thus, the room has restricted improvement for ancient Chinese women. The room has a sort of seemingly invisible but apparent glass ceiling limiting how feminist these Chinese kung fu movies can be. The glass ceiling is usually created from those artificial barriers based on attitudinal or organizational bias that prevent qualified individuals from advancing upward in their organizations into [controlling, dominating, deciding, or] management-level positions.[18]

If the glass ceiling is what women continually run into, the glass ceiling of the Chinese cinematic martial arts room includes Xiaomei's death in exchange for Jin's life in *House of Flying Daggers*, Flying Snow's sacrifice of her life for Nameless's assassination of the king and Moon's fatal battle with Flying Snow for Broken Sword in *Hero*, Wan'er's death at the end of *The Banquet*, the gradually poisoned queen's death at the end of *Curse of the Golden Flower*, and Yü Jiaolong's leap into the abyss for Xiao Hu's wish in *Crouching Tiger Hidden Dragon*.

The inclusion of the same upper limitation for ancient Chinese women's rights in so many kung fu films cinematically visualizes the glass ceiling. It is no longer merely a coincidence for so many ancient Chinese women to sacrifice themselves, take suicidal actions, and lose their lives at the end of these films. Rather, it is a clear showcase of the unquestionable existence of the glass ceiling. These movies cannot help but include these types of endings precisely because of the necessity to show how these ancient Chinese women's freedom is limited by the glass ceiling.

The "Job Ceiling" that the Heads of Shakespeare's Chinese Sisters Bump On

In addition to the glass ceiling, there is a "job ceiling." Jobs are not neutral. Jobs are not gender-free. Occupations are usually gendered and sexually biased. For instance, Wan'er in *The Banquet* and the queen in *Curse of the Golden Flower* are perhaps the most ambitious career women among all the female protagonists in these Chinese martial arts films. Wan'er becomes a female ruler of the whole nation and the queen plans to overthrow the original king and establish a new dynasty under the name of her favorite son. Unfortunately, Wan'er never really becomes a successful ruler in *The Banquet* because she dies immediately upon formal initiation of her political kingship. Wan'er's death may illustrate how superior rank of political administration and kingship usually belongs to men. This may be one of the reasons why Wan'er is assassinated. In *Curse of the Golden Flower*, the queen fails to overthrow the original king and establish her son's own dynasty for the same reason. Even in real life Empress Wu Zetian (624-705), who established her own dynasty, Da Zhou, in 690 A.D., gave up that dynasty in 705 A.D., and returned to her original status as a royal spouse of the emperor of the Tang Dynasty. Her favorite female governmental officer, whose name was Shangguang Wan'er (664-710), the same as that of the female protagonist in *The Banquet*, died a miserable death at a relatively young age, just like Wan'er in *The Banquet*, because the Emperor Xün of the Tang Dynasty, Li Longji (685-762), killed her when she was only forty-six years old.

Ironically, in all these martial arts films, the only queen not to die is exactly the one who neither has her own career nor competes with men for political kingship. Qingcheng in *The Promise* is perhaps the only female protagonist who is not truly a career woman and the only one without any job and political ambition. As a beautiful housewife married to the king, she is entirely within the private sphere and not subject to the job ceiling of her female counterparts in other films. If this is not a coincidence, the fact that Qingcheng does not compete with men on the job market seems to explain why she escapes from the hurtful glass ceiling or job ceiling. This phenomenon results in the following reasonable feminist questions: Does the ceiling apply to women who do not pursue a career? Does the cinematic vision of the patriarchal society effectively kill career women? Pygmalion loves the attractive appearance of his ivory beauty named Galatea but does not seem to clearly show much interest in or concern for her spiritual parts in the Greco-Roman myth. This begs the feminist question of whether the cinematic Pygmalion permits only superficial beauty and downplays the value of ancient Chinese women's spiritual pursuits to expand their capabilities, especially when their spiritual needs exceed what is approved by society.

Feminist theorists, like Virginia Woolf, believe that the job ceiling limits talented women with William Shakespeare's potentiality. Among all the ancient Chinese women in the kung fu movies, Qing Nü in *The Banquet* is closest to Judith Shakespeare because they share a talent for performing and have potential for stage management. Qing Nü is a singer with amazing on-stage performing talents and a successful stage manager who plans the surprising entertainment for Emperor Li and Queen Wan'er in the royal banquet. Unfortunately, she dies on the stage after her excellent performance.

Both Jade Fox in *Crouching Tiger Hidden Dragon* and Liu Yüfang in *Seven Swords* are teachers. Jade Fox works as Yü Jiaolong's private tutor; she is almost like the "teachers of the inner chambers" that Dorothy Ko[19] mentions, though she teaches not reading and writing but martial arts. Unfortunately, the teacher of the inner chamber named Jade Fox in Ang Lee's *Crouching Tiger Hidden Dragon* does not win any respect, which the five-thousand-year Confucianism awards to educators, from Li Mubai and other male knights. On the contrary, the content of her teaching methods, teaching styles, and curriculum plans are seen as negative by Li Mubai and other male experts of kung fu. Liu Yüfang in Tsui Hark's *Seven Swords* wins her villagers' esteem and gratitude not because of her status as a teacher but primarily because of the surprising fact that she finds the true betrayer, kills him, and saves the children's lives. She turns out to be chiefly a mother-like or sister-like figure who looks after children and protects their lives when all the people knowing martial arts travel away from her village. Her teaching contents seem to be trivialized or marginalized byproducts, because the film does not clearly focus on her curriculum designs or teaching materials. Jade Fox's and Liu Yüfang's relationships with their students apparently contains less authority than male masters' or teachers' relationship with their female students. Their students neither sacrifice life nor offer sexual service in the way female students do to their male masters or teachers in the kung fu movies in the manner of Moon who enters into suicidal combat as a disciple to avenge Broken Sword and cooperates when Broken Sword requests sex in *Hero*; and Jiang Chan who has sex with the crown prince to fulfill the wish of her father, who is her teacher of pharmacology in *Curse of the Golden Flower*.

In *Curse of the Golden Flower*, both Jiang Chan and her mother, the king's first wife, have professional knowledge of pharmaceutics and medicine. Jiang Chan is a professional pharmacist with good kung fu. She is hired to work in the royal pharmacy department. Her mother, the king's first wife, also has professional training in medicine and accurately diagnoses that the king has poisoned the queen. Both the queen and the king's first wife end up being killed in spite of the queen's efforts to rescue them in the film, just like the tragic ending of Judith Shakespeare's life according to Virginia Woolf's *A Room of One's Own*.

Both Lüzhu in *Seven Swords* and Xiaomei in *House of Flying Daggers* are secret agents with experience serving either as sexual or entertaining comfort women. Lüzhu is originally a military prostitute whom Fenghuo Liangcheng selected to replace his former girlfriend, Yüzhu. After falling in love with Chu Zhaonan, Yüzhu provides Fenghuo Liangcheng with military secrets. In *House of Flying Daggers*, Xiaomei works as an assassin and a well-trained spy; moreover, her jobs include pretending to be a dancer, a blind courtesan in a brothel, and an outlaw who escapes from prison. Both Yüzhu and Xiaomei die in the films, as Judith Shakespeare did.

Look Back and Bump Heads on the Ceilings: Directors' Controlling Power

Another way to visualize the glass ceiling and job ceiling is that moment when the prisoners in the Platonic cave are unlocked and allowed to turn their heads and see what is behind them in the Platonic cave:

> And now look again, and see what will naturally follow if the prisoners are released and disabused of their error. At first, when any of them is liberated and compelled suddenly to stand up and turn his neck round and walk and look towards the light, he will suffer sharp pains; the glare will distress him, and he will be unable to see the realities of which in his former state he had seen the shadows; and then conceive someone saying to him, that what he saw before was an illusion, but that now, when he is approaching nearer to being and his eye is turned towards more real existence, he has a clearer vision—what will be his reply? And you may further imagine that his instructor is pointing to the objects as they pass and requiring him to name them—will he not be perplexed? Will he not fancy that the shadows which he formerly saw are truer than the objects which are now shown to him?
>
> Plato The Republic Book VII

I contend that unchained viewers who are permitted to turn their necks and look toward the directors or producers of puppet shows could be compared to the Chinese women whose feet were tied in the past but are released now. Directors' control of everything on the screen is the visible glass ceiling or job ceiling. Ancient Chinese women's rewritten biographies in the kung fu movies on the silver screen are simply the shows under the glass- and job ceiling.

Cinematic Sculpting Power: the Mythological Pygmalion and the Cinematic Pygmalion

The directors who arrange dummies to produce the images and shows on the wall in the Platonic cave could be compared to the filmmakers who direct actresses to create the cinematic biographies of ancient Chinese women. The actresses, such as Xü Feng (b. 1950), Zhang Ziyi (b. 1979), Gong Li (b. 1965), Maggie Man-yuk Cheung (b. 1964), and Cecilia Pak-chi Cheung (b. 1980), parallel the dummies, mannequins, or raw materials that directors or artists use to produce their works of art. Directors need actresses as much as actresses need filmmakers. Take Gong Li for example: "many people said that Gong Li's success requires Zhang Yimou's stage direction... [but] Zhang Yimou's success also has a lot to do with Gong Li."[20] No matter how much actresses and directors depend on one another, however, the roles actresses play in the films are under the filmmakers' or storytellers' control. Wan'er in *The Banquet*, Xiaomei in *House of Flying Daggers*, Flying Snow in *Hero*, Qingcheng in *The Promise*, and the queen in *Curse of the Golden Flower*—the roles of ancient Chinese women that the actresses play—are the directors' imaginings of these women.

Because the ancient Chinese women whom viewers see on the silver screen are the directors' creations or products according to the ideal of ladies in the directors' minds, the images produced are the outcomes of the directors' artistic sculpting powers. The directorial sculpting power is the same as a sculptor's power over raw materials, such as ivory, marble, stone, clay, metal, or wood. The ancient Chinese ladies whom viewers see in the theater are thus similar to the statues that sculptors create.

I would like to extend this parallel to the Greco-Roman mythological legend of Pygmalion. Pygmalion is a talented sculptor who carves a perfect lady that he has in his mind by using a piece of ivory as his raw material in his studio. He is so obsessed with the statue of his ideal fair lady that he falls in love with his creation, naming it Galatea and treating it as if the statue were a real woman. Pygmalion begs Goddess Venus to bring the statue to life. The ivory statue of the fair lady is as beautiful as Goddess Venus herself; therefore, Goddess Venus agrees to turn the ivory statue into a real woman. Pygmalion finally marries Galatea and lives a happy marital life with her with Goddess Venus's blessing.

The directors of the Chinese martial arts films are cinematic versions of Pygmalion. Whereas Pygmalion possesses the artistic sculpting power in the Greco-Roman myth, the directors of Chinese martial arts films cinematically share the same sculpting power. Actresses, such as Xü Feng, Gong Li, Maggie Man-yuk Cheung, Zhang Ziyi, and Cecilia Pak-chi Cheung, are like the ivory in the cinematic Pygmalions' hands. The roles of ancient Chinese women that the actresses play—such as Wan'er in *The Banquet*, Xiaomei in *House of Flying Daggers*, Flying Snow in *Hero*, Qingcheng in *The Promise*, and the queen in *Curse of the Golden Flower*—mirror the ivory statues of ancient Chinese fair ladies that the cinematic Pygmalion sculpts. The cinematic martial arts world resembles the sculpting studio of Pygmalion's own. But Pygmalion's sculpting studio is not a room of Galatea's own. Throughout the mythological story, it is unclear whether Galatea loves Pygmalion, whether she desires to marry him as much as he desires to marry her, whether she has other choices before deciding who her husband will be, how she transforms herself from a statue to a woman, what kind of fate she would like to have, or what she thinks about herself. Similar to the ancient Chinese women in the martial arts films, Galatea does not write or rewrite her own life story or autobiography at all. The true writer of Galatea's biography is not Galatea herself but Pygmalion, who sculpts and marries her.

Educational Sculpting Power and Cultivating Power: My Fair Ladies on the Silver Screen

In addition to the Greco-Roman myth of Pygmalion, I would like to widen this metaphorical parallel or intertextuality to George Bernard Shaw's *My Fair Lady* (*Pygmalion*), the musical that won the Academy Award in 1964. It is the story of Henry Higgins, a professor of phonetics who successfully educates and corrects the Cockney[21] accent of Eliza Doolittle's spoken English.

Eliza Doolittle, the flower girl with a strong Cockney accent, in this film functions as the raw material for Professor Higgins to reshape in his "classroom" or teaching studio. Audrey Hepburn (1929-1993) functioned as the puppet or model for the director to manage to produce the movie in the studio the same way Chinese actresses—Xü Feng, Zhang Ziyi, Gong Li, Cecilia Pak-chi Cheung, and Maggie Man-yuk Cheung—serve as the "dummies" under Chinese filmmakers' control in the film studios. They are like the ivory sculpted by Pygmalion.

In this sense, the directors who manage the projected images on the wall in the Platonic cave are all following men who create their works of art or "products" and achieve success: Pygmalion, whose product is an ivory statue of a beautiful woman, Professor Higgins, whose product is the elegant accent of spoken English from Eliza Doolittle's mouth in *My Fair Lady*, George Cukor (1899-1983), whose success was turning Audrey Hepburn into Eliza Doolittle in the film *My Fair Lady*, and all the Chinese filmmakers who successfully direct Chinese actresses, such as Gong Li, Xü Feng, or Zhang Ziyi, and turn them into the ancient Chinese fair ladies that they have in their minds. These men all share the same power.

Shakespeare's Sister under the Glass Ceiling in the Room of Pygmalion's Own

My Fair Lady shares the same glass ceiling, after the female protagonist completes her phonetic education, with almost all the other martial arts films and stories that this chapter covers. At the end of *My Fair Lady*, Eliza Doolittle finds nowhere else to go, achieves no career success, and returns to the control of Professor Higgins. The film ends at the moment when Professor Higgins apparently complains about the misplacement of his slippers to Eliza Doolittle; this ending trivializes Eliza Doolittle's potential for success in the flower business and her talent in phonetics and almost equates her with nothing but a housekeeper or housewife inside of the private sphere. Although Eliza Doolittle may willingly return to Professor Higgins because she breaks through the 19th-century British sociocultural taboo for a cockney flower girl's romantic love relationship with a male professor, her romantic love for Professor Higgins should still not hinder her flower business or talent in phonetics, especially when Professor Higgins does not sacrifice his career or teaching position for their romantic relationship.

Goddess Venus fulfills Pygmalion's wish and turns Galatea into his wife, but the story offers no opportunity for Galatea to express herself. Is Galatea going to be a housewife kept in the private sphere for the rest of her life? Is Galatea happy about this kind of life? What if Galatea would like to have or would be given other choices? What else can Galatea do? The storytellers who unconsciously adopt the male-centered point of view to delineate the mythological story are probably the glass ceiling that Galatea encounters.

Are Eliza Doolittle, Galatea, and all the ancient Chinese women in the kung fu movies truly fair ladies who "do little" outside of the parameters of their creators' approval or outside of the room of their Pygmalion's own? Are they going to be like Judith Shakespeare who has talents but lacks success? Do they also encounter the same glass ceiling? What can the released viewers or prisoners do for women and feminism with their untied feet and unlocked necks in the Platonic cave? What can the directors, filmmakers, and cinematic Pygmalions do for their fair ladies and how do they react to their fair ladies, after ancient Chinese women unbind their feet, unlock their necks, turn their heads, and witness the process used to artificially produce the projected images on the wall of the Platonic cave? The surname of the fair lady in *My Fair Lady* seems to foretell the answer to these riddles. The glass ceiling is like the Chinese cinematic Pygmalion's male-centered camera lens to turn women into objects or playthings of a male gaze on the silver screen.[22] Under the glass ceiling and in the room of Pygmalion's own, ladies on the silver screen or the wall for projection in the cave can "do little"—including Eliza Doolittle in *My Fair Lady*, Galatea in the Greco-Roman myth, Judith Shakespeare in feminist theoretical discourses, Wan'er in *The Banquet*, Xiaomei in *House of Flying Daggers*, Jade Fox and Yü Jiaolong in *Crouching Tiger Hidden Dragon*, Moon and Flying Snow in *Hero*, Liu Yüfang and Lüzhu in *Seven Swords*, Qingcheng in *The Promise*, the queen in *Curse of the Golden Flower*, and so on.[23]

Conclusion

After my combination of all the above-mentioned Western theories and Chinese martial arts films in this article and after the audience turn back and witness the truth of how directors arrange puppets in the Platonic cave, here is my answer to the gender question of how feminist Chinese martial arts films can be at the beginning of the new millennium: The fair ladies in these kung fu films at movie theaters, which parallel the puppet show in the cave, can "do little" under the glass ceiling and male filmmakers' control. The feminism in these Chinese martial arts films is limited; it is within the parameter of male filmmakers' approval for women's rights.

After discussing Chinese cinematic martial arts room of Pygmalion-like King Hu's, Ang Lee's, and Zhang Yimou's own, the second part of this book interrogates how much the ancient Chinese fair ladies, whom Pygmalion-like filmmakers cinematically sculpts, can do from feminist standpoints. I contend that the fair lady's surname, "Doolittle," in *Pygmalion* (*My Fair Lady*) foretells the cruel truth that ancient Chinese women in the films can do little outside of Pygmalion's authorization.

What ancient Chinese women in the kung fu films can really do outside of Pygmalion's cinematic control of their destiny. For example, what can Shakespeare's two Chinese sisters, Wan'er and Qing Nü in *The Banquet*, do in order to avoid their death? What can they do to avoid repeating Judith Shakespeare's footsteps? What can Wan'er in *The Banquet* and the Queen in *Curse of the Golden Flower* do to secure the continuation of their own political empowerment? What can they do to avoid repeating Empress Wu Zetian's failure to maintain her dynastic regime? What can Qingcheng do to change her doomed lack of true love by herself, without depending on Kunlun in *The Promise*? What can Lüzhu do about her status as a military slave, comfort woman, and foreigner facing the disbelief of almost everyone, including Chu Zhaonan in *Seven Swords*? What can Liu Yüfang, as a female teacher, do about Pygmalion's male-centered teacher-student complex in *Seven Swords*? What can she do about the undeniable fact that a female schoolteacher is sometimes only an educational nanny to mother village children when everybody else with kung fu goes out for combat? The fair lady's surname, "Doolittle," in *Pygmalion* (*My Fair Lady*) foretells that these ancient Chinese fair ladies in the martial arts films can do little. The word, "Doolittle," is thus not merely a surname but also a key word to refer to the "glass ceiling" of how little these ancient Chinese fair ladies can do in the cinematic martial arts room of Pygmalion's own.

References

Armanet, François. *Ciné Kung Fu*. Paris: Ramsay, 1988, pp. 51-52.
Brians, Paul. *Reading about the World, Vol. I*. Orlando, FL: Harcourt Brace, 1999.
Birrell, Anne. *New Songs from a Jade Terrace: An Anthology of Early Chinese Love Poetry*. New York: Penguin Books, 1986, p. 231.
Bordwell, David. "Richness through Imperfection: King Hu and the Glimpse." *Transcending the Times: King Hu and Eileen Chang*. Hong Kong: The 22nd Hong Kong International Film Festival hosted by the provisional Urban Council of Hong Kong, 1998, p. 34.

Chen, Mo. *Zhang Yimou dianying lun (Discourses of Zhang Yimou's Films)*. Beijing: Zhongguo dianying, 1995, p. 203-205.
---. *Zhongguo wuxia dianying shi (History of Chinese Martial Arts Films)*. Beijing: Zhongguo dianying (Chinese Films), 2005, pp. 146; 150.
Chen, Ya-chen. *This Chinese Feminism Which Is Not "One": Feminist Scholars and Academic Feminism across the Taiwan Strait in the 1990s* (forthcoming).
Chow, Rey. *Primitive Passions: Visuality, Sexuality, Ethnography and Contemporary Chinese Cinema*. New York: Columbia University Press, 1995, p. 149.
Chung, Ling and King Hu. *Shanke ji (Visiting the Mountain)*. Taipei: Yuanjing, 1979, p. 147.
Ciment, Michel. "Entretien avec King Hu." *Positif* (May 1975): 169; Du San-gae trans. *Influence* (Fall 1975): 13.
Elley, Derek. "King Hu." *Inernaitonal Film Guide*. London: Tantivy Press, 1978, p. 27.
Frankel, Hans H. "The Development of Han and Wei *Yüeh-fu* as a High Literary Genre." *The Vitality of the Lyric Voice: Shih Poetry from the Late Han to the Tang*. Lin Shuen-fu and Stephen Owen edt. Princeton: Princeton University Press, 1986.
Hu, Jinquan and Koichi Yamada. *A Touch of King Hu*. Li He and Ma Songzhi trans. Hong Kong: Zhengwen, 1998, pp. 68-97.
Jia, Leilei. *Zhongguo wuxia dianying shi (A History to Chinese Martial Arts Films)*. Beijing: Wenhua yishu, 2005, pp. 14-19, 87.
---. *Wu zhi wu—zhongguo wuxia dianying de xingtai yu shenhun (The Dance of Martial Arts—The Figure and Soul of Chinese Martial Arts Films)*. Zhengzhou: Henan renmin, 1998, pp. 105-110.
Jiao, Xiongping. *Taigang dianying zhong de zuozhe yü leixing (Authors and Genres in Taiwanese and Hong Kong Films)*. Taipei: Yuanliu, 1991, p. 17.
Ko, Dorothy. *Teachers of the Inner Chambers: Women and Culture in Seventeenth-Century China*. Stanford: Stanford University Press, 1994.
Lu, Xun. *Kuangren riji (Diary of A Mad Man)*. Hong Kong: Sanlian, 2004.
---. *Diary of A Mad Man*. William A. Lyell trans. Honolulu: University of Hawaii Press, 1990.
Ma, Guoguang. "Xie ran cheng shi hua *xia nü*" (Blood on Poetry and Discourse on *A Touch of Zen*). *Zhongguo shibao (China Times)* August 30, 1975. This article also appears in Huang Ren's *Hu Jinquan de shijie (King Hu's World)*. Taipei: Yatai, 1999, p. 254.
Plato and P. Shorey. *The Republic*. London: W. Heinemann, 1930.
Plato and B. Jowett. *Plato's The Republic*. New York: The Modern library, 1941.
Rance, P. T. J.. *Martial Arts*. London: Virgin Books, 2005, p. 128.
Rubin, Gayle. "The Traffic in Women." *Toward an Anthropology of Women*. Rayna R. Reiter edt. New York: Monthly Review, 1975. pp. 157-210.
Sato, Tadao. *Zhongguo dianying bainian (One Hundred Years of Chinese Films)*. Qian Hang trans. Shanghai: Shanghai Books, 2005, pp. 199-200.
Schubart, Rikke. " 'Beautiful Vase Made of Iron and Steel': Micheele Yeoh." *Super Bitches and Action Babes: The Female Hero in Popular Cinema, 1970-2006*. Jefferson, NC: McFarland, 2007, p. 124.

Tam, Kwok-kan and Wimal Dissanayake. *New Chinese Cinema*. New York: Oxford University Press, 1998, pp. 23-34.
Teo, Stephen. "Only the Valiant: King Hu and His *Cinema Opera*." *Transcending the Times: King Hu and Eileen Chang*. Hong Kong: The 22nd Hong Kong International Film Festival hosted by the provisional Urban Council of Hong Kong, 1998, pp. 21-22.
West, David. *Chasing Dragons: An Introduction to the Martial Arts Films*. London: I.B. Tauris, 2006, p. 101.
Woolf, Virginia. *A Room of One's Own*. New York: Harcourt, Brace, 1929.
Yang, Jeff. *Once Upon a Time in China: A Guide to Hong Kong, Taiwanese, and Mainland Chinese Cinema*. New York: Atria Books, 2003, p. 49.
Zhuo, Boshang. "Dianying yüyan de kaichuangzhe—lun Hu Jiquan de jianjie fengge" (The Founder of the Cinematic Language—King Hu's Stylistic Editing of Films). *Hu Jinquan de shijie* (*King Hu's World*). Huang Ren edt. Taipei: Yatai, 1999, pp. 221-224.

Notes

1. For details, consult the following books:
Plato and P. Shorey, *The Republic*. (London: W. Heinemann, 1930).
Plato and B. Jowett, *Plato's The Republic*. (New York: The Modern library, 1941).
2. King Hu is the filmmaker of the first Chinese award-winning kung fu movie, *A Touch of Zen* (1971). He "enjoyed critical success in the West, with *A Touch of Zen* winning the Grand Technical Prize at the... Cannes Film Festival, although he never achieved the mass popularity attained by Bruce Lee or the Shaolin films of Shaw Brothers during the kung fu boom of the 1970s." For details, consult David West's *Chasing Dragons: An Introduction to the Martial Arts Films*. (London: I.B. Tauris, 2006), 101. Also consult François Armanet's *Ciné Kung Fu*. (Paris: Ramsay, 1988), 51-52, 82-83.
David West says that King Hu won the award in 1969 in his book; however, other scholars believe that King Hu did not win this award until 1975 according to their publications. See Jia Leilei's *Wu zhi wu—zhongguo wuxia dianying de xingtai yu shenhun* (*The Dance of Martial Arts—The Figure and Soul of Chinese Martial Arts Films*). (Zhengzhou, China: Henan renmin, 2005), 105. See also Chen Mo's *Zhongguo wuxia dianying shi* (*History of Chinese Martial Arts Films*). (Beijing: Zhongguo dianying / Chinese Films, 2005), 146.
3. These Chinese martial arts films of the new millennium are successors that follow the martial arts films King Hu (1932-1997 A.D.) directed to amaze the participants of international film festivals and film critics in the 1960s and 1970s. Many scholars in film studies have already explored the interrelations between King Hu's cinematic martial arts world and the martial arts world Ang Lee, Zhang Yimou, Chen Kaige, and other Chinese filmmakers created in the new millennium; therefore, I will avoid repetition of their research.
4. Zheng Peipei (b. 1952) plays both Yang Huizhen in *A Touch of Zen* and Jade Fox in *Crouching Tiger Hidden Dragon*. "Her presence in the film creates a direct link be-

tween *Crouching Tiger Hidden Dragon* and the [martial arts films] of earlier decades." For details, consult P. T. J. Rance's *Martial Arts*. (London: Virgin Books, 2005), 128.

5. Rey Chow, *Primitive Passions: Visuality, Sexuality, Ethnography and Contemporary Chinese Cinema*. (New York: Columbia University Press, 1995), 149.

6. King Hu mentions that the wushu in his kung fu movies is not "real fighting" but dancing in the tradition of Peking Opera, just like cinematic ballet shows or balletic fights. Derek Elley clearly evinces, "It is the action sequences in Hu's films that bear the strongest imprint of a Peking Opera influence." The dancing elements of King Hu's martial arts films remind viewers of Zhang Ziyi's and Michelle Yeoh's backgrounds as dancers and balletic swordplay in *Crouching Tiger Hidden Dragon*, *House of Flying Daggers* and *The Banquet*. For example, Sato Tadao points out that in *House of Flying Daggers* Zhang Ziyi's marvelous acrobatic skills and choreographic training enable Xiaomei to do a "straddle split" horizontally and then stand up vertically from the floor. Rikke Schubart also mentions that Michelle Yeoh studied ballet, jazz, and contemporary dance and earned her bachelor's degree from London's Royal Academy of Dance. For details, consult Michel Ciment's "Entretien avec King Hu" in *Positif* (May 1975): 169; Du San-gae's translation in *Influence* (Fall 1975): 13. See Derek Elley's "King Hu" in *Inernaitonal Film Guide*. (London: Tantivy Press, 1978), 27. Consult Sato Tadao's *Zhongguo dianying bainian* (*One Hundred Years of Chinese Films*). trans. Qian Hang. (Shanghai: Shanghai Books, 2005), 199-200. See also Rikke Schubart's "'Beautiful Vase Made of Iron and Steel': Micheele Yeoh" in *Super Bitches and Action Babes: The Female Hero in Popular Cinema, 1970-2006*. (Jefferson, NC: McFarland, 2007), 124.

King Hu is also one of the earliest filmmakers to use spring mattresses and editorial work on brief film clips to create the martial arts performance or combat scenes that real martial arts experts or swordsmen cannot make possible. For instance, in *A Touch of Zen*, there is a scene in which the female protagonist, played by Xü Feng, jumps from somewhere lower onto somewhere higher. King Hu honestly confesses that it is impossible for the actress to do this and that it is merely a symbolic representation of martial arts skills. Xü Feng does not know any martial arts. She is a silent woman in everyday life. King Hu believes that through her serenity and her roles as a martial arts lady in films, she can achieve a sort of balanced beauty. Among all the actresses, King Hu feels that Xü Feng's thoughts match his thoughts the best. For details, consult Hu Jinquan and Koichi Yamada's *A Touch of King Hu*. Li He and Ma Songzhi trans. Hong Kong: Zhengwen, 1998, pp. 68-97. Also consult Jia Leilei's *Zhongguo wuxia dianying shi* (*A History to Chinese Martial Arts Films*). (Beijing: Wenhua yishu, 2005), 14-19.

David Bordwell also comments on Hu's cinematic representation of kung fu and compares it with other filmmakers' representations:

> Hu used long-shots that allow the actors to vault in and out of blocking material in the foreground. Instead of 1-2-3 constructive editing like Zhang Che's in *One-Armed Swordsman*, Hu gives us only a phase 1 or 2 or 3—launch *or* leap *or* landing, or only two of them. And by making the shots extraordinarily brief, he goes beyond his contemporaries; blink and you miss the stunt.

For details, consult David Bordwell's "Richness through Imperfection: King Hu and the Glimpse" in *Transcending the Times: King Hu and Eileen Chang*. (Hong Kong: The

22nd Hong Kong International Film Festival hosted by the provisional Urban Council of Hong Kong, 1998), 34.

7. Jeff Yang, *Once upon a Time in China: A Guide to Hong Kong, Taiwanese, and Mainland Chinese Cinema*. (New York: Atria Books, 2003), 49.

8. Boshang Zhuo, "Dianying yüyan de kaichuangzhe—lun Hu Jiquan de jianjie fengge" (The Founder of the Cinematic Language—King Hu's Stylistic Editing of Films) in *Hu Jinquan de shijie* (*King Hu's World*). ed. Huang Ren. (Taipei: Yatai, 1999), 221-224.

9. Xiongping Jiao, *Taigang dianying zhong de zuozhe yü leixing* (*Authors and Genres in Taiwanese and Hong Kong Films*). (Taipei: Yuanliu, 1991), 17.

10. Ling Chung and King Hu, *Shanke ji* (*Visiting the Mountain*). (Taipei: Yuanjing, 1979), 147.

11. King Hu neglects Yang Huizhen's emotions for her severely ill mother-in-law, husband, and newborn. Yang Huizhen does what a filial daughter-in-law does for Gu Shengzhi's mother by spinning cotton into yarns and decocting medical herbs for her. She cares about her moterh-in-law's wish to have a grandchild so much that she volunteers to serve as a birth machine at the beginning of the story; it is unreasonable and irrational that she shows no concern for Gu Shengzhi's mother after giving birth to her child at the end of the story. It is also unconvincing that she has no emotional ups and downs when facing Gu Shengzhi at the moment of her seduction, sexuality, pregnancy, and childbirth. As a mother, it is even unpersuasive for Yang Huizhen to have no maternal or motherly love for her child and turn from an attractive and well-educated Chinese lady into a ruthless mother who cruelly orphans her child. For details, consult Ma Guoguang's "Xie ran cheng shi hua *xia nü*" (Blood on Poetry and Discourse on *A Touch of Zen*). *Zhongguo shibao* (*China Times*) August 30, 1975. This article also appears in Huang Ren's *Hu Jinquan de shijie* (*King Hu's World*). (Taipei: Yatai, 1999), 254. Also see Chen Mo's *Zhongguo wuxia dianying shi* (*History of Chinese Martial Arts Films*). (Beijing: Zhongguo dianying / Chinese Films, 2005), 150.

12. Leilei Jia's *Wu zhi wu—zhongguo wuxia dianying de xingtai yu shenhun* (*The Dance of Martial Arts—The Figure and Soul of Chinese Martial Arts Films*). (Zhengzhou: Henan renmin, 1998), 109-110.

13. Stephen Teo's analysis of King Hu's two-sided cinematic portrait of ancient Chinese women in *A Touch of Zen* may be an illustration. On the one hand, Yang Huizhen, the female protagonist, is equal to men in terms of kung fu skills, courage, or determination. On the other hand, she "conforms to the Confucian [patriarchal] ideal of womanhood: the silent, chaste woman, conversant with arts of song and poetry." For details, consult Stephen Teo's "Only the Valiant: King Hu and His *Cinema Opera*" in *Transcending the Times: King Hu and Eileen Chang*. (Hong Kong: The 22nd Hong Kong International Film Festival hosted by the provisional Urban Council of Hong Kong, 1998), 21-22.

14. Leilei Jia, *Zhongguo wuxia dianying shi* (*A History to Chinese Martial Arts Films*). (Beijing: Wenhua yishu, 2005), 87.

15. Mo Chen, *Zhang Yimou dianying lun* (*Discourses of Zhang Yimou's Films*). (Beijing: Zhongguo dianying, 1995), 202.

16. Mo Chen, *Zhang Yimou dianying lun* (*Discourses of Zhang Yimou's Films*). (Beijing: Zhongguo dianying, 1995), 205.

17. Kwok-kan Tam and Wimal Dissanayake, *New Chinese Cinema.* (Oxford and New York: Oxford University Press, 1998).

18. In 1991 A.D., the U. S. Department of Labor defined glass ceiling as "those artificial barriers based on attitudinal or organizational bias that prevent qualified individuals from advancing upward in their organization into management-level positions." For details, consult the Report on the Glass Ceiling Initiative at the U. S. Department of Labor in the 1991 A.D.. The Department of Labor had also its Glass Ceiling Commission from 1991 A.D. to 1996 A.D..

19. For details, consult Dorothy Ko's *Teachers of the Inner Chambers: Women and Culture in Seventeenth-Century China.* (Stanford: Stanford University Press, 1994).

20. Chen, Mo. *Zhang Yimou dianying lun (Discourses of Zhang Yimou's Films).* (Beijing: Zhongguo dianying, 1995), 203.

21. Cockney is a dialect spoken primarily by working-class or poor London inhabitants.

22. Jia, Leilei. *Wu zhi wu—zhongguo wuxia dianying de xingtai yu shenhun (The Dance of Martial Arts—The Figure and Soul of Chinese Martial Arts Films).* (Zhengzhou: Henan renmin, 1998), 110.

23. The glass ceiling in the Chinese cinematic martial arts room of Pygmalion's own applies not merely to the Chinese kung fu movies of the new millennium but also to the limitations on feminist developments in the new millennium. One of the best illustrations may be the Mainland Chinese political leaders' promotion of feminist N.G.O.s before 1995 to showcase Chinese Communist feminist developments to the world in the United Nations' World Women's Congress, but their lack of systematic assistance to continue running these feminist organizations after worldwide media reporters' departure from China after 1995. On the one hand, there are some truly feminist developments, such as the women's hotline or other feminist service offices. On the other hand, feminist developments are restricted to and cannot transcend the boundary of censors' agreement and support—just look how little the feminist N.G.O.s with financial difficulties could do without any sponsorship at the moment of their "death" at the end of the twentieth century and the beginning of the twenty-first century. The Mainland Chinese interviewees in *This Chinese Feminism Which Is Not "One"* (forthcoming) clearly evince this feminist developmental predicament. Another illustration is how the glass ceiling functions in workplaces. I call it the job ceiling or class ceiling. Men usually tend to be those who successfully jockey positions with superior authority or power, and have women as their assistants. For instance, presidents of nations, companies, and universities are chiefly male in patriarchal societies, though there are some exceptions. That is, jobs are gendered and the ruling class is usually male.

PART 3

INTERVIEWS

Chapter Eleven
Interview with Chung Ling, King Hu's Spouse and Screenwriter

Bellow is the translation and transcription of an interview with Chung Ling (Zhong, Ling) in Hong Kong during summer 2009:
My formal occupation is not a screenwriter. *Legend of the Mountain* is an exceptional case; King Hu was my husband at that time, and I, therefore, cooperated with him. I was not familiar with the film industry. When I co-worked with him, I was like his disciple. I was more a disciple than a professional screenwriter. When I was drafting the screenplay, King Hu did not dominate my decision of female protagonists' destinies. I asked him how to make it a screenplay, and he advised me to divide the story into different scenes and add descriptions of different characters' actions. I provided the outline of the story, characters' dialogues, and description of characters' actions. King Hu made a lot of changes after I gave him what I had written. He added his own opinions about the traditional Chinese ghost stories. His changes are inevitable and unavoidable because he was facing practical issues when shooting the film. For instance, when he saw a pavilion, he changed my description of the location and replaced it with the pavilion. Characters' actions also changed because of the pavilion. Hence, the story plot related to the pavilion was also different. I did not require King Hu not to change details. I gave him a lot of flexibility for his revisions of my screenplay.

King Hu was a professional filmmaker, so I did not touch anything about his professional control of his films, but I followed him to the shooting spots, joined his preparation, and witnessed his film-shooting processes. For instance, we went to Korea, where he shot scenes on locations for the film *Legend of the Mountain*. When he drew the outdoor scenes, his drawing was already the appearance of the scenes on the silver screen. We communicated about different outdoor scenes and decided whether they would be suitable for the outline of the story. King Hu added small details to my original screenplay. For example, my original screenplay did not include Yiyun's musical performance near the foggy brook, yet King Hu added it to my screenplay after he discovered the nice-looking scene to shoot on location. As for the English version of the screenplay, I did not screenplay in English. It was later translated into English by King Hu's friend who taught in National Tsing Hua University, Taiwan, and proofread by me.

The input that I contributed as a screenwriter was the new topic about gender issues because the main focuses of King Hu's previous films had not been interactions between men and women. Even if King Hu's previous movies included romantic relations, they were neither the main focus nor deeply explored in detail. For instance, the scholar and the lady expert of martial arts in *A Touch of Zen* had sexual gratification and produced a child, but the scenes of their sexuality and romantic interactions were limited. In *Valiant Ones* (1975), the romantic relation between the male protagonist and the female protagonist was vague, ambiguous, and not clearly delineated. King Hu had to focus on gender issues in *Legend of the Mountain* because the original version of the story focused on them. I based my screenplay on a ghost story in Zheng Chengduo's literary work in the Song Dynasty. The female protagonists, especially the woman named Yüenian, are basically the same as the original version in the literary work. Yiyun, the role that Sylvia Ai-chia Chang played, was my own invention. Because of the female role Yiyun, there were comparisons and contracts between the two female characters and there was a love triangle among the male protagonist and the two female protagonists.

In *Legend of the Mountain*, the two female protagonists are extremely strong and eye-catching roles, while the male protagonist is a pretty weak character. The male protagonist is not masculine at all. He is cowardly and passive. It had not been difficult for King Hu to cinematically portray tough women in his films since *Dragon Gate Inn* (1976). Take *Nianyü guanyin* (*The Smashed Jade Guanyin*), another story in the same collection of literary works in the Song Dynasty, for instance. The female protagonist is forcefully autonomous, but the male protagonist is irresponsible and fearful. *Ernü yingxiong zhuan* (*Stories of Heroes and Heroines*), the literary masterpiece deriving from legends or folklore at the level of non-aristocratic, non-governmental and ordinarily civil circles in the Qing Dynasty, also includes tough women and weak men. This repetitive pattern of strong women and cowardly men probably resulted from suppressed wishful thinking. In ancient China, women were severely oppressed; therefore, there came hopes and literary imaginings of tough women and weak men to balance the gender inequality. Male artists and writers probably shared the same hopes and imagination.

Why would male artists, including King Hu, create cinematic images of tough women, instead of strong men or heroes? How tough do they allow women to be in their works of arts? These are interesting questions. I agree with you on the argument of the limitation set up for women's toughness or emancipation—namely, incompletion of what you mean by "Chinese martial arts feminism." There is truly still a "prison" for these tough women partially released from traditional Chinese chauvinism. For instance, in King Hu's *A Touch of Zen*, the monk tames evildoers and the female protagonist, whom the male protagonist mistakes as a female ghost at the beginning of the story. In

Legend of the Mountain, the Tibetan Buddhist lama subdues the two female protagonists, who transform from goblins into beauties, with Buddhist sutra and sorcery. In *Raining in the Mountain* (1979), there is also a monk taming bandits. These monks are male. After the cinematic creation of tough women and release of them from ancient Chinese gender inequality, there is always someone male to control and restrict these women. Who are these men? They are not the weak, cowardly, irresponsible, and fearful male protagonists. They are not ordinary men. They are senior monks. They are sexually neutral because monks do not have sex with women. To put this in a frank and direct way, they are semi-castrated men because of their lack of sex with women. To put this in a euphemistic way, they experienced deep Buddhist epiphanies. Buddhist exorcists are usually the men, whom King Hu has in his film texts, to cinematically tame and limit tough women. In this sense, these tough women who enjoyed their feminist emancipation or liberation are subconsciously demonized.

With reference to fox spirits, they usually refer to not merely ghost-like fox spirits but also women involved in immoral romantic or sexual relations with men. Pu Songling's *Liaozhai zhiyi* (*Strange Stories from a Chinese Studio*) in the Qing Dynasty included a lot of good fox spirits and evil fox spirits. King Hu's *Legend of the Mountain* has also a good fox spirit and a bad one; Yüenian is portrayed as the malevolent fox spirit, while Yiyun is the benevolent one. Both Yüenian and Yiyun in *Legend of the Mountain* are originally based on the traditional Chinese archetypal belief of fox spirits and female scapegoats because the male protagonist's transcription of Buddhist sutra aims to benefit humans and the original goal of both Yüenian and Yiyun is to steal his Buddhist sutra, but Yiyun changes and becomes a good fox spirit. At the end of the film, she cares only about the male protagonist's safety and sacrifices her life to protect him and his Buddhist sutra. In other words, King Hu creates a good fox spirit that violates the cliché of bad fox spirits and scapegoats.

I agree with you on the argument that fox spirits or women are usually turned into scapegoats. As long as there are national disasters, adulteries, or crises, chauvinistic or male-centered traditions often blame women, not men. Details of Yüenian's evil schemes to have sex with the male protagonist and force him to marry her are what King Hu added to my original screenplay. King Hu ascribed the blame to Yüenian and discarded the male protagonist's responsibility. In many Chinese martial arts films and fictions, male teachers immorally enjoy sex with female students but still maintain good reputations and Confucian images. Female teachers end up with notorious or scandalous tragedies, such as Jade Fox's miserable death in Ang Lee's *Crouching Tiger Hidden Dragon* and the public criticism of Xiao Long Nü's romantic love for her disciple in Jin Yong's *The Return of the Condor Heroes*. These are men's patriarchal limitations, in my viewpoint.

The female protagonists in *A Touch of Zen* and *Dragon Gate Inn* are cinematically portrayed as positive female images to justify innocent female scapegoats. In the past, upright characters in King Hu's films have usually been male, such as *The Valliant Ones* and *The Fate of Lee Khan* (1987). King Hu's cinematic creation of so many tough women and great heroines is to help ancient Chinese women win their justice back, just like what Li Ruzhen (1762-1830) or Cao Xueqin (1716?-1763) do to their female protagonists in literary masterpieces. Even when the female protagonist in *Raining in the Mountain* is a thief, King Hu turns her into a female *yi zei* (thief with admirable integrity and justness). King Hu's cinematic creation of upright and respectful female experts of martial arts influenced other well-known directors of kung fu films, such as Zhang Che (Chang, Che, 1923-2009), who directed *The Golden Swallow* in 1968, and Li Xing (Li, Hsing, b. 1930).

In my viewpoint, there are two major components in the tradition of Chinese martial arts films: combats of kung fu and artistic representations. I feel that women can play important roles in the artistic representations though fighting is traditionally men's world. This is why women's space in so many decades of tradition of Chinese martial arts film can be larger and larger. Ang Lee's *Crouching Tiger Hidden Dragon*, for instance, reserves a far more significant space for women than Zhang Che's *The Golden Swords*. This is perhaps why it is so meaningful for Ang Lee to invite Zheng Peipei (Cheng, Pei-pei, b. 1946) to play Jade Fox in *Crouching Tiger Hidden Dragon* after she successfully played the Golden Swallow in Zhang Che's *The Golden Swallow*.

A lot of female protagonists in King Hu's martial arts films, especially those played by Xu Feng (Hsü Feng; b. 1950), are King Hu's own fantasy or imagination of lofty and beautiful women. I do not think that the source of his fantasy or imagination was true women in his life. For example, King Hu's mother was not the same as the heroine-like mother of Bai Xianyong (Pai, Hsian-yung, b. 1937). His mother painted, but did not have strong personality. She was not the first wife of King Hu's father. King Hu's older sisters grew up with him in the mines because his father was the owner of the mines. I do not think that I was a part of the source of his fantasy or imagination because we did not know each other when Xu Feng became the female protagonist in his *A Touch of Zen*. According to my understanding of his experience in Hong Kong, female friends were like buddies to King Hu. So I believe that the female protagonists in his films are only his own fantasy or imagination, not extractions from women he encountered or interacted with in his everyday life.

If there is a "prison" for these female protagonists, it must be the subconscious chauvinistic beliefs remaining in King Hu's heart. This is why King Hu creates monks, instead of nuns or other women, to regulate these female protagonists and curb the Chinese martial arts feminism, which these female protagonists enjoy, at the end of his films. King Hu still has residuals of patriarchal thoughts in his mind. Generally speaking, it is already a great accomplishment for King Hu to create so many touching women and respectful heroines in his films. He deserves this credit.

Chapter Twelve
Interview with Pan Hua, a Female Classmate and Peer-Director of Zhang Yimou, Chen Kaige, Tian Zhuangzhuang, Wu Ziniu, Li Shaohong, Hu Mei, and Peng Xiaolian

Bellow is the translation and transcription of an interview with Pan Hua in Beijing during summer 2009:
I was a teenager during the Cultural Revolution and saw only a small number of good Mainland Chinese feature films before the end of my high school period. There were no foreign films for ordinary folks. Descendents of high-level governmental officers, such as Chen Kaige, Tian Zhuangzhuang (b. 1952), and Peng Xiaolian (b. 1953), were exceptions permitted to see movies from Euro-America, Hong Kong, and Taiwan. Born and raised to parents who are educated elites rather than governmental officers, I had no opportunity to see non-Mainland Chinese films.

The Cultural Revolution was over in 1976, and Mainland Chinese higher education restarted in 1977. The Beijing Film Academy did not start to teach students until 1978, however, because the school was waiting for professors' return from the countryside. At the age of eighteen in 1978, I passed the entrance examination and became one of the one hundred thirty-five undergraduate students in the Beijing Film Academy. There were five departments: screenwriting, filmmaking, photography/cinematography, performing, and fine arts. There were twenty to thirty students in every department. The age of students was eighteen to twenty-eight. The original maximum of students' age was twenty-two, but it was lifted to twenty-eight because of Zhang Yimou's letter of petition to Huang Zhen (1909-1989), the Minister of Culture, who was a professional photographer. In the eight years after 1978, except for the Department of Performance, there were no new students.

As for the ratio of female students and male students, I would say that around ten to twenty percent of students were female. The Department of Photography/Cinematography had the smallest number of female students because of the heavy equipment, such as video recorders, cameras, and so on.

There were thirty-five students in the Department of Photography/Cinematography; only three of the thirty-five students were female at that time. The Department of Screenwriting had around thirty students, and four or five of the thirty students were female. I belonged to the Department of Filmmaking. There were thirty students in my department, and nine of the thirty students were female. Among the nine female students in our department, three became award-winning and well-anthologized female directors: Li Shaohong (b. 1955), Hu Mei (b. 1958), and Peng Xiaolian (b. 1953). The Department of Fine Arts shared almost the same ratio with my department. The Department of Performance probably had the largest number of female students because of the inevitable necessity for drama and cinema to include female protagonists or characters. The proportion of female students in the Department of Performance was a little bit more than one-third, but not yet half. Female students in the Department of Performance were trained to become female protagonists because our professors believed that students could easily play other female roles after learning how to become successful female protagonists.

Except for special courses about different majors, all the one hundred and thirty-five undergraduate students shared the same classes. Every day, we were together with one another in the same classrooms, dining rooms, and dormitory halls. We were very familiar with one another at that time. Once per month, the Department of Fine Arts and Department of Photography/Cinematography held a joint exhibition. Zhang Yimou's photographical works always attracted a considerable number of student viewers. Zhang Yimou is a silent person, but his works of art always catch viewers' eyes and vibrate their hearts in the most impressive way. At that time, we had no money to purchase films and other materials for videocassette recorders; therefore, we simply learned everything by going to the television station to observe how professional staff members edited their films and raw materials from their own tuner for direct TV reception and programmable timers. At our graduation, we finally had an opportunity to practically edit our film clips and complete our own motion pictures. I feel proud to say that we depended purely on our marvelous filmmaking skills, not computer software or special high-tech devices, at that time.

Although Zhang Yimou belonged to the Department of Photography/Cinematography, his true goal was to be a filmmaker, not simply a photographer or cinematographer. He audited all the courses regarding screenwriting, adaption of original literary pieces, filmmaking, performance, and fine arts. He learned everything and discussed everything with us.

Zhang Yimou came to the Beijing Film Academy at the age of twenty-eight. Wu Ziniu (b. 1953) did not come until he was twenty-five. These senior students were impressively excellent. Zhang Yimou and Wu Ziniu were both born to well-educated parents with a lot of books at their homes. They read a lot before the Cultural Revolution. I believe that Zhang Yimou even memorized a great number of well-anthologized literary classics, including poetry from the Tang and Song Dynasties. In addition, they had extraordinary and unbelievable experiences when they were sent down during the Cultural Revolution. Zhang

Yimou served as a blue-collar laborer at a textile mill in Yunnan. Wu Ziniu worked as a porter and witnessed how the lack of sufficient food starved senior people into miserable deaths. Their drafts of screenplays outshone all the other students' works. Tian Zhuangzhuang's parents are Tian Fang (1911-1974), a famous actor, and Yu Lan (b. 1921), a well-known actress; I believe that he has his parents' special gene or DNA about screenplays and on-stage performance. His brother, Tian Xinxin, shares the same gene and works as a professional sound recordist. Tian Zhuangzhuang was a soldier and then a professional cinematographer with successful experience in dealing with documentary films related to local agriculture in a film studio before passing the entrance examination of the Beijing Film Academy. Early, when we were only undergraduate students, it was already not surprising to believe that some of our excellent students would become winners of Oscars, Academy Awards, or other significant awards in the Cannes, Toronto, Asian-Pacific, or other important international film festivals.

People in the Chinese film industry, especially female filmmakers, can seldom have normal family lives. The job and workplace are particularly inappropriate for women or married people. Zhang Yimou, for instance, is single after the end of his marriage with Xiao Hua and romantic relation with Gong Li, a famous and award-winning Chinese actress. Hu Mei also gives up her opportunity to be married. Ann Hui, an award-winning Hong Kong female filmmaker, and Wang Xiaoli (Wang, Hsiao-li), a well-known Taiwanese female filmmaker, not only remain single but also look masculine.

Being a director takes a lot of talent, wisdom, and physical energy. Unlike Hollywood in America or other aspects of the Western film industry, the Chinese film industry has no break on Saturdays and Sundays. The requirement of endless physical energy in the Chinese film industry even includes sleeplessness for 18 or 20 hours every day during film-shooting periods. This is not what most women can physically afford to do. Even after some educational institutions offer special fellowships or scholarships for female students to learn how to become female filmmakers, it will not change the cruel fact that the job disallows female filmmakers to enjoy normal family lives and play good wives, mothers, and daughters-in-law in the patriarchal society.

Take me, for instance; I have a child and other family members to take care of. I cannot live that kind of life. I did not know that being a successful or award-winning female filmmaker would make me have to sacrifice so much when I became a student in the Beijing Film Academy. At that time, I naively enjoyed the works of arts on the silver screen and believed that I could also make up wonderful stories, but had no idea about how much more efforts should be made before films could be successful. When I graduated from the Beijing Film Academy in 1982, various film studios came to look for their potential employees, but I preferred to be a teacher in the Chinese Broadcast Academy because of the following two reasons: First, my mother's job as a principle of elementary school influenced me and resulted in my favor for a teaching position. Second, the Chinese Broadcast Academy established their brand new

Department of Television, and my professor recommended them to hire me as their faculty member in the division of stage direction. I also produced screenplays and directed several television soap operas during summer and winter breaks. As a female director, I of course prefer more flexibility and space for feminist emancipation. My female classmate and an award-winning female filmmaker, Peng Xiaolian, is also good at producing motion pictures about women and gender concerns.

Right now I am teaching in the Communication University of China. One third to half of my current students are female. The ratio of 1:3 applies in most educational institutions related to the Chinese film industry. I believe that the deciding factor of this ratio is the survival on the job market. A lot of my female students struggled between their family lives and occupations related to films; they could not help but work as editors in newspaper offices or fictionists. I think around half of my female students remain active in the film industry. Male students also suffered. For example, Lu Chuan (b. 1971)—son of Lu Tianming (b. 1943), a famous screenwriter—could not find financial support for his films until Jiang Wen's friend persuaded Jiang Wen (b. 1963) to take a look at, invest money in, and play the male protagonist in Lu Chuan's film. Before Jiang Wen's support, Lu Chuan financially depended on his parents because he was reluctant to have a job that he did not truly love. Lu Chuan's unhappy past is similar to Ang Lee's experience because Ang Lee depended on his wife's financial support before his films were successful.

Choosing a spouse, who also works in and is familiar with the Chinese film industry, can probably alleviate the difficulties for people working in Chinese film studios. For example, most of our female classmates who became well-known and award-winning filmmakers sacrificed their family lives, but Li Shaohong is an exception. She envisioned the predicament of her balance between the Chinese film industry and family life; therefore, she married Zeng Nianping, an award-winning cinematographer. Chen Kaige is lucky because his wife, Chen Hong (b. 1968), is always an actress or a co-producer in the same work-team. Without Chen Hong, Chen Kaige would not have made so many contributions.

With reference to the martial arts world, it is mainly men's world, and female characters usually function as decorations, in my viewpoint. Male masters of martial arts outnumber female experts of kung fu. Female directors seldom show strong interest in martial arts films. My current female students in the Beijing Film Academy are less interested in martial arts stories and films than male students are. Even though you use Ann Hui's martial arts films as counter-examples in your book, kung fu movies are still not Ann Hui's main focus. I believe that Ann Hui still prefers topics related to women and gender differences, such as her representative work, *Summer Snow*, in 1995.

Zhang Yimou's films focus on a number of women; however, I think his gender ideology is stereotypically patriarchal and male-centered. As his female classmate, I witnessed his true attitude toward women in his everyday life.

When we were undergraduate students, I witnessed that his girlfriend came to clean his room and wash his blanket, pants, and socks on holidays. He usually collected dirty clothes and waited for his girlfriend to wash them for him. In that year, he was already twenty-eight years old. He would have already married that girl if he had not had the opportunity to go to college at that time. He is patriarchal and male-centered in not merely my point of view but also his own perspective. He honestly admitted his patriarchy and male-centeredness when we were classmates in our college. He defines women's responsibilities as cooking, cleaning, and housekeeping. He loves women who cook, wash dishes, clean house, do laundry, produce offspring, raise children, and look after family members. The women who sacrifice themselves for men or romantic love in his films are exactly ideal women in his gender ideology. These are women that he, as a man, would like to see.

Chen Kaige is the same as Zhang Yimou in terms of patriarchal and male-centered gender ideology. His wife, Chen Hong, is exactly his almighty personal secretary, washing machine, dishwasher, Dutch wife, babysitter, and housekeeper. For instance, if Chen Hong tells Chen Kaige to dress in green today, Chen Kaige would undoubtedly still put on green clothes even if he does not like to be in green. Chen Kaige is completely an idiot, taking Chen Hong's advice in the domestic aspects of their everyday life. Chen Hong gave birth to two sons; she takes care of and decides everything in the private sphere and their family life. Inside of their home, Chen Hong is the controller of all the domestic details; outside of their home, Chen Kaige is the decider of everything. Chen Hong is Chen Kaige's "little woman." This is what I witnessed as Chen Kaige's female classmate and peer-director.

Jia Zhangke (b. 1970) was born and brought up in a countryside village in Shanxi. He is probably even more male-centered and patriarchal because of his hometown and family background. Jia Zhangke's parents are a stereotypical model-pair of traditional Chinese husband and wife.

Other Chinese male fifth-generation filmmakers are similar to Zhang Yimou and Chen Kaige in terms of gender ideology. It is not true that they do nothing inside of their homes. They sometimes help do some housework; however, the division of labor is unchangeably patriarchal and male-centered. As a female classmate and peer-director of most male fifth-generation filmmakers, I see no exception. This kind of patriarchal and male-centered gender ideology is reflected in these male filmmakers' works on the silver screen. The audience members who accept this sort of gender ideology become their conspiracy.

Younger Chinese male filmmakers such as Wang Quanan (b. 1965) might be less patriarchal. Younger Chinese audience members tend to be also less male-centered. For instance, my current female students in the Beijing Film Academy may share your questions: Why should Yü Jiaolong jump into the abyss to fulfill her boyfriend's wish at the end of Ang Lee's *Crouching Tiger Hidden Dragon*? Why does Luo Xiaohu not leap into the abyss and sacrifice himself for his girlfriend in the film? Younger Chinese female filmmakers may refuse to design the storyline and conclude their films in such a male-centered and patriarchal way. Unfortunately, the current proportion of these young people is too limited to alter the overall condition of Chinese film industry.

Furthermore, investors who provide financial supports to filmmakers possess a lot of controlling power. Ninety-nine percent of current investors in the Chinese film industry are men with male-centered and patriarchal gender ideology.[1] Zhang Weiping and Zhang Yimou, for example, are a well-known sponsor-director pair. Sponsors barely hesitate to reject directors who share your feminist questions about the gender inequality. Without investors, nothing can be done. Female or feminist directors who aim to shoot films that challenge gender inequality undoubtedly face problems of investors' financial supports.

Even male directors give way to investors because of financial concerns. For instance, Huayi Brothers Media Group is a famous company established by Wang Zhongjun and Wang Zhonglei, two brothers who were born and brought up by high-level governmental officers and returned from the US after their master's degrees. The media group sponsored Feng Xiaogang and had dominating power over his films, such as how the storyline develops and which actors and actress would play which roles in *The Banquet.*

As for actresses who play the self-sacrificial women in films or female screenwriters, they may express their opinions in meetings, but they rarely fight against filmmakers or sponsors for the possibility for the plot to include more feminist emancipation. Most people show no conflicts with directors or sponsors after the final decision of the screenplay.

The People's Republic of China (P.R.C.) is different from other countries. She is a nation that claimed the ideal of gender egalitarianism at the beginning of her national history in 1949. Current Chinese Mainlanders do not tolerate sexual violence, which is a frequently seen problem in South Africa and thus what South African female filmmakers expose in their films. But current Chinese Mainlanders' subconscious acceptance of traditional patriarchy has not yet faded; for example, it remains in the subconscious appreciation for the tragedies of women's self-sacrifice for men on the silver screen. The cinematic or fictional representations of women's self-sacrifice for men is more appreciated by current Mainland Chinese mainstream audience members and hence financially better rewarded than that of men's self-sacrifice for women. Men who sacrifice themselves for women are defined as useless jerks, and films that highlight this kind of men are not blockbusters. The mainstream Mainland Chinese audience members feel that it is romantic for women to sacrifice themselves for men; therefore, stories and movies that include this kind of women sell well. This is how financial benefits and the box office decide the impossibility of Luo Xiaohu's sacrifice for his girlfriend's wish in Ang Lee's *Crouching Tiger Hidden Dragon* and Jin's and Liu's self-sacrifices for Xiaomei in Zhang Yimou's *House of Flying Daggers*. Financial benefits and the box office result in the tragic and so-called romantic endings in which Yü Jiaolong self-sacrificially jumps into the abyss to make her boyfriend's wish come true and Xiaomei sacrifices her own life to keep both Jin and Liu alive. This cruel fact became an unequaled obstacle for an influential call for stronger collective objection to the gender inequality that still remains in the subconscious patriarchy and male-centered-ness of mainstream audience members.

In addition to financial sponsorship and the box office, the current P.R.C. censorship is a governmental obstacle[2] to what you mean by "Chinese martial arts feminism" in films. Administratively speaking, the priority of emancipation for Mainland Chinese multi-media is websites, literature (such as fictions), television, newspapers, and finally motion pictures. In other words, motion pictures suffer from the most severe censorship. Ang Lee's *Lust Caution* (2007), for instance, suffered from problems of Mainland Chinese censorship. The leading actress, Tang Wei (b. 1979), in this film was severely criticized by the Mainland Chinese public and blacklisted by Beijing authorities and financial sponsors in 2008.[3]

Censors take turns deciding the destinies of films and remain anonymous to prevent bribery. They are divided into various groups but belong to three governmental branches: first, the division of broadcast, films, and television; second, the division of the central political propaganda; third, the division of culture. The Bureau of Films decides where censors come from every year. Most censors are male governmental officers because they have a good sense of the political atmosphere that regulates and influences films. The office of censorship in the Bureau of Films will collect comments from anonymous censors and give the reviews to directors of every Mainland Chinese film. Nobody can have a narrow escape from this censorship in Mainland China. For instance, the Chinese film industry in the past had a censorial rule that Hollywood was a taboo. When the television station's reporters interviewed me, I could mention only American films, but not Hollywood. Generally speaking, censors are more difficult to work with than sponsors in most Mainland Chinese directors' viewpoints because sponsors are more negotiable but censors are not flexible.

I personally hope that there will be a better-supportive system, including censorship, sponsorship, investment, national policies, political and sociocultural atmospheres, marketing mechanisms, educational curriculum about gender egalitarianism, ceaseless efforts, passions and patience for films and multimedia. As a female classmate and peer-director of so many successful fifth-generation filmmakers in China, I certainly look forward to a brighter future of Chinese film industry, especially when I am also educating future Chinese directors as a professor in Chinese academy.[4]

Notes

1. Lu Yan (b. 1957) is an exception. With working experience as an actress and a master's degree in drama and cinema, she is a female Chinese sponsor of recent American films. Hu An is another exception. She received her academic degree in business administration at New York University in 1985, established her own real estate

company, attended intensive courses about cinema, and successfully became an award-winning female director in 2000.

2. Current Mainland Chinese female governmental officers are usually women who share the following experience and background: *wu dangpai* (no special preference for any specific political groups), *zhi shi jie* (educated elites), *xia guo xiang* (experience in being "sent down" or politically brainwashed in the marginalized countryside), *liu guo xue* (abroad studies in foreign countries). The Chinese-language abbreviation of these four kinds of experience and background in this context happens to be *wu zhi xia liu*—a pun for another Chinese phrase that means ignorance and low-down-ness in other context. More often than not, at the administrative levels of towns, villages, and cities, this kind of female governmental officer oversees five or six male subordinate staff members, yet you can hardly see these female administrative heads' existence at or above the provincial level. The difference between the P.R.C. and other places is obvious if one compares Mainland China with Taiwan or Euro-America. Taiwan had already a female vice president from 2000 to 2008; Englishmen have a queen, instead of a king, as their ruler; Americans have female Secretaries of State and female candidates for presidency. However, there has been no symptom for any influential positions to be occupied by women at the national level in Mainland China. What do the comparisons and contrasts mean? They refer to the lack of enough space for women's leadership. Whether these Mainland Chinese women occupy administrative positions still heavily depends on male deciders' preference and the politically correct requirement to slightly balance the male-to-female ratio. Female administrative heads' political ideals or gender ideology still cannot be directly and widely spread to or influential toward the public.

3. Jane Macartney, "Tang Wei Blacklisted for 'Glorifying Traitors,'" in *Times Online*: http://www.thetimes.co.uk/tto/arts/film/article2426823.ece (online data accessed in July 2009).

4. Dorothy Kehl and Simon Xiaomin Chen helped the interviewer reach and communicate with Pan Hua.

Chapter Thirteen
Interview with Tsai Kuo-jung, a Coplanner and Screenwriter of Ang Lee's *Crouching Tiger Hidden Dragon*

Bellow is the translation and transcription of an interview with Tsai Kuo-jung (Cai, Guojung) in Taipei during summer 2009:
My role as a co-planner and screenwriter of Ang Lee's *Crouching Tiger Hidden Dragon* started in 1995. My wife and I visited Ang Lee in New York State during that summer. At Ang Lee's home after our dinner, we chatted about the martial arts fictions and other banned books that we had read as adolescents and teenagers in the 1950s and 1960s. We mentioned Wang Dulu's martial arts story and could not stop our conversation until midnight. In the next morning, Ang Lee suggested turning Wang Dulu's work into a kung fu film. So we started to plan this movie.

This is Ang Lee's first martial arts film. It is entirely different from other directors' kung fu movies. Ang Lee said that *jiang hu*—that is, the ideal and imaginary world of kung fu that you pointed out in your chapter—exists in every Chinese boy's and man's heart. Our preparation for *Crouching Tiger Hidden Dragon*, however, was slow because Ang Lee was shooting other films, such as *The Ice Storm* (1997) and *Ride with the Devil* (1999).

Wang Dulu's original martial arts story includes five volumes. Ang Lee and I shared the same interest in the first and fourth volume. *Crouching Tiger Hidden Dragon* belongs to the fourth volume. We decided to focus on the fourth volume instead of the first volume because Yü Jiaolong deserves our cinematic portrait.

Yü Jiaolong is different from most female experts of martial arts. She is a Manchurian without any Han biological heritage. Manchurian women neither tied feet nor suffered from as much gender inequality as Han women, but it did not mean that Manchurian women, like Yü Jiaolong, never experienced any restriction. For instance, when she meets Luo Xiaohu in the desert, Yü Jiaolong's love is entirely free from limitation, but she ends up with all kinds of restrictions after her return to Beijing, including her dissatisfaction with Luo

Xiaohu because what Luo Xiaohu can offer to her is not as much as the pampered sons of wealthy and influential families in Beijing can provide.

Wang Dulu is also biologically a Manchurian. He knows Manchurian culture, personality, and conventions better than other writers do, and hence has a better fictional portrait of Yü Jiaolong as a Manchurian woman than almost anyone else. Wang Dulu's fictional design of Yü Jiaolong in the authentic Manchurian tradition is like Lao She's literary delineation of Beijing as a true native in Beijing.

We believe that there are at least two major factors for *Crouching Tiger Hidden Dragon* to sell well in the Western market: first, exoticism; second, combats of kung fu. I am sure I can successfully deal with how the film touches Chinese audience members' hearts. For example, Chinese viewers can easily comprehend the ancient Chinese match-making principle that Luo Xiaohu's background as a parentless outlaw does not fit into Yü Jiaolong's wealthy family. I do not need to elaborate this and prepare our Chinese audience for this sort of background information; however, I am not sure about current Western audience members. It is incorrect to naively believe that nothing similar to this appears in the West. Princesses usually married prices in the West during the medieval era, and even now, it is not an impossible phenomenon for wealthy Western parents to marry daughters to wealthy men, though the frequency for wealthy parents to do so in modern Western societies is different from that in the medieval period. But the West is still not the same as ancient China; therefore, we asked James Schamus to take care of our Western viewers and market. I firmly believe that James Schamus was a good choice. He has been happily cooperating with Ang Lee for a long time. His Jewish heritage and cultural background can smoothly bridge him and Chinese traditions because Jewish traditions share a lot of similarities with Chinese traditions, such as match-making and parental insist on descendants' education. I think the most important part of his contribution was his control of how this film attracted and impressed Western audience members.

After James Schamus joined us and became one of the screenwriters for *Crouching Tiger Hidden Dragon*, I suggested that Ang Lee include one more screenwriter: Wang Hui-ling. Wang Hui-ling has also been harmoniously cooperating with Ang Lee for a long time. One of the main reasons for Ang Lee and me to include her was the fact that I was unable to leave my position as the associate editor-in-chief of *China Times* to accompany Ang Lee to find and decide on Mainland Chinese filming locations at that time. I told Ang Lee that Wang Hui-ling would be a good screenwriter to replace me when I was unavailable. Without Wang Hui-ling, the screenplay would not have been so successful.

In addition to Wang Hui-ling and me, there was one more Chinese consultant: A Cheng, a Mainland Chinese fictionist. A Cheng offered his opinions between my participation in the preparation for the film and Wang Hui-ling's arrival at this work team. That is to say, there were totally four men and one woman to adapt Wang Dulu's original literary work: Ang Lee, James Schamus, A Cheng, and me as the male group; Wang Hui-ling as the only female screenwriter. In this sense, only twenty percent of the workforce was female.

At the beginning of our process to adapt Wang Dulu's fiction for this film, the first bottleneck was the inconsistency of Yü Jiaolong's personality because Wang Dulu wrote and published around one thousand words of the same story in the newspapers every day. We had to reshape many details. I confess that I worked as a male screenwriter and coped with Yü Jiaolong's story from men's perspectives, not women's. I interpreted Yü Jiaolong from men's standpoints. It was too difficult for me to explore Yü Jiaolong from women's viewpoints.

In my point of view, Yü Jiaolong has nowhere to go at the end of the film. It is impossible for her to return to her parents or the man, whom she was married to, in Beijing. Martial arts experts in the *jiang hu* cannot forgive and accept her, either. She cannot find her salvation anywhere. Because of the lack of salvation, she can only escape from her dilemma. She has two choices of escape: first, leap into the abyss; second, return to the desert to live her marital life with Luo Xiaohu. As a male screenwriter, I did not think of your feminist questions about why Luo Xiaohu does not sacrifice himself to fulfill Yü Jiaolong's dream at that time, but I felt that Yü Jiaolong's leap into the abyss would be more tragic and powerful than her return with Luo Xiaohu to the desert in terms of how this film catches the audience before viewers' departure from theaters.

I understand that most current American viewers cannot tolerate tragic endings and that most Hollywood films have happy endings; however, the original version of Wang Dulu's fiction has already a tragic ending in terms of Yü Jiaolong's romantic love and life story. In addition, tragedies can win audience members' hearts more forcefully than comedies. This literary theory derives from Plato in the Greco-Roman era of Western cultural history.

Jade Fox is an important character in *Crouching Tiger Hidden Dragon*. I agree with you that she represents fox spirits or female scapegoats of chauvinistic Chinese men's immoral sexuality. I also agree with you that there must be a sufficient space for Jade Fox to metaphorically reverse the miscarriage of all the fox spirits' justice. I attribute this to Wang Hui-ling's contribution, because she was the only female screenwriter of this film. Otherwise, male screenwriters seldom interpret the problem between Jiang Nanhe and Jade Fox as something unfair for women. You probably also notice that all the male characters, throughout the film, define Jade Fox as a villain regardless of Jiang Nanhe's sexual irresponsibility and lie. I agree with you that one of the earliest Chinese cultural origins of fox spirits is Daji, the most famous royal concubine of Emperor Zhou of the Shang Dynasty. Daji is transformed from a fox to a beautiful woman. The belief in fox spirits is popular in not merely China but also East Asia or Southeast Asia. Even nowadays there are temples of fox spirits in Japan and China.

I myself believe that it is inevitable and indispensible for Jade Fox to accuse Jiang Nanhe of lying to exchange advanced martial arts skills for their sexual relation. Even as a male screenwriter, I do not feel hurt by Jade Fox's accusation of men. I understand how unfair Jade Fox feels it is when she becomes a female scapegoat of Jiang Nanhe's sexual irresponsibility and chauvinism, though I, as a man speaking from men's perspectives, doubt whether Jade Fox's version of this story is true because it is impossible for viewers to verify or double-check anything with Jiang Nanhe.

When I was planning this film with Ang Lee and working with other screenwriters to adapt the original martial arts novel, we discussed how heavy or how light the part of Jade Fox's accusation should be. I personally feel that this proportion of her defense for fox spirits and accusation of injustice is appropriate. If it had been enlarged, it would have been too much and weakened other boyfriend-girlfriend pairs in the same film. If it had been decreased, it would have been too little to draw viewers' attention. When we were planning the female character Jade Fox in *Crouching Tiger Hidden Dragon*, our reference was Rebecca's omnipresent ghost in Alfred Hitchcock's film *Rebecca* (1940). Our plan was to use the deal, sexuality, and hatred between Jiang Nanhe and Jade Fox as the ubiquitous background so there would be enough space to cinematically portray diverse kinds of young people's romances.

In this book, you contend that male filmmakers tend to shut the gate of complete and unlimited feminist emancipation at the end of kung fu movies after slightly opening the door of "Chinese martial arts feminism." I cordially agree with you on this argument. Ang Lee's *Crouching Tiger Hidden Dragon* is undoubtedly an illustration of what you highlight. As a man, however, I feel that it is already extremely revolutionary for Ang Lee and his male screenwriters to open the door for Chinese women in such a martial arts film that focuses on how Chinese patriarchal society looked two hundred years ago. Except for ghost films, kung fu movies allow a larger space and more flexibility for ancient Chinese feminist liberation than all the other kinds of films about ancient China. Even in the ideal world of *jiang hu*, most martial arts ladies usually put on men's sportswear or disguise themselves as men just like Mulan; therefore, they are still not completely released from patriarchal domination.

As for whether filmmakers, including award-winning and well-anthologized male directors, and other influential people in the Chinese film industry will eventually remove the outer gate of unlimited liberation for women at the end of films after they slightly open the door of "Chinese martial arts feminism," my answer is yes. I believe that the door of emancipation, once opened, cannot be closed. Yet the completion of door-opening processes and the unlimitedness of feminist emancipation on the silver screen take time and hence will not happen in only one decade. To hastily complete the cinematic dream of "Chinese martial arts feminism" is not good for true feminist awakening of every filmmaker, because true epiphany does not easily and immediately occur. More and more female staff members in film studios are playing influential roles, though women and married people, just like what Pan Hua said when you interviewed her, do still suffer in the current Chinese film industry. More and more undergraduate and graduate students take different levels of courses about women's and gender studies. I have confidence in the eventual arrival of feminist epiphany or awakening in filmmakers', censors', sponsors', and producers' future lives. In my prediction, it will even not take one century for this to complete.[1]

Notes

1. Wang Wei assisted the interviewer to contact and reach Tsai Kuo-jung. Tsai Kuo-jung also offered his photo with Ang Lee in the Oscar Award party.

Chapter Fourteen
Interview with Wang Wei, a Judge in the Golden Horse Film Festival

Bellow is the translation and transcription of her interview with Wang Wei in Taipei during summer 2009:
The earliest Golden Horse Film Festival resulted from Chiang Kai-cheh's intention to draw the non-Mainland film industry to his side because the Chinese name of the film festival, Jin Ma, clearly indicated Jinmen and Matzu, the two Taiwanese frontlines facing the Mainland Chinese communist power. People in the Taiwanese film industry also took advantage of the ceremony of film festival to celebrate Chiang Kai-cheh's birthday.

When James Song directed the Government Information Office in 1979, he decided that the Golden Horse Film Festival would follow the format of the Oscar Awards, nominating candidates first and then announcing the winners during the ceremony. In the early 1990s, the managing group of the film festival became the TGHFF Executive Committee (Taipei Golden Horse Film Festival Executive Committee) administratively under the Motion Picture Development Foundation, Republic of China.[1] The TGHFF Executive Committee is not governmental, but there are forever governmental officers in the Motion Picture Development Foundation. Judges include screenwriters, filmmakers, actors, actresses, soundmen, choreographers, film editors, and so on. Name lists of judges are usually not confidential, especially after the announcement of nominees. When Li Xing (b. 1930), a well-known professional filmmaker, and I coplanned the thirtieth Golden Horse Film Festival in 1992, our goals were professionalism and globalization. Li Xing used a video camera to simultaneously show the procedure of how judges voted for, negotiated, and decided their favorite nominees to various journalists or reports, who were prohibited to disclose the names of winners until the end of the ceremony.

Details of judges' nominating, voting, negotiating, and deciding processes are seldom recorded in academic publications. I can provide some examples of my own experience to you. In 1992, Yang Kui-mei, the professional actress playing the female protagonist in *Hill of No Return*, and Lindsey Chan, the amateur actress playing the female protagonist in Evans Chan's *To Liv(e)*, were both nominated as candidates for best actress. The final choice was Lindsey

Chan regardless of her lack of working experience in the past and Yang Kui-mei's abundant and excellent working experience for more than one decade. I did not understand why an amateur Hong Kong actress beat a professional Taiwanese actress. In 1998, I also did not understand why Li Xiaolu, a fourteen-year-old actress playing the female protagonist in Chen Chong's *Xiu Xiu* (1997), beat Yang Kui-mei in Tsai Ming-liang's *The Hole* (1997).

Serving as a judge in the Golden Horse Film Festivals,[2] I think actresses can barely win any significant award in feature films or commercial films whose main focus is not women. Observing global film industry and various film festivals in the West, I assure you that even well-known Western actresses such as Nicole Mary Kidman (b. 1967), can hardly win anything important unless they play female protagonists in movies focusing on gender issues or women.

Recalling all the award-winning filmmakers in the Golden Horse Film Festivals, I believe that films directed by Stanley Kwan (b. 1957) brought the largest number of Golden Horse Awards to actresses. Working as Ann Hui's assistant director in 1979, Stanley Kwan began directing in 1984 and made a considerable number of feature films or commercial films focusing on women or gender concerns, such as *Women* (1984), *Love unto Waste* (1986), *Rouge* (1987), *Full Moon in New York* (1988), *Center Stage* (1991), and *Red Rose White Rose* (1994).[3] Almost every one of his films successfully produced an award-winning actress in the Golden Horse Film Festivals.[4]

Even Stanley Kwan's gay film, *Lan Yu* (2002), produced two nominees for best actor: Liu Ye (b. 1978) and Hu Jun (b. 1968). I served as a judge in the Golden Horse Film Festival at that time. There were twelve judges in that year though the total number of judges in the Golden Horse Film Festivals is usually an odd number, not an even number. In the first and second voting processes, there were six votes for Liu Ye and six votes for Hu Jun. In the third voting, Liu Ye won seven votes and Hu Jun got five votes, so the Golden Horse Award for the Best Actor went to Liu Ye.

In my experience in working as a judge in the Golden Horse Film Festivals, there were usually twelve or thirteen judges, and two or three of them were female. The proportion of female judges is around one-sixth only. The largest ratio of female judges, according to my memory, was three women among seven judges.

I agree that there is truly gender inequality and sexual discrimination against women. The film industry is incredibly inappropriate for married women. In current Taiwanese, Hong Kong, or Mainland Chinese societies, will parents-in-law happily encourage daughters-in-law to work eighteen to twenty hours in film studios and filming locations every day? No, they will not. The union of the Hollywood film industry regulates reasonable working hours for staff members; however, the union of the Mainland Chinese, Hong Kong and Taiwanese film industry does not do the same thing now. I am not optimistic in terms of the future possibility for the Mainland Chinese, Hong Kong, and Taiwan union to achieve the same thing. Screenwriting is already the best choice for married women because creative writing and adaptation of literary works do not require them to leave home, neglect their parents-in-law and children, and stay up at midnight. Unfortunately, screenwriting does not always guarantee any steady or monthly income; therefore, most female and married screenwriters inevitably depend on their spouses' steady incomes.

In the current Taiwanese film industry, it is still a taboo for women or female filmmakers to sit on containers of filming equipments or to view a view finder though there has been a little improvement in the past decades. Behind the taboo is the sexually discriminatory assumption that women's bodies are unclean or polluting. This taboo functions like the frequently seen phenomenon that women are prohibited to worship gods in temples during their menstrual periods.

After finishing my graduate degree in cinema studies, I became a screenwriter and producer of some martial arts films and soap operas. I have to honestly tell you that women play marginal and decorative roles in the cinematic world of kung fu. The female protagonist in Chang Che's *The One-Armed Swordsman* (1967) is the best illustration, in my viewpoint. Even martial arts ladies, such as the Golden Swallow or Mulan, put on men's sportswear, disguise themselves as men, or experience their mysterious loss of excellent martial arts skills and success in combats after people discover that they are actually female. This patriarchal tradition to marginalize women continues and influences current Hong Kong films. For instance, female protagonists in Andrew Wai-Keung Lau's and Alan Siu-Fai Mak's *The Infernal Affairs* (2002) are like two decorative flowers watching male protagonists' power struggles against each other. They do not participate in any influential, critical, powerful, or significant turning point of the entire storyline. On the contrary, its Hollywood counterpart, Martin Scorsese's *The Departed* (2006) inserts a woman between the two male protagonists and has their love triangle as a selling point though William Monahan, the screenwriter, confesses that he bases this film on the Hong Kong film, *The Infernal Affairs*. I therefore create my own theory about contemporary Hong Kong films: Martial arts films' tendency to marginalize and trivialize women is the foundation of current Hong Kong cinema.

It is almost a cinematic routine that male masters of kung fu become less powerful if they enjoy sexuality or romantic relations with women; therefore, monks and eunuchs are usually the most influential men with astonishing martial arts skills in a number of Chinese kung fu films. I think that sexuality, private parts, or romances in Chinese martial arts world are taboos that signify the centuries-long patriarchal traditions of sexual oppression. Corey Yuen's *The Legend of Fong Sai-yuk* (1993) is the first and best example that immediately comes to my mind. The male protagonist's mother soaks him in a special medical liquid since his childhood so that his kung fu overpowers everybody else's; however, his private part is his only weakness. He dies because his private part is injured.

In my point of view, the most revolutionary gender ideology in recent cinematic representations of the martial arts world is probably *Swordsman II: Remastered Version* (2002; Director: Ching Siu-tung; Producer: Tsui Hark), focusing on the gender issues about queer, homophobia, transsexuality, transgender, and heterosexuality. The plot about transsexuality and transgender reminds the audience of Wong Kar-wai's *Ashes of Time* (1994). Today (July 4, 2009) we will be able to see Wong Kar-wai's *Ashes of Time Redux* in Taipei.

With reference to recent Chinese martial arts films, I do not think Mainland Chinese filmmakers' grasps of the true martial arts chivalric spirit in kung fu movies exceed that of Hong Kong or Taiwanese directors. The Cultural Revolution and educational problems that most fifth-generation filmmakers experienced were obstacles of their complete understanding and genuine epiphany of the authentic essence of traditional Chinese culture in my point of view.

Generally speaking, female protagonists or characters function as troublemakers, helpers, and sexual—or at least romantic—reward for male protagonists in the global film industry. This is a cinematic formula that applies in almost every film studio. For example, the indispensably clichéd ending of Roland Emmerich's *ID4* (1996) includes sexuality as the reward for the male protagonist. Why? I believe that the box office and the market are the dominators. Even in the Western film industry, the market and box office decide female roles' destinies in most commercial films. Michael Bay's *Transformers* (2007) is an example that I think of now. Financial factors determine how influential or how decorative the female protagonist is.

Even if female screenwriters or actresses raise feminist questions and disagree with investors or producers on the patriarchal decision about female roles' destinies in the storylines on the silver screen, their opinions will seldom overpower practical financial concerns. Taiwanese soap operas in the SETTV illustrate this. Su Li-mei, the producer and the wife of the boss of the television station, decided female protagonists to be poor and ordinary women meeting wealthy men, just like the female protagonist in Denis Lee's *Pretty Woman* (1990). After Su Li-mei, Chen Yu-shan became the producer, and she started to allow female protagonists' flaws, such as their slight mammonism, in the storylines of soap operas.

The background information of producers' audience research is interesting. In the 1950s to early 1990s, the mainstream viewers of soap operas, which derived from screenwriting and romantic fictions by Chiung Yao (b. 1938), were middle-aged housewives or career women. But nowadays, the mainstream audience members of recent and current Taiwanese "trendy TV drama" (soap operas that focus on romantic love and feature a lot of young and nice-looking actors and actresses; similar to *Beverly Hills* in the US and *The 101th Proposal* or *Love 2000* in Japan) are young girls from elementary schools to high schools or at the undergraduate level. As for the famous local Taiwanese soap opera, *Taiwan Tornado* (2004-2005), producers divulge that they assume the mainstream audience members are divorced women, wealthy men's underground mistresses, or women whose jobs were usually unacceptable by mainstream social norms, such as sex workers, bargirls, club ladies, and strippers, according to surveys of viewers. On the survey forms, there are three choices related to viewers' marital status: married, unmarried, or other. The mainstream female audience members of *Taiwan Tornado* selected "other," instead of a clear boundary between "married" and "unmarried."

My own working experience is also a good example. When I wrote screenplays of the soap opera *The Lie* (2002; CTV/China Television Station; rating: the top), the producer and director, Li Lei, always decided the development of female protagonists' life stories. For instance, in one of our soap operas, the female protagonist encounters a man she loves after her husband's extramarital love affair. Li Lei, as the director and producer, decided that she wanted the female protagonist to have such a similar experience. In our discussions about the female protagonist's fate, the key point was Li Lei's estimation of whether the contemporary Taiwanese public and social norms permit such a woman to have sexual relation with the man she loves. She believed that the Taiwanese audience can accept this kind of sexual relation but requested me, as the screenwriter, to make their sexual scene as vague as possible. After the female protagonist's sex with the man she loves, Li Lei required that this female protagonist divorce her husband and thus commit no crime of adultery, because she anticipated that Taiwanese society could still not accept the female protagonist's extramarital love affair. Li Lei approved my suggestion that the female protagonist's mother-in-law encourages the divorce and financially supports the female protagonist, because we both tried to avoid the cliché of conflicts between mothers-in-law and daughters-in-law in not only Chinese/Taiwanese drama and cinema but also Korean soap operas. At the end of the soap opera, Li Lei and I did not let the female protagonist continue her romantic relation with the man she loves; instead, we turned the female protagonist into an independent and strong single mother who brought up her own children by having a store of her own. From the beginning to the end, Li Lei's concerns about the market and viewers' acceptability dominated the female protagonist's life story. The maximum that I could do as a screenwriter was to offer my suggestions to Li Lei.

Producers have to be practical in terms of financial concerns. Let me tell you one more experience. When I suggested that producers create tailor-made films, soap operas, or commercial advertisements for female superstars, they honestly told me their preference to replace female superstars with male superstars. Why? Male superstars will easily bring in more companies' financial investments than female superstars. Companies will generously sponsor the soap opera or commercial advertisement as long as male superstars use or include their products, such as watches, belts, shampoo, eyeglasses, shoes, socks, clothes, ties, hats, sportswear, wine, soft drinks, and so on—in their on-stage performances. Actors who play James Bond in the film series of 007, for example, attracted countless companies' investment. Even Tony Chiu-Wai Leung (b. 1962), a male superstar with short hair, beat female superstars with long and attractive hair and won the opportunity and unbelievable salary (15 million RMB) to advertise the anti-dandruff shampoo "Head and Shoulders."

Compared with male superstars, female superstars usually end up with less sponsorship and therefore fewer opportunities for their tailor-made soap opera or commercial advertisements.

Here is another example. Gu Long (1937-1985; real name: Xiong, Yaohua), one of the most famous male writers of Chinese martial arts fictions, did not experience good romantic relations.[5] He hardly has an ordinary woman as the female protagonist in his fictions. Almost every female protagonist in his martial arts stories is a prostitute or courtesan. When adapting his martial arts fictions for kung fu films or television soap operas, I suffered from difficulties in changing this stereotype of female protagonists. The market and box office forced me to replace his original female protagonists with ordinary women because the audience no longer loved to see so many prostitutes or courtesans in martial arts films. Compared with Gu Long, I, as a screenwriter, felt that Jin Yong is better and more flexible. I suffer less when adapting the story plot about female protagonists in Jin Yong's martial arts fictions.

Notes

1. Consult the website of the Motion Picture Development Foundation, Republic of China: http://www.taiwancinema.com/ct_12966_40 (online data accessed in July 2009). Also see the website related to the Taipei Golden Horse Film Festival Executive Committee: http://www.goldenhorse.org.tw (online data accessed in July 2009).

2. Wang Wei served as a judge in 1992, 1996, and 2002. He received his master's degree in film studies from the City College of New York in the late 1980s. Jerry W. Carlson helped make this interview possible.

3. *Yang ± Yin: Gender in Chinese Cinema* (1996) is Stanley Kwan's documentary film. Because of this film, he came "out of the closet" for the first time. After finishing the gay film, *Lan Yu*, in 2002, Stanley Kwan repeated the announcement of his homosexuality to the public.

4. *Still Love You After All These* (1997) and *Everlasting Regret* (2005) are rare exceptions. Actresses in these two films directed by Stanley Kwan did not win any awards in the Golden Horse Film Festivals.

5. Gu Long wrote his first novelette in 1949—right after his first failure in love in 1948. In 1952, his parents' marriage ended in divorce. His second failure in love in 1956 initiated his ceaseless creations of Chinese martial arts fictions. He did not stop writing martial arts fictions until his death.

Chung Ling and the author of this book. Photo courtesy of Ya-chen Chen.

Ang Lee and Tsai Kuo-jung at a celebratory party after the Oscar Awards in 2000. Photo courtesy of Tsai Kuo-jung.

Appendix 1
Chinese Martial Arts Films for Narrative Analyses in This Book

A Touch of Zen 俠女/侠女 directed by King Hu in 1971
Legend of the Mountain 山中傳奇/山中传奇 directed by King Hu in 1979
Crouching Tiger Hidden Dragon 臥虎藏龍/卧虎藏龙 directed by Ang Lee in 2000
Hero directed 英雄 by Zhang Yimou in 2002
House of Flying Daggers 十面埋伏 directed by Zhang Yimou in 2004
The Promise 無極/无极 directed by Chen Kaige in 2005
Seven Swords 七劍/七剑 directed by Tsui Hark in 2005
The Banquet 夜宴 directed by Feng Xiaogang in 2006
Curse of the Golden Flower 滿城盡帶黃金甲/满城尽带黄金甲 directed by Zhang Yimou in 2006

Appendix 2
Crouching Tiger Hidden Dragon
臥虎藏龍　卧虎藏龙

Basic Credit List
Director: Ang Lee
Fictionist: Wang Dulu
Screenwriters: Wang Hui-ling, James Schamus, Tsai Kuo-jung, A Cheng, and Ang Lee
Producers: Ang Lee, Li-Kung Hsu, and Bill Kong
Choreographer: Yuen Wo-ping
Custom Designer: Tim Yip
Running Time: 120 minutes

MPAA Rating: PG-13 for martial arts violence and some sexuality
Distribution Company: Sony Pictures Classics
Year of Copyright: 2000

Cast:
Li Mubai: Chow Yun-fat
Yü Xiulian: Michelle Yeoh
Yü Jiaolong: Zhang Ziyi
Jade Fox: Cheng Pei-pei
Luo Xiaohu: Chang Chen

Website:
http://www.sonypictures.com/cthv/crouchingtiger/main.htm
(online data accessed in August 2009)

Story Plot:
Li Mubai falls in love with Yü Xiulian, but does not clearly express his love for her because of his friendship with Yü Xiulian's dead fiancée, Meng Sizhao. His teacher, Jiang Nanhe, promised Jade Fox to exchange their sexual relationship for Jade Fox's advanced martial arts lessons, but he ate his words after enjoying Jade Fox's sexual service. Jade Fox was so angry that she poisoned Jiang Nanhe and stole his manual of kung fu. Police Chief Cai Jiu, his daughter Cai Xiangmei, and his daughter's boyfriend tried to arrest and punish Jade Fox. Li Mubai also tried to revenge Jiang Nanhe after he discovered that Jade Fox's secret student, Yü Jiaolong, stole his precious sword, Green Destiny Sword. Yü Jiaolong is Lord Yü's only daughter. She secretly learned martial arts with Jade Fox, who worked as a housekeeper in the Yü family, since her childhood. Her martial arts skills exceeds Jade Fox's kung fu later on because Jade Fox is illiterate and therefore cannot learn anything from the written parts of the kung fu manual without depending on Yü Jiaolong's reading abilities. Lord Yü would like to marry Yü Jiaolong to Lu Junpei, another royal relative's son; however, Yü Jiaolong started her secret romantic relationship with Luo Xiaohu during her trip to Xinjiang. Yü Jiaolong keenly desires to enjoy her freedom. During Yü Jiaolong's own trip to escape from the arranged marriage, she was poisoned by Jade Fox. Li Mubai rescued Yü Jiaolong by killing Jade Fox, but died because of Jade Fox's poison. Yü Xiulian gave Green Destiny Sword and her own hairpin to Yü Jiaolong and arranged the reunion of Yü Jiaolong and Luo Xiaohu after Li Mubai's death. At the end of the film, Yü Jiaolong asks Luo Xiaohu to make a wish, and then she jumps into the abyss in order to make Luo Xiaohu's wish come true according to Luo Xiaohu's description of the mythological belief that wishes would come true if faithful wish-makers jump into the abyss.

Appendix 3
Hero 英雄

Basic Credit List
Director: Zhang Yimou
Screenwriters: Wang Bin and Li Feng
Producers: Dou Shoufang, William Kong, Philip Lee, Zhang Weiping, and Zhang Yimou
Music: Tan Dun
Choreographer: Tony Siu-Tung Ching
Cinematographer: Christopher Doyle
Custom Designer: Emi Wada
Running Time: 99 minutes (extensive version: 107 minutes)
MPAA Rating: PG-13 for martial arts violence and some sexuality
Distribution Companies: Beijing New Picture Film Co. and Miramax Films
Year of Copyright: 2002 in Chinese-speaking areas; 2004 in the West

Cast:
Nameless: Jet Li
Broken Sword: Tony Chiu-Wai Leung
Flying Snow: Maggie Cheung
Ying Zheng: Chen Daoming
Long Sky: Donnie Yen
Moon: Zhang Ziyi

Website:
http://www.miramax.com/hero (online data accessed in August 2009)

Story Plot:
Nameless wins Long Sky's trust and agreement to present his head to Ying Zheng, the Emperor of the Qin, and approach Ying Zheng at the distance of one hundred steps. Later on, Nameless tries to defeat Flying Snow in order to approach Ying Zheng at the distance of only ten steps.
However, this film includes diverse version of how Nameless defeats Flying Snow. The first version is the red-colored version on the silver screen. Due to jealousy and love triangle, Flying Snow kills Broken Sword and Moon. Therefore, Nameless easily defeats Flying Snow because of Flying Snow's deep melancholy after the complication. Ying Zheng disbelieves this version presented by Nameless. Instead, he presents his own version. This version is the blue-colored version. In this version, Flying Snow wins her competition with Broken Sword as a volunteer to be defeated by Nameless in front of Ying Zheng's army troops. But Nameless corrects Ying Zheng and presents the green-

colored and white-colored version. In the green-colored version, Broken Sword almost successfully assassinates Ying Zheng, but he gives up at the last moment. Flying Snow is so angry with Broken Sword that she stops speaking with Broken Sword for three years. After that, it is the white-colored version. Nameless promises Flying Snow and Broken Sword that his martial arts skills can assure the life of either one of them though it would seem to be his successful defeat in front of Ying Zheng's army troops. Flying Snow stops Broken Sword and volunteers to play the role of the defeated in Ying Zheng's army camp. Moon brings Broken Sword's sword to Nameless and tells him about Broken Sword's two words as a gift for Nameless: "Our Land," indicating that Ying Zheng's unification of all the warring states can probably bring good future to fellow folks on our land. This changes Nameless's mind and stops him from assassinating Ying Zheng at the Royal Palace of Qin. Flying Snow is again so furious that she fights against Broken Sword, but Broken Sword does nothing to defend himself and thus is killed by Flying Snow in order to prove his true love for her. At the end of the film, Flying Snow kills herself and dies with Broken Sword. At the same time, Ying Zheng's army troops also kill Nameless in the State of Qin.

Appendix 4
House of Flying Daggers 十面埋伏

Basic Credit List
Director: Zhang Yimou
Screenwriters: Wang Bin, Li Feng, and Zhang Yimou
Producers: William Kong, Zhang Zhanyan, Zhang Weiping, and Zhang Yimou
Music: Shigeru Umebayashi
Choreographer: Tony Siu-Tung Ching
Cinematographer: Zhao Xiaoding
Custom Designer: Emi Wada
Running Time: 119 minutes (Australian version: 118 minutes)
MPAA Rating: PG-13 for sequences of stylized martial arts violence and some sexuality
Distribution Company: Beijing New Picture Film Co.
Year of Copyright: 2004 in Chinese-speaking areas; 2005 in the West

Cast:
Xiaomei: Zhang Ziyi
Jin: Takashi Kaneshiro
Liu: Andy Lau

Website:
http://www.sonypictures.com/classics/houseofflyingdaggers/trailer-open.html
(online data accessed in August 2009)

Story Plot:
House of Flying Daggers (Feigao men) is an outlaw organization against the governmental corruption. Xiaomei is a young female member of the House of Flying Daggers. She pretends to be a blind courtesan as well as the blind daughter of the ex-head of the House of Flying Daggers. Liu is a young male member of the House of Flying Daggers, pretending to be a police chieftain. Jin is a true police headman co-working with Liu, and his mission is to visit Xiaomei at the whorehouse, win her trust and follow her all the way to the headquarter of the House of Flying Daggers.

Liu does everything to win Xiaomei's love; however, Xiaomei is attracted to Jin during her three-day journey with Jin from the brothel, police station and jail to the House of Flying Daggers. The romantic triangle echoes the well-known poetic lines at the beginning and the end of the film. During the film, Liu and Xiaomei play the game of "fairies point out the way" several times, indirectly reflecting Xiaomei's need to be directed to the right choice between Liu and Jin inside of the love triangle. At the end of the movie, Xiaomei's final decision is to sacrifice herself and give up her own life in order to rescue both Jin and Liu from the mutual fight and bring them out of the emotional labyrinth of romantic triangle.

Appendix 5
The Promise 無極 无极

Basic Credit List
Director: Chen Kaige
Screenwriters: Chen Kaige and Zhang Tan
Producer: Chen Hong
Music: Guan Xia
Choreographer: Lin Dian
Cinematographer: Bao Dexi (Peter Pau)
Custom Designer: Tim Yip
Running Time: 123 minutes
MPAA Rating: PG-13 for stylized violence, martial arts actions, and some sexual contents
Distribution Company: 21st Century Shenkai Film
Year of Copyright: 2005

Cast:
Kunlun: Jiang Dong-kun
Qingcheng: Cecilia Cheung
Guangming: Hinoyuki Sanada
Wuhuan: Nicolas Tse
Snow Wolf: Liu Ye
Goddess Manshen: Chen Hong
King: Cheng Qian

Website:
http://www.thepromise.sina.com.cn/ (online data accessed in August 2009)

Story Plot:
When Qingcheng is a little girl, she tricks Wuhuan in order to have his bun as her food. She also promises Goddess Manshen to exchange true love for food and beauty. Goddess Manshan tells Qingcheng that there would not be true love unless the snow falls in spring, time moves backward, and the dead comes back to life. After Qingcheng grows up, she becomes a beautiful queen without true love. Kunlun is a talented runner from the snow country and General Guangming's slave but mistaken as General Guangming when he kills the king and rescues Qingcheng because General Guangming requests Kunlun to put on his crimson armor. Because of this misunderstanding, Qingcheng mistakes her love for Kunlun as her love for General Guangming. Wuhuan knows the truth and regards Qingcheng's lack of true love and this misunderstanding as his revenge. At the end of the story, Qingcheng discovers that the person she truly loves is actually Kunlun, instead of General Guangming. Kunlun carries Qingcheng and tries to run so fast that the time can move backward in order to change Qingcheng's destiny, cancel her childhood promise to Goddess, and help Qingcheng win true love.

Appendix 6
Seven Swords 七劍 七剑

Basic Credit List
Director: Tsui Hark
Fictionist: Liang Yüsheng
Screenwriters: Cheung Chi-sing, Chun Tin-nam, and Tsui Hark
Producer: Lee Joo-ick, Pan Zhizhong, and Ma Zhong-jun
Music: Kenji Kawai
Choreographer: Lau Kar-leung

Cinematographer: Keung Kwok-man
Custom Designer: Poon Wing-yan
Running Time: 153 minutes (Singaporean version: 141 minutes)
MPAA Rating: PG-13 for stylized violence, martial arts actions, and some sexual contents
Distribution Company: Dragon Dynasty
Year of Copyright: 2005

Cast:
Chu Chaonan: Donnie Yen
Wu Yuanying: Charlie Young
Han Zhibang: Lu Yi
Fenghuo Liancheng: Sun Honglei
Duan Lüzhu: Kim So-Yeon
Liu Yüfang: Zhang Jingchu
Yang Yunchong: Leon Ming Lai

Website:
http://www.sevenswordsthefilm.com/ (online data accessed in August 2009)

Story Plot:
The Manchurian government imposes a ban to stop citizens from practicing martial arts. Fenghuo Liancheng takes advantages of this to kill innocent people and win his own financial benefits. Fu Qingzhu used to be an executor and Fenghuo Liancheng's supervisor in the previous dynasty, but he would like to rescue people in the martial village from Fenghuo Liancheng's misdeeds thanks to Wu Yuanying's help for his narrow escape from death. He brings Wu Yuanying and Han Zhibang to a sword-forger at Mt. Heaven. This sword-forger asks his four disciples, Chu Zhaonan, Yang Yuncong, Xin Longzi and Mulang, to return with Fu, Wu, and Han to the martial village and help all the villagers. He also gives a sword to each of the above-mentioned seven people and initiates the union of "seven swords." The village chief's daughter, Liu Yüfang, is in love with Han Zhibang but attracted to Chu Zhaonan. However, Chu Zhaonan starts his romantic relationship with Lüzhu, Fenghuo Liancheng's Koren comfort woman, because of the Korean background that they have in common. After Chu Zhaonan brings Lüzhu from Fenghuo Liancheng's place to the martial village, a spy poisons villagers' water and Lüzhu is mistaken as the poisoner. In fact, Lüzhu discloses Fenghuo Liancheng's top secret to Chu Zhaonan and goes to steal it with Chu Zhaonan. Fenghuo Liancheng captures Chu. Lüzhu returns to inform people in the martial village before her death. When almost all the people with martial arts skills leave the martial village to rescue Chu Zhaonan, the spy, Qiu Dongluo, begins his plans to kill the remaining villagers, including children. Liu Yüfang, the only adult staying there to protect children, is forced to fight against and kill Qiu Dongluo. Although Chu Zhaonan is finally rescued and brought back to the martial village, all the people with martial arts skills in

the village still have to travel to the Forbidden City in order to persuade the King to withdraw the martial arts ban. Liu Yüfang stays in the village to protect children again at the end of the film.

Appendix 7
The Banquet 夜宴

Basic Credit List
Director: Feng Xiaogang
Screenwriters: Qiu Guangjian and Shen Heyu
Producer: John Chong and Wang Zhongjun
Music: Tan Dun
Choreographer: Yuen Wo-ping
Cinematographer: Zhang Li
Custom Designer: Tim Yip
Running Time: 131 minutes
MPAA Rating: PG-13 for stylized violence, martial arts actions, and some sexual contents
Distribution Companies: Huayi Brothers and Media Asia Films
Year of Copyright: 2006

Cast:
Empress Wan'er: Zhang Ziyi
Emperor Li: Ge You
Prince Wuluan: Daniel Wu
Qing Nü: Zhou Xun
Grand Marshal: Ma Jingwu
Grand Marshal's son and Qing Nü's brother: Huang Xiaoming

Website:
http://ent.sina.com.cn/yeyan.html (online data accessed in August 2009)

Story Plot:
Wan'er and Prince Wuluan are in love since childhood; however, Wan'er is married to the original Emperor, Wuluan's biological father, and then Emperor Li. Emperor Li is Prince Wuluan's uncle and kills the original Emperor in order to win the royal thrown. He tries to also kill Wuluan in order to secure his own political power. Wan'er does everything to rescue Wuluan, but she is aware that Qingnü also loves Wuluan. When Wan'er tries to poison Emperor Li, Qingnü inadvertently drinks the poisoned wine and dies at the end of the on-stage per-

formance to celebrate Emperor Li's inauguration. Emperor Li insists to drink the poisoned wine after Wan'er confirms her poison. Prince Wuluan dies because of the poison on the sword later on. Wan'er becomes the female ruler of the country, but is assassinated at the end of the film.

Appendix 8
Curse of the Golden Flower
满城尽带黄金甲　满城尽带黄金甲

Basic Credit List
Director: Zhang Yimou
Playwright/Dramatist: Cao Yu
Screenwriter: Zhang Yimou
Producers: William Kong, Zhang Weiping, and Zhang Yimou
Music: Shigeru Umebayashi
Choreographer: Yuen Wo-ping
Cinematographer: Zhao Xiaoding
Custom Designer: Huo Tingxiao
Running Time: 114 minutes
MPAA Rating: R
Distribution Companies: Sony Picture Classics and Edko Film
Year of Copyright: 2006

Cast:
Empress Liang: Gong Li
Emperor Ping: Chow Yun-Fat
Crown Prince: Liu Ye
Second Prince: Jay Chou
Little Prince: Qin Junjie
Jiang Chan: Li Man
Emperor's first wife: Chen Jin

Website:
http://www.sonyclassics.com/curseofthegoldenflower/
(online data accessed in August 2009)

Story Plot:
　　Emperor Ping abandons his first wife, lies that his first wife dies, and marries Empress Liang in order to strengthen his political power. Emperor Ping's first wife escapes from the palace, runs into the royal medical doctor Jiang, mar-

ries Dr. Jiang, and gives birth to Jiang Chan. However, Empress Liang has a secret love affair with Crown Prince, who later on betrays Empress Liang and falls in love with Jiang Chan. Emperor Ping is also aware of the unusual relationship between Empress Liang and the Crown Prince; therefore, he slowly and secretly poisons Empress Liang by adding poison into Empress Liang's hourly medicine. Dr. Jiang and Jiang Chan both work in the royal pharmacy to deal with the poison for Emperor Ping. Emperor Ping's first wife discloses the secret about Emperor Ping's poison to Empress Liang. Gradually, the Second Prince also knows Emperor Ping's poison added to Empress Liang's hourly medicine. He agrees with Empress Liang to plan a riot to overthrown Emperor Ping's dynasty. Empress Liang embroiders golden chrysanthemum blossoms on scarves for the Second Prince's army troops.

One day, Emperor Ping's first wife discovers the romantic relationship between the Crown Prince and Jiang Chan. In order to stop the potential incest and embarrass Emperor Ping, Empress Liang exposes the truth that Jiang Chan is actually the Crown Prince's half sister because they share the same biological mother. Emperor Ping's army troops kill Jiang Chan, her mother, and Dr. Jiang.

The Little Prince kills the Crown Prince and asks Emperor Ping to step down and turn him into the new emperor, but he is whipped to death by Emperor Ping. The Second Prince's military action fails. Emperor Ping does not put the Second Prince to death, but he requests that Second Prince forces Empress Liang to take the poisoned medicine till death. It is so painful for the Second Prince that he commits suicide in front of the Emperor and the Empress. At the end of the film, Empress Liang pours the poisonous medicine out of her cup to display the fact that the medicine is actually poisonous.

Appendix 9
Audience Research

In spring 2009, thirty adult viewers saw Ang Lee's *Crouching Tiger Hidden Dragon* and joined this survey in the US. The outcome of this audience research, basically speaking, supports my academic arguments in this book. Most participants in this survey remark that they recognize the Chinese martial arts feminism that female protagonists enjoy in the film and notice the limitation or incompletion of this liberation for women in the martial arts world.

In this group, thirteen of the members are male, while seventeen of them are female. Ten male viewers and two female audience members are interested in martial arts. Ten women, but no men, show interest in love stories and gender issues in the films. Twenty-five of the viewers say that they like the Chinese cultural elements and atmosphere on the silver screen and that they see the movies for fun.

In terms of biological and cultural heritage backgrounds, there are ten Caucasians, two bi-racial viewers, seventeen Asians, and an African-American. Some of them are Christians or Catholics. One of them is Muslim. Most Asians are Buddhists. All of the viewers can speak fluent American English. Thirteen of them can speak Mandarin Chinese and other Chinese dialects, such as Cantonese or Fujianese. One of them is a native speaker of Japanese. One of them can speak Korean. Six of them can speak Spanish.

After the thirty viewers saw the movie, they filled out survey forms including the questions noted below. Here is a list of my basic statistical data regarding their answers.

Questions	Strong Disagreement		Average		Strong Agreement	Mean Average	Standard Deviation
	1	2	3	4	5		
Do you recognize the feminist freedom	1 person	0 persons	6 persons	5 persons	18 persons	4.3	1.005

that female protagonists enjoy in the film, such as their choices of spouses and the lack of foot-binding?	3.33%	0%	20%	16.67%	60%		
Do you agree that female protagonists deserve the feminist emancipation that you witness in the film?	0 persons 0%	0 persons 0%	4 persons 13.33%	6 persons 20%	20 persons 66.67%	4.53	0.718
Do you think that there is already some gender egalitarianism in the film?	1 person 3.33%	1 person 3.33%	9 persons 30%	6 persons 20%	13 persons 43.33%	3.967	1.079
Do you agree that the female protagonist (Yu Xiulian) should sacrifice the rest of her life for her dead fiancé?	19 persons 63.33%	7 persons 23.33%	2 persons 6.67%	2 person 6.67%	0 persons 0%	1.633	1.079
Are you aware that Yu Jiaolong's wish and her boyfriend's wish are opposite (namely, Yu wishes to leave her home but her boyfriend wishes to return to his home)?	1 person 3.33%	3 persons 10%	2 persons 6.67%	9 persons 30.22%	15 persons 50%	4.133	1.175
Do you agree that the female protagonist (Yu Jialong/Jen) should die for the wish that her boyfriend makes at the end of the film?	16 persons 3.33%	7 persons 23.33%	5 persons 16.67%	1 person 3.33%	1 person 3.33%	1.8	1.046
Do you question why the female protagonist's boyfriend does not jump into the abyss for the wish that she makes if men and women are truly treated equal in the film?	12 persons 40%	2 persons 6.67%	8 persons 26.67%	4 persons 13.33%	4 persons 13.33%	2.533	1.454
Do you notice that	2	4	3	10	11	3.8	1.249

female educators have a worse image than male teachers in the film or on the silver screen?	persons 6.67%	persons 13.33%	persons 10%	persons 33.33%	persons 36.67%		
Are you aware that most ancient Chinese educators and students should be male and that the female teachers and students in the film should be exceptional?	1 person 3.33%	2 persons 6.67%	3 persons 10%	6 persons 20%	19 persons 63.33%	4.267	1.093
Do you agree that there is a disproportionate ratio of men's teaching positions, women's teaching positions, men's learning opportunities and women's access to education in imperial China?	1 person 3.33%	2 persons 6.67%	3 persons 10%	7 persons 23.33%	17 persons 56.67%	4.23	1.086
Do you agree on the cinematic representation of the relation between the male teacher and the male student (namely, Jiang Nanhe and Li Mubai)?	0 persons 0%	3 persons 10%	2 persons 6.67%	14 persons 46.67%	11 persons 36.67%	4.1	0.907
Do you agree on the cinematic representation of the relation between the female teacher and the female student (namely, Jade Fox and Yu Jiaolong/Jen)?	2 persons 6.67%	2 persons 6.67%	9 persons 30%	6 persons 20%	11 persons 36.67%	3.733	1.209
Do you agree on the cinematic representation of the relation between the male teachers and the female students (namely, Jiang	12 persons 40%	12 persons 40%	3 persons 10%	3 persons 10%	0 persons 0%	1.9	0.943

Nanhe and Jade Fox; and Li Mubai and Yu Jiaolong/Jen)?							
Are you aware of the Chinese cultural indication of "fox" (or "fox-spirit") in terms of the senior woman's name?	7 persons 23.33%	1 person 3.33%	8 persons 26.67%	1 person 3.33%	13 persons 43.33%	3.4	1.604
Do you agree that the senior woman should be portrayed as an evil person?	21 persons 70%	2 persons 6.67%	4 persons 13.33%	3 persons 10%	0 persons 0%	1.633	1.048
Do you agree that male teachers exchange female students' sexuality with their teaching contents (martial arts skills)?	18 persons 60%	2 persons 6.67%	7 persons 23.33%	2 persons 6.67%	1 person 3.33%	1.867	1.176
Do you agree with Jade Fox that Jiang Nanhe deserves the punishment (that is, death) because he asks her to exchange their sexual relation with his kung fu but fails to teach her the advanced martial arts skills after having sex with her?	1 person 3.33%	4 persons 13.33%	5 persons 16.67%	7 persons 23.33%	13 persons 43.33%	3.9	1.193
Do you agree that Jiang Nanhe should be portrayed as a good person/teacher and deserve Li Mubai's respect for him?	12 persons 40%	5 persons 16.67%	8 persons 26.67%	3 persons 10%	2 persons 6.67%	2.267	1.263
Do you believe that the gender egalitarianism is already enough in the film?	11 persons 36.67%	10 persons 33.33%	4 persons 13.33%	4 persons 13.33%	1 person 3.33%	2.133	1.469

Appendix 10
Awards

Oscar Award: Best Directors

1929 Dramatic Picture: Frank Borzage (*Seventh Heaven*)
     Comedy Picture: Lewis Milestone (*Two Arabian Knights*)
1930 Frank Lloyd (*The Divine Lady*)
1931 Lewis Milestone (*All Quiet on the Western Front*)
1932 Norman Taurog (*Skippy*)
1933 Frank Borzage (*Bad Girl*)
1934 Frank Lloyd (*Cavalcade*)
1935 Frank Capra (*It Happened One Night*)
1936 John Ford (*The Informer*)
1937 Frank Capra (*Mr. Deeds Goes to Town*)
1938 Leo McCarey (*The Awful Truth*)
1939 Frank Capra (*You Can't Take It with You*)
1940 Victor Fleming (*Gone with the Wind*)
1941 John Ford (*The Grapes of Wrath*)
1942 John Ford (*How Green Is My Valley*)
1943 William Wyler (*Mr. Miniver*)
1944 Michael Curtiz (*Casablanca*)
1945 Leo McCarey (*Going My Way*)
1946 Billy Wilder (*The Lost Weekend*)
1947 William Wyler (*The Best Years of Our Lives*)
1948 Elia Kazan (*Gentleman's Agreement*)
1949 John Huston (*The Treasure of the Sierre Madre*)
1950 Joseph L. Mankiewicz (*A Letter to Three Wives*)
1951 Joseph L. Mankiewicz (*All about Eve*)
1952 George Stevens (*A Place in the Sun*)
1953 John Ford (*A Quiet Man*)
1954 Fred Zinnemann (*From Hero to Eternity*)
1955 Elia Kazan (*On the Waterfront*)
1956 Delbert Mann (*Marty*)
1957 George Stevens (*Giant*)

1958 David Lean (*The Bridge on the River Kwai*)
1959 Vincente Minnelli (*Gigi*)
1960 William Wyler (*Ben-Hur*)
1961 Billy Wilder (*The Apartment*)
1962 Robert Wise and Jerome Robbins (*West Side Story*)
1963 David Lean (*Lawrence of Arabia*)
1964 Tony Richardson (*Tom Jones*)
1965 George Cukor (*My Fair Lady*)
1966 Robert Wise (*The Sound of Music*)
1967 Fred Zinneman (*A Man of All Seasons*)
1968 Mike Nichols (*The Graduate*)
1969 Carol Reed (*Oliver!*)
1970 John Schlesinger (*Midnight Cowboy*)
1971 Franklin J. Shafferner (*Patton*)
1972 William Fredkin (*The French Connection*)
1973 Bob Fosse (*Cabaret*)
1974 George Roy Hill (*The Sting*)
1975 Francis Ford Coppola (*The Godfather Part II*)
1976 Milos Forman (*One Flew Over the Cuckoo's Nest*)
1977 John G. Avildsen (*Rocky*)
1978 Woody Allen (*Annie Hall*)
1979 Michael Cimino (*The Deer Hunter*)
1980 Robert Benton (*Kramer vs. Kramer*)
1981 Robert Redford (*Ordinary People*)
1982 Warren Beatty (*Reds*)
1983 Richard Attenborough (*Gandhi*)
1984 James L. Brooks (*Terms of Endearment*)
1985 Milos Forman (*Amadeus*)
1986 Sydney Pollack (*Out of Africa*)
1987 Oliver Stone (*Platton*)
1988 Bernardo Bertolucci (*The Last Emperor*)
1989 Berry Lavinson (*Rain Man*)
1990 Oliver Stone (*Born on the Fourth of July*)
1991 Kevin Costner (*Dances with Wolves*)
1992 Jonathan Demme (*The Silence of the Lamb*)
1993 Client Eastwood (*Unforgiven*)
1994 Steven Spielberg (*Schindler's List*)
1995 Robert Zemeckis (*Forrest Gump*)
1996 Mel Gibson (*Braveheart*)
1997 Anthony Minghella (*The English Patient*)
1998 James Cameron (*Titanic*)
1999 Steven Spielberg (*Saving Private Ryan*)
2000 Sam Mendes (*American Beauty*)
2001 Steven Soderbergh (*Traffic*)
2002 Ron Howard (*A Beautiful Mind*)

2003 Roman Polanski (*The Pianist*)
2004 Peter Jackson (*The Lord of the Ring: The Return of the King*)
2005 Client Eastwood (*Million Dollar Baby*)
2006 Ang Lee (*Brokeback Mountain*)
2007 Martin Scorsese (*The Departed*)
2008 Joel Coen and Ethan Coen (*No Country for Old Man*)
2009 Danny Boyle (*Slumdog Millionaire*)
2010 Kathryn Bigelow (*Hurt Locker*)
2011 Tom Hopper (*The King's Speech*)
2012 Michel Hazanavicius (*The Artist*)

台灣金馬獎最佳導演
Golden Horse Award: Best Directors

1962 陶秦（千嬌百媚）Tao, Qin / Tao, Chin (*Les Belles*)
1963 李翰祥（梁山伯與祝英臺）Li, Hanxiang / Li, Han-hsiang (*The Love Eterne*)
1965 李行（養鴨人家）Li, Xing / Li, Hsing (*Beautiful Duckling*)
1966 李翰祥（西施）Li, Hanxiang / Li, Han-hsiang (*Xi Shi*)
1967 李嘉（我女若蘭）Li, Jia / Li, Chia (*Orchids and My Love*)
1968 白景瑞（寂寞的十七歲）Bai, Jingrui / Pai, Ching-rui (*Lonely Seventeen*)
1969 吳桓（小鎮春回）Wu, Huan (*Town of Spring*)
1970 張曾澤（路客與刀客）Zhang, Zengze / Chang, Tzeng-tze (*From the Highway*)
1971 丁善璽（落鷹峽）Ding, Shangxi / Ting, Shan-hsi (*The Ammunition Hunter*)
1972 李行（秋決）Li, Xing / Li, Hsing (*Autumn Summary*)
1973 程剛（十四女英豪）Cheng, Kang / Cheng, Gang (*The Fourteen Amazons*)
1975 劉藝（長情萬縷）Liu, Yi / Liu, I (*Long Way From Home*)
1976 張佩成（狼牙口）Zhang, Peicheng / Chang, Pei-cheng (*The Venturer*)
1977 張曾澤（筧橋英烈傳）Zhang, Zengze / Chang, Tzeng-tze (*Heroes of the Eastern Skies*)
1978 李行（汪洋中的一條船）Li, Xing / Li, Hsing (*He Never Gives Up*)
1979 胡金銓（山中傳奇）Hu, Jinquan / Hu, Chin-chuan / King Hu (*Legend of the Mountain*)
1980 王菊金（六朝怪談）Wang, Jujin / Wang, Chu-chin (*Six Dynasties Strange Discussion*)

1981 徐克（夜來香）Tsui, Hark (*All the Wrong Clues*)
1982 章國明（邊緣人）Zhang, Guoming / Chang, Kuo-ming (*Edge*)
1983 陳坤厚（小畢的故事）Chen, Kunhou / Chen, Kun-hou (*Growing Up*)
1984 麥當雄（省港旗兵）Mai, Dangxiong / Johnny Mak (*Long Arm of the Law*)
1985 張毅（我這樣過了一生）Zhang, Yi / Chang, I (*Kuei-mei, A Woman*)
1986 吳宇森（英雄本色）Wu, Yusen / John Woo (*A Better Tomorrow*)
1987 王童（稻草人）Wang, Tong / Wang, Tung (*Strawman*)
1988 羅啟銳（七小福）Luo, Qirui / Alex Kai-Yui Law (*Painted Faces*)
1989 侯孝賢（悲情城市）Hou, Xiaoxian / Hou, Hsiao-hsien (*City of Sadness*)
1990 嚴浩（滾滾紅塵）Yan, Hao (*Red Dust*)
1991 王家衛（阿飛正傳）Wang, Jiawei / Wong, Kar-wai (*Days of Being Wild*)
1992 王童（無言的山丘）Wang, Tong / Wang, Tung (*Hill of No Return*)
1993 李安（囍宴）Li, An / Ang Lee (*The Wedding Banquet*)
1994 蔡明亮（愛情萬歲）Cai, Mingliang / Tsai, Ming-liang (*Love Is Elsewhere*)
1995 侯孝賢（好男好女）Hou, Xiaoxian / Hou, Hsiao-hsien (*Good Men Good Women*)
1996 姜文（陽光燦爛的日子）Jiang, Wen (*In the Heat of the Sun*)
1997 陳果（香港製造）Chen, Guo / Chan, Gor (*Made in Hong Kong*)
1998 陳沖（天浴）Chen, Chong / Joan Chen (*Xiu Xiu—The Sent Down Girl*)
1999 許鞍華（千言萬語）Xu, Anhua / Ann Hui (*Ordinary Heroes*)
2000 杜琪峰（鎗火）Du, Qifeng / Johnnie Kei-fung To (*The Mission*)
2001 關錦鵬（藍宇）Guan, Jinpeng / Stanley Kam-pang Kwan (*Lan Yu*)
2002 李安（推手） Li, An / Ang Lee (*Pushing Hands*)
2003 劉偉強／麥兆輝（無間道）Liu, Weiqiang / Lau, Wai-keung and Mai, Zhaohui / Mak, Siu-fai (*Infernal Affairs*)
2004 杜琪峰（大事件）Du, Qifeng / Johnnie Kei-fung To (*Breaking News*)
2005 周星馳（功夫）Chou, Xingchi / Stephen Chow (*Kung Fu*)
2006 陳可辛（如果愛）Chen, Kexin / Peter Ho-Sun Chan (*Perhaps Love*)
2007 李安（色戒）Li, An / Ang Lee (*Lust Caution*)
2008 陳可辛（投名狀）Chen, Kexin / Peter Ho-Sun Chan (*The Warlords*)
2009 戴立忍（不能沒有你）Dai, Li-jen / Leon Dai (*No Pudeo Visir Sin Ti*)
2010 鍾孟宏（第四張畫）Chung, Monghong (*The Fourth Portrait*)
2011 許鞍華（桃姐）Hui, Ann (*A Simple Life*)

香港金像獎最佳導演
Hong Kong Film Awards: Best Directors

1982 方育平（父子情）Fang, Yuping / Allen Yuk-ping Feng (*Father and Son*)
1983 許鞍華（投奔怒海）Xu, Anhua / Ann Hui (*Boat People*)
1984 方育平（半邊人）Fang, Yuping / Allen Yuk-ping Fong (*Ah Ying*)
1985 嚴浩（似水流年）Yan, Hao / Yim Ho (*Homecoming*)
1986 張婉婷（非法移民）Zhang, Wanting / Mabel Cheung (*Illegal Immigrant*)
1987 方育平（美國心）Fang, Yuping / Allen Yuk-ping Fong (*Just Like Weather*)
1988 林嶺東（龍虎風雲）Lin, Lingdong / Ringo Lam (*City on Fire*)
1989 關錦鵬（胭脂扣）Guan, Jinpeng / Stanley Kwan (*Rouge*)
1990 吳宇森（喋血雙雄）Wu, Yusen / John Woo (*The Killer*)
1991 王家衛（阿飛正傳）Wang, Jiawei / Wong, Kar-wai (*Days of Being Wild*)
1992 徐克（黃飛鴻）Xu, Ke / Tsui, Hark (*Once upon a Time in China*)
1993 張之亮（籠民）Zhang, Zhiliang / Jacob Chi Leung Cheng (*Cageman*)
1994 爾冬陞（新不了情）Er, Dongsheng / Derek Tung-Sing Yee (*C'est la vie, mon chéri*)
1995 王家衛（重慶森林）Wang, Jiawei / Wong, Kar-wai (*Chung King Express*)
1996 許鞍華（女人四十）Xu, Anhua / Ann Hui (*Woman Forty*)
1997 陳可辛（甜蜜蜜）Chen, Kexin / Peter Ho-Sun Chan (*Comrade, Almost a Love Story*)
1998 陳果（香港製造）Chen, Guo / Chan, Gor (*Made in Hong Kong*)
1999 陳嘉上（野獸刑警）Chen, Jiashang / Gordon Car-Seung Chan (*Beast Cop*)
2000 杜琪峰（鎗火）Du, Qifeng / Johnnie Kei-fung To (*The Mission*)
2001 李安（臥虎藏龍）Li, An / Ang Lee (*Crouching Tiger Hidden Dragon*)
2002 周星馳（少林足球）Chou, Xingchi / Stephen Chow (*Shaolin Soccer*)
2003 劉偉強/麥兆輝（無間道）Liu, Weiqiang / Lau, Wai-keung & Mai, Zhaohui / Mak, Siu-fai (*Infernal Affairs*)
2004 杜琪峰（PTU）Du, Qifeng / Johnnie Kei-fung To (*PTU*)
2005 爾冬陞（旺角黑夜）Er, Dongsheng / Derek Tung-Sing Yee (*One Night in Mongkok*)
2006 杜琪峰（黑社會）Du, Qifeng / Johnnie Kei-fung To (*Triad Election*)
2007 譚家明（父子）Tan, Jiaming / Patrick Tam (*After This, Our Exile*)
2008 陳可辛（投名狀）Chen, Kexin / Peter Ho-Sun Chan (*The Warlords*)
2009 許鞍華（天水圍的夜與霧）Xu, Anhua / Ann Hui (*Night and Fog*)
2010 陳德森（十月圍城）Chen, Teddy (*Bodyguards and Assassins*)

2011 徐克（狄仁傑之通天帝國）Tsui, Hark (*Di Renjie*)

中国內地金鸡奖最佳导演
Golden Rooster Award: Best Directors

1981 N/A
1982 成荫（西安事变）Cheng, Yin (*Xi'an Incident*)
1983 吴贻弓（城南旧事）Wu, Yigong (*Memories of Old Peking*)
1984 汤晓丹（廖仲恺）Tang, Xiaodan (*Liao Zhongkai*)
1985 凌子风（边城）Ling, Zifeng (*Border City*)
1986 颜学恕（野山）Yan, Xueshu (*In the Wild Mountains*)
1987 丁荫楠（孙中山）Ding, Yinnan (*Sun Zhongshan* / *Sun Yat-sen*)
1988 吴天明（老井）Wu, Tianming (*Old Well*)
1989 吴子牛（晚钟、欢乐英雄、阴阳界）Wu, Ziniu
  (*Evening Bell, To Die*, and *Between Life and Death*)
1990 李前宽、肖桂云（开国大典）、谢铁骊、赵元（红楼梦）
  Li, Qiankuang and Xiao, Guiyun (*Founding Ceremony*) as well as
  Xie, Tieli and Zhao, Yuan (*Dream of the Red Chamber*)
1991 N/A
1992 孙周（心香、大决战）Sun, Zhou (*Heartfelt* and *Final Battle*)
1993 王兴东（蒋筑英）Wang, Xingdong (*Jiang Zhuying*)
1994 何平（炮打双灯）He, Ping (*Red Firecracker, Green Firecracker*)
1995 黄建新、杨亚洲（背靠背，脸对脸）Huang, Jianxin and Yang Yazhou
  (*Back to Back, Face to Face*)
1996 吴天明（变脸）Wu, Tianming (*King of Masks*)
1997 韦廉（大转折）Wei, Lian (*The Breakthrough*)
1998 胡炳榴（安居）Hu, Bingliu (*Live in Peace*)
1999 张艺谋（一个都不能少）Zhang, Yimou (*Not One Less*)
2000 张艺谋（我的父亲母亲）Zhang, Yimou (*The Road Home*)
2001 霍建起（蓝色爱情）Huo, Jianqi (*A Love of Blueness*)
2002 杨亚洲（美丽的大脚）、陈凯歌（和你在一起）Yang, Yazhou
  (*Beautiful Big Feet*) and Chen, Kaige (*Together*)
2003 张艺谋（英雄）Zhang, Yimou (*Hero*)
2004 彭小莲（美丽上海）Peng, Xiaolian (*Beautiful Shanghai*)
2005 马俪文（我们俩）Ma, Liwen (*We Both*)
2006 N/A

2007 戚健（天狗）、尹力（云水）Qi, Jian (*Nintendogs*) and Yin, Li (*Cloud Water Song*)
2008 N/A
2009 冯小刚（集结号）Feng, Xiaogang (*The Assembly*)
2010 冯小刚（非诚勿扰）Feng, Xiaogang (*If You Are the One*)
2011 陈力（爱在廊桥）Chen, Li (*Love on Gallery Bridge*)

Academy Award for Writing Original Screenplays: Best Original Scripts (not based upon previously published material)

1940 *The Great McGinty* by Preston Sturges
1941 *Citizen Kane* by Herman Mankiewicz and Orson Welles
1942 *Woman of the Year* by Michael Kanin and Ring Lardner Jr.
1943 *Princess O'Rourke* by Norman Krasna
1944 *Wilson* by Lamar Trotti
1945 *Marie-Louise* by Richard Schweizer
1946 *The Seventh Veil* by Muriel Box and Sydney Box
1947 *The Bachelor and the Bobby-Soxer* by Sidney Sheldon
1948 *none given* (Instead of the categories "Original Screenplay" and "Screenplay," it was combined into one category, called "Screenplay.")
1949 *Battleground* by Robert Pirosh (In 1949, the category was renamed "Story and Screenplay")
1950 *Sunset Boulevard* by Charles Brackett, D.M. Marshman, Jr. and Billy Wilder
1951 *An American in Paris* by Alan Jay Lerner
1952 *The Lavender Hill Mob* by T.E.B. Clarke
1953 *Titanic* by Charles Brackett, Richard Breen and Walter Reisch
1954 *On the Waterfront* by Budd Schulberg
1955 *Interrupted Melody* by Sonya Levien and William Ludwig
1956 *The Red Balloon* by Albert Lamorisse
1957 *Designing Woman* by George Wells
1958 *The Defiant Ones* by Nathan E. Douglas and Harold Jacob Smith
   (Upon request of his widow and upon recommendation of the Writers Branch Executive Committee, the Board of Governors voted to restore the name of Nedrick Young to the nomination and award presented to Nathan E. Douglas, which was a pseudonym for Mr. Young during the blacklisting period.)
1959 *Pillow Talk* by Clarence Greene, Maurice Richlin, Russell Rouse and Stanley Shapiro

1960 *The Apartment* by I.A.L. Diamond and Billy Wilder
1961 *Splendor in the Grass* by William Inge
1962 *Divorce, Italian Style* by Ennio de Concini, Pietro Germi and Alfredo Giannetti
1963 *How the West Was Won* by James Webb
1964 *Father Goose* by Peter Stone and Frank Tarloff
1965 *Darling* by Frederic Raphael
1966 *A Man and a Woman*: Story by Claude Lelouch; Screenplay by Claude Lelouch and Pierre Uytterhoeven
1967 *Guess Who's Coming to Dinner* by William Rose
1968 *The Producers* by Mel Brooks
1969 *Butch Cassidy and the Sundance Kid* by William Goldman (In 1969, the category was renamed: "Story and Screenplay based on material not previously published or produced.")
1970 *Patton* by Francis Ford Coppola and Edmund H. North
1971 *The Hospital* by Paddy Chayefsky
1972 *The Candidate* by Jeremy Larner
1973 *The Sting* by David S. Ward
1974 *Chinatown* by Robert Towne
1975 *Dog Day Afternoon* by Frank Pierson
1976 *Network* by Paddy Chayefsky (In 1976, the category was renamed: "Screenplay written directly for the Screen Based on factual material or on story material not previously published or produced.")
1977 *Annie Hall* by Woody Allen and Marshall Brickman
1978 *Coming Home*: Screenplay by Robert C. Jones and Waldo Salt; Story by Nancy Dowd (In 1978, the category was renamed: "Screenplay written directly for the screen.")
1979 *Breaking Away* by Steve Tesich
1980 *Melvin and Howard* by Bo Goldman
1981 *Chariots of Fire* by Colin Welland
1982 *Gandhi* by John Briley
1983 *Tender Mercies* by Horton Foote
1984 *Places in the Heart* by Robert Benton
1985 *Witness*: Screenplay by William Kelley, Earl Wallace; Story by William Kelley, Pamela Wallace, and Earl Wallace
1986 *Hannah and Her Sisters* by Woody Allen
1987 *Moonstruck* by John Patrick Shanley
1988 *Rain Man* by Ronald Bass and Barry Morrow
1989 *Dead Poets Society* by Tom Schulman
1990 *Ghost* by Bruce Joel Rubin
1991 *Thelma and Louise* by Callie Khouri
1992 *The Crying Game* by Neil Jordan
1993 *The Piano* by Jane Campion
1994 *Pulp Fiction* by Quentin Tarantino (story and screenplay) and Roger Avary (story)

1995 *The Usual Suspects* by Christopher McQuarrie
1996 *Fargo* by Ethan and Joel Coen
1997 *Good Will Hunting* by Ben Affleck and Matt Damon
1998 *Shakespeare in Love* by Marc Norman and Tom Stoppard
2000 *Almost Famous* by Cameron Crowe
2001 *Gosford Park* by Julian Fellowes
2002 *Talk to Her (Hable con ella)* by Pedro Almodóvar
2003 *Lost in Translation* by Sofia Coppola
2004 *Eternal Sunshine of the Spotless Mind* by Pierre Bismuth, Michel Gondry and Charlie Kaufman
2005 *Crash* by Paul Haggis and Bobby Moresco
2006 *Little Miss Sunshine* by Michael Arndt
2007 *Juno* by Diablo Cody (Brook Busey)
2008 *Milk* by Dustin Lance Black
2009 *Hurt Lock* by Mark Boal
2010 *The King's Speech* by David Seidler
2011 *Midnight in Paris* by Woody Allen

Academy Award for Writing Adapted Screenplays: Best Adapters

1927/1928 *Seventh Heaven*: Benjamin Glazer from a play by Austin Stong
1928/1929 *The Patriot*: Hanns Kräly from a play by Ashley Dukes translated from the play *Der Patriot* by Alfred Neumann derived from the story *Paul I* by Dmitri Merezhkovsky
1929/1930 *The Big House*: Joseph Farnham, Martin Flavin, Frances Marion, Lennox Marion original
1930/1931 *Cimarron*: Howard Estabrook from the novel by Edna Ferber
1931/1932 *Bad Girl*: Edwin J. Burke from the novel and play by Viña Delmar
1932/1933 *Little Women*: Victor Heerman, Sarah Y. Mason from the novel by
1934 *It Happened One Night*: Robert Riskin from the story *Night Bus* by Samuel Hopkins Adams
1935 *The Informer*: Dudley Nichols from the novel by Liam O'Flaherty. This was the first Academy Award ever to be declined.
1936 *The Story of Louis Pasteur*: Pierre Collings and Sheridan Gibney from their own story
1937 *The Life of Emile Zola*: Heinz Herald, Geza Herczeg and Norman Raine from the book *Zola and His Time* by Matthew Josephson
1938 *Pygmalion*: Ian Dalrymple, Cecil Lewis, W.P. Lipscomb and George Bernard Shaw from the play by George Bernard Shaw
1939 *Gone with the Wind*: Sidney Howard from the novel by Margaret Mitchell

Appendix 10

1940 *The Philadelphia Story*: Donald Ogden Stewart from the play by Philip Barry
1941 *Here Comes Mr. Jordan*: Sidney Buchman and Seton Miller from the play Heaven Can Wait by Harry Segall
1942 *Mrs. Miniver*: George Froeschel, James Hilton, Claudine West and Arthur Wimperis based on the novel by Jan Struther
1943 *Casablanca*: Philip Epstein, Julius J. Epstein, Howard Koch from the play Everybody Comes to Rick's by Murray Burnett and Joan Alison
1944 *Going My Way*: Frank Butler and Frank Cavett from the story by Leo McCarey
1945 *The Lost Weekend*: Charles Brackett, Billy Wilder from the novel by Charles R. Jackson
1946 *The Best Years of Our Lives*: Robert Sherwood from the novel Glory for Me by MacKinlay Kantor
1947 *Miracle on 34th Street*: George Seaton from the story by Valentine Davies
1948 *The Treasure of the Sierra Madre*: John Huston from the novel by B. Traven
1949 *A Letter to Three Wives*: Joseph Mankiewicz from the novel Letter to Five Wives by John Klempner
1950 *All About Eve*: Joseph Mankiewicz from the short story The Wisdom of Eve by Mary Orr
1951 *A Place in the Sun*: Harry Brown and Michael Wilson from the novel An American Tragedy by Theodore Dreiser and the play An American Tragedy by Patrick Kearney
1952 *The Bad and the Beautiful*: Charles Schnee from the story Tribute to a Badman by Charles Bradshaw
1953 *From Here to Eternity*: Daniel Taradash from the novel by James Jones
1954 *The Country Girl*: George Seaton from the play by Clifford Odets
1955 *Marty*: Paddy Chayefsky based on his teleplay
1956 *Around the World in Eighty Days*: John Farrow, S. J. Perelman, James Poe from the novel by Jules Verne
1957 *The Bridge on the River Kwai*: Carl Foreman, Michael Wilson and Pierre Boulle) based on the novel by Pierre Boulle
1958 *Gigi*: Alan Jay Lerner based on the novel by Colette
1959 *Room at the Top*: Neil Paterson from the novel by John Braine
1960 *Elmer Gantry*: Richard Brooks from the novel by Sinclair Lewis
1961 *Judgment at Nuremberg*: Abby Mann from his teleplay
1962 *To Kill a Mockingbird*: Horton Foote from the novel by Harper Lee
1963 *Tom Jones*: John Osborne from the novel The History of Tom Jones, a Foundling by Henry Fielding
1964 *Becket*: Edward Anhalt from the play by Jean Anouilh
1965 *Doctor Zhivago*: Robert Bolt from the novel by Boris Pasternak
1966 *A Man for All Seasons*: Robert Bolt from his play
1967 *In the Heat of the Night*: Stirling Silliphant from the novel by John Ball
1968 *The Lion in Winter*: James Goldman from his play

1969 *Midnight Cowboy*: Waldo Salt from the novel by James Leo Herlihy
1970 *MASH*: Ring Lardner Jr. from the novel by Richard Hooker
1971 *The French Connection*: Ernest Tidyman from the novel by Robin Moore
1972 *The Godfather*: Mario Puzo and Francis Coppola from the novel by Mario Puzo
1973 *The Exorcist*: William Peter Blatty from the novel of William Blatty
1974 *The Godfather, Part II*: Francis Coppola, Mario Puzo from the novel The Godfather by Mario Puzo
1975 *One Flew Over the Cuckoo's Nest*: Bo Goldman, Laurence Hauben from the novel by Ken Kesey
1976 *All the President's Men*: William Goldman from the book by Carl Bernstein and Bob Woodward
1977 *Julia*: Alvin Sargent from the novel Pentimento by Lillian Hellman
1978 *Midnight Express*: Oliver Stone from the book by Billy Hayes and William Hoffer
1979 *Kramer vs. Kramer*: Robert Benton from the novel by Avery Corman
1980 *Ordinary People*: Alvin Sargent from the novel by Judith Guest
1981 *On Golden Pond*: Ernest Thompson from his play of the same title
1982 *Missing*: Constantin Costa-Gavras, Donald Stewart from the book by Thomas Hauser
1983 *Terms of Endearment*: James L. Brooks from the novel by Larry McMurtry
1984 *Amadeus*: Peter Shaffer from the play by Peter Shaffer
1985 *Out of Africa*: Kurt Luedtke from the memoirs of Isak Dinesen, the book Silence Will Speak by Errol Trzebinski and the book Isak Dinesen: The Life of a Storyteller by Judith Thurman
1986 *A Room with a View*: Ruth Prawer Jhabvala from the novel by E.M. Forster
1987 *The Last Emperor*: Bernardo Bertolucci and Mark Peploe from the autobiography *From Emperor to Citizen: The Autobiography of Aisin-Gioro Pu Yi* by Henry Pu Yi
1988 *Dangerous Liaisons*: Christopher Hampton from the novel by Choderlos de Laclos and the play by Christopher Hampton
1989 *Driving Miss Daisy*: Alfred Uhry from the play by Alfred Uhry
1990 *Dances with Wolves*: Michael Blake from the novel by Michael Blake
1991 *The Silence of the Lambs*: Ted Tally from the novel by Thomas Harris
1992 *Howards End*: Ruth Prawer Jhabvala from the novel by E.M. Forster
1993 *Schindler's List*: Steven Zaillian from the novel by Thomas Keneally
1994 *Forrest Gump*: Eric Roth from the novel by Winston Groom
1995 *Sense and Sensibility*: Emma Thompson from the novel by Jane Austen
1996 *Sling Blade*: Billy Bob Thornton from the play by Billy Bob Thornton
1997 *L.A. Confidential*: Curtis Hanson and Brian Helgeland from the novel by James Ellroy
1998 *Gods and Monsters*: Bill Condon from the novel Father of Frankenstein by Christopher Bram

1999 *The Cider House Rules*: John Irving from the novel by John Irving
2000 *Traffic*: Stephen Gaghan from the teleplay *Traffik* by Simon Moore
2001 *A Beautiful Mind*: Akiva Goldsman from the biography by Sylvia Nasar
2002 *The Pianist*: Ronald Harwood from the book by Władysław Szpilman
2003 *The Lord of the Rings: The Return of the King*- Fran Walsh
2004 *Sideways*: Alexander Payne and Jim Taylor from the novel by Rex Pickett
2005 *Brokeback Mountain*: Larry McMurtry and Diana Ossana from the short story by E. Annie Proulx
2006 *The Departed*: William Monahan from the Hong Kong film *Infernal Affairs*. At the 79th Oscar Award night, the Commentator incorrectly stated that the movie was adapted from a Japanese film.
2007 *No Country for Old Men*: Ethan and Joel Coen from the novel by Cormac McCarthy
2008 *Slumdog Millionaire*: Simon Beaufoy from the novel *Q & A* by Vikas Swarup
2009 *Precious*: Geoffrey Fletcher from the novel *Push* by Sapphire
2010 *The Social Work*: Aaron Sorkin from the book *The Accidental Billionaire* by Ben Metzrich
2011 *The Descendants*: Alexander Payne, Nat Faxon and Jim Rash

Golden Globe Award: Best Screenwriters

1965 *Doctor Zhivago*: Robert Bolt
1966 *A Man for All Seasons*: Robert Bolt
1967 *In the Heat of the Night*: Sterling Silliphant
1968 *Charly*: Stirling Silliphant
1969 *Anne of the Thousand Days*: Bridget Boland, John Hale and Richard Sokolove
1970 *Love Story*: Erich Segal
1971 *The Hospital*: Paddy Chayefsky
1972 *The Godfather*: Francis Ford Coppola and Mario Puzo
1973 *The Exorcist*: William Peter Blatty
1974 *Chinatown*: Robert Towne
1975 *One Flew Over the Cuckoo's Nest*: Lawrence Hauben and Bo Goldman
1976 *Network*: Paddy Chayefsky
1977 *The Goodbye Girl*: Neil Simon
1978 *Midnight Express*: Oliver Stone
1979 *Kramer vs. Kramer*: Robert Benton
1980 *The Ninth Configuration*: William Peter Blatty
1981 *On Golden Pond*: Ernest Thompson
1982 *Gandhi*: John Briley
1983 *Terms of Endearment*: James L. Brooks

1984 *Amadeus*: Peter Shaffer
1985 *The Purple Rose of Cairo*: Woody Allen
1986 *The Mission*: Robert Bolt
1987 *The Last Emperor*: Bernardo Bertolucci, Mark Peploe and Enzo Ungari
1988 *Running on Empty*: Naomi Foner
1989 *Born on the Fourth of July*: Oliver Stone and Ron Kovic
1990 *Dances with Wolves*: Michael Blake
1991 *Thelma & Louise*: Callie Khouri
1992 *Scent of a Woman*: Bo Goldman
1993 *Schindler's List*: Steven Zaillian
1994 *Pulp Fiction*: Quentin Tarantino
1995 *Sense and Sensibility*: Emma Thompson
1996 *The People vs. Larry Flynt*: Scott Alexander and Larry Karaszewski
1997 *Good Will Hunting*: Ben Affleck and Matt Damon
1998 *Shakespeare in Love*: Marc Norman and Tom Stoppard
1999 *American Beauty*: Alan Ball
2000 *Traffic*: Stephen Gaghan
2001 *A Beautiful Mind*: Akiva Goldsman
2002 *About Schmidt*: Alexander Payne and Jim Taylor
2003 *Lost in Translation*: Sofia Coppola
2004 *Sideways*: Alexander Payne and Jim Taylor
2005 *Brokeback Mountain*: Larry McMurtry and Diana Ossana
2006 *The Queen*: Peter Morgan
2007 *No Country for Old Men*: Ethan and Joel Coen
2008 *Slumdog Millionaire*: Simon Beaufoy
2009 *Up in the Air*: Jason Reitman and Sheldon Turner
2010 *The Social Network*: Aaron Sorkin
2011 *Midnight in Paris*: Woody Allen

Golden Horse Award: Best Screenwriters

1962 秦亦孚《星星月亮太陽》(*Sun, Moon, Star*: Chin, I-fu)
1963 葛瑞芬《為誰辛苦為誰忙》(lack of English translation)
1964 江榴照《諜海四壯士》(lack of English translation)
1965 N/A
1966 胡金銓《大地兒女》(*Sons of Good Earth*: King Hu)
1967 秦亦孚《蘇小妹》(*Wife of a Romantic Scholar*: Chin, I-fu)
1968 胡金銓《龍門客棧》(*Dragon Inn*: King Hu)
1969 吳桓《小鎮春回》(*Gain Sons, Not Losing Daughter*: Wu, Huan)
1970 魯稚子《歌聲魅影》(*Phantom of the Paradise*: Lu, Chih-tzi)

1971 李翰祥《緹縈》(*The Story of Ti-Ying*: Lee, Han-hsiang)
1972 張永祥《還君明珠雙淚垂》
(*Indebt for Life and Love*: Chang, Young-hsiang)
1973 鳳鳴編劇小組《忍》
1974 N/A
1975 張永祥《吾土吾民》(*Our Land, Our People*: Chang, Young-hsiang)
1976 鄧育昆《梅花》(*Victory*: Teng, Yu-kung)
1977 何曉鍾《筧橋英烈傳》(*Heroes of the Eastern Skies*: He, Hsiao-chung)
1978 張永祥《汪洋中的一條船》(*Never Gives Up*: Chang, Young-hsiang)
1979 Best Original screenplay: 張永祥《小城故事》;
Best Adapted Screenplay: 李翰祥《乾隆下揚州》
1980 Best Original Screenplay: 宋項如《候鳥之愛》;
Best Adapted Screenplay: 宋項如《候鳥之愛》
1981 Best Original Screenplay: 吳念真《同班同學》;
Best Adapted Screenplay: 張永祥《假如我是真的》
1982 Best Original Screenplay: 張鍵《邊緣人》
1983 Best Original Screenplay: 蔡繼光、許默《男與女》;
Best Adapted Screenplay: 朱天文、侯孝賢、丁亞民、許淑真《小畢的故事》(*Growing Up*: Chu, Tien-wen; Hou Hsiao-hsien; Ting, Ya-min; Hsu Shu-chen)
1984 吳念真《老莫的第二個春天》(*Old Mo's Second Spring*: Wu, Nien-chen); 侯孝賢、廖輝英《油麻菜籽》(*Ah Fei*: Hou, Hsiao-hsien; Liao, Hui-ying)
1985 朱天文、侯孝賢《童年往事》(*A Time to Love, A Time to Die*: Chu, Tien-wen; Hou, Hsiao-hsien); 蕭颯、張毅《我這樣過了一生》(*Kuei-mei, A Woma:* Hsiao, Sa; Chang, I)
1986 小野《我們都是這樣長大的》(*Reunion*: Hsiao-yeh); 吳念真《父子關係》(*The Two of Us*: Wu, Nien-chen)
1987 王小棣、宋紘《稻草人》(*Strawman*: Wang, Hsiao-li; Chu, Hung); 阮繼志《倩女幽魂》(*A Chinese Ghost Story*: Ruan, Chi-chih)
1988 羅啟銳、張婉婷《七小福》
(*Painted Face*: Luo, Chi-rui; Chang, Wan-ting)
1989 邱戴安平《三個女人的故事》(*Full Moon in New York*: Qiu Dai An-ping)
1990 吳念真《客途秋恨》(*Song of the Exile*: Wu, Nien-chen); 小野《刀瘟》(*The Story of A Gangster*: Hsiao-yeh)
1991 楊德昌、閻鴻亞、楊順清、賴銘堂《牯嶺街少年殺人事件》(*A Brighter Summer Day*: Edward Yang/Yang, Te-chang; Yen, Hung-ya; Yang, Shun-ching; Lai, Ming-tang)
1992 吳念真《無言的山丘》(*Hill of No Return*: Wu, Nien-chen); 賴聲川《暗戀桃花源》(*The Peach Blossom Land*: Stanley Lai/Lai, Shen-chuan)

1993 馮光遠、李安《喜宴》(*Wedding Banquet*: Feng, Kwang-yuan; Ang Lee); 胡大為、鄧碧燕、林紀陶、於仁泰《白髮魔女傳》(*The Bride with White Hair*: Hu, Ta-wei; Teng, Pi-yen; Lin, Chi-tao; Yu, Ren-tai)
1994 楊德昌《獨立時代》(*A Confucian Confusion*: Edward Yang/Yang, Te-chang); 林奕華《紅玫瑰白玫瑰》(*Red Rose White Rose*: Lin, I-hua)
1995 陳玉勳《熱帶魚》(*Tropical Fish*: Chen, Yu-hsun); 朱天文《好男好女》(*Good Man Good Women*: Chu, Tien-wen)
1996 張澤鳴《月滿英倫》(*Foreign Moon*: Chang, Tze-ming); 姜文《陽光燦爛的日子》(*In the Heat of the Sun*: Jiang, Wen)
1997 陳果《香港製造》(*Made in Hong Kong*: Chan, Gor); 杜國威《南海十三郎》(*The Mad Phoenix*: To, Kwok-wai)
1998 張婉婷、羅啟銳《玻璃之城》(*City of Glasses*: Chang, Wan-ting; Luo, Chi-rui); 陳沖、嚴歌苓《天浴》(*Xiu Xiu, the Sent Down Girl*: Chen, Chong; Yan Geling)
1999 張作驥《黑暗之光》(*Darkness and Light*: Chang, Tzuo-chi)
2000 陳果《細路祥》(*Little Cheung*: Chan, Gor); 胡安、黃丹、唐婁彝、Kate Raisz、Bob McAdrew《西洋鏡》(*Shadow Magic*: Hu, An; Huang, Dan; Tang, Louyi, Kate Raisz and Bob McAdrew)
2001 陳果《榴槤飄飄》(*Durian Durian*: Chan, Gor); 魏紹恩《藍宇》(*Lan Yu*: Jimmy Ngai)
2002 岸西《男人四十》(*July Rhapsody*: Ivy Ho)
2003 游乃海、歐健兒《PTU 機動部隊》(*PTU*: Yau, Nai-Hoi; Au, Kin-Yee); 李揚《盲井》(*Blind Shaft*: Li, Yang)
2004 游乃海、葉天成、歐健兒《柔道龍虎榜》(*Throw Down*: Yau, Nai-Hoi; Yip Tin-Shing; Au, Kin-Yee); 林正盛《月光下，我記得》(*The Moon Also Rises*: Lin, Cheng-sheng)
2005 游乃海、葉天成《黑社會》(*Election*: Yau, Nai-Hoi; Yip, Tin-Shing); 馮小剛、王剛、林黎勝、張家魯《天下無賊》(*A World without Thieves*: Feng, Xiaogang; Wang, Gang; Lin, Lisheng; Zhang, Jialu)
2006 寧浩《瘋狂的石頭》(*Crazy Stone*: Ning, Hao); 寧岱、張元《看上去很美：小紅花》(*Little Red Flowers*: Ning, Dai; Zhang, Yuan)
2007 Tony Ayres《意》(*The Home Song Stories*: Tony Ayres); 王蕙玲、詹姆斯·夏姆斯《色，戒》(*Lust Caution*- Wang, Hui-ling; James Schamus)
2008 蔡宗翰、林書宇《九降風》(*Winds of September*: Tsai, Tzung-han; Lin, Shu-yu); 劉恒《集結號》(*Assembly*: Liu, Huan)
2009 戴立忍、陳文彬《不能沒有你》(*No Puedo Vivir Sin Ti*: Leon Dai; Chen, Wen-Pin)
2010 張作驥《當愛來的時候》(*When Love Comes*: Chang, Tso-chi)

2011 楊南倩、鄧勇星、秦海璐、葛文喆、席然《到阜陽六百里》(Return Ticket: Yang, Nanqian; Deng, Yongxing; Qin, Hailu; Ge, Wenzhe; Xi, Ran)

Hong Kong Film Critics Society Award: Best Screenwriters and Adapters

1994 王家衛（東邪西毒）*Ashes of Time*: Wong, Kar-wai
1995 技安（西遊記）*The Journey to the West*: Jeff Lau
1996 郭偉鐘（旺角風雲）*Mongkok Story*
1997 陳慶嘉（熱血最強）*Task Force*: Chan, Hing-kar
1998 司徒錦源、游乃海、周燕嫻（非常突然）*Expect the Unexpected*: Szeto, Kam-Yuen; Yau, Nai-Hoi; Chow, Hin-yan 技安（超時空要愛）*Timeless Romance*: Jeff Lau
1999 鄒凱光、葉偉信、張問（爆裂刑警）*Bullets over Summer*: Chow, Hoi-kwong, Yip Wai-shun and Cheung Man
2000 陳慶嘉、錢小蕙（江湖告急）*Jiang Hu: The Triad Zone* Chan, Hin-kar; Chin, Siu-wai
2001 卓韻芝（初戀嗱喳麵）*Merry Go Round*: Gc, Goo-Bi
2002 陳果（香港有個荷李活）*Hollywood Hong Kong*: Chan Gor
2003 韋家輝、游乃海、歐健兒、葉天成（大隻佬）*Running on Karma*: Wai, Ka-fai; Yau, Nai-hoi; Au, Kin-yee; Yip, Tin-Shing
2004 陳嘉上、鍾繼昌（A1頭條）*A1 Headline*: Chan, Kar-seung; Chung, Kai-cheong
2005 王晶（黑白戰場）*Color of the Loyalty*: Wong, Jing
2006 王晶、鄧特希（臥虎）*Woho*: Wang, Jing
2007 韋家輝、歐健兒（神探）*Med Detective*: Wai, Ka-fai; Au, Kin-yee
2008 岸西（親密）*Claustrophobia*: Ivy Ho
2009 韋家輝、歐健兒（再生號）*Written By*: Wai, Ka-fai; Au, Kin-yee
2010 羅啟銳（歲月神偷）*Echoes of the Rainbow*: Law, Alex
2011 岸西（月滿軒尼詩）*Hennessey*: Ivy Ho

Nobel Prize Laureates in Literature

2011 Tomas Tranströmer

2010 Mario Vargas Llosa
2009 Herta Müller
2008 Jean-Marie Gustave Le Clézio
2007 Doris Lessing
2006 Orhan Pamuk
2005 Harold Pinter
2004 Elfriede Jelinek
2003 J. M. Coetzee
2002 Imre Kertész
2001 V. S. Naipaul
2000 Gao Xingjian
1999 Günter Grass
1998 José Saramago
1997 Dario Fo
1996 Wislawa Szymborska
1995 Seamus Heaney
1994 Kenzaburo Oe
1993 Toni Morrison
1992 Derek Walcott
1991 Nadine Gordimer
1990 Octavio Paz
1989 Camilo José Cela
1988 Naguib Mahfouz
1987 Joseph Brodsky
1986 Wole Soyinka
1985 Claude Simon
1984 Jaroslav Seifert
1983 William Golding
1982 Gabriel García Márquez
1981 Elias Canetti
1980 Czeslaw Milosz
1979 Odysseus Elytis
1978 Isaac Bashevis Singer
1977 Vicente Aleixandre
1976 Saul Bellow
1975 Eugenio Montale
1974 Eyvind Johnson, Harry Martinson
1973 Patrick White
1972 Heinrich Böll
1971 Pablo Neruda
1970 Alexandr Solzhenitsyn
1969 Samuel Beckett
1968 Yasunari Kawabata
1967 Miguel Angel Asturias
1966 Shmuel Agnon, Nelly Sachs

1965 Mikhail Sholokhov
1964 Jean-Paul Sartre
1963 Giorgos Seferis
1962 John Steinbeck
1961 Ivo Andric
1960 Saint-John Perse
1959 Salvatore Quasimodo
1958 Boris Pasternak
1957 Albert Camus
1956 Juan Ramón Jiménez
1955 Halldór Laxness
1954 Ernest Hemingway
1953 Winston Churchill
1952 François Mauriac
1951 Pär Lagerkvist
1950 Bertrand Russell
1949 William Faulkner
1948 T.S. Eliot
1947 André Gide
1946 Hermann Hesse
1945 Gabriela Mistral
1944 Johannes V. Jensen
1943 The prize money was with 1/3 allocated to the Main Fund and with 2/3 to the Special Fund of this prize section
1942 The prize money was with 1/3 allocated to the Main Fund and with 2/3 to the Special Fund of this prize section
1941 The prize money was with 1/3 allocated to the Main Fund and with 2/3 to the Special Fund of this prize section
1940 The prize money was with 1/3 allocated to the Main Fund and with 2/3 to the Special Fund of this prize section
1939 Frans Eemil Sillanpää
1938 Pearl Buck
1937 Roger Martin du Gard
1936 Eugene O'Neill
1935 The prize money was with 1/3 allocated to the Main Fund and with 2/3 to the Special Fund of this prize section
1934 Luigi Pirandello
1933 Ivan Bunin
1932 John Galsworthy
1931 Erik Axel Karlfeldt
1930 Sinclair Lewis
1929 Thomas Mann
1928 Sigrid Undset
1927 Henri Bergson
1926 Grazia Deledda

1925 George Bernard Shaw
1924 Wladyslaw Reymont
1923 William Butler Yeats
1922 Jacinto Benavente
1921 Anatole France
1920 Knut Hamsun
1919 Carl Spitteler
1918 The prize money was allocated to the Special Fund of this prize section
1917 Karl Gjellerup, Henrik Pontoppidan
1916 Verner von Heidenstam
1915 Romain Rolland
1914 The prize money was allocated to the Special Fund of this prize section
1913 Rabindranath Tagore
1912 Gerhart Hauptmann
1911 Maurice Maeterlinck
1910 Paul Heyse
1909 Selma Lagerlöf
1908 Rudolf Eucken
1907 Rudyard Kipling
1906 Giosuè Carducci
1905 Henryk Sienkiewicz
1904 Frédéric Mistral, José Echegaray
1903 Bjørnstjerne Bjørnson
1902 Theodor Mommsen
1901 Sully Prudhomme

Anthologized Writers in *the Columbia Anthology of Modern Chinese Literature*

1918-1949
Lu Xun 魯迅
Xu Dishan 徐第山
Ye Shaojun 葉紹鈞
Yu Dafu 郁達夫
Mao Dun 茅盾
Lao She 老舍
Shen Congwen 沈從文
Ling Shuhua 凌叔華
Ba Jin 巴金

Shen Zhicun 沈蟄存
Ding Ling 丁玲
Wu Zuxiang 吳祖緗
Xiao Hong 蕭紅
Zhang Ailing/Eileen Chang 張愛玲

1949-1976
Zhu Xining/ Chu Hsi-ning 朱西甯
Chen Yingzhen/Chen Ying-chen 陳映真
Bai Xianyoung/Pai Hsian-yung 白先勇
Wang Wenxing/Wang Wen-hsing 王文興
Huang Chunming/Huang Chun-ming 黃春明
Wang Zhenhe/Wang Chen-ho 王禎和

After 1976
Liu Yichang 劉以鬯
Wang Zenqi 汪曾祺
Qiao Dianyun 喬典雲
Wang Meng 王蒙
Chen Ruoxi/Chen Juo-hsi 陳若曦
Xi Xi/Hsi Hsi 西西
Li Youngping 李永平
Yuan Qiongqiong/Yuan Chiung-chiung 袁瓊瓊
Li Rui 李瑞
Li Ang 李昂
Xiao Sa/Hsiao Sa 蕭颯
Can Xue 殘雪
Han Shaogong 韓少功
Chen Cun 陳村
Liu Heng 劉衡
Mo Yan 莫言
Zhu Tianwen/Chu Tien-wen 朱天文
Zhang Dachun/Chang Ta-chun 張大春
Tie Ning 鐵寧
Yu Hua 余華
Su Tong 蘇童

Selected Bibliography

Abrams, M. H. *Glossary of Literary Terms* (Eighth Edition). Boston: Thomson Wadsworth, 2005.
Adair, Carole K. "Cracking the Glass Ceiling: Factors Influencing Women's Attainment of Senior Executive Positions" (Ph.D. Dissertation). Colorado State University, 1994, p. 32.
Adelman, Janet. *Suffocating Mothers: Fantasies of Maternal Origin in Shakespeare's Plays, Hamlet to the Tempest*. London: Routledge, 1992.
Aguirre, Adalberto. *Women and Minority Faculty in the Academic Workplace: Recruitment, Retention, and Academic Culture*. San Francisco: Jossey-Bass, 2000, p. 61.
Alexander, Peter. *Hamlet: Father and Son*. Oxford: Clarendon Press, 1955.
Andrew, Geoff. *10*. London: British Film Institute, 2005.
Armanet, François. *Ciné Kung Fu*. Paris: Ramsay, 1988, pp. 51-52.
Ashliman, D. L. "Cinderella" or "The Little Glass Slipper" in "Folklore and Mythology Electronic Texts.": http://www.pitt.edu/~dash/type0510a.html#perrault (online data retrieved in April 2011).
Astruc, Alexander. "The Birth of a New Avant-garde: La caméra stylo." *The New Wave: Critical Landmarks*. Peter Graham. New York: Doubleday, 1968, pp. 17-23.
Bailey, Julie James. "Women's History in Film." *Reel Women Working in Film and Television*. New South Wales, Australia: Australian Film Television & Radio School, 1999, p. viii.
Banh, Meina. "Oh My Hero!" UCLA Asia Institute: *Asian Pacific Arts*. 9/3/2004. http://goo.gl/3tzTu (online data retrieved in April 2011).
Banke, Cécile De. *Shakespeare Stage Production Then and Now*. London: Hutchinson, 1954.
Baskin, Ellen. "Cracking the Glass Ceiling in the Film Industry." *Los Angels Times*. June 2, 2003.
Bate, Jonathan and Russell Jackson. *The Oxford Illustrated History of Shakespeare on Stage*. Oxford: Oxford University Press, 2001, pp. 11, 13, 102, 118, 145, 152, 153, 155.

bell hooks. *Black Looks: Race and Representation*. Boston: South End Press, 1992, p. 21.
Berry, Chris. "Calm in the Eye of the Storm." *Cinemaya* 30, 1995.
Berry, Chris and Mary Farquhar. *China on Screen: Cinema and Nation*. New York: Columbia University Press, 2006, pp. 54; 70; 139.
Berry, Michael. "Chen Kaige: Historical Revolution and Cinematic Rebellion." *Speaking in Images: Interviews with Contemporary Chinese Filmmakers*. New York: Columbia University Press, 2005, p. 87.
---. "Ang Lee: Freedom in Films." *Speaking in Images: Interviews with Contemporary Chinese Filmmakers*. New York: Columbia University Press, 2005, p. 327; 347.
---. "Introduction: Speaking in Images." *Speaking in Images: Interviews with Contemporary Chinese Filmmakers*. New York: Columbia University Press, 2005, pp. 10-18.
Birrell, Anne. *New Songs from A Jade Terrace: An Anthology of Early Chinese Love Poetry*. New York: Penguin Books, 1986, p. 231.
---. *Erotic Decor: A Study of Love Imagery in the Sixth Century A. D. Anthology*. New York: S. N., 1979.
---. *The Classic of Mountains and Seas*. New York: Penguin, 1999.
Bordwell, David. "Aesthetics in Action: Kungfu, Gunplay, and Cinematic Expressivity." *At Full Speed: Hong Kong Cinema in a Borderless World*. Esther C. M. Yau edt. Minneapolis: University of Minnesota Press, 2001, pp. 78-79.
---. "Richness through Imperfection: King Hu and the Glimpse." *Transcending the Times: King Hu and Eileen Chang*. Hong Kong: The 22nd Hong Kong International Film Festival hosted by the provisional Urban Council of Hong Kong, 1998, p. 34.
Braester, Yomi. "Chinese Cinema in the Age of Advertisement: The Filmmaker as a Cultural Broker." *China Quarterly* 183 (September 2005): 549-564.
Brians, Paul. *Reading about the World, Vol. I*. Orlando, FL: Harcourt Brace, 1999.
Birrell, Anne. *New Songs from a Jade Terrace: An Anthology of Early Chinese Love Poetry*. New York: Penguin Books, 1986, p. 231.
Brontë, Charlotte. *Jane Eyre*. New York: Norton, 2001.
Browne, Nick, Paul G. Pickowicz, Vivian Sobchack, and Esther Yau. *New Chinese Cinemas: Forms, Identities, Politics*. Cambridge: Cambridge University Press, 1994, p. 5.
Cai, Rong. "Gender Imaginations in *Crouching Tiger, Hidden Dragon* and the Wuxia World." *Positions: East Asian Cultural Critique* 13, no. 2 (Fall 2005): 441–71.
Cao, Yü. *Lei yü* (*Thunderstorm*). Wang Zuoliang and Barnes trans. Beijing: Foreign Language Press, 2003.
Chai, Ying. *Wenhua shiyu zhong de Zhang Yimou*. Beijing: Zhongguo shehui kexue, 2011.
Chan, Felicia. "Crouching Tiger Hidden Dragon: Cultural Migrancy and Translatability." *Chinese films in Focus: 25 New Takes*. Chris Berry edt. London: BFI, 2003, pp. 56-64. This article also appears in Chris Berry's *Chinese Films in Focus II*. Basingstoke: BFI / Palgrave MacMillan, 2008, pp. 73-81.
Chan, Kenneth. "The Global Return of the *Wu Xia Pian* (Chinese Sword-Fighting Movie): Ang Lee's *Crouching Tiger Hidden Dragon*." *Cinema Journal* 43.4 (2004): 3-17.
Chang Sun, Kang-I and Huan Saussy. *Women Writers of Traditional China: An Anthology of Poetry and Criticism*. Stanford: Stanford University Press, 1999.
Chen, Chen. *Gong Fu* (*Kung Fu*). Beijing: Wenhua yishu, 2006.
Chen, Dongyuan. *Zhongguo funü shenghuo shi* (*History of Chinese Women's Life*). Shanghai: Shanghai Bookstore, 1984, p. 118.

Chen, Jingliang and Zou Jianwen. *Bainian zhongguo dianying jingxuan* (*The Best of Centennial Chinese Cinema*). Beijing: Zhongguo shehui kexue, 2005, pp. 608; 227.
Chen, Kaige. "Qinguo ren" (The Person with Heritage of the Qin State). *Zhongguo dianying yishujia yenjiu congkan: lun Zhang Yimou* (*The Book Series of Research on Chinese Film Artists: Zhang Yimou*). Beijing: Zhongguo dianying (Chinese Films), 1994.
Chen, Mo. *Zhang Yimou dianying lun* (*Discourses of Zhang Yimou's Films*). Beijing: Zhongguo dianying, 1995, p. 203-205.
---. *Zhongguo wuxia dianying shi* (*History of Chinese Martial Arts Films*). Beijing: Zhongguo dianying (Chinese Films), 2005, pp. 146; 150.
Chen, Shan. *A History of Chinese Martial Arts Heroes*. Shanghai: Sanlian Bookstore, 1992.
Chen, Xihe. "On the Father Figures in Zhang Yimou's Films: From *Red Sorghum* to *Hero*." *Asian Cinema* (Fall/Winter 2004): 133–40.
Chen, Ya-chen. *The Many Dimensions of Chinese Feminism*. New York: Palgrave MacMillan, 2011.
Cheng, Huizhe. *Dianying dui xiaoshuo de kuayue: Zhang Yimou yingpian yanjiu* (*Filmic Strides across Fictions: Research of Zhang Yimou's Films*). Beijing: Zhongguo dianying, 2010.
Chiu, Tzu-hsiu (Beryl). "Public Secrets: Geopolitical Aesthetics in Zhang Yimou's *Hero*." *The Electronic Journal of the Asian Studies on the Pacific Coast* (2004/5): http://mcel.pacificu.edu/easpac/2005/tzuchiu.php3 (online data retrieved in April 2011).
Chow, Rey. *Primitive Passions: Visuality, Sexuality, Ethnography, and Contemporary Chinese Cinema*. New York: Columbia University Press, 1995, pp. 39; 149; 151-152.
Chung, Ling. *Dadi chunyu: Chung Ling zixuanji* (*Spring Rain on the Earth: Self-Selected Collections by Chung Ling*). Hong Kong: Tiandi tushu, 2004, pp. 11-16.
Chung, Ling and King Hu. *Shanke ji* (*Visiting the Mountain*). Taipei: Yuanjing, 1979, p. 147.
Chung, Tsai-chun. *Chuancheng yu chuangxin* (*Heritage and Originality*). Taipei: Institute of Chinese Literature and Philology, Academia Sinica, 1999.
Ciment, Michel. "Entretien avec King Hu." *Positif* (May 1975): 169; Du San-gae trans. *Influence* (Fall 1975): 13.
Cixous, Hélène. "The Laugh of the Medusa." Keith Cohen and Paula Cohen trans. *Signs* 1, no. 4 (1976): 875-893.
Clark, Paul. *Chinese Cinema: Culture and Politics Since 1949*. Cambridge: Cambridge University Press, 1987, p. 180.
---. *Reinventing China: A Generation and Its Films*. Hong Kong: Chinese University Press, 2005, p. 140.
Clark, S & M. Corcoran. "Perspectives on the Professional Socialization of Women Faculty." *Journal of Higher Education* 57 (I): 21-43.
Clark, William. *Academic Charisma and the Origin of the Research University*. Chicago: University of Chicago Press, 2006.
Clements, Jonathan. *Wu: The Chinese Empress Who Schemed, Seduced and Murdered Her Way to Become a Living God*. Stroud: Sutton, 2007.
Cornelius, Sheila. *New Chinese Cinema: Challenging Representations*. London Wallflower: 2004, p. 71.
Crump, James Irving. *Chan-Kuo Ts'e* (*The Stratagems of the Warring States*). Ann Arbor: University of Michigan Press (Center for Chinese Studies), 1996 (Revised Edition).

---. *Intrigues: Studies of the Chan-kuo Ts'e*. Ann Arbor: University of Michigan Press, 1964.
---. "The Assassins." *Legends of the Warring States: Persuasions, Romances, and Stories from Chan-kuo Ts'e*. Ann Arbor: University of Michigan (Center for Chinese Studies), 1998.
Culler, Jonathan. *The Pursuit of Signs—Semiotics, Literature, Deconstruction*. Ithaca, New York: Cornell University Press, 1981, p. 105.
Curtin, Michael. "The Future of Chinese Cinema: Some Lessons from Hong Kong and Taiwan." *Chinese Media, Global Contexts*. Chin-Chuan Lee edt. New York: Routledge, 2003, p. 237.
Dariotis, Wei Ming and Eileen Fung. "Breaking the Soy Sauce Jar: Diaspora and Displacement in the Films of Ang Lee." *Transnational Chinese Cinemas: Identity, Nationhood, Gender*. Sheldon Hsiao-peng Lu edt. Honolulu: University of Hawaii Press, 1997, p. 187.
Davies-Netzley, Sally Ann. "Women above the Glass Ceiling: Perceptions on Corporate Mobility and Strategies for Success." *Understanding Inequality: The Intersection of Race/Ethnicity, Class and Gender*. Barbara A. Arrighi edt. Lanham: Rowman & Littlefield, 2007, p. 210.
Davison, Peter. *Hamlet: Text and Performance*. London: Macmillan, 1983, p. 44.
Donaldson, Peter S. "Oliver, Hamlet, and Freud." *Shakespeare on Film: New Casebooks*. R. Shaughnessy edt. London: Macmillan, 1998.
Draper, John W. "The Elder Hamlet and the Ghost." *The Hamlet of Shakespeare's Audience*. New York: Octagon Books, 1970, pp. 97-108.
Du, Shanshan. *Chopsticks Only Work in Pairs*. New York: Columbia University Press, 2002.
Elley, Derek. "King Hu." *International Film Guide*. London: Tantivy Press, 1978, p. 27.
Eng, Robert Y. "Is Hero a Paean to Authoritarianism?" UCLA Asian Institute: *Asian Media: Media News Daily* (9/7/2004): http://goo.gl/dLWSN (online data retrieved in April 2011).
Erlich, Avi. *Hamlet's Absent Father*. Princeton: Princeton University Press, 1977.
Fang, Shouchu. *Muoxue yuanliu (The Origin of the Mohist Studies)*. Shanghai: Zhonghua shuju, 1937.
Feng, Xiaosheng Lin. "Chow Yun-fat: Hong Kong's Modern TV." *Chinese Film Starts*. Mary Farquhar and Yinjing Zhang edt. London: Routledge, 2010.
Feng, Youlan. *Zhongguo zhexue shi (History of Chinese Philosophy)*. Hong Kong: Zhongguo tushu, 1959.
---. *History of Chinese Philosophy*. Derk Bodde trans. Princeton: Princeton University Press, 1959.
Fennema, Elizabeth and Penelope Peterson. "Autonomous Learning Behavior: A Possible Explanation of Gender-Related Differences in Mathematics." *Gender Influences in Classroom Interaction*. Louise Cherry Wilkinson and Cora B. Marrett edt. New York: Academic Press, 1985, p. 26.
Fitzgerald, C. P. *The Empress Wu*. London: Cresset, 1968.
Frankel, Hans H. "The Development of Han and Wei *Yüeh-fu* as a High Literary Genre." *The Vitality of the Lyric Voice: Shih Poetry from the Late Han to the Tang*. Lin Shuen-fu and Stephen Owen edt. Princeton: Princeton University Press, 1986, p. 256.
Freud, Sigmund. *The Interpretation of Dreams*. James Strachey trans. New York: Avon,

1965. p.298.
---. "Some psychopathic Characters on the Stage." *The Penguin Freud Library: Volume 14: Art and Literature*. James Strachey edt. Harmondswoth: Penguin, 1985, p. 126.
Friedan, Betty. *The Feminine Mystique*. NY: Dell, 1974, p. 50.
Frye, Roland Mushat. "The 'Questionable' Ghost." *The Renaissance Hamlet: Issues and Responses in 1600*. Princeton: Princeton University Press, 1984, pp. 14-29.
Fu, Poshek. *Between Shanghai and Hong Kong: The Politics of Chinese Cinemas*. Stanford: Stanford University Press, 2003, p. 91.
Gallehugh, D. Sue and Allen Gallehugh. *Bedtime Stories for Grown-ups: Fairy-Tale Psychology*. Deerfield Beach, Florida: Health Communication, 1995, pp. 17-24.
Gilbert, Sandra and Susan Gubar. *The Madwoman in the Attic: The Woman Writer and the Nineteenth-Century Literary Imagination*. New Haven: Yale University Press, 2000.
Gilman, Charlotte Perkins. *The Yellow Wallpaper and Other Writings*. New York: Modern Library, 2000.
Goddard, Harold. "Hamlet: His Own Falstaff." *William Shakespeare's Hamlet*. Harold Bloom edt. New York: Chelsea House, 1986, pp. 11.
Grigg, Russell. *Lacan, Language, and Philosophy*. Albany: SUNY Press, 2008.
Grimm, Jacob and Wilhelm. "Snow White." *Folk & Fairy Tales*. Martin Hallett and Barbara Karasek edt. Second Edition. New York: Broadview Press, 2000, p. 68.
Gubar, Susan. *Rooms of Our Own*. Urbana: University of Illinois Press, 2006.
Gubar, Suan and Sandra Gilbert. *The Madwomen in the Attic: Women Writers and the Nineteenth Century Literary Imagination*. New Haven: Yale University Press, 1979.
---. Shakespeare's Sisters: Feminist Essays on Women Poets. Bloomington: Indiana University Press, 1979.
Guilford, Gwynn. "All in the Thread." *That's Beijing* (April 29, 2006): http://www.zhouxun.tv/bbs/redirect.php?tid=7889&goto=lastpost (online data retrieved in April 2011).
Guo, Jingming. *Wu ji (The Promise)*. Bejing: Renmin wenxue, 2006, p. 152.
Guo, Zhiyu. *Zhongguo wushu shi jian bian (Concise History of Chinese Martial Arts)*. Beijing: Renmin tiyu, 2007.
Gurr, Andrew. *The Shakespearian Playing Companies*. Oxford: Clarendon, 2003.
---. *The Shakespeare Stage*. Cambridge: Cambridge University Press, 1992.
---. *The Shakespeare Company, 1594-1642*. Cambridge: Cambridge University Press, 2004, pp. 48, 60, 61.
Han, Yunbo. *The Culture of the Martial Arts Hero*. Chongqing: Chongqing Publishing Company, 2004.
Harries, Elizabeth Wanning. *Twice upon a Time: Women Writers and the History of the Fairy Tale*. Princeton, N.J.: Princeton University Press, 2001, p. 13.
Harris, Kristine. "The Romance of the Western Chamber and the Classical Subject Film in 1920s Shanghai." *Cinema and Urban Culture in Shanghai, 1922-1943*. Yingjin Zhang edt. Stanford: Stanford University Press, 1999, p. 56.
Hideki, Mori. *Bokkou*. Sakemi Kenichi (Chinese translation) edt. Taipei: Tongli, 2006.
Hsu, Li-gong and Ling-i Kung. *Rang women zai ai yi ci—Hsu Li-gong de dianying shijie (Let's Fall in Love Again—Hsu Li-gong's Cinematic World)*. Taipei: Tianxia yuanjian, 2006, p. 263.
Hu, Jinquan and Koichi Yamada. *A Touch of King Hu*. Li He and Ma Songzhi trans. Hong Kong: Zhengwen, 1998, pp. 68-97.
Huang, Alexander C. Y. *Chinese Shakespeares: Two Centuries of Cultural Exchange*.

New York: Columbia University Press, 2008.
Huang, Qi. *The Martial Arts Hero in Ancient China.* Taipei: The Commercial Publishing Company, 1998.
Huang, Xiaoyang. *Yingxiang zhongguo: Zhang Yimou zhuan (Impressions on China: Zhang Yimou's Biography).* Beijing: Huaxia, 2008.
Hutchuel, Sarah. *Shakespeare, From Stage to Screen.* Cambridge: Cambridge University Press, 2004.
Irigaray, Luce. *This Sex Which Is Not One.* Ithaca: Cornell University Press, 1985.
---. *Speculum of the Other Women.* Ithaca: Cornell University Press, 1985.
---. *An Ethics of Sexual Difference.* Ithaca: Cornell University Press, 1993.
---. *Luce Irigaray: Key Writings.* London and New York: Continuum, 2004.
---. *Luce Irigaray: Teaching.* London and New York: Continuum, 2008.
Jameson, R.D. "Cinderella in China." *Cinderella: A Folklore Casebook.* Alan Dundes edt. New York: Garland, 1982, p. 74.
Jay, Jennifer W. "*Crouching Tiger Hidden Dragon:* (Re)packaging China and Selling the Hybridized Culture in an Age of Transnationalism." *Reading Chinese Transnationalisms: Society, Literature, and Films.* Maria Ng and Philip Holden edt. Hong Kong: Hong Kong University Press, 2006.
Jia, Leilei. "Yingxiang yüyan de ganxing xingshi yü biaoshu yüjing—Zhang Yimou yingpian zhong de shijue/sinli yiyi" (The Sensational Forms and Expressive Contexts of the Cinematic Language—The Visual/Psychological Meanings in Zhang Yimou's Films). *Zhongguo dianying yishujia yenjiu congkan: lun Zhang Yimou (The Book Series of Research on Chinese Film Artists: Zhang Yimou).* Beijing: Zhongguo dianying (Chinese Films), 1994.
---. *Zhongguo wuxia dianying shi (A History to Chinese Martial Arts Films).* Beijing: Wenhua yishu, 2005, pp. 14-19, 87.
---. *Wu zhi wu—zhongguo wuxia dianying de xingtai yu shenhun (The Dance of Martial Arts—The Figure and Soul of Chinese Martial Arts Films).* Zhengzhou: Henan renmin, 1998, pp. 105-110.
Jiao, Xiongping. *Taigang dianying zhong de zuozhe yü leixing (Authors and Genres in Taiwanese and Hong Kong Films).* Taipei: Yuanliu, 1991, p. 17.
Jin, Yong (Cha, Louis). *Tianlong babu (Demi-Gods and Semi-Devils).* Beijing: Wenhua yishu, 1998.
---. *Yitian tulong ji (The Heaven Sword and Dragon Sabre).* Hong Kong: Minghe she, 1985.
---. *Xueshan feihu (Fox Volant in the Snowy Mountain).* Hong Kong: Chinese University Press, 1996.
---. *The Book and the Sword.* Graham Earnshaw trans. Oxford: Oxford University Press, 2005.
Johnson, Kay A. *Women, the Family and Peasant Revolution in China.* Chicago: University of Chicago Press, 1983, p. 24.
Johnson, Michael J. "Perspectives on Tranformational Leadership and the Modern Glass Ceiling." *Dancing on the Glass Ceiling: Women, Leadership and Technology.* Don Olcott, Jr. and Darcy W. Hardy edt. Madison, WI: Atwood, 2006, p. 43.
Jones, Ernest. *Hamlet and Oedipus.* New York: Norton, 1976, p. 22.
Kang, Zhengguo. *Congshen fengyüe jian— xing yü zhongguo gudian wenxue (Aspects of Sexuality and Literature in Ancient China).* Shenyang: Liaoning, 1998, pp. 124-127.
Kennedy, Dennis and Li Lan Young. *Shakespeare in Asia: Contemporary Performance.*

Cambridge: Cambridge University Press, 2010.
Kiarostami, Abbas. *10 on Ten* (DVD). 2004.
Kim, L. S. "*Crouching Tiger Hidden Dragon:* Making Women Warriors—A Transnational Reading of Asian Female Action Heroes." *Jump Cut: A Review of Contemporary Media*. 48 (Winter 2006): http://www.lib.berkeley.edu/MRC/cjkfilmbib.html (online data retrieved in April 2011).
Kingston, Maxine Hong. "No Name Woman." *The Woman Warrior: China Men*. New York: Everyman's Library, 2005, pp. 1-16.
Ko, Dorothy. *Teachers of the Inner Chamber: Women and Culture in Seventeenth-Century China*. Stanford: Stanford University Press, 1994.
---. *Cinderella's Sisters: A Revisionist History of Footbinding*. Berkeley: California University Press, 2005.
---. *Every Step a Lotus: Shoes for Bound Feet*. Berkeley: University of California Press, 2001.
Kovacsics, Violeta. "Agit Pop: The 52nd San Sebastián International Film Festival." *Senses of Cinema* (December 2004): http://goo.gl/rRkqv (online data retrieved in April 2011).
Kraicer, Shelly. "Absence as Spectacle: Zhang Yimou's *Hero*." *Cinema Scope* 5.1 (2003): 9-11.
Kristeva, Julia. *Desire in Language: A Semiotic Approach to Literature and Art*. New York: Columbia University Press, 1980, p. 13.
Kuang, Shi. *Tianxia wuji Chen Kaige*. Beijing: Zhongguo guangbo dianshi, 2005, p. 132.
Lang, Andrew. *The Blue Fairy Book*. New York: Random House, 1959, pp. 96-104.
Lau, Joseph M. S. and Howard Goldblatt. *The Columbia Anthology of Modern Chinese Literature*. New York: Columbia University Press, 2007.
Lauzen, Martha M. *The Celluloid Ceiling: Behind-the-Scenes Employment of Women on the Top 250 Films of 2006*. San Diego: San Diego State University, 2007.
Lee, Hwanhee. "House of Flying Daggers: A Reappraisal." *Senses of Cinema* 35 (April-June 2005): www.sensesofcinema.com.
Levith, Murray J. *Shakespeare in China*. London and New York: Con-tinnum, 2004.
Levitin, Jacqueline. "*Crouching Tiger Hidden Dragon, Hero,* and *House of the Flying Daggers*: Interpreting Gender Thematics in the Contemporary Swordplay Film—View from the West." *Asian Cinema* 17:1 (Sping/Summer 2006): 166–182.
Li, Erwei. *Zhi mian Zhang Yimou: Zhang Yimou de dian ying shi jie* (*Facing Zhang Yimou: Zhang Yimou's Cinematic World*). (Beijing: Economic Daily Press, 2002), 134–48, 322-29.
Li, Feng. *Ying Xiong* (*Hero*). (Hong Kong: Mingchuang / Bright Windows, 2002), 4, 53, 120-56, 334.
Li, Ning and Bailong Jiang. *Zhongguo wushu shi lue* (*A Brief Historical Survey of Chinese Martial Arts*). Beijing: Renmin tiyu, 2003.
Li, Ruru. *Shashibiya: Staging Shakespeare in China*. Hong Kong: Hong Kong University Press, 2003.
Li, Shaohong. "Wo de nüxing juewu" (My Feminist Awakening). *Jiushi niandai de "di wu dai"* (*The 5th Generation of Chinese filmmakers in the 1990s*). Yang Yüanying, Pan Hua, Zhang Zhuan, and Shen Yun edt. Beijing: Beijing Broadcast Academy Press, 2000, p. 54.
Li, Zongwei. *Tangren chuanqi* (*Legends of People in the Tang Dynasty*). Beijing: Zhonghua, 2004.

Lim, Lin Lean. *More and Better Jobs for Women: An Action Guide.* Geneva: International Labor Organization, 1996, p. 39.

Lo, Kwai-cheung. *Chinese Face/Off: The Transnational Popular Culture of Hong Kong.* Urbana: University of Illinois Press, 2005, pp. 21; 186-187; 247.

Lu, Sheldon H. *Transnational Chinese Cinemas: Identity, Nationhood, Gender.* Honolulu: University of Hawaii Press, 1997, p. 10.

---. *China, Transnational Visuality, Global Postmodernity.* Stanford: Stanford University Press, 2001, p. 50.

Lu, Xun. *Kuangren riji (Diary of a Mad Man).* Hong Kong: Sanlian, 2004.

---. *Diary of A Mad Man.* William A. Lyell trans. Honolulu: University of Hawaii Press, 1990.

Lu, Yüan-chun. *Shuo yüan jinzhu jinyi (Current Annotation and Translation of Collections of Words).* Taipei: Sanmin, 1991, pp. 348-385.

Lunneborg, Patricia W. *Women Changing Work.* New York: Greenwood, 1990, p. 187.

Luo, Lichun. *A History of Chinese Martial Arts Fiction.* Liaoning: People's Publishing Society, 1990.

Lyons, Donald. "Passionate Precision: Sense and Sensibility." *Film Comment* 32.1 (1996): 36-42, p. 40.

Ma, Guoguang. "Xie ran cheng shi hua *xia nü*" (Blood on Poetry and Discourse on *A Touch of Zen*). *Zhongguo shibao (China Times)* August 30, 1975. This article also appears in Huang Ren's *Hu Jinquan de shijie (King Hu's World).* Taipei: Yatai, 1999, p. 254.

Macfarlane, Bruce. *The Academic Citizen: the Virtue of Service in University Life.* London and New York: Routledge, 2007.

Mair, Victor. *The Shorter Columbia Anthology of Traditional Chinese Literature.* New York: Columbia University Press, 2000.

Mann, Susan and Yu-yin Cheng. *Under Confucian Eyes: Writings on Gender in Chinese History.* Berkeley: University of California Press, 2001.

Mao, Yinkun. *Sichuang wushu da chuan (Complete Collections of Martial Arts in Sichuan).* Chengdu: Sichuan keji, 1989.

Menasche, Ann. "Women Need Affirmative Action to Overcome Discrimination." *Working Women: Opposing Viewpoints.* San Diego: Greenhaven Press, 1998, p. 89.

Mencius. *The Book of Mencius.* Lionel Giles trans. J. L. Cranmer-Byng edt. London: Butler & Tanner, 1949, pp. 79-80.

---. D. C. Lau trans. London: Penguin Books, 2004, pp. 97-80.

Michaeldfelder, Diane P. and Richard E. Palmer. *Dialogue and Deconstruction: The Gadmar-Derrida Encounter.* Albany: SUNY Press, 1989.

Mo Mo. *Zhongguo dianying jiaofu: Zhang Yimou zhuan (Godfather of Chinese Films: Zhang Yimou's Biography).* Beijing: Zhongguo dianshi guangbo, 2008.

Morris, Gary. "Beautiful Beast: Crouching Tiger Hidden Dragon." *Bright Lights Film Journal* 31 (2001): http://brightlightsfilm.com/31/crouchingtiger.html (online data retrieved in April 2011).

Mulvey, Laura. "The Myth of Pandora: A Psychoanalytical Approach." *Feminisms in the Cinema.* Laura Pietropaolo and Ada Testaferri edt. Bloomington: Indiana University Press, 1995, p. 3.

---. "Visual Pleasure and Narrative Cinema." *Screen* 16.3(Autumn 1975): 6-18.

---. *Visual and Other Pleasures.* Basingstoke: Palgrave MacMillan, 2008.

Munt, Alex. "Digital Kiarostami and The Open Screenplay." *Scan: Journal of Media Arts Culture* 3:2 (2006): hdl.handle.net/1959.14/11067.
Neipris, Janet. "A Small Delegation." *Plays by Janet Neipris*. New York: Broadway Play Publishing, 2000, pp. 1-60.
Palmer, Barbara and Dennis Simon. *Breaking the Political Glass Ceiling: Women and Congressional Elections*. New York: Routledge, 2008, p. 177.
Pang, Laikwan. *Building a New China in Cinema*. (New York: Rowman and Littlefield, 2002), 128.
Perrault, Charles. "Cinderella, or the Little Glass Slipper." *Cinderella: A Folklore Casebook*. Alan Dundes edt. New York: Garland, 1982, p. 18.
---. "The Sleeping Beauty in the Wood." *Folk & Fairy Tales*. Martin Hallett and Barbara Karasek edt. Second Edition. New York: Broadview Press, 2000, p. 44.
Perna, Laura. "The Relationship between Family and Employment Outcomes." *The Challenge of Balancing Faculty Careers and Family Work*. John W. Curtis edt. San Francisco: Jossey-Bass, 2005, p. 17.
Petroff, Jane and Bob Morris. *Women on Top*. New York: WNET TV Station (S.l.: s.n.), 1985.
Plato and P. Shorey. *The Republic*. London: W. Heinemann, 1930.
Plato and B. Jowett. *Plato's The Republic*. New York: The Modern library, 1941.
Poole, Gregory S. and Ya-chen Chen. *Ethnographies of the Professoriate in East Asia: The Cultural Translation of Faculty Tradition in the Face of Globalizing Reforms*. Rotterdam, the Netherlands: Sense Publishers, forthcoming.
Prosser, Eleanor. "Enter Ghost." *Hamlet and Revenge*. Second Edition. Stanford: Stanford University Press, 1971, pp. 101-117.
Pu, Songling. *Liaozhai zhiyi* (*Strange Stories from a Chinese Studio*). Beijing: Beijing shi yue wen yi, 1997.
---. *Liaozhai zhiyi* (*Strange Stories from a Chinese Studio*). Herbert A. Giles's English trans. New York: Boni and Liveright, 1925.
---. *Strange Tales from a Chinese Studio*. John Minford trans. London: Penguin, 2006.
Quan tang shu (*The Whole Book of the Tang Dynasty*). Beijing: Zhonghua, 1982.
Rance, PTJ. *Martial Arts*. London: Virgin Books, 2005, p. 128.
Rawnsley, Gary D. and Ming-yeh T. Rawnsley. *Global Chinese Cinema: the Culture and Politics of "Hero."* New York: Routledge, 2010.
Rosser, Sue V. *The Science Glass Ceiling: Academic Women Scientists and the Struggle to Succeed*. New York: Routledge, 2004, p. 54.
Rothschild, N. Harry. *Wu Zhao: China's Only Woman Emperor*. New York: Pearson Longman, 2008.
Rosenman, Ellen Bayuk. *A Room of One's Own: Women Writers and the Politics of Creativity*. New York: Twayne Publishers, 1995.
Rubin, Gayle. "The Traffic in Women: Notes on the 'Political Economy' of Sex." *Toward an Anthropology of Women*. Rayna Reiter edt. New York: Monthly Review Press, 1975, pp. 157-210.
Samimy, Keiko Komiya. "Multiple Mentors in My Career as a University Faculty." *"Strangers" on the Academy: Asian Women Scholars in Higher Education*. Guofang Li and Gulbahar H. Beckett edt. Sterling, VA: Stylus, 2006, p. 112.
Sang, Tze-lan Deborah. "Wang Dulu de jingwei nüxing chengzhang xiaoshuo" (The Bildungsroman of Beijing Women by Wang Dulu). *Beijing: Dushi xiangxiang yü wenhua jiyi* (*Beijing: Urban Imagination and Cultural Memory*). Chen Pingyuan and

David Der-wei Wang edt. Beijing: Beijing University Press, 2005, pp. 210-212.
---. "Women's Work and Boundary Transgression in Wang Dulu's Popular Novels." *Gender in Motion: Divisions of Labor and Cultural Change in Late Imperial and Modern China*. Bryna Goodman and Wendy Larson edt. Lanham, MD: Rowman & Littlefield, 2005, pp. 289-291.
Sato, Tadao. *Zhongguo dianying bainian (One Hundred Years of Chinese Films)*. Qian Hang trans. Shanghai: Shanghai Books, 2005, pp. 199-200.
Schubart, Rikke. "'Beautiful Vase Made of Iron and Steel': Micheele Yeoh." *Super Bitches and Action Babes: The Female Hero in Popular Cinema, 1970-2006*. Jefferson, NC: McFarland, 2007, p. 124.
Serban, George. *The Tyranny of Magical Thinking*. New York: E. P. Dutton, 1982.
Shi, Nai'an and Luo Guanzhong. *Shuihuzhuan (Outlaws of the Marsh)*. Sidney Shapiro trans. Volume I. Bloomington: Indiana University Press, 1981, pp. 353-356.
Silbergeld, Jerome. *China into Film: Frames of Reference in Contemporary Chinese Cinema*. London: Reaktion Books, 1999, p. 9.
Sibu congkan (The Four Treasures Series). (Shanghai: Commercial Press, 1921), 9.41b.
Sima, Qian. *Shi ji (Records of the Grand Historian of China)*. Original Version Published in the Han Dynasty. Shanghai: Hanyü da cidian, 2004.
Smith, Sharon. "The Image of Women in Film: Some Suggestions for Future Research." *Feminist Film Theory: A Reader*. Sue Thornham edt. New York: New York University Press, 1999, p. 14.
Spalding, Douglas A. "Instinct: With Original Observations on Young Animals." *Macmillan's Magazine* 27 (1837): 282-297.
---. "On Instinct." *Nature* 6 (1972): 485-486.
Stone, Judy. *Eye on the World: Conversations with International Filmmakers*. Los Angeles: Silman-James Press, 1997, pp. 93; 597.
Styan, J. L. *The English Stage: A History of Drama and Performance*. Cambridge: Cambridge University Press, 1996.
Sun, Lin and Shi Feng. *Yüwen yanjiu conglun (A Series of Studies on Languages and Literature)*. 7 (1997): 57-65.
Tam, Kwok-kan and Wimal Dissanayake. *New Chinese Cinema*. New York: Oxford University Press, 1998, pp. 23-34.
Teo, Stephen. "Only the Valiant: King Hu and His *Cinema Opera*." *Transcending the Times: King Hu and Eileen Chang*. Hong Kong: The 22nd Hong Kong International Film Festival hosted by the provisional Urban Council of Hong Kong, 1998, pp. 21-22.
---. "Tsui Hark: National Style and Polemic." *At Full Speed: Hong Kong Cinema in a Borderless World*. Esther C. M. Yau edt. Minneapolis: University of Minnesota Press, 2001, p. 143.
The Chicago Area Partnerships (CAPS). *Pathways and Progress: Corporate Best Practices to Shatter the Glass Ceiling*. Chicago: the Chicago Area Partnerships, 1996, p. 11.
Thomson, Peter. *Shakespeare's Theatre*. Second Edition. New York: Routledge, 1992.
Thornham, Sue. "Women and Film: A Discussion of Feminist Aesthetics." *Feminist Film Theory: A Reader*. New York: New York University Press, 1999, p. 117.
Treut, Monika. "Female Misbehavior." *Feminisms in the Cinema*. Laura Pietropaolo and Ada Testaferri edt. Bloomington: Indiana University Press, 1995, p. 115.

Trinh, Minh-ha. "Who Is Speaking: Of Nation, Community, and First Person Interview." *Feminisms in the Cinema*. Laura Pietropado and Ada Testaferri edt. Bloomington: Indiana University Press, 1995.
Tsouluhas, Litsa. "The Cost of Caring: Female Beginning Teachers, Occupational Stress and Coping" (Ph.D. Dissertation). Department of Curriculum, Teaching and Learning, University of Toronto, 2005.
Tung, Chi. "To America, With Love: Zhang Yimou's One-Note Rhapsody." UCLA Asian Institute: *Asian Pacific Arts* 9/3/2004. For details, consult http://goo.gl/9OZXP (online data retrieved in April 2011).
Vardac, Nicholas. *Stage to Screen*. Cambridge: Harvard University Press, 1949.
Wang Bin. *Zhang Yimou zhege ren (A Biographical Sketch of Zhang Yimou)*. (Beijing: Tuanjie, 1998), 85-90.
Wang, Georgette and Emily Yueh-yu Yeh. "Globalization and Hybridization in Cultural Products: The Cases of *Mulan* and *Crouching Tiger, Hidden Dragon*." *International Journal of Cultural Studies* 8.2 (2005): 175-193.
Wang, John Ching-yu. "Cung *Cike liezhuan Jing Ke zhuan* kan *Shi Ji* de xüshi tece yu chengjiu" (On the narrative characteristics and achievements of *Records of the Historian* from *The Biography of Jing Ke* in *The Biography of Assassins*). Chung Tsaichun's *Chuancheng yu chuangxin (Heritage and Originality)*. Taipei: Institute of Chinese Literature and Philology, Academia Sinica, 1999.
Wang, Xiaoxin. *Ciyü yüanliu manbi (Scripts on the Origins of Words and Phrases)*. Guangzhou: Guangdong Education, 1990, p. 75.
Wei, Long. *Mou tian xia (Zhang Yimou: from a Man of Northwest China to the Chief Director of the 2008 Beijing Olympic Games)*. Beijing: China Pictorial Publishing House, 2009.
Wei, Qingwen. "*Yüeren ge* yü zhuangyü de guangxi shiyi" (Explanations of the Relations between *A Song from Yüe* and the Language of the Zhuang Tribe). *Minzu yüwen lunji (Anthology of Critical Essays on People's Languages and Literatures)*. Beijing: Shehui kexue, 1981, p. 23-46.
---. "Shi lun baiyüe minzu de yüyan" (On the Languages of Hundreds of Tribes of the Yüe State). *Baiyüe minzushi lunji (Anthology of Essays on Hundreds of Tribes of the Yüe State)*. Beijing: Shehui kexue, 1982, pp. 276-288.
West, David. *Chasing Dragons: An Introduction to the Martial Arts Films*. London: I.B. Tauris, 2006, p. 101.
Westermarck, Edward Alexender. *The History of Human Marriage*, 5th edn. London: Macmillan, 1921.
---. *Marriage Ceremonies in Morocco* (microfilm). Woodbridge, Conn.: Research Publications, 1977. Also consult Edward Westermarck's *The History of Human Marriage* (microfilm). Woodbridge, Conn.: Research Publications, 1977.
Wolf, Margery. "The People's Republic of China." *Women Workers in Fifteen Countries*. Jennie Farley edt. Ithaca: ILR Press, Cornell University, 1985, p. 33.
Woolf, Virginia. *A Room of One's Own*. San Diego: Harcourt Brace Jovanovich, 1989.
Wright, Elizabeth. *Psychoanalytic Criticism: A Reappraisal*. Second Edition. Cambridge: Polity Press, 1998.
Xü, Shiyi. "Explanations on Some Words in History about the Han, Wei, Jin, Northern and Southern Dynasties." *Journal of Nanyang Normal University* 5.7 (2006): 32-38.
Xü, Zhonglin. *Fengshan yanyi (The Creation of the Gods)*. Beijing: Xinshijie (New World Press), 2000.

Yang, Jeff. *Once Upon A Time in China: A Guide to Hong Kong, Taiwanese, and Mainland Chinese Cinema.* New York: Atria, 2003, pp. 41; 49; 103.

Yang, Mayfair Mei-hui. "Of Gender, State, Censorship, and Overseas Capital: An Interview with Chinese Director Zhang Yimou." *Zhang Yimou Interviews.* Frances Gateward, ed. (Jackson: University Press of Mississippi, 2001), 38.

Yau, Kinnia Shuk-ting. *Japanese and Hong Kong Film Industries: Understanding the Origins of East Asian Film Networks.* London: Routldge, 2010.

Yolen, Jane. *Favorite Folktales from Around the World.* New York: Pantheon Books, 1986, p. 1.

Yu, Sabrina Qiong. "Jet Li: Star Construction and Fan Discourse on the Internet." *Chinese Film Stars.* Mary Farquhar and Yingjin Zhang edt. London: Routledge, 2010.

Yu, Shuiqing. *Zhongguo wushu shi gaiyao (Historical Outline of Chinese Martial Arts).* Wuhan: Hubei kexue jishu, 2006.

Yu, Zhijun. *Zhongguo tuantong wushu shi (History of Traditional Chinese Martial Arts).* Beijing: Renmin University Press, 2006.

Yun, Youke. *Jianghu cong tan (Legends of Jiang Hu).* Tianjin: Baihua wenyi, 1996.

Zhang, Huijun. *Fengge chuangzao: Zhang Yimou dianying chuangzuo lun (Creation of Styles: Analyses of Zhang Yimou's Films).* Beijing: Zhongguo dianying, 2010.

---. *Xingshi zhuisuo yu shijue chuangzao: Zhang Yimou dianying chuangzuo yanjiu (Searches for Forms and Creations of Visions: Studies of Zhang Yimou's Creative Works).* Beijing: Zhongguo dianying, 2008.

Zhang, Jihe. *The Martial Arts Hero in Chinese Literary History.* Beijing: Chinese Social Science Press, 1994.

Zhang, Jiuying. *Fanpai Zhang Yimou.* (Beijing: Zhongguo mangwen, 2001), 246–49.

Zhang, Yimou and Li Erwei. "Wei zhongguo dianying zouxiang shijie pulu" (To Pave the Way toward the World for Chinese Films). *Zhang Yimou, di wudai daoyan congshu: wei yi mou buwei daoliang mou (Zhang Yimou, the Fifth Generation Filmmaker in Book Series: For Art's Sake, Not For Rice and Sorghum's Sake).* (Changsha: Hunan wenyi, 1997), 389.

Zhang, Yingjin. *Chinese National Cinema.* New York: Routledge, 2004, pp. 278; 287; 296.

Zhang, Youhe. *Tang Song chuanqi xuan (Selected Legends of the Tang and Song Dynasties).* Beijing: Renmin wenxue, 1998, p. 221.

Zhang, Zhen. "An Amorous History of the Silver Screen: The Actress as Vernacular Embodiment in Early Chinese Film Culture." *A Feminist Reader in Early Cinema.* Jennifer M. Bean and Diane Negra edt. Durham: Duke University Press, 2002, p. 524.

Zheng, Qunyuan. *History of Martial Arts Heroes.* Shanghai: Shanghai Literary Publishing Society, 1999.

Zheng, Zhang Shangfang. "Decipherment of *Yüeren ge.*" *Chaiers de Linguistique Asie Orientale.* Centre de Recherches Linguistiques sur l'Asie Orientale (Paris). Vol. 2. 20. No.1, 1991, pp. 159-168.

Zhenguan zhengyao (Significant Policies During the Zhenguan Era). Chengdu: Sichuan renmin, 1987.

Zhou, Feng. *Zhongguo gudai fuzhuang cankao ziliao (Reference for Clothes in Ancient China).* Beijing: Yanshan, 1988.

Zhou, Weiliang. *Zhongguo wushu shi (History of Chinese Martial Arts).* Beijing: Gaodeng jiaoyu, 2003.

Zhu, Xi. *Zhuzi yülei (Categories of Zhuzi's Words).* Beijing: Zhonghua, 1986.

Zhu, Ying. "A Culture and an Economy in Disarray." *Chinese Cinema During the Era of Reform*. Westport, Connecticut: Praeger, 2003, p. 17.

Zhuo, Boshang. "Dianying yüyan de kaichuangzhe—lun Hu Jiquan de jianjie fengge" (The Founder of the Cinematic Language—King Hu's Stylistic Editing of Films). *Hu Jinquan de shijie (King Hu's World)*. Huang Ren edt. Taipei: Yatai, 1999, pp. 221-224.

Zipes, Jack. "Setting Standards for Civilization through Fairy Tales: Charles Perrault and His Associates." *Fairy Tales and the Art of Subversion: The Classical Genre for Children and the Process of Civilization*. New York: Wildman Press, 1983, p. 14.

Zuo, Qiuming. *Zuozhuan (Zuo's Commentary)*. Changsha, Hunan: yüelu shushe, 2001.

---. *Guo yü*. Jinan: Qilu shushe, 2000.

Index

Ang Lee, 1, 5-8, 13, 15, 20, 24n2, 25n16, 35, 38, 40, 43n1, 44n11, 93n1, 153, 156, 160-161, 165-166, 170n1, 175, 178, 190, 196, 197, 202, 208, 210n3, 219-220, 224-227, 229-230, 232, 233n1
Ann Hui, 156, 167, 223-224, 236

The Banquet, 1-2, 4-5, 12-13, 20, 22, 115, 117-126, 130n8, 131n17, 160, 196-199, 201-202, 204-205, 207-208, 211n6, 226
Beijing Film Academy, 110n1, 221-225
Buddha, 183

castration fear, 118, 159-160, 176, 179-180, 184-185, 187, 190
Chang Che, 5, 44n11, 220, 237
chastity, 12, 15, 17, 20, 33, 37, 76, 78, 147, 198
Chen Kaige, 1, 5, 12, 20-21, 61, 65n1, 66n8, 66n10, 97-99, 101-104, 106, 108-109, 110n1, 111n2, 112n18, 113nn26-27 160, 170n1, 196-197, 210n3, 221, 224-225
Chinese cinematic martial arts feminism, 1-2, 12, 16, 18, 21-22, 195
Chinese martial arts films, 1-2, 5, 7-9, 16, 20-22, 24n2, 25n16, 44n11, 75-76, 83-84, 92, 153-154, 157-158, 160, 166-168, 178, 196, 201, 205, 207-208, 210n3, 219-220, 238
Chu, Tien-hsin 163, 172n30

Chu, Tien-wen, 161-163, 172n28, 172n30
cinematic pen, 153-155, 158-160, 165-166, 168
Come Drink with Me, 5
Confucius, 11, 60, 82n12, 177-178, 183
Crouching Tiger Hidden Dragon, 1-2, 5-8, 13, 15, 20, 24n2, 31-32, 38-39, 41, 43n1, 44n11, 45n23, 53, 83-84, 93n1, 153-155, 160-161, 165-166, 175, 178, 180-182, 184-186, 189-190, 196-202, 207, 210n4, 211n6, 219-220, 225-226, 229-232
Curse of the Golden Flower, 1-2, 4, 13, 15, 20-21, 133-137, 139-147, 160, 196-197, 199, 201, 203-205, 207-208

E Mei, 6-7, 19
Eileen Chang, 161, 163, 165, 172n30

femininity, 84, 118
feminism, 1-2, 4, 6-7, 9-10, 12, 14-16, 18, 21-22, 24n1, 26n21, 27n22, 43n3, 82n4, 94n11, 94n13, 155, 166, 181, 184, 195, 207-208, 213n23, 218, 220, 227, 232
Feng Xiaogang, 1, 4-5, 9, 12-13, 20, 22, 115, 120, 126, 129n4, 160, 196-197, 226
fifth-generation filmmakers, 225, 227, 238
Fuxi, 10

gender, 1, 7-9, 16, 33-34, 56, 84, 92, 118, 135-136, 138-141, 159-160, 178-180, 186, 188, 196, 201, 207, 232, 238; equality, 2, 6, 182, 184, 190; ideology, 11, 76-78, 91, 103, 113n27, 176, 195, 224-226, 228n2, 237; inequality, 10-11, 13, 17, 103, 133, 147, 175, 200, 218-219, 226-227, 229, 236
glass ceiling, 2, 21, 157-158, 168, 184, 190, 195-196, 200-204, 206-208, 213n18, 213n23; cinematic, 160; for ancient Chinese women in the films, 180
Golden Globes, 161
Golden Horse, 24n3, 156-157, 161-162, 235-236, 240n1, 240n4
Golden Rooster, 156-157, 170n1
Golden Swallow, 5, 220, 237

Han Dynasty, 4, 12-14, 18, 24n10, 27n26, 75, 77-78, 82n5, 98-99, 116, 119, 124, 177
Hero, 1-3, 12-13, 20, 47-63, 67n22, 153-155, 160, 175, 177, 181-182, 184, 186, 189-190, 196-199, 201, 203-205, 207
Hong Fu Nü, 18-21
Hong Kong Film Critics Society, 161
Hou Hsiao-hsien, 163, 172
House of Flying Daggers, 1-2, 4, 12-13, 20, 55, 69, 71, 75-76, 78, 81, 82n11, 150n16, 153-155, 160, 196-201, 203-205, 207, 211, 226
King Hu, 1, 5-6, 24n2, 84, 163, 166, 170n1, 196, 199, 210nn2-3, 211n6, 212n11, 212n13, 217-220
Hu Mei, 221-223

Kung fu, 5, 10, 17-18, 25n16, 32-35, 38, 55-56, 57, 71, 82n8, 84-85, 87-88, 92, 122, 147, 155, 178, 182-184, 186, 190, 198-199, 212n13, 230; film, 1-2, 197, 201, 207-208, 220, 229, 237, 240; filmmaker, 196; instructor, 15, 19; movie, 7-8, 25n17, 167, 196, 201-204, 207, 210n2, 211n6, 213n23, 224, 229, 232, 238; training, 6, 19, 31; in the Tang Dynasty, 75, 77

Laura Mulvey, 43, 82, 159, 171
Legend of the Mountain, 1, 5, 163, 166, 175, 180-182, 184, 186, 188-190, 217-219
Li Ang, 43n2
Li Shaohong, 94n4, 221-222, 224
Li Yannian, 12-13, 22, 69, 70, 72, 74-75, 77-78, 80, 81n1, 82n15, 97-99, 101-102, 106, 108, 119

martial arts fiction, 10, 26, 77, 200, 229, 240n5
Mencius, 11, 133, 143-144, 147, 177
Ming Dynasty, 5, 7, 15, 17, 76
Mo Yan, 54, 161
My Fair Lady, 206-208

Nie Yinniang, 18-21, 77
Nobel Prize Laureates in literature, 164
Nüwa, 10

Oedipus, 118, 179
Oscars, 83, 156-157, 223, 233, 235

Pearl Buck, 164
Peng Xiaolian, 156, 221-222, 224
penis envy, 179-180, 187-188; cinematic 159-160
Princess Fragrance, 167
The Promise, 1, 5, 12, 20-21, 97-104, 106-108, 111nn2-3, 112n18, 113nn26-27, 153-155, 160, 196-197, 202, 204, 207-208

Pygmalion, 195-196, 202, 204-208, 213n23

Qing Dynasty, 5, 7, 14-18, 76, 90, 218-219

Red Lantern, 55, 67n22, 161
Red Sorgham, 161
The Romance of the Book and the Sword, 167

Seven Swords, 1-2, 5, 13, 21, 83-89, 91-92, 93n3, 160, 175, 181, 183-184, 190, 196-197, 202-203, 207-208
Shakespeare, 4, 9, 115, 118, 124-126, 129n1, 130n6, 130n9, 131nn16-17, 201-203, 206-208
Shaolin, 6, 178, 210n2
Shaw Brothers, 210
Song Dynasty, 6-7, 14-15, 44n12, 60, 76, 130n6, 177, 218
Sui Dynasty, 177
Su Tong, 161

Tang Dynasty, 4, 6, 10, 14, 17-19, 21, 68n48, 75-78, 82n8, 82n11, 117-119, 121-122, 130n12, 145-147, 150n16, 177-178, 202
Tian Zhuangzhuang, 211, 213

A Touch of Zen, 1-2, 5, 153-155, 160, 196-199, 210n2, 210n4, 211n6, 212n11, 212n13, 218-220
Tsui Hark, 1, 5, 13, 21, 84, 93n3, 160, 196-197, 203, 237

union, 20, 35, 38, 121, 236

Wang Dulu, 43n1, 45n23, 161, 165-166, 229-231
Wudang, 6-7, 35, 38, 40-41, 155, 178, 185-186
Wu Emperor, 12-13
Wu Tianming, 156
Wu Zetian, 4, 17, 27n30, 75, 77, 82n7, 117-119, 121-122, 146-147, 177, 202, 208
Wu Ziniu, 221-223

Yellow Emperor, 10-11

Zhang Yimou, 1, 3-4, 12-13, 15, 20, 47-63, 65n1, 66n8, 66n10, 67n22, 68n38, 69-71, 74-78, 80-81, 133, 156, 160-162, 170n1, 175, 177, 190, 196-197, 200, 204, 208, 201n3, 221-226
Zhou Dynasty, 3, 5, 11-12, 17, 24n9, 77, 82n12, 116, 122, 178

About the Author: Chen, Ya-chen

Ya-chen Chen is an assistant professor of foreign languages and literature and director of the Chinese Language Program at Clark University, and formerly affiliated with the City University of New York (with the same titles and Asian studies director), in both of which this book was prepared. Her academic books include *The Many Dimensions of Chinese Feminism* (2011); *Women and Gender in Contemporary Chinese Societies: Beyond the Han Patriarchy* (2011); *Higher Education in East Asia: Neoliberalism and the Professoriate* (2009); *Women in Taiwan: Sociocultural Perspectives* (2009); and *Farewell My Concubine: Same-Sex Readings and Cross-Cultural Dialogues* (2004).

Ya-chen Chen's academic interests include Sino-Western comparative literature, Asian Studies, women's and gender studies, (multi)cultural studies, and film studies. Ya-chen Chen is the recipient of *Fu Cheng* Literary Award (1995), CCA (Council for Cultural Affairs) Modern Literary Research Award (1997-1998), Lynn Interdisciplinary Research Fellowship in Women's and Gender Studies (2001-2005), Faculty Fellowship Publication Program (FFPP) Grant (2009), William Stuart Research Award (2009), Taiwan Studies Research Travel Grant (the first and so far the only Chinese-heritage winner, 2010), and NCID (National Center of Institutional Diversity) Award (2010-2011). Her academic articles appear in *China Quarterly*; *American Journal of Chinese Studies* (*AJCS*); *Borrowers and Lenders: Journal of Shakespeare and Appropriation*; *Asian Cinema*, *Mediascape: Journal of Cinema and Media Studies*; *Feminism/o*; *Dangdai* (*Contemporary*); *Shijie dianying* (*World Cinema*) and so forth. Most of them are also included in Ohio State University's MCLC (Modern Chinese Literature and Culture) online resource center.